THE LAW OF RESTITUTION
IN ENGLAND AND IRELAND

Third Edition

Cavendish
Publishing
Limited

THE LAW OF RESTITUTION
IN ENGLAND AND IRELAND

Third Edition

Andrew Tettenborn, MA, LLB
Barrister
Bracton Professor of Law,
University of Exeter

Cavendish
Publishing
Limited

London • Sydney

First published in Great Britain 2002 by Cavendish Publishing Limited, The Glass House, Wharton Street, London WC1X 9PX, United Kingdom
Telephone: +44 (0)20 7278 8000   Facsimile: +44 (0)20 7278 8080
Email: info@cavendishpublishing.com
Website: www.cavendishpublishing.com

© Tettenborn, A   2002
First edition   1993
Second edition   1996
Third edition   2002

British Library Cataloguing in Publication Data

Tettenborn, AM
Law of restitution in England and Ireland – 3rd ed
1 Restitution – England 2 Restitution – Wales 3 Restitution – Ireland
I Title
346.4'2'029

ISBN 1 85941 567 9

Printed and bound in Great Britain

PREFACE

Restitution law continues to advance at a gallop. The Anglo-Irish case law, much of it unreported, has burgeoned alarmingly; we have important new books from England and the Commonwealth; and there is ever more speculation on the subject in the reviews and on the Internet. This third edition of *The Law of Restitution in England and Ireland* has expanded in sympathy. Substantive law has been thoroughly mobile, at least in England, and it is a fair inference that this development will in due course be reflected on the other side of the Irish Sea. The fall-out from *Westdeutsche* has forced our courts into more precision in deciding what to do about ineffective contracts. The mistake of law bar has finally fallen, as everyone said it would, rendering urgent problems that were previously hypothetical playthings for academics. *Jones* and *Parc* have set tracing and subrogation on clear lines for future development. Since *Attorney General v Blake* we also know we are going somewhere on disgorgement damages for breach of contract, though precisely where nobody seems to know – yet.

The aim of this book is the same as ever: to give a succinct yet thoughtful account of Anglo-Irish restitution law, to take sides on controverted points, and to set its readers' thinking further. Coverage has been widened and deepened in a number of places. But, like any book, it cannot be the last word. Further changes already loom: the requirement of total failure of consideration must be on its last legs, and merger of the legal and equitable rules on identification in tracing cases is a racing certainty. The next edition, no doubt, will be yet fatter than this one: but that is the way with law books.

I owe widespread debts of gratitude. To Exeter University for providing an extraordinarily congenial environment for writing in; to members of the Law Faculty of my alma mater, Cambridge, for continued stimulation, albeit at a distance; and to the multifarious correspondents of the Restitution Discussion Group in cyberspace, who have constantly produced new ideas to chew over (some of them even good ones). But perhaps most of all to my family, for putting up with long periods of absence from normal duties.

As far as possible the law is stated as at August 2001.

Andrew Tettenborn
Exeter
October 2001

CONTENTS

Preface   *v*

Table of Cases   *xv*

Table of Statutes   *xli*

1 THE CONCEPT OF RESTITUTION   1

  I WHAT IS RESTITUTION ABOUT?   1

    Historical note   2

    Unjust enrichment today   4

  II THE ESSENTIALS OF A CLAIM FOR RESTITUTION OF

    UNJUST ENRICHMENT   5

      (a) The first requirement: enrichment   6

      (b) The second requirement: a gain which is 'unjustified'   13

      (c) The third requirement: enrichment 'at the claimant's

        expense'   17

  III FACTORS JUSTIFYING RETENTION   20

    (a) Forced exchange, subjective devaluation and

      'incontrovertible benefit'   21

    Forced exchange: 'incontrovertible benefit'   21

    'Subjective devaluation'   23

    (b) *Bona fide* purchase   25

    (c) Lawful receipt from a third party   27

    (d) Incidental benefit   30

    (e) Receipt under contract with the claimant   31

    (f) Donative intent   31

    (g) A questionable factor: 'officiousness'   32

  IV THE RELATION BETWEEN UNJUST ENRICHMENT AND

    OTHER SOURCES OF LIABILITY   32

    Restitution and the law of property   34

  V RESTITUTION: A COHERENT LEGAL CATEGORY?   36

    (a) 'Unjust enrichment': a coherent idea?   37

    (b) The coherence of the concept of 'gain'   38

    (c) Unjust enrichment: worth discussing separately?   40

2 REMEDIES   43

  I INTRODUCTION   43

  II PECUNIARY RESTITUTION   44

  III PROPRIETARY CLAIMS   45

    The boundary between personal and proprietary restitution   48

    When is a proprietary remedy available?   50

      (a) Rescission   50

      (b) Claim in respect of claimant's property or its proceeds   51

      (c) Mistake   51

      (d) Land improvement cases   52

	(e) Gains in breach of duty	52
	(f) Payments and transfers made *ultra vires*	53
	(g) Miscellaneous	54
IV	SUBROGATION	54
	Definition	54
	When will the right to subrogation arise?	56
	(a) Property claims and analogous cases	57
	(b) Defective loan cases	57
	(c) Unauthorised debits	60
	(d) Sureties	61
	(e) More general applications	62
	Is the concept of subrogation worth keeping as a restitutionary remedy?	63
	Other cases of 'subrogation'	64
	(a) Insurance	65
	(b) Two oddities: businesses operated by insolvent trustees, and the Third Parties (Rights against Insurers) Act 1930	66

3	**MISTAKE**	**69**
I	WHAT MISTAKES SHOULD GROUND RESTITUTION?	69
	(a) Present and future mistakes	69
	(b) Mistake of fact and mistake of law	70
	Mistake of law – definition	72
	The effect of changes in the law	73
	Limitations on recovery for mistake of law	74
	(c) The nature of the mistake	74
II	THE RELEVANCE OF CONTRACT	77
III	MONEY PAID BY MISTAKE	78
	(a) The principle of recovery	78
	(b) Mistaken payments: the availability of a proprietary remedy	79
IV	PROPERTY TRANSFERRED BY MISTAKE	80
	(a) General	80
	(b) Property transferred by mistake: remedies	81
	(c) Forced exchange and subjective devaluation: property cases	83
V	SERVICES AND MISTAKE	84
	(a) Generally	84
	(b) Services, mistake and acquiescence	86
	(c) Services: non-pecuniary remedies	88
VI	RESTITUTION FOR MISTAKE WHERE NEITHER ACCEPTANCE NOR ACQUIESCENCE	88
VII	EXCEPTIONS TO RECOVERY FOR MISTAKE	89
	(a) Risk	89
	(b) Compromise	90
	(c) Benefits rendered in the face of litigation	90

4   DURESS AND UNCONSCIENTIOUS DEALING   **91**

I   BENEFITS RENDERED UNDER DURESS   92
Forms of duress   92
   (a) Direct violence   92
   (b) Other unlawful pressure ('economic duress')   92
II OTHER FORMS OF PRESSURE   101
   (a) Undue influence   102
   Generally   102
   'Defences' to undue influence claims   106
   (b) An extension of undue influence: the 'poor and ignorant' cases   106
   (c) Demands contrary to legislative provisions   108
III REMEDIES   109
   (a) Money paid   109
   (b) Property transferred   109
   (c) Services rendered   110
   (d) The position of third parties   111

5   FREE ACCEPTANCE   **113**

I   THE FUNCTION OF FREE ACCEPTANCE   113
II FREE ACCEPTANCE IN OPERATION   116
   (a) The idea of acceptance   116
   Request   116
   Acquiescence   117
   Advantage-taking   119
   (b) The need for 'free' acceptance   120
   (c) Lack of gratuitous intent   122

6   FAILURE OF ASSUMPTIONS (1)   **125**

I   INTRODUCTION   125
   (a) Free acceptance and failure of assumptions   126
   (b) Contractual and non-contractual expectations   126
   (c) Forms of benefit covered by failure of assumptions   127
   (d) The problem of counter-restitution   128
   (e) Proprietary claims and failure of consideration   129
II BENEFITS RENDERED UNDER VALID CONTRACTS   131
   (a) Contract cases: 'failure of consideration'   131
   Generally   131
   'Consideration'   132
   Valid contracts: money paid   133
   Valid contracts: goods provided and services rendered   139

7	**FAILURE OF ASSUMPTIONS (2)**	**153**
I	VITIATED CONTRACTS IN GENERAL	153
	(a) Vitiated contracts and failure of consideration	153
	(1) Background	153
	(2) Voidable contracts: failure of consideration and counter-restitution	154
	(3) Void contracts: counter-restitution and the place of failure of consideration	157
	(b) Void contracts: claims for benefits in kind	159
	(1) Generally	159
	(2) The effect of a losing bargain	159
II	CONTRACTS AFFECTED BY MISTAKE	160
	(a) Generally	160
	(b) Contracts void for mistake	161
	(1) Money paid	161
	(2) Benefits in kind	161
	(c) Contracts voidable for mistake	162
	(1) Money paid	162
	(2) Benefits in kind	163
III	CONTRACTS AFFECTED BY DURESS AND UNDUE INFLUENCE	163
IV	CONTRACTS AFFECTED BY MINORITY	164
	(a) Contractual capacity: the general law	164
	(b) Claims by minors: money paid	165
	(c) Claims by minors: property and services	166
	(d) Claims against the minor	167
V	CONTRACTS AFFECTED BY ILLEGALITY	168
	(a) In general	168
	(b) Illegality as an unjust factor: protective illegality	169
VI	CONTRACTS AFFECTED BY *ULTRA VIRES*	171
	(a) Restitutionary claims by the corporation	171
	(b) Claims against the corporation	172
VII	CONTRACTS AFFECTED BY LACK OF FORMALITY	174
VIII	NON-CONTRACTUAL CASES	175
8	**RECOUPMENT AND CONTRIBUTION**	**181**
I	GENERALLY	181
	(a) Discharge of obligation	182
	Discharge: the problem of unrequested payment of another's obligation	183
	(b) Compellability	184
	(c) An obligation lying primarily on the defendant	187

Contents

II PARTICULAR CASES OF RECOUPMENT 188
    (a) Sureties 188
    (b Leases 189
    (c) Co-owners 190
    (d) Other rights of recourse 192
III THE RIGHT TO CONTRIBUTION 193
    (a) Concurrent debtors 193
    (b) Co-sureties 193
    (c) Concurrent insurers 194
    (d) Concurrent wrongdoers and trustees 195
    (e) Other cases of contribution 196
IV POSSIBLE EXTENSIONS OF RECOUPMENT AND CONTRIBUTION 197
V A SPECIAL CASE – GENERAL AVERAGE 198

9 **NECESSITY** 199
  I NECESSITOUS INTERVENTION: THE GENERAL RULE
    OF NON-RECOVERY 199
  II NECESSITOUS INTERVENTION: THE EXCEPTIONS
    TO NON-RECOVERY 200
    (a) Agency of necessity 200
    (b) Bailment 202
    (c) Trustees' rights 202
    (d) Liquidators and receivers 203
    (e) Medical attention 204
    (f) Supply of necessaries to incompetents 204
    (g) Caring for animals 205
    (h) Performance of public duties 206
    (i) Ireland: the doctrine of 'salvage' 207
    (j) Other cases 207
  III A GENERAL PRINCIPLE? 208
  IV MARITIME SALVAGE: A FURTHER ISSUE 209
    (a) In general 209
    (b) The place of salvage in restitution law 212

10 **BENEFITS CONFERRED THROUGH THIRD PARTIES:**
'TRACING' 213
  I GENERALLY 213
  II 'TRACING' 213
    (a) In general 213
    (b) Tracing: the common law rules 215
    Common law – the nature of the claimant's rights in
      substitute assets 215
    Common law – identifying the proceeds 219

Common law money claims and change of position   220
(c) Tracing: the equitable jurisdiction   220
Equitable personal claims   221
Equitable claims to substitute property   223
(a) The nature of the claimant's interest in the substitute   223
(b) The equitable proprietary base   225
(c) Sufficient connection: identifying the proceeds   227
(d) Mixing assets: bank accounts and 'first in, first out'   228
(e) A conundrum: 'backwards tracing'   230
(f) A special rule in equity: the lien against property in
    the wrongdoer's hands   230
(g) Equitable tracing: change of position and *bona fide* purchase 232
III DIVERSION CASES   232
(a) Generally   232
(b) Profits of property or office   232
(c) Other cases   234

11 RESTITUTION FOR WRONGS   **237**

I   GENERALLY   237
II   THE POINT OF PRINCIPLE: WHEN SHOULD RESTITUTION
     FOR WRONGS BE PERMITTED?   238
     (a) Infringement of tradable rights   240
     (b) Obligations of loyalty   241
III CASES WHERE RESTITUTION FOR WRONGS IS AVAILABLE   242
     (a) Restitution for torts   242
         The availability of exemplary damages   242
         Tort damages: gain masquerading as loss   243
         Waiver of tort   244
         Waiver of tort: non-cash gains   246
     (b) Restitution for breach of contract   247
         Contracts providing for payment over of profits arising
             from breach   248
         Breach of contract amounting also to infringement of a
             property or tradable right   248
         Breach of contract not to do something without consent:
             the covenant cases   249
         Breach of contract and breach of fiduciary duty   250
         Other cases   250
     (c) Restitution for breach of trust or fiduciary duty   251
         Trustees   251
         Other fiduciaries   252
     (d) Infringement of intellectual property rights   253

IV	RESTITUTIONARY REMEDIES AVAILABLE FOR WRONGS	255
	(a) Form	255
	(b) The exceptions: *Taylor v Plumer*	255
	(c) The exceptions: 'property benefits'	255
	(d) Other fiduciary profits	256
	(e) Profits and losses	257

12 RESTITUTION AND PUBLIC AUTHORITIES | | **259**

I	GENERALLY	259
II	PARTICULAR PUBLIC LAW RIGHTS TO RESTITUTION	261
	(a) Payments *colore officii*	261
	(b) Overpaid taxes	262
	(c) Recovery by the State or Crown of unauthorised payments	264
	(d) Restrictions on recovery against public authorities	265
	Procedural	265
	Substantive – change of position and analogous arguments	266
	Substantive – unjust enrichment of the claimant if recovery permitted	268

13 DEFENCES | | **269**

I	GENERALLY	269
II	EXCLUSION OF RESTITUTION BY AGREEMENT AND SIMILAR CASES	269
	(a) Exclusion by contract or compromise	269
	(b) Finality: intent to close a transaction	270
	(c) Donative intent	270
III	CHANGE OF POSITION	271
	(a) Generally	271
	(b) Change of position: extent and scope of the defence	273
	(c) Does change of position require an act by the defendant?	275
	(d) Change of position and double recovery	276
	(e) Change of position: acts other than paying money	277
	(f) Prior and subsequent change of position	277
	(g) Who can invoke change of position? – the problem of 'wrongdoers'	278
	(h) Possible other exceptions to change of position	279
IV	ESTOPPEL	279
V	ILLEGALITY AND STATUTORY INVALIDITY	282
	(a) Generally	282
	(b) Exception: unknowing participation	283
	(c) Exception: 'repentance cases'	283

(d) Exception: claimant not *in pari delicto*   285
(e) A particular case: restitution and the impact of existing
    property rights   286
(f) Statutory bars to recovery   287

Selected bibliography   291

Index   295

TABLE OF CASES

United Kingdom and Ireland

19th Ltd, Re [1989] ILRM 652 ....56, 61

Aas v Benham [1891] 2 Ch 244 253

AB v South West Water Services Ltd [1993] QB 507 246

Adam v Newbigging (1886) 34 Ch D 582; (1888) 13 App Cas 308 155

AG for Hong Kong v Reid [1994] 1 AC 324 ....7, 13, 34, 47, 52,
53, 225, 256, 257

AG v Blake [2001] 1 AC 268 ....33, 238, 239, 247,
249, 250, 254

AG v Guardian Newspapers Ltd (No 2) [1990] 1 AC 109 254

AG v Ryan's Car Hire [1965] IR 642 ....2, 182

AG's Reference (No 1 of 1985) [1986] 2 All ER 219 256

Agip (Africa) Ltd v Jackson [1991] Ch 547 ....29, 216, 218, 220,
223, 226, 227

Ahearne v McSwiney (1858) IR 8 CL 568 190

Aiken v Short (1856) 1 H and N 210 ....26, 27, 74

Albionic, The [1942] P 81 210

Alder v Moore [1961] 2 QB 57 248

Alev, The [1989] 1 Lloyd's Rep 138 93

Alexander v Rayson [1936] 1 KB 169 284

Alexander v Vane (1836) 1 M & W 511 118

Allwood v Clifford (2001) unreported, 28 June, Ch D 253

Allcard v Skinner (1887) 36 Ch D 145 ....104, 105, 105, 106

Allied Carpets plc v Nethercott (2000) unreported, 28 January 53

Allied Discount Card v Bord Failte [1991] 2 IR 185 4

Allied Irish Banks Ltd v Glynn [1973] IR 188 83

Allison v Jenkins [1904] 1 IR 341 ....190, 192

Alston, Ex p (1868) LR 4 Ch App 168 187

Aluminium Industrie BV v Romalpa Ltd [1976] 2 All ER 552 ....19, 233

Amoco (UK) Exploration Co v Teesside Gas
Transportation Ltd (1999) unreported, 30 July, CA
(reversed on unconnected grounds: [2001] 1 All ER (Comm) 883) 37

Anderson v Ryan [1967] IR 34 26

Andrews v Patriotic Insurance Co of Ireland (1886) LR Ir 335 65

Angel Bell, The [1980] 1 All ER 480 47

Anson v Anson [1953] 1 QB 636 187

Appleby v Myers (1867) LR 3 CP 651 ....148, 151

Arab Monetary Fund v Hashim [1993] 1 Lloyd's Rep 543 253

Arcedeckne, Re (1883) 24 Ch D 709 193
Argos, The (1873) LR 5 PC 134 201
Armagas Ltd v Mundogas SA [1986] AC 717 161
Armstrong v Jackson [1917] 2 KB 822 156
Arrale v Costain Ltd [1976] 1 Lloyd's Rep 98 104
Arris v Stukeley (1677) 2 Mod 260 ....19, 233
Arterial Drainage Co v Rathangan Drainage Board (1880) 6 LR Ir 513 140
Ashbury Carriage and Wagon Co v Riche (1875) LR 7 HL 653 171
Asher v Wallis (1707) 11 Mod 146 233
Associated Japanese Bank (International) Ltd
    v Crédit du Nord SA [1988] 3 All ER 902 ....156, 160, 161
Astley v Reynolds (1731) 2 Str 915 ....93, 109
Athel Line Ltd v Liverpool & London War
    Risks Association Ltd [1944] KB 87 198
Atkinson v Denby (1862) 7 H & N 934 ....170, 286
Atlantic Baron, The [1979] QB 705 ....94, 97, 100, 163
Atlantic Shipping Ltd v Finagrain Ltd
    (1999) unreported, 15 January 119
Atlas Express Ltd v Kafco Ltd [1989] 1 All ER 641 ....93, 94, 97
Aubert v Walsh (1810) 3 Taunt 277 ....283, 284
Auckland Harbour Board v R [1924] AC 318 ....53, 71, 265, 272, 279
Avon CC v Howlett [1983] 1 All ER 1073 ....280, 281
Aylesford (Earl) v Morris (1873) LR 8 Ch App 473 107

Bahin v Hughes (1886) 31 Ch D 390 195
Bainbrigge v Browne (1881) 18 Ch D 188 ....109, 111
Baker v Medway Building Supplies Ltd [1958] 2 All ER 533 222
Banco Exterior Internacional v Mann [1995] 1 All ER 936 112
Bank of America v Arnell [1999] Lloyd's Rep Bank 399 ....52, 80
Bank of Credit and Commerce
    International Ltd v Aboody [1990] 1 QB 923 104
Bank of Ireland Finance Ltd v Daly [1978] IR 79 60
Bank of Nova Scotia v Hogan [1996] 3 IR 239 (Supreme Court) 112
Bank Tejarat v Hong Kong and Shanghai Bank
    [1995] 1 Lloyd's Rep 239 ....271, 274
Bankers Trust v Namdar (1997) unreported, 14 February, CA 56
Bannatyne v MacIver [1906] 1 KB 103 58
Banque Belge pour l'Étranger v Hambrouck [1921] 1 KB 321 ....217, 218

Table of Cases

Banque Financière de la Cité v Parc
  (Battersca) Ltd [1999] 1 AC 221 ....55, 56, 56, 59,
                                                                        62, 63, 65, 88
Barclays Bank Ltd v Quistclose
  Investments Ltd [1970] AC 567 130
Barclays Bank Ltd v WJ Simms Ltd [1979] 3 All ER 522 ....61, 75, 79, 111, 272
Barclays Bank plc v Buhr [2001] EWCA 1223 214
Barclays Bank plc v O'Brien [1994] 1 AC 180 ....27, 105, 111, 112
Barlow Clowes International Ltd v Vaughan
  [1992] 4 All ER 22 ....226, 229
Barton v Armstrong [1976] AC 104 ....92, 93, 96, 101, 164
Basham, Re [1987] 1 All ER 405 176
Batis, The [1990] 1 Lloyd's Rep 345 33
Daylis v Bishop of London [1913] 1 Ch 127 272
Becerra v Close Bros Ltd (1999) unreported, 25 June, QBD 22, 115, 118
Beckingham and Lambert v Vaughan (1616) 1 Rolle Rep 391 235
Becton Dickinson (UK) Ltd v Zwebner [1989] QB 208 189
Behrend v Produce Brokers Ltd [1920] 3 KB 530 ....134, 145, 147
Bekhor (AJ) Ltd v Bilton Ltd [1981] 2 All ER 564 47
Belger v Belger (1989) unreported, 17 July, CA 186, 187, 193
Bell Houses Ltd v City Wall Properties Ltd [1966] 1 QB 207 ....171, 172
Bell v Lever Bros [1932] AC 761 ....31, 77, 154, 160
Belshaw v Bush (1851) 11 CB 191 183
Beresford v Kennedy (1887) 21 Ir LTR 17 ....185, 186, 187
Berg v Sadler & Moore [1937] 2 KB 158 ....282, 284
Bergin v Farrell (1999) unreported,
  17 December, HC (Ireland) 116
Berkeley Applegate (Investment Consultants) Ltd, Re [1989] Ch 32 203
Bigos v Bousted [1951] 1 All ER 92 ....282, 284
Bilbie v Lumley (1801) 2 East 469 ....70, 71, 74
Binstead v Buck (1777) 2 W Bl 1117 205
Birse Construction Ltd v Haiste [1996] 2 All ER 1 ....183, 195
Bishop, Ex p (1880) 15 Ch D 400 192
Bishopsgate Investment Trust Ltd v Homan [1995] Ch 211 ....229, 230
Biss, Re [1903] 2 Ch 40 251
Black v Freedman (1910) 12 CLR 105 227
Blackburn Benefit Building Society
  v Cunliffe Brooks & Co (1882) 22 Ch D 61 ....58, 59
Blackwood's Lessee v Gregg (1831) Hayes 277 92

Boardman v Phipps [1967] 2 AC 46 ....251, 256

Bolton v Mahadeva [1972] 1 WLR 1009 144

Bonner v Tottenham Building Society [1899] 1 QB 161 190

Boodle Hatfield v British Films Ltd [1986] BCC 99 60

Bookmakers' Afternoon Greyhound Service Ltd
    v Gilbert [1994] FSR 723 ....22, 24, 118, 121

Boscawen v Bajwa [1995] 4 All ER 769 ....57, 63, 215

Boston Deep Sea Fishing Co v Ansell (1888) 39 Ch D 339 ....45, 253

Boulton v Jones (1857) 2 H and N 564 ....25, 83, 85, 120

Boustany v Pigott (1993) 69 P and CR 298 108

Bovis Construction Ltd v Commercial Union
    Assurance Co plc [2001] Lloyd's Rep IR 321 ....184, 194, 195

Bowell v Milbank (1772) 1 TR 399 234

Bowmaker Ltd v Barnet Instruments Ltd [1945] KB 65 286

Box v Barclays Bank plc (1998) The Times, 30 April 48, 129, 219, 225

Boyter v Dodsworth (1796) 6 TR 681 234

BP (Exploration) Ltd v Hunt [1983] 2 AC 352 ....11, 12 , 13, 150, 151, 152, 272

Bradford Corp v Pickles [1895] AC 587 102

Brady v Flood (1841) 6 Circuit Cases 309 ....96, 282

Brewer Street Investments Ltd v Barclays Woollen Co Ltd
    [1954] 1 QB 428 ....177, 178

Bridgewater v Griffiths [2000] 1 WLR 524 159

Brisbane v Dacres (1813) 5 Taunt 143 70

British Bank for Foreign Trade v Novinex Ltd [1949] 1 KB 623 116

British Red Cross Balkan Fund, Re [1914] 2 Ch 419 229

British Steel Corp v Cleveland Bridge &
    Engineering Co Ltd [1984] 1 All ER 504 ....29, 117, 131,
                                                           177, 178, 179

British Steel plc v Customs and Excise Comrs [1997] 2 All ER 366 266

Broadway Approvals v Odhams Press Ltd [1965] 1 WLR 805 243

Brook's Wharf and Bull Wharf Ltd v Goodman Bros [1937] 1 KB 534 192

Brown & Davis Ltd v Galbraith [1972] 1 WLR 997 123

Browning v Morris (1778) 2 Cowper 790 ....169, 170

BSkyB plc v Comrs of Customs & Excise [2001] STC 437 263

Buchan v Ayre [1915] 2 Ch 474 203

Buller v Harrison (1777) 2 Cowp 565 271

Bullingdon v Oxford Corp [1936] 3 All ER 875 74

Bullock v Lloyds Bank Ltd [1955] Ch 317 88

Burston Finance Ltd v Speirway Ltd [1974] 3 All ER 735 59

Butler v Broadhead [1974] 2 All ER 401 222
Butler v Rice [1910] 2 KB 277 90
Butler's Wharf Ltd, Re [1995] 2 BCLC 43 188
Butlin's Settlement Trusts, Re [1976] 2 All ER 483 80
Butlin-Sanders v Butlin (1985) 15 Fam Law 126 108
Butterworth v Kingsway Motors Ltd [1954] 1 WLR 1286 136
Byfield, Re [1982] 1 All ER 249 28
Byrne v Rudd [1920] 2 IR 12 . . . . .70, 72

Cadaval (Duke) v Collins (1836) 4 A and E 858 100
Callan v Marum (1871) 5 IR CL 315 143
Callinan v VHI Board [1994] 3 CMLR 796. . . . . .160, 204, 206
Callisher v Bischoffsheim (1870) LR 5 QB 449 270
Calveley v Merseyside Chief Constable [1989] 1 All ER 1025 266
Camellia, The (1884) 9 PD 27 211
Car and Universal Finance Co Ltd v Caldwell [1965] 1 QB 525 . . . . .47, 50, 82
Casey (A Bankrupt), Re (1993) unreported, 1 March, HC (Ireland) .65
Casey v Irish Sailors Land Trust [1937] IR 208 71
Cassell & Co Ltd v Broome [1972] AC 1027 . . . . .33, 242, 258
Castellain v Preston (1883) 11 QBD 380 65
Cavalier Insurance Ltd, Re [1989] 2 Lloyd's Rep 450 . . . . .70, 284, 285
Chalmers v Pardoe [1963] 3 All ER 552 176
Chandler v Webster [1904] 1 KB 493 132
Chaplin v Leslie Frewin Ltd [1966] Ch 71 166
Chartered Trust (Ireland) Ltd v Healy
     (1985) unreported, 10 December, HC (Ireland) 136
Chase Manhattan NA v Israel-British Bank Ltd [1981] Ch 105 . . . . .29, 32, 36,
                                                                                                     43, 48, 51, 52,
                                                                                                     70, 79, 80, 83,
                                                                                                     101, 109, 130, 286
Cheese v Thomas [1994] 1 All ER 35 129
Chesters, Re [1935] 1 Ch 77 190
Chesworth v Farrer [1967] 1 QB 107 245
Chettiar v Chettiar [1962] AC 294 . . . . .286, 287
Chetwynd v Allen [1899] 1 Ch 353 58
Chichester Diocesan Board Fund v Simpson [1944] AC 341 221
Chieb v Carter (1987) unreported, 3 June 117

Chillingworth v Esche [1924] 1 Ch 97 ....127, 175
Chipboard Products Ltd, Re [1994] 3 IR 164 ....61, 188
Choko Star, The [1990] 1 Lloyd's Rep 506 201
Christy v Row (1808) 1 Taunt 299 146
CIBC Mortgages Ltd v Pitt [1994] 1 AC 200 ....103, 104, 105, 106, 111, 112
Clarke v Dickson (1858) 8 EB & E 148 155
Clarke v Shee (1774) 1 Cowp 197 218
Clayton's Case (1816) 1 Mer 572 ....228, 229, 230, 231, 232
Cleadon Trust Ltd Re [1939] Ch 286 85
Clough Mill Ltd v Martin [1984] 3 All ER 982 255
Clowes Developments Ltd v Mulchinock
    (2001) unreported, 24 May, Ch D 135
Cocks v Masterman (1829) 9 B & C 902 272
Coldunell Ltd v Gallon [1986] 1 All ER 429 ....103, 104, 112
Colley v Overseas Exporters Ltd [1921] 3 KB 302 139
Collins (Philip) Ltd v Davis [2000] 3 All ER 808 ....274, 278, 280, 281
Combe v Combe [1951] 2 KB 215 277
Commercial Banking Co of Sydney v Mann [1961] AC 1 216
Commercial Union Assurance Co Ltd v Hayden [1977] QB 804 195
Comr of Stamp Duties v Livingston [1965] AC 694 226
Conway v Irish National Teachers' Organisation [1991] 2 IR 305 243
Cooke v Wright (1861) 1 B and S 559 ....90, 270
Coomber, Re [1911] 1 Ch 723 252
Cooper v O'Connell (1997) unreported, 5 June 243
Cooper v Phibbs (1865) 17 Ir R Ch 73, (1867) LR 2 HL 149 ....73, 78, 163
Copis v Middleton (1823) Turn & R 224 61
Cork & Youghal Rly Co, Re (1869) LR 4 Ch App 748 57
Corpe v Overton (1833) 10 Bing 252 165
Cotronic v Dezonie [1991] BCLC 721 283
Cotter v Minister of Agriculture (1991) unreported, 31 July, HC (Ireland) 131
Coughlan v Moloney (1905) 39 ILTR 153 143
Cowern v Nield [1912] 2 KB 419 ....4, 167, 289
Crabb v Arun DC [1976] Ch 179 87
Crantrave Ltd v Lloyds Bank plc [2000] 4 All ER 273 ....61, 84, 117, 183
Craven-Ellis v Canons Ltd [1936] 2 KB 403 ....120, 123
Craythorne v Swinburne (1807) 14 Ves 160 ....61, 187, 188
Creagh v Sheedy [1955–1956] Ir JR 85 143
Crédit Lyonnais Nederland NV v Burch [1997] 1 All ER 144 105
Cresswell v Potter (1968) [1978] 1 WLR 255n 107, 108

Croker v Croker (1874) 4 ILT 181 105
Cronmire, Re [1898] 2 QB 383 288
Crown House Ltd v Amec plc
  (1989) 48 Build LR 37 179
CTN Cash and Carry Ltd v Gallagher Ltd [1994] 4 All ER 714 ....95, 102, 103
Cullen v Cullen [1962] IR 268...87, 114
Cundy v Lindsay (1878) 3 App Cas 459 ....14, 25, 82, 98, 130, 162
Cutter v Powell (1795) 6 TR 320 ....148, 149

D & C Builders Ltd v Rees [1966] 2 QB 617 ....94, 98, 101
Dakin v Oxley (1864) 15 CBNS 646 144
Davies v London & Provincial Marine Insurance Co
  (1878) 8 Ch D 469 96
Davis & Co (Contractors) Ltd v Fareham UDC [1956] AC 696 139
Dempsey v Ward [1899] 1 IR 463 251
Denton, Re [1904] 2 Ch 178 188
Dickinson v Burrell (1866) LR 1 Eq 337 109
Dickson v Buller (1859) 9 Ir CLR 205
Dies v British International Mining & Finance Corp [1939] 1 KB 724 138
Dillwyn v Llewellyn (1862) 4 De G F and J 517 87
Dimond v Lovell [2000] 2 All ER 897 ....175, 289, 290
Diplock, Re [1948] Ch 465 ....9, 57, 226, 228, 229, 271
Dolan v Neligan [1967] IR 247 ....70, 71, 72, 260, 261
Douglas v Hello! Ltd [2001] 2 All ER 289 119
Downer Enterprises Ltd, Re [1974] 2 All ER 1074 62
Dowse v Gorton [1891] AC 190 67
Drane v Evangelou [1978] 2 All ER 437 243
Dublin Corp v Building & Allied Trades Union [1996] 1 IR 468 ....4, 72
Dublin Corp v Trinity College [1985] ILRM 84 ....71, 72
Duke of Norfolk's Settlement Trusts, Re [1982] Ch 61 203
Duncan Fox and Co v North and South Wales Bank
  (1880) 6 App Cas 1 ....55, 62, 188, 192
Durrant v Ecclesiastical Comrs (1880) 6 QBD 234 272

Eagle Trust plc v SBC Securities Ltd (No 2) [1996] 1 BCLC 121 222
Earl of Shrewsbury's case (1610) 9 Rep 46b 233
Easat Ltd v Racal plc (2000) unreported 10, 24
East Cork Foods Ltd v O'Dwyer [1978] IR 103 ....5, 16, 184, 192

Eastbourne BC v Foster [2001] EWCA 1091 ....265, 278
Eastern Capital Futures Ltd, Re [1989] BCLC 371 203
Eastgate v Lindsey Morden Group plc [2001] PNLR 953 195
Eaton v Donegal Tweed Co Ltd (1934) LJCCR 81 190
Edelsten v Edelsten (1863) 1 DJ and Sm 185 254
Edgington v Fitzmaurice (1885) 29 Ch D 459 70
Edmonds (1862) Ex p 4 De G F and J 488 67
Edward Owen Ltd v Barclays Bank Ltd [1978] QB 159 18
El Ajou v Dollar Land Holdings plc [1993] 3 All ER 717 ....48, 52, 130, 220, 222, 226
Eldan Services Ltd v Chandag Motors Ltd
    [1990] 3 All ER 459 ....79, 219, 257
Electricity Supply Nominees Ltd
    v Thorn EMI plc (1991) 63 P & CR 143 ....189, 190
Elf Enterprises (Caledonia) Ltd v London Bridge
    Engineering Ltd (1997) The Times, 28 November 63
Ellesmere Brewery Co v Cooper [1896] 1 QB 75 194
Ellis v Barker (1871) LR 7 Ch App 104 105
Ellis v Ellis (1909) 26 TLR 166 83
Elvin & Powell Ltd v Plummer Roddis Ltd (1933) 50 TLR 158 ....82, 162
England v Guardian Insurance Ltd [1999] 2 All ER (Comm) 481 66
English v Dedham Vale Properties Ltd [1978] 1 All ER 382 233
Ennis, Re [1893] 3 Ch 238 194
Erlanger v New Sombrero Phosphate Co (1878) 3 App Cas 1218 ....134, 156
Esso Bernicia, The [1989] 1 AC 643 ....184, 192
ET Ltd v Fashion Gossip Ltd (2000) unreported, 29 July, CA 120
Euroactividade AG v Moeller (1995) unreported, 1 February, CA 276
Evans v Llewellin (1787) 1 Cox Eq Cas 333 107
EVTR Ltd, Re [1987] BCLC 646 225
Exall v Partridge (1799) 8 TR 308 ....41, 187, 191

Fahey v Frawley (1890) 26 LR Ir 78 188
Falcke v Scottish Imperial Insurance Co
    (1881) 34 Ch D 234 ....21, 85, 88, 191, 199, 208
Fanning v Wicklow CC (1984) unreported, 30 April 162, 176
Fell v Whitaker (1871) LR 7 QB 120 95
Felthouse v Bindley (1862) 11 CB (NS) 869 118
Ferguson (DO) Associates Ltd v Soh (1992) 62 Build LR 95 134

Fetherstone v Mitchell (1848) 11 Ir Eq R 35 ....191, 192

Ffrench's Estate, Re (1887) 21 LR Ir 283 ....26, 224

Fibrosa Spolka Akcyjna v Fairbairn Lawson
   Combe Barbour [1943] AC 32 ....3, 132, 147, 149

Fielding & Platt Ltd v Najjar [1969] 2 All ER 150 283

Fitt v Cassanet (1852) 4 M & G 898 138

Flannery v Dean [1995] 2 ILRM 393 201

Folans and Co v Minister of Education [1984] 1 ILRM 265 141

Forman & Co Pty Ltd v The Liddesdale [1900] AC 190 121

Foskett v McKeown [1998] Ch 265 230

Foskett v McKeown [2001] 1 AC 102 ....7, 9, 214, 215, 216, 227

Founds Estate, Re [1970] NI 139 104

Frederick Inns Ltd, Re [1981] ILRM 582 172

Freeman & Lockyer v Buckhurst Park
   Properties Ltd [1964] 2 QB 480 282

French's Wine Bar Ltd, Re [1987] BCLC 499 ....47, 83, 162

Friends' Provident Life Office v Hillier Parker [1997] QB 805 ....196, 221

Fry v Lane (1888) 40 Ch D 312 ....107, 108

Gabbett v Lauder (1883) LR 11 Ir 295 ....252, 255

Gamerco v ICM/Fair Warning Ltd [1995] 1 WLR 1226 152

Garvey v Ireland (1979) unreported, 19 December,
   Supreme Court (Ireland) 247

Garvey v McMinn (1846) 9 Ir Eq R 526 107

Gebhardt v Saunders [1892] 2 QB 452 206

General Tire and Rubber Co v Firestone Tyre
   and Rubber Co Ltd (No 2) [1975] 2 All ER 173 244

Ghana Commercial Bank Ltd v Chandiram [1960] AC 732 58

Gilbert v Knight [1968] 2 All ER 248 122

Glubb, Re [1900] 1 Ch 354 82

Godley v Perry [1960] 1 WLR 9 164

Goldcorp Exchange Ltd, Re [1995] 1 AC 74 ....48, 49, 50, 51, 70,
                                                                     129, 224, 225

Golightly v Reynolds (1772) Lofft 88 215

Goole & Hull Steam Towing Ltd
   v Ocean Marine [1928] 1 KB 589 66

Gore v Gore [1901] 2 IR 269 ....188, 193

Goring, The [1988] AC 431 ....200, 210

Gormley v Johnston (1895) 29 ILTR 69 186

Gosbell v Archer (1835) 2 Ad & El 500 . . . . .174, 288
Goss v Chilcott [1996] AC 788 . . . . .128, 133, 134, 136, 275
Gowers v Lloyds & National Provincial
    Foreign Bank Ltd [1938] 1 All ER 766 271
Graham v Thompson (1867) IR 2 CL 64 288
Gray v Richards Butler & Co (1996) The Times, 23 July 45, 85, 274, 277
Gray v Southouse [1949] 2 All ER 1019 170
Grealish v Murphy [1946] IR 35 . . . . .107, 108
Greasley v Cooke [1980] 3 All ER 710 176
Great Northern Rly Co v Swaffield (1874) LR 9 Ex 132 . . . . .201, 202, 205, 212
Great Western Rly Co v Sutton (1869) LR 4 HL 226 .108, 260, 261
Greenwood v Bennett [1973] QB 195 . . . . .22, 86, 89
Greer v Downs Supply Co Ltd [1927] 2 KB 28 25
Gregg v Kidd [1956] IR 183 . . . . .104, 107
Grey v Southouse [1949] 2 All ER 1019 285
Griffiths v Owen [1907] 1 Ch 195 252
Gt Southern & Western Rly Co
    v Robertson (1878) 2 LR Ir 548 . . . . .108, 260
Guinness Mahon & Co Ltd v Kensington BC [1999] QB 215 . . . . .72, 158, 161, 169
Guinness plc v Saunders [1990] 2 AC 663 . . . . .121, 123, 252
Guinness v CMD Ltd (1995) 45 Con LR 48 193
Guppys (Bridport) Ltd v Brookling (1984) 14 HLR 1 243

Hain SS Co v Tate and Lyle Ltd [1936] 2 All ER 597 144
Halifax Building Society v Muirhead (1998) 76 P&CR 418 58
Halifax Building Society v Thomas [1996] Ch 217 . . . . .239, 245
Hallett's Estate, Re (1880) 13 Ch D 696 231
Hambly v Trott (1776) 1 Cowp 371 245
Hancock v Smith (1889) 41 Ch D 456 228
Harberton (Lord) v Bennett (1829) Beatty 386 189
Hardie and Lane Ltd v Chiltern [1928] 1 KB 663 . . . . .96, 102
Hardoon v Belilios [1901] AC 118 . . . . .45, 203
Hargreave v Everard (1856) 6 Ir Ch R 678 . . . . .104, 105
Harnedy v National Greyhound Racing Co [1944] IR 160 164
Harris v Sheffield United Football Club Ltd [1987] 2 All ER 838 .118
Harry Parker v Mason [1940] 4 All ER 199 284
Harse v Pearl Life Assurance Co [1904] 1 KB 558 70
Hart v O'Connor [1985] AC 1000 204
Hasan v Willson [1977] 1 Lloyd's Rep 431 27

Hassard v Smith (1872) IR 6 Eq 429 204

Hatch, Re [1919] 1 Ch 351 73

Hay v Carter [1935] Ch 397 194

Hayes v Stirling (1863) 14 Ir CLR 277 127

Hazell v Hammersmith & Fulham LBC [1992] 2 AC 1 .72

Head v Tattersall (1871) LR & Ex 7 155

Hedley Byrne & Co Ltd v Heller & Partners Ltd [1964] AC 462 237

Henderson v Folkestone Waterworks Co (1885) 1 TLR 329 71

Henehan v Courtney (1966) 101 ILTR 25 116

Henry v Hammond [1913] 2 KB 515 53

Hermann v Charlesworth [1905] 2 KB 123 . . . . .170, 285

Hickey v Roches Stores Ltd (1976) [1993] RLR 196 . . . . .3, 4, 239, 243

Hicks v Hicks (1802) 3 East 16 172

Highland Finance Ltd v Sacred Heart College
    of Agriculture [1992] 1 IR 472 . . . . .54, 60

Highland Loch, The [1912] AC 312 197

Hill v Browne (1843) 6 Ir Eq R 406 192

Hill v Perrott (1810) 3 Taunt 274 . . . . .245, 246

Hillesden Securities Ltd v Ryjack Ltd [1983] 2 All ER 184 243

Hinckley and Bosworth BC v Shaw [2000] LGR 9 278

Hobbs v Marlowe [1978] AC 16 65

Hoenig v Isaacs [1952] 1 All ER 176 . . . . .139, 144

Hogan v Steele & Co Ltd [2000] 1 ESC 26 182

Holt v Markham [1923] 1 KB 504 . . . . .2, 272, 280

Hood of Avalon (Lady) v Mackinnon [1909] 1 Ch 476 . . . . .75, 80, 83

Hooper v Exeter Corp (1887) 56 LJQB 457 . . . . .261, 262

Hopper v Burness (1876) 1 CPD 137 . . . . .145, 146

Horry v Tate & Lyle Ltd [1982] 2 Lloyd's Rep 417 106

Hortensius v Bishops [1989] ILRM 294 169

House of Spring Gardens Ltd v Point Blank Ltd [1984] IR 611 4

Hudson v Robinson (1816) 4 M & S 475 217

Hughes v Liverpool Victoria Friendly Society [1916] 2 QB 482 285

Hughes, Re [1970] IR 237 229

Hulton v Hulton [1917] 1 KB 813 156

Hunt v Silk (1804) 5 East 449 133

Hunter v Hunt (1845) 1 CB 300 190

Hunter, Re (1998) unreported, Ch D, NI 8, 190

Hussey v Palmer [1972] 3 All ER 744 .52, 114, 127, 140, 176

Hyundai Heavy Industries Co Ltd
v Papadopoulos [1980] 2 All ER 29 ....135, 139, 147

Inche Noriah v Shaik Allie Bin Omar [1929] AC 127 105
Industrial Development Consultants Ltd
v Cooley [1972] 2 All ER 162 252
Industries & General Mortgage Co Ltd v Lewis [1949] 2 All ER 573 248
International Sales Ltd v Marcus [1982] 3 All ER 551 222
Inverugie Investments Ltd v Hackett [1995] 1 WLR 713 8
Inwards v Baker [1965] 2 QB 29 176
Iran Shipping Co v Denby [1987] 1 Lloyd's Rep 367 ....45, 256
Irish National Insurance Co v Scannell [1959] Ir Jur Rep 41 188
Irish Shipping Ltd, Re [1986] ILRM 518.....................26, 29, 43, 79, 80, 286
Italia Express, The [1992] 2 Lloyd's Rep 281 194

Jackson Stansfield v Butterworth [1948] 2 All ER 558 283
Jacob v Allen (1703) 1 Salk 27 ....19, 233
Jaggard v Sawyer [1995] 2 All ER 189 ....243, 247
James, Ex p (1874) LR 9 Ch App 609 ....70, 260
Jegon v Vivian (1871) LR 6 Ch App 742 244
Jenkins v Tucker (1788) 1 H Bl 90 206
Jennings v Woodman [1952] 2 TLR 309 178
John v James [1991] FSR 397 104
John v MGN Ltd [1998] QB 598 ....242, 243
Johnson, Re (1880) 15 Ch D 548 67
Johnson v Royal Mail Steam Packet Co (1867) LR 3 CP 38 187
Johnson v Wild (1890) 44 Ch D 146 190
Jones (FC) and Sons (Trustee) v Jones [1997] Ch 159 ....51, 53, 79, 214,
215, 216, 217, 220
Jones (RE) Ltd v Waring & Gillow Ltd [1926] AC 670 27
Jones v Stroud DC [1988] 1 All ER 5 ....184, 268

K, Re [1988] 1 All ER 358 204
Kangaroo, The [1918] P327 ....24, 211
Kasumu v Baba-Egbe [1956] AC 539 ....170, 171
Kayford Ltd, Re [1975] 1 All ER 604 130
Kearley v Thomson (1890) 24 QBD 742 ....282, 284
Keech v Sandford (1726) 1 Eq Cas Abr 741 ....251, 252, 255
Keeler's Settlement Trusts, Re [1981] 1 All ER 889 203

Kelly v Solari (1841) 9 M and W 54 . . . . .71, 74, 78, 270

Kelly v Staunton (1826) 1 Hogan 393 191

Kenny v Cosgrave [1926] IR 515 265

Ker v Ker (1869) 4 Ir R Eq 15 . . . . .8, 62, 187, 190, 191, 197

Key v Harwood (1846) 2 CB 905 128

Khan v Permayer (2000) unreported, 22 June, CA 28

Kincora Builders Ltd v Cronlin
        (1973) unreported, 5 March, HC (Ire) 144

King v Alston (1848) 12 QB 971 233

Kingsnorth Trust Ltd v Bell [1986] 1 All ER 423 11

Kiriri Cotton v Dewani [1960] AC 192 285

Kirwan v Cullen (1854) 2 Ir Ch R 322 . . . . .105, 170

Kleinwort Benson Ltd v Birmingham CC [1997] QB 380 . . . . .19, 40, 174, 268

Kleinwort Benson Ltd v Lincoln CC [1999] 2 AC 349 . . . . .37, 72, 73, 74,
                                                                                                                                        75, 130, 161

Kleinwort Benson Ltd v Sandwell BC [1994] 4 All ER 890 173

Kleinwort Benson Ltd v South Tyneside MBC [1994] 4 All ER 972 .40

Kleinwort Benson Ltd v Vaughan
        (1995) unreported, 13 December, CA 186, 187

Kleinwort, Sons and Co v Dunlop Rubber Co (1907) 97 LT 263 271

Kuddus v Chief Constable of Leicestershire [2001] 3 All ER 193 243

Lagunas Nitrate Co v Lagunas Syndicate [1899] 2 Ch 392 155

Lamb v Bunce (1815) 4 M & S 275 . . . . .114, 115, 118

Lancashire Loans Ltd v Black [1934] 1 KB 380 . . . . .105, 109, 111

Langton v Langton [1995] 2 FLR 890 . . . . .103, 108

Larner v London CC [1949] 2 KB 683 75

Lawlor v Alton (1873) IR 8 CL 160 233

Lazard Bros v Midland Bank Ltd [1933] AC 289 73

Leader v Leader (1874) IR 6 CL 20 . . . . .3, 234

Lecky v Walter [1914] IR 326 . . . . .78, 133, 137, 156

Lee-Parker v Izzett [1971] 1 WLR 1688 . . . . .48, 86, 130

Legal & General Assurance Soc Ltd v Drake
        Insurance Co Ltd [1992] QB 877 . . . . .182, 184, 194, 195

Legge v Croker (1811) 1 Ball & B 506 137

Leslie (J) Engineers Co Ltd, Re [1976] 2 All ER 85 . . . . .221, 222

Leslie (R) Ltd v Shiell [1914] 3 KB 607 . . . . .34, 46, 167, 168, 289

Leslie, Re (1883) 23 Ch D 552 . . . . .191, 199

Lewis v Averay [1972] 1 QB 198 ....26, 82, 160
Lewisham BC v Masters (1999) unreported, 25 November, CA 160
Liberian Insurance Agency Inc v Mosse [1977] 2 Lloyd's Rep 560 184
Liggett v Barclays Bank Ltd [1928] 1 KB 48 61
Lightly v Clouston (1808) 1 Taunt 112 2456
Linden Gardens Developments Ltd v Lenesta Sludge
    Disposals Ltd [1994] 1 AC 85 268
Linz v Electric Wire Co of Palestine Ltd [1948] AC 371 154
Lipkin Gorman v Karpnale Ltd [1991] 2 AC 548 ....4, 26, 27, 29–30,
                                                          40, 57, 71, 148, 149,
                                                    216, 217, 218, 220, 221, 223
                                                       227, 232, 265, 267, 271,
                                                           272, 273, 274, 277,
                                                           278, 279, 280, 281

Lister & Co v Stubbs (1890) 45 Ch D 1 ....45, 52, 53, 256
Liversidge v Broadbent (1859) 4 H and Nor 603 235
Livingstone v Rawyards Coal Co Ltd (1880) 5 App Cas 25 88
Lloyds Bank Ltd v Bundy [1975] QB 326 156
Lloyds Bank plc v Independent
    Insurance Co Ltd [2000] QB 110 ....75, 90
Locke v Evans (1823) 11 Ir Eq R 52n 190, 191
Lodder v Slowey [1904] AC 442 ....140, 142
Lodge v National Union Investment Co [1907] 1 Ch 300 170
Logan v Uttlesford DC (1986) 136 NLJ 541 181
London Commercial County Reinsurance, Re [1922] 2 Ch 67 288
London United Breweries Ltd, Re [1907] 2 Ch 511 67
Lonrho Exports Ltd v Export Credit
    Guarantee Dept [1996] 4 All ER 673 66
Lonrho Exports Ltd v Export Credit
    Guarantee Dept [1999] Ch 158 47
Lonrho plc v Fayed (No 2) [1992] 1 WLR 1 48
Lowis v Wilson [1949] IR 347 127
Lowry v Bourdieu (1780) 2 Doug 468 169
Lusty v Finsbury Securities Ltd (1991) 58 Build LR 66 140
Lydon v Coyne (1946) 12 Ir JR 64 107

M'Mehan v Warburton [1896] 1 IR 435 28
Macadam, Re [1946] Ch 73 ....235, 251
Macclesfield Corp v Great Central Rly Co [1911] 2 KB 528 206
Mackenzie v Royal Bank of Canada [1934] AC 468 156

Macmillan Inc v Bishopsgate Investment
  Trust Ltd [1995] 3 All ER 747 35
Madden v Kempster (1807) 1 Camp 12 245
Maher v Collins [1975] IR 232 245
Mahesan v Malaysia Government Housing Society [1979] AC 374 258
Mahoney v Purnell [1996] 3 All ER 61 109
Manila, The [1988] 3 All ER 843 . . . . .22, 121
Manson v Associated Newspapers Ltd [1965] 1 WLR 1038 242
Mara v Browne [1896] 1 Ch 199 233
Marley, Re [1976] 1 WLR 952 188
Marlow v Pitfeild (1719) 1 P Wms 558 58
Marsh v Keating (1834) 1 Bing NC 198 217
Marston Construction Ltd v Kigass Ltd
  (1989) Build LR 109 . . . . .10, 22, 178
Martin v Porter (1839) 5 M & W 351 88
Maskell v Horner [1915] 3 KB 106 . . . . .93, 99, 100
Massalia, The [1961] 2 QB 278 149
Massey v Midland Bank plc [1995] 1 All ER 929 112
Matheson v Smiley [1932] 2 DLR 787 204
Mavor v Pyne (1825) 3 Bing 285 175
Maxwell v Pressdram Ltd (1986) The Times, 22 November 242
Mayfield v Llewellyn [1961] 1 WLR 119 196
Mayhew v Crickett (1818) 2 Swan 185 188
McCormack v Bennett (1973) unreported, 2 July, HC (Ireland) .105
McNeil v Millen [1907] 2 IR 328 3
Mecca, The [1897] AC 286 229
Merryweather v Nixan (1799) 8 TR 186 195
Metall und Rohstoff AG v Donaldson [1989] 3 All ER 14 227
Metcalfe v Britannia Ironworks Co (1877) 2 QBD 423 144
Metropolitan Police Receiver v Croydon Corp [1957] 1 All ER 78 . . . . .182, 192
Middleton v Magnay (1864) 2 H and M 233 . . . . .48, 130
Midland Bank plc v Brown Shipley Ltd [1991] 2 All ER 690 272
Midland Bank plc v Shepherd [1988] 3 All ER 17 105
Midland Great Western Railway Co v Benson
  (1878) 2 LR (Ir) 548 183
Miles v Wakefield MBC [1987] AC 539 . . . . .145, 146
Ministry of Defence v Ashman [1993] 2 EGLR 102 . . . . .8, 119, 244
Ministry of Health v Simpson [1951] AC 251 . . . . .15, 45, 221, 222, 223, 279
Mohamed v Alaga and Co [1999] 3 All ER 699 289

Money Markets International
  Stockbrokers Ltd, Re [2000] 3 IR 437 229
Monnickendam v Leanse (1923) 39 TLR 445 138
Montagu's Settlement Trusts, Re [1987] Ch 264 222
Mooney v Ó Coindealbhóin [1992] 2 IR 23 260
Moore v Fulham Vestry [1895] 1 QB 399 ....90, 100
Morgan Guaranty Trust v Lothian Regional Council 1995 SC 151 71
Morgan v Ashcroft [1938] 1 KB 49 ....75, 288, 290
Morgan v Palmer (1824) 2 B & C 729 261
Morgan v Seymour (1638) 1 Ch R 120 188
Moriarty v Regent's Garage Co [1921] 1 KB 423 144
Morley v Morley (1855) de Gex, M & G 610 190
Morris v Ford Motor Co Ltd [1973] 2 All ER 1084 56
Moseley v Cressey's Co (1865) LR 1 Eq 405 ....129, 225
Moule v Garrett (1872) LR 7 Ex 10 189
Muckley v Ireland [1985] IR 472 260
Mulhallen v Marum (1843) 3 Dr and W 317 ....105, 105
Murphy v AG [1982] IR 241 ....16, 37, 45, 101, 109,
                                                  260, 264, 267, 272
Mutual Finance Ltd v Wetton & Sons Ltd [1937] 2 KB 389 ....95, 103
My Kinda Town Ltd v Soll [1982] FSR 147 254

NAD v TD [1985] ILRM 153 52
Napier and Ettrick (Lord) v Hunter [1993] AC 713 ....65, 66
Nash v Inman [1908] 2 KB 1 205
National Bank v O'Connor (1966) 103 ILTR 73 ....27, 75, 78
National Oilwell v Davy Offshore Ltd [1993] 2 Lloyd's Rep 582 65
National Pari-Mutuel Ltd v R (1930) 47 TLR 110 70
National Permanent Benefit Building
  Society, Re (1869) LR 5 Ch App 309 58
National Westminster Bank Ltd v Barclays
  Bank International Ltd [1974] 3 All ER 834 ....90, 274, 280
National Westminster Bank Ltd v Morgan [1985] AC 686 ....58, 106
National Westminster Bank plc v Somer [2001] EWCA 970 281
Naumann v Northcote (1978) unreported, 7 February, CA 194
Nelson v Larholt [1948] 1 KB 339 222
Neste OY v Lloyds Bank plc [1983] 2 Lloyd's Rep 658 ....48, 130, 225
Nevill's case (1870) LR 6 Ch App 43 ....188, 192
Nicholson v Chapman (1793) 2 H Bl 254 ....199, 205

North British & Mercantile Insurance Co v London,
   Liverpool & Globe Insurance Co (1876) 5 Ch D 569 194
Northern Banking Co v Carpenter [1931] IR 268 105
Norwich Union Fire Insurance Society
   Ltd v Price [1934] AC 455 ....75, 78, 79
Notara v Henderson (1872) LR 7 QB 225 201
Nurdin & Peacock plc v Ramsden & Co Ltd
   [1999] 1 All ER 941 ....73, 74, 78, 94
NZ Netherlands Society v Kuys [1973] 1 WLR 1126 253

O'Callaghan v Ballincollig Holdings Ltd
   (1993) unreported, 31 March 22, 199, 208
O'Donnell v Dún Laoghaire Corp [1991] ILRM 301 262
O'Flanagan v Ray-Ger (1983) unreported, 28 April, HC (Ireland) 104
O'Kelly v Glenny (1846) 9 Ir Eq R 25 106
O'Loghlen v O'Callaghan (1874) IR 8 Ch 116 ....70, 73
O'Reilly v Mackman [1983] 2 AC 237 ....262, 265
O'Rourke v Revenue Comrs [1996] 2 IR 1 37
O'Sullivan v Management Agency Ltd [1985] 3 All ER 351 ....104, 134, 156, 159
Oatway, Re [1903] 2 Ch 356 231
Official Custodian of Charities v Mackey
   (No 2) [1985] 2 All ER 1016 ....15, 19, 233, 234
Oom v Bruce (1810) 12 East 225 283
Orakpo v Manson Investments Ltd [1978] AC 95 ....34, 54, 56, 60, 289
Orchis, The (1890) 15 PD 38 187
Oriental Finance Corp v Overend Gurney & Co
   (1874) LR 7 HL 348 186
Oriental Hotels Co Ltd, Re [1908] 1 IR 473 203
Otter v Lord Vaux (1856) 6 de Gex, M & G 637 191
Owen v Tate [1976] QB 402 ....85, 183, 185, 186

P v P [1916] 2 IR 400 ....127, 136
Pao On v Lau Yiu Long [1980] AC 614 ....92, 94, 95, 96, 97,
                                                                     101, 110, 163
Paradise Motor Co Ltd, Re [1968] 2 All ER 625 83
Parkinson v College of Ambulance [1925] 2 KB 1 ....282, 284
Parry v Cleaver [1970] AC 1 66
Pascoe v Turner [1979] 2 All ER 945 87
Patten v Bond (1889) 60 LT 583 60

Patten v Hamilton [1911] IR 46 253
Patterson v Murphy [1978] ILRM 85 196
Paul v Speirway Ltd [1976] Ch 220 60
Paynter v Williams (1833) 1 C & M 810 118
Pearce v Brain [1929] 2 KB 310 ....134, 154, 165, 166
Penarth Dock & Eng Co Ltd v Pounds [1963] 1 Lloyd's Rep 359 ....3, 248
Pennell v Deffell (1853) 4 De G M & G 372 228
Perera v Vandiyar [1953] 1 WLR 672 247
Peter Lind Ltd v Mersey Docks and
    Harbour Board [1972] 2 Lloyd's Rep 234 176
Peter Pan Mfg Co v Corsets Silhouette Ltd [1963] 3 All ER 402 254
Petrinovic v Mission Française (1942) 71 Lloyd's List LR 208 148
Pfeiffer Weinkellerei GmbH v Arbuthnot
    Factors Ltd [1991] BCC 484 ....19, 233
Phelan v Stewards of Kilmacthomas Races (1896) ICT 36 288
Phillips v Homfray (1871) LR 6 Ch App 770 ....3, 8, 245, 246
Phillips v Phillips (1862) 4 De G, F and J 208 ....26, 83, 112, 224
Phillips v Phillips (1885) 29 Ch D 673 252
Phipps v Boardman [1967] 2 AC 46 252
Pigot's Case (1614) 11 Co Rep 26b 135
Pike, Re (1889) 23 LR Ir 9 ....204, 207
Pindaros, The [1983] 2 Lloyd's Rep 635 192
Pine Valley Ltd v Minister of the Environment [1987] IR 23 71
Planché v Colburn (1831) 8 Bing 14 ....10, 141, 151
Platt v Casey's Drogheda Brewery Ltd [1912] 1 IR 271 73
PMPA Garages (Longmile) Ltd , Re [1992] 1 IR 332 ....4, 5, 173
PMPA Insurance Co Ltd, Re [1986] ILRM 524 ....14, 217
Pollard v Bank of England (1871) LR 6 QB 623 90
Polly Peck Ltd (No 2), Re [1998] 3 All ER 812 ....49, 80, 225
Pontypridd Union v Drew [1927] 1 KB 214 ....204, 205
Portman Building Society v Hamlyn Taylor Neck [1998] 4 All ER 202 ....5, 7
Portreath, The [1923] P 155 210
Power, Re [1899] 1 IR 6 85
Power's Policies, Re [1899] 1 IR 6 ....190, 191, 204
Prager v Blatspiel Stamp & Heacock Ltd [1924] 1 KB 566 201
Premier Dairies Ltd v Jameson
    (1983) unreported, 1 March, HC (Ireland) 141
Price v Neal (1762) 3 Burr 1364 272
Pride, Re [1891] 2 Ch 135 ....8, 190

Proodos C, The [1980] 2 Lloyd's Rep 390 96
Protheroe v Protheroe [1968] 1 All ER 1111 . . . . .252, 253, 255

Quistclose Investments Ltd v Barclays Bank Ltd [1970] AC 567 . . . . .36, 130, 225

R (J) (A Ward of Court), Re [1993] ILRM 657 87
R v Richmond LBC ex p McCarthy & Stone Ltd [1992] 2 AC 48 . . . . .103, 261
R v Secretary of State for the Environment ex p London
    Borough of Camden (1995) unreported, 17 February, QBD 260, 265, 272,
                                    273, 278, 279
R v Shadrokh-Cigari [1988] Crim LR 465 51
Radcliffe v Price (1902) 18 TLR 466 105
Rae v Joyce (1892) 29 LR Ir 500 107
Raffles v Wichelhaus (1864) 2 H & C 906 161
Ramsden v Dyson (1866) LR 1 HL 129 . . . . .87, 114
Ramskill v Edwards (1885) 31 Ch D 100 197
Randolph v Tuck [1962] 1 QB 175 196
Ranelagh (Lord's) Will, Re (1994) 26 Ch D 590 252
Rathdonnell (Lord) v Colvin [1952] IR 297 207
Ravald v Russell (1830) You 9 71
Reading v AG [1951] AC 507 . . . . .20, 276, 277
Regal (Hastings) Ltd v Gulliver [1942] 1 All ER 378 252
Regalian Properties Ltd v London Docklands
    Development Corp [1995] 1 All ER 1005 . . . . .177, 178
Reilly (orse O'Reilly), Re
    (1989) unreported, 11 January, HC (Ireland) 56
Reversion Fund and Insurance Co Ltd
    v Maison Cosway Ltd [1913] 1 KB 364 . . . . .44, 58, 59
Rhodes, Re (1890) 44 Ch D 94 204
Richardson, Re [1911] 2 KB 712 188
Riches v News Group Newspapers Ltd [1985] 2 All ER 845 243
Richmond Gate Property Co Ltd, Re [1964] 3 All ER 936 . . . . .31, 123, 131
Roche v Sherrington [1982] 1 WLR 599 105
Rogers v Louth County Council [1981] ILRM 144 . . . . .70, 261, 262
Rookes v Barnard [1964] AC 1129 . . . . .238, 242, 243
Roscoe (Bolton) Ltd v Winder [1915] 1 Ch 62 . . . . .224, 229

Rover International Ltd v Cannon Film
 Sales Ltd (No 3) 3 All ER 423 . . . . .15, 74, 75, 76, 78, 79,
 81, 84, 129, 133, 136, 142
 155, 157, 158, 159, 161
Rowland v Divall [1923] KB 500 . . . . .136, 137
Roy v Kensington FPC [1992] 1 All ER 705 . . . . .265, 266
Royal Bank of Australia, Re (1856) D M & G 572 . . . . .193, 196
Royal Bank of Scotland plc v Etridge (No 2) [1998] 4 All ER 705 105
Royal Brunei Airlines Sdn Bhd v Tan [1995] 2 AC 378 253
RPH Ltd v Mirror Group Ltd (1993) 65 P & CR 252 189
Ruabon SS Co v London Assurance Co [1900] AC 6 39
Rumsey v North Eastern Rly Co (1863) 14 CB (NS) 641 119
Rusden v Pope (1868) LR 3 Ex 269 . . . . .19, 234
Ryan v Byrne (1880) 17 ILTR 102 190

Saleh Farid v Theodorou (1992) unreported, 30 January, CA 243
Salting, Ex p (1883) 25 Ch D 148 187
Saronic v Liberia Huron [1979] 1 Lloyd's Rep 341 . . . . .273, 278
Satnam Investments Ltd v Dunlop
 Heywood & Co Ltd [1999] 3 All ER 652 226
Savage v Canning (1867) IR 1 CL 434 . . . . .175, 289
Scaptrade, The [1983] 2 AC 694 138
Schiesser International Ltd v Gallagher (1971) 106 ILTR 22 248
Scott v Pattison [1923] 2 KB 723 289
Scott v Scott (1962) 109 CLR 649 . . . . .228, 230
Scott v Surman (1742) Willes 40 219
Scottish Equitable plc v Derby [2001] 3 All ER 793 . . . . .74, 267, 270, 274,
 275, 276, 277, 281
Seager v Copydex Ltd [1967] 2 All ER 415 254
Sebel Products Ltd v Comrs of
 Customs and Excise [1949] Ch 409 . . . . .78, 79
Seddon v North Eastern Salt Co Ltd [1905] 1 Ch 326 . . . . .78, 137, 155
Shamia v Joory [1958] 1 QB 448 235
Shanahan v Redmond, (1994) unreported, 21 June, HC (Ireland) 28, 30
Shanahan's Stamp Auctions Ltd v Farelly [1962] IR 386 226
Shansal v Al-Kishtaini (1999) unreported, 9 June 130
Sharpe (A Bankrupt), Re [1980] 1 All ER 198 52
Shaw v Shaw [1965] 1 All ER 638 . . . . .168, 169, 284
Shelley v Paddock [1980] 1 All ER 1009 285
Siboen, The and The Sibotre [1976] 1 Lloyd's Rep 293 . . . . .94, 96, 99, 100, 271

Silverwood v Silverwood (1997) 74 P & CR 453 287
Simpson v Thomson (1877) 3 App Cas 279 192
Sims v Midland Rly Co [1913] 1 KB 103 201
Sinclair v Brougham [1914] AC 398 ....4, 5, 46, 173, 225
Singh v Ali [1960] AC 167 169
Slator v Nolan (1876) IR 11 Eq 367 107
Sleigh v Sleigh (1850) 5 Ex 514 192
Smith New Court Securities Ltd v Scrimgeour Vickers
    (Asset Management) Ltd [1994] 4 All ER 225; [1997] AC 254 155
Smith v Bruning (1700) 2 Vern 392 170
Smith v Compton (1832) 3 B & Ad 407 188
Smith v Wood [1929] 1 Ch 14 ....188, 193
Smith's Estate Re [1937] Ch 636 202
Smyth v Smyth (1919) 53 ILTR 145 107
Sneath v Valley Gold [1893] 1 QB 477 270
Société Nouvelle d'Armement v Spillers and
    Bakers Ltd [1917] 1 KB 865 198
Solle v Butcher [1950] 1 KB 671 73
Solomons v Williams (2001) unreported, 23 May, Ch D 220
Sorrell v Paget [1950] 1 KB 252 199
South of Scotland Electricity Board
    v BOC Ltd (No 2) [1959] 2 All ER 225 ....108, 259, 261
South Tyneside Metropolitan BC v Svenska International plc
[1995] 1 All ER 545 ....148, 172, 222, 266, 2378
South West Water Services Ltd v International
    Computers Ltd (1999) unreported, 26 June, QBD 136
Space Investments Ltd v CIBC [1986] 3 All ER 75 49
Spiers & Pond v Finsbury BC (1956) 1 Ryde's Rating Cas 219 266
St Enoch Co v Phosphate Co [1916] 2 KB 624 148
Stapleton v Prudential Assurance Co (1928) 62 ILTR 56 ....132, 154
Steele v Williams (1853) 8 Ex 625 261
Steinberg v Scala (Leeds) Ltd [1923] 2 KB 452 ....154, 165
Stevens v Hill (1805) 5 Esp 247 235
Stevenson v Snow (1761) 3 Burr 1237 ....138, 283, 284
Stimpson v Smith [1999] 2 All ER 833 ....185, 194
Stocks v Wilson [1913] 2 KB 235 167
Stocznia Gdanska SA v Latvian
    Shipping Co [1998] 1 All ER 883 ....132, 134, 135
Stoke-on-Trent CC v W and J Wass Ltd [1988] 3 All ER 394 244

Stott v West Yorkshire Road Car Co Ltd [1971] 2 QB 651 ....182, 196
Stovin-Bradford v Volpoint Ltd [1971] 3 All ER 571 244
Strachan v Universal Stock Exchange (No 2) [1895] 2 QB 69 288
Strand Electric Ltd v Brisford
    Entertainments Ltd [1952] 2 QB 246 ....20, 33, 34, 243, 248
Strang Steel & Co v Scott and Co (1889) 14 App Cas 601 198
Streiner v Bank Leumi (1985) unreported, 31 October, QBD 276
Strickland v Turner (1852) 7 Ex 208 ....137, 161
Stronge v Johnston (1997) unreported, Ch D (NI), 16 April 108
Stroud Architectural Systems Ltd v John Laing
    Construction Ltd [1994] 2 BCLC 276 36
Sumner v Sumner (1935) 69 ILTR 101 169
Sumpter v Hedges [1898] 1 QB 673 143
Surrey Breakdown Ltd v Knight [1999] RTR 84 201
Surrey CC v Bredero Homes Ltd [1993] 3 All ER 705 ....239, 247, 249
Sutherland Publishing Co Ltd v Caxton
    Publishing Co Ltd [1936] Ch 323 ....254, 258
Swordheath Properties Ltd v Tabet [1979] 1 All ER 240 244
Sybron Corp v Rochem Ltd [1983] 2 All ER 707 ....79, 80

Tagus, The [1903] P 44 64
Tailby v Official Receiver (1887) 18 QBD 25 19
Tang Man Sit v Capacious Investments Ltd [1996] AC 514 258
Tate v Williamson (1866) LR 2 Ch App 55 104
Taylor v Bowers (1876) 1 QBD 291 283
Taylor v Laird (1856) 25 LJ Ex 329 ....84, 121
Taylor v Plummer (1815) 3 M & S 562 ....215, 216, 255
Tempany v Hynes [1976] IR 101 48
Tetley v British Trade Corp (1922) 10 Lloyd's List LR 678 201
Texaco (Ireland) Ltd v Murphy (No 2) [1992] 1 IR 399 260
Texaco (Ireland) Ltd v Murphy (No 3) [1992] 2 IR 300 260
TH Knitwear (Wholesale) Ltd, Re [1987] 1 WLR 371 182
Thomas v Brown (1876) 1 QBD 714 ....138, 284
Thompson's Trustee v Heaton [1974] 1 All ER 1239 ....252, 253
Thorne v Motor Trade Ass'n [1937] AC 797 ....96, 102, 165
Thurstan v Nottingham Permanent
    Building Society [1902] 1 Ch 1; [1903] AC 6 58
Tilley's Will Trusts, Re [1967] Ch 1179 ....228, 232

Tinker v Tinker [1970] P 136 ....286, 287
Tinsley v Milligan [1994] 1 AC 340 ....286, 287
Tito v Waddell (No 2) [1977] Ch 106 247
Tojo Maru, The [1972] AC 242 199
Toner v Livingston (1896) 30 ILTR 80 288
Tottenham v Bedingfield (1572) Owen 35 233
Tower Hamlets BC v Chetnik
    Developments Ltd [1988] 1 AC 858 264
Towey, (A Bankrupt), Re (1994) unreported, 24 March, HC (Ireland) 28, 182
Travers Construction Ltd v Lismore Homes Ltd
    (1990) unreported, 9 March, HC (Ireland) 146
Treacy v Corcoran (1874) IR 8 CL 40 ....144, 146
Tribe v Tribe [1996] Ch 107 ....284, 286
Trident Beauty, The [1994] 1 All ER 470 ....127, 133
Troilus, The [1951] AC 820 210
Tsakiroglou & Co Ltd v Noblee Thorl GmbH [1962] AC 93 139
Tugwell v Heyman (1812) 3 Camp 298 206
Turquand, Ex p (1876) 3 Ch D 445 ....56, 61
Twinsectra Ltd v Yardley [1999] Lloyd's Rep Banking 438 130
Twyford v Manchester Corp [1946] Ch 236 ....100, 262
Tyrie v Fletcher (1777) 2 Cowp 666 132

UDT (Ireland) Ltd v Shannon Caravans Ltd [1976] IR 225 136
United Australia Ltd v Barclays Bank Ltd [1941] AC 1 ....244, 258
United Overseas Bank v Jiwani [1977] 1 All ER 733 ....274, 275, 280
Unity Joint Stock Banking Co v King (1858) 25 Beav 72 ....46, 52, 86, 110, 287
Universal Stock Exchange v Strachan [1896] AC 166 288
Universe Sentinel, The [1983] AC 366 ....93, 95, 97, 110
Upton-on -Severn RDC v Powell [1942] 1 All ER 220 ....86, 271

Valentini v Canali (1889) 24 QBD 166 ....154, 165
Van Zeller v Mason Catley (1907) 25 RPC 37 254

Walford v Miles [1992] 2 AC 128 177
Walter v James (1871) LR 6 Ex 124 ....84, 117, 183
Wandsworth LBC v Winder [1985] AC 461 103
Ward v National Bank of New Zealand (1883) 8 App Cas 755 194
Warman International Ltd v Dwyer (1995) 182 CLR 544 253

Warman v Southern Counties Hire &
Finance Co [1949] 2 KB 576 ....18, 136
Watson & Son Ltd v Fireman's Fund Insurance
Co of San Francisco [1922] 2 KB 355 198
Watson v Russell (1862) 5 B & S 968 26
Way v Latilla [1937] 3 All ER 759 116
Weatherby v Banham (1832) 5 C & P 228 117
Webber v Smith (1689) 2 Vern 103 190
Weingarten v Bayer (1903) 22 RPC 341 254
Wenlock (Baroness) v River Dee Co (1887) 19 QBD 155 57
West Ham Union v Pearson (1890) 62 LT 638 204
West Midlands Chief Constable v White
(1992) The Times, 25 March 169
Westdeutsche Landesbank Girozentrale
v Islington BC [1996] AC 669 ....5, 15, 26, 29, 32,
36, 46, 47, 51, 53,
79, 80, 130, 133, 157,
158, 171, 172, 173, 225,
227, 259, 265, 266, 267
Whelan v Madigan [1978] ILRM 136 243
Whincup v Hughes (1871) LR6 CP 78 147
White v Meade (1840) 2 Ir R Eq 420 105
Whitham v Bullock [1939] 2 KB 81 189
Whitwham v Westminster Brymbo Coal Co [1892] 2 Ch 538 ....8, 244
Wilkinson v Lloyd (1845) 7 QB 27 137
William Brandt's Sons v Dunlop Rubber Co [1905] AC 454 19
William Lacey (Hounslow) Ltd v Davis
[1957] 1 WLR 932; [1957] 2 All ER 712 ....114, 126, 176
William Whiteley Ltd v R (1909) 101 LT 741 ....74, 90
Williams v Bayley (1866) LR 1 HL 200 ....96, 103
Williams v Everett (1811) 14 East 582 234
Williams v Moor (1843) 11 M & W 256 165
Williams v Roffey Bros Ltd [1991] 1 QB 1 270
Willis and Son (A Firm) v British Car
Auctions Ltd [1978] 2 All ER 392 217
Willmott v Barber (1880) 15 Ch D 96 86
Wiluszynski v Tower Hamlets LBC [1989] ICR 493 ....118, 145, 146
Wimpey v BOAC [1955] AC 169 195
Winson, The [1982] AC 939 ....200, 202
Wolenberg v Royal Co-operative Collecting Society (1915) 83 LJ KB 1316 132

Wood v Morewood (1841) 3 QB 440n 88
Woolwich Building Society v IRC (No 2) [1993] AC 70 .4, 13, 16, 53, 71,
                    78, 90, 94, 100, 101, 103,
                  109, 153, 260, 261, 263,
                 264, 265, 266, 267, 268
Workers Trust Ltd v Dojap [1993] AC 573 138
Wrexham, Mold and Connah's Quay Rly Co, Re [1899] 1 Ch 440 . . . . .54, 55, 57, 60, 64
Wright v Carter [1903] 1 Ch 27 . . . . .105, 105
Wrotham Park Estates Ltd v Parkside
  Homes Ltd [1974] 2 All ER 321 . . . . .248, 249
Wylie v Carlyon [1922] 1 Ch 51 60

Yardley v Arnold (1842) C & M 434 233
Yaxley v Gotts [2000] 1 All ER 711 140
Yorkshire Insurance Co v Nisbet Shipping Ltd [1962] 2 QB 330 65
Young v Holt (1947) 65 RPC 25 254
Ypatia Halcaussi, The [1985] 2 Lloyd's Rep 364 90

Zuhal K, The [1987] 1 Lloyd's Rep 151 186
Zurich Insurance Co v Shield Insurance Co
  (1987) unreported, 18 December, Supreme Court (Ireland) 194

Australia

ANZ Banking Group Ltd v Westpac Ltd (1988) 164 CLR 662 . . . . .4, 26, 75
Brenner v FAM [1993] 2 VR 221 141
Chan v Zacharia (1984) 154 CLR 178 251
Commonwealth v Burns [1971] VR 825 . . . . .265, 279
Comr of Revenue v Royal Insurance
  Australia Ltd (1994) 69 ALJR 51 . . . . .19, 40, 73, 267, 268
Crescendo Ltd v Westpac Ltd (1988) 19 NSWLR 40 97
David Securities Pty Ltd v Commonwealth
  Bank of Australia (1992) 175 CLR 353 71
Foran v Wright (1989) 64 ALJR 1 39
Gertsch v Atsas (1999) unreported, 1 October, SC (NSW) 221, 279
Latec Investments Ltd v Hotel Terrigal
  Pty Ltd (1965) 113 CLR 265 . . . . .26, 48
Mason v NSW (1959) 102 CLR 108 . . . . .99, 262
Pavey and Matthews Pty Ltd v Paul (1987) 162 CLR221 . . . . .4 , 5, 16, 34,
                    114, 175, 290
Roxborough v Rothmans Australia Ltd (1999) 161 ALR 253 . . . . .78, 134, 268

Sabemo v North Sydney Municipal Council (1977) 2 NSWLR 880 ....177, 259
US Surgical Corp v Hospital Products Corp (1984) 58 ALJR 587 250
Victoria Park Racing Ltd v Taylor (1937) 58 CLR 479 121
York Air Conditioning v Commonwealth (1949) 80 CLR 11 ....76, 77

Canada

Air Canada v British Columbia [1989] 1 SCR 1133 ....4, 71, 259, 262,
263, 266, 267, 268
Deglman v Guaranty Trust Co of Canada [1954] 3 DLR 785 ....4, 5, 174, 289
Dusik v Martin (1985) 62 BCLR 1 109
Fox v Royal Bank of Canada (1975) 59 DLR (3d) 258 188
Gidney v Shark [1995] 5 WWR 385 89
Hastings v Seaman's Village [1946] 4 DLR 695 206
Lac Minerals Ltd v International Corona
    Resources Ltd [1989] 2 SCR 574 250
More (James) v University of Ottawa (1974) 49 DLR (3d) 666 4
Peter Kiewit's Sons v Eakins Commission Co Ltd [1960] SCR 361 98
Petro-Canada Ltd v Capot-Blanc (1992) 95 DLR (4th) 69 32
Royal Bank of Canada v Dawson (1994) 111 DLR (4th) 230 281
Storthoaks Rural Municipality
    v Mobil Oil Canada Ltd (1975) 55 DLR (3d) 1 272

New Zealand

Auckland CC v Henderson District Court [1998] 1 NZLR 253 (NZ) 4
Equiticorp Industry Corp Ltd v The Crown [1998] 2 NZLR 481 4
Moyes and Groves Ltd v Radiation (NZ) Ltd [1982] 1 NZLR 368 93
Samson v Proctor [1975] NZLR 665 (NZ) 241

USA

Boomer v Muir, 24 P 2d 570 (1933) 143
City of New Orleans v Firemen's Charitable Association, 9 So 486 (1891) 241
Du Pont de Nemours v Christopher, 431 F 2d 1012 (1970) 119, 122
Snepp v US, 444 US 507 (1980) 247
Ulmer v Farnsworth, 16 Atl 65 (1888) (Supreme Court of Maine) 30
US v Butler, 297 US 1 (1935) 266
Vickery v Ritchie, 88 NE 835 (1909) 161
Vincent v Erie Transport Co, 124 NW 221 (1910) 197

TABLE OF STATUTES

Apportionment Act 1870
 (Eng, Ire, NI) 144, 144, 149
 s 2 ....140, 146

Betting and Lotteries
 Act 1956 (Ire)
 s 36.............................27
Bills of Exchange Act 1882
 (Eng, Ire, NI)
 s 28.............................186
 s 55(2) 192
 s 56.............................208
 s 59(2) 55
 s 65.............................207
 s 68(5) 207
Bill of Rights 1688 (Eng, NI) 263
 Art 4 263

Carriage of Goods
 by Sea Act 1971 (Eng, NI) 198
Civil Liability Act 1961 (Ire) 35
 s 2 ....195, 196
 s 7.............................8
 s 8.............................246
 s 21(2) 196
 s 22.............................196
 s 23(4) 181
 s 25.............................196
 s 29(1) 182, 184, 196
 s 29(8) 195
 s 30.............................181
 s 31.............................181
 s 34(2)(d) 35
 s 46.............................195
 s 46(2) 195
 s 62.............................67
 Chp 2.............................195
Civil Liability (Contribution)
 Act 1978 (Eng, NI) 195
 s 1 ....194, 195
 s 1(2), (3) 181
 s 1(4) 182, 184, 196

 s 1(5) 195
 s 2.............................196
 s 2(1) 196
Companies Act 1963 (Ire)
 s 8.............................53
 s 8(1) 57, 171
 s 285(6) 56, 64
Companies Act 1985 (Eng)
 s 35 ....53, 57
 s 35(1) 171
 s 35(4) 171
 s 322A 171
Consumer Credit
 Act 1974 (Eng, NI) 175, 289, 290
 ss 60, 61 174
 s 127 175
Contracts (Rights of
 Third Parties) Act 1999
 (Eng, NI) 234
Conveyancing Act 1892 (Ire)
 ss 4, 5 190
Copyright Act 1963 (Ire)
 s 22(2) 254
 s 23(3) 254
Copyright, Designs and
 Patents Act 1988 (Eng, NI)
 s 297(1) 122
 s 96(2) 254
 s 97(1) 254
 s 233(1) 254
Courts Act 1981 (Ire)
 s 22(1) 13
Criminal Law Act 1967 (Eng)
 s 5 103
Criminal Law (NI) Act 1967 (NI)
 s 5.............................103
Customs Consolidation
 Act 1876 (Ire) 260

Estate Agents Act 1979 (Eng, NI)
 s 18 ....174, 175

Finance Act 1986 (Eng, NI)
  s 114 263
Financial Services Act 1986
  (Eng, NI)
  s 132 285
Fire Services Act 1947 (Eng)
  s 30 197
Frustrated Contracts
  (NI) Act 1947 (NI) 147
Frustrated Contracts
  Act 1974 (British Columbia)
  s 5(3) 152

Gaming Act 1845 (Eng, NI) 27
  s 18 . . . . .27, 288, 290
Gaming and Lotteries
  Act 1956 (Ire)
  s 36 288

Highways Act 1980 (Eng)
  s 165(3) 206, 290
Hire Purchase Act 1946 (Ire)
  s 3(2) 289
Housing Act 1988 (Eng)
  s 28 . . . . .238, 243

Industrial Relations
  Act 1990 (Ire) 195
Infants' Relief Act 1874 (Ire) 289
  s 1 . . . . .34, 164–65
  s 2 165
Insolvency Act 1986 (Eng) 47
  s 234(4) 34, 203, 245
  Sched 6, s 11 . . . . .56, 64

Judicature Act 1908 (NZ)
  s 94A(2) 71

Landlord and Tenant Law
  (Amendment) Act 1860 (Ire, NI))
  s 16 189

Landlord and Tenant
  (Covenants) Act 1995 (Eng)
  s 5 189
Law of Property Act 1925 (Eng)
  s 146 190
Law of Property
  (Miscellaneous
  Provisions) Act 1989 (Eng)
  s 2 . . . . .174, 288
Law Reform (Frustrated
  Contracts) Act 1943 (Eng) 11, 131,
                                        147, 148
  s 1(2) .148, 149, 150,
                                        151, 152
  s 1(3) .148, 150, 151,
                                        152, 272
  s1(3)(b) 151
Law Reform
  (Miscellaneous
  Provisions) Act 1934 (Eng)
  s 1(1) 8, 246
Law Reform (Property,
  Perpetuities and
  Succession) Act 1962 (WA)
  s 23 71
Law of Property Act 1925 (Eng)
  s 40 288
  s 49(2) 138
Limitation Act 1980 (Eng)
  s 32(1)(c) 72

Marine Insurance Act 1906
  (Eng, Ire, NI)
  s 84 283
Matrimonial
  Causes Act 1973 (Eng)
  s 25 24
Mercantile Law
  Amendment Act 1856
  (Eng, Ire, NI)
  s 5 . . . . .61, 185, 188

Merchant Shipping
  Act 1947 (Ire) 198
Merchant Shipping Act 1995
  (Eng, NI)
  ss 92, 93 210
  s 187 195
  Sched 11 210
  Sched 11, s 6(1) 210
  Sched 11, s 19 211
  Sched 11, Pt I, s 1(a) 210
  Sched 11, Pt I, s 6.2 201
  Sched 11, Pt I, s 12(1) 211
  Sched 11, Pt I, s 13 211
  Sched 11, Pt II, s 2(1) 210
  Sched 11, Pt II, s 5 211
Merchant Shipping
  (Salvage and Wreck)
  Act 1993 (Ire)
  s 23...............................210
  s 25...............................211
  s 26...............................211
  s 29...............................211
  s 30...............................210
  s 32...............................211
  Pt III 209, 210
Minors' Contracts
  Act 1987 (Eng) 58, 167
  s 3 ....168, 289
  s 3(1) 45, 46, 165
Misrepresentation
  Act 1967 (Eng)
  s 1 ....78, 155
  1(b) 137
Misrepresentation
  (NI) Act 1967 (NI) 78, 137, 155
Moneylenders Act 1927 (Eng)
  s 6(1) 290

Patents Act 1977 (Eng, NI)
  s 61(1)(d)........................254
  s 62(1) 254

Patents Act 1992 (Ire)
  s 47..............................254
  s 49(1) 254

Rent Act 1977 (Eng)
  s 57 ....170, 285

Sale of Goods and
  Supply of Services
  Act 1980 (Ire)
  s 44(b) 137, 155
Sale of Goods Act
  1893 (Ire) 25, 80, 143, 145
  s 2...............................205
  s 4 ....174, 288
  s 8(2) 117
  s 30(1) 149
  s 30(2) 81
  s 49(1) 139
  s 55(4) 269
Sale of Goods Act 1979
  (Eng, NI).....................80, 139
  s 3(2) 205
  s 8(2) 117
  s 30(1) 143, 145
  s 30(3) 25, 81
Social Security
  (Recovery of Benefits)
  Act 1997 (Eng) 182
Solicitors (Amendment)
  Act 1960 (Ire)
  s 21(8) 56
Statute of Frauds
  1677 (Eng)
  s 4...............................288
Statute of Frauds
  (Ireland) 1695 (Ire, NI)
  s 2 ....174, 288
Statute of
  Limitations 1957 (Ire)
  s 72...............................72

Supreme Court Act 1981 (Eng)
  s 35 13

Taxes Consolidation
  Act 1997 (Ire)
  s 930 263
  s 930(2) 264
Taxes Management
  Act 1970 (Eng, NI)
  s 33 263
  s 33(2A)(a) 264
Third Parties (Rights
  Against Insurers)
  Act 1930 (Eng) 66
  s 1 67
Torts (Interference with
  Goods) Act 1977 (Eng, NI) 22
  s 2(1) 25
  s 6 . . . . .22, 89
  s 10 35

Trustee Act 1925 (Eng)
  s 30(2) 202
  s 57 203

Unfair Contract Terms
  Act 1977 (Eng, NI) 269

Value Added Tax Act 1972 (Ire)
  s 20 263
  s 20(5)(b) 268
Value Added Tax
  Act 1994 (Eng, NI)
  s 80 263
  ss 80(3), 80(3A–3C) 268

CHAPTER 1

THE CONCEPT OF RESTITUTION

I WHAT IS RESTITUTION ABOUT?

1-1   Restitution can be defined as the area of civil law concerned with reversing unjust enrichment on the part of a defendant. More precisely, it involves removing from him some accretion to his wealth which, in the eyes of the law, he should not be entitled to retain, or making him pay for some non-money benefit on the basis that it would be wrong to allow him to retain it for nothing.

A few concrete examples will clarify matters. If you are lucky, you may end today better off than you started it. You may receive a sum of money or a car. Someone else may discharge a debt of yours, thus freeing you from an obligation you would otherwise be under, or render you a service, such as repairing your roof after a gale (or paying a builder to do it). Again, if you have obtained information of commercial or other interest, you may turn it to your advantage and make a profit from it. And so on. Now, in the majority of such cases, the law has nothing to say about this. Gains, like losses, are a fact of social and commercial life. Respect for institutions such as contracts, gifts and other means of transferring wealth means that, like losses, they must *prima facie* be allowed to lie where they fall. But, this will not always be so: there may well be good reasons not to leave matters as they are. Suppose your payment to me is for a car which I do not deliver, or imagine that it results from nothing more than a computer error by your bank. In such a case, I cannot keep it and must repay you what I received. Or take another instance. Suppose the payment is a genuine gift from you, but that it represents money you have stolen from X; if so, I must repay X. And, as with payments of money, so with other more indirect benefits. If you pay my debt to some third party as a simple gift to me, nothing more need be said: but if you pay it because you have stood surety for me, I must reimburse you the amount you paid. You may give me valuable know-how as a matter of benevolence: but if, in fact, you transferred it to me in confidence because I was your employee, or because we envisaged a joint venture which did not, in the event, come off, I cannot use it for my personal benefit, and I must normally account to you for any profit I make out of it. Yet again, if you mend my roof because you wrongly think there was a contract between us and I encourage you in that belief, I am likely to have to pay you for doing so.

It is cases of this latter type that the law of restitution is about. More formally, restitution will be defined in this book as the response of the law to gains which it regards as unjustified – or, more simply, the law concerning the rectification of unjust enrichment.[1] We will be concerned with the rules of law which (a) decide which gains by a defendant should be left to stand, and which should be regarded as unjustified and therefore reversed or compensated; and (b) in the latter case, where the defendant is not allowed to keep his gain, determine (a) who should be given a remedy against him; and (b) what form that remedy should take.

Historical note

1-2 Roman law recognised, a least on occasion, a doctrine that '*natura aequum est neminem cum alterius detrimento fieri locupletiorem*'.[2] The concept of recovery for unjust enrichment has also been a feature of many European systems for some time.[3] A general provision to that effect appears in the German Civil Code,[4] where it has given rise to considerable litigation and comment, and also in the Dutch code.[5] French law has codal provisions governing a number of isolated cases which we would regard as restitutionary, but has developed a much more general doctrine in case law.[6]

In Anglo-Irish law, by contrast, until some 30 years ago the idea that a claimant might be able to found an action on a general principle of unjust enrichment received a pretty consistently bad press. Examples of this attitude include Kingsmill Moore J's scathing reference as late as 1965 to 'the somewhat vague brocards of unjust benefit or restitution or quasi-contract',[7] and Scrutton LJ's well known castigation of the idea of unjust enrichment in 1922 as a case of 'well-meaning sloppiness of thought'.[8] Few books in either jurisdiction were

---

1   In this book, the terms 'unjust enrichment' and 'unjustified enrichment' will be used interchangeably. If anything, the latter term is slightly more adequate, in that it emphasises that the basis of recovery is not 'justice' in the broad sense, but the fact that the claimant has shown some specific feature which renders the defendant's enrichment unjustified and hence justifies the law in reversing it. In the absence of a perfect system of law these questions must, of course, remain distinct.

2   Pomponius, D 12 6 14. See too Justinian, D 50 17 206.

3   It features explicitly in German law (see § 812 of the German Civil Code) and has been extensively developed in France by judicial decision. Useful comparative coverage appears in, eg, Dawson, *Unjust Enrichment: A Comparative Survey*: see, also, Gallo (1992) 40 AJCL 431; Zimmerman (1995) 15 OJLS 403.

4   § 812.

5   § 6.203.

6   See, eg, Malaurie and Aynès, *Droit Civil*, §§ 940–55.

7   *AG v Ryan's Car Hire Ltd* [1965] IR 642, p 664.

8   *Holt v Markham* [1923] 1 KB 504, p 513. To be fair, this reference was, strictly, limited to attempts to use the common law action for money had and received as a general means of reversing unjust enrichment.

written specifically about it:[9] the subject tended to be covered superficially as an adjunct to books on, for example, contract[10] or equity.[11] True, there were also early expressions of a more encouraging nature: apart from Lord Mansfield's famous apophthegm in *Moses v McFerlan*,[12] one need merely mention Lord Wright's recognition in 1943[13] that 'any system is bound to provide remedies for cases of what has been called unjust enrichment or unjust benefit'. But, in practice, little notice was taken of them.

1-3　Moreover, this unwillingness to embrace a general principle of recovery was perhaps understandable. The majority of situations now regarded as restitutionary had long been catered for, albeit under different names: most unjust enrichment was, in fact, reversed. Between them, the venerable common law actions for money had and received, the actions known as *quantum valebat* and *quantum meruit*, the doctrine of waiver of tort, the rule that damages could in certain cases take account of the defendant's profits,[14] common law and statutory rights to contribution, and various equitable duties to account, covered a great deal of the field. Faced with this situation, it is not surprising that the judges chose to remain within the existing categories of recovery rather than postulate any new theory of liability.[15]

There was also a further doctrinal difficulty. The notion that many of the common law restitutionary actions had to be subsumed under the rubric of 'quasi-contract'[16] distinctly hampered development of any coherent theory of liability. The idea of 'quasi-contract' was inherently vacuous, reflecting little more than a convenient pigeon hole for ideas that did not fit neatly anywhere else. In so far as it meant that the defendant had to pay as if he had contracted to do so when he had not, it was simply uninformative, in that it did not say *why* he had to pay.[17] And, although a lot of restitutionary claims do indeed have an affinity with contract (for example, the duty to pay for benefits rendered under a

---

9　Stoljar, *Quasi-Contract*, published in 1964, was a notable early exception. American scholarship was quicker off the mark: the *Restatement of Restitution* was published in 1936, and Dawson and Palmer's *Cases on Restitution* in 1957. For an overview of the situation before the general recognition in England of the principle of unjust enrichment, see the first edition of Goff & Jones, *The Law of Restitution*, 1966, p 11 et seq.

10　Where a chapter on 'quasi-contract' was regularly tacked onto the end of textbooks.

11　In particular, as regards claims to substituted assets using the technique of 'tracing'.

12　'This kind of equitable action, to recover back money, which ought not in justice to be kept, is very beneficial, and therefore much encouraged. It lies only for money which, *ex aequo et bono*, the defendant ought to refund ...': see (1760) 2 Burrows 1005, p 1012.

13　In *Fibrosa Spolka Akcyjna v Fairbairn Lawson Combe Barbour* [1943] AC 32, p 61.

14　Eg, *Phillips v Homfray* (1871) LR 6 Ch App 770; *Penarth Dock and Eng Co Ltd v Pounds* [1963] 1 Lloyd's Rep 359; *Hickey v Roches Stores Ltd* (1976) [1993] RLR 196. See, generally, below, Chapter 11.

15　For Irish examples of this tendency see, eg, *Leader v Leader* (1874) IR 6 CL 20; *McNeil v Millen* [1907] 2 IR 328.

16　For a brief historical excursus, see Goff & Jones, *The Law of Restitution*, 5th edn, p 5 et seq (hereafter, 'Goff & Jones').

17　Cf Jackson, *History of Quasi-Contract*, p 127.

contract terminated for breach), the result was even more disastrous when the name 'quasi-contract' was invoked by the House of Lords in *Sinclair v Brougham*[18] to hold that a deposit taker which borrowed money *ultra vires* could not be sued for money had and received in any circumstances, for no better reason than that it could not have been made liable in contract.

Unjust enrichment today

1-4   Today, there is no doubt that courts do in fact recognise the existence of the principle of unjust enrichment. It is established beyond doubt in both jurisdictions (a) that recovery in respect of unjust enrichment is a recognised category of law,[19] (b) that it unites at least some categories of liability previously thought to be disparate and unconnected,[20] and (c) that there are rules applicable on principle to all such claims which can be brought under this rubric.[21] Importantly, it is also accepted that on principle, new heads of recovery for unjustified enrichment may be created,[22] at least where there is room for development by analogy with existing cases where there already is liability.[23] Similar developments have taken place in other common law countries.[24]

In addition, it is now well established that this head of liability is free standing. The old idea that it was somehow vestigially connected with contract

---

18   [1914] AC 398. Compare the scarcely more defensible decision in *Cowern v Nield* [1912] 2 KB 419 (contractual non-liability of minor held to prevent quasi-contractual recovery of money paid for goods not supplied). The reasoning in *Sinclair v Brougham* is now effectively discredited in England, the Irish courts having rightly disowned it in 1991: *Re PMPA Garages (Longmile) Ltd* [1992] 1 IR 332.

19   England: *Lipkin Gorman v Karpnale Ltd* [1991] 2 AC 548, p 572 (Lord Goff); *Woolwich Building Society v Inland Revenue Comrs (No 2)* [1993] AC 70, 196–97. Ireland: *House of Spring Gardens v Point Blank* [1984] IR 611, p 707 (Griffin J); *Allied Discount Card v Bord Fáilte* [1991] 2 IR 185, p 190 (Lynch J); *Dublin Corp v Building and Allied Trade Union* [1996] 1 IR 468. Cf also, *Hickey v Roches Stores Ltd* (1976) [1993] RLR 196. See Birks [1991] LM and CLQ 473.

20   'Although as yet there is in English law no general rule giving the plaintiff a right of recovery from a defendant who has been unjustly enriched at the plaintiff's expense, the concept of unjust enrichment lies at the heart of all the individual instances in which the law does give a right of recovery' – Lord Browne-Wilkinson in *Woolwich Building Society v IRC (No 2)* [1993] AC 70, pp 196–97. See, too, the reference to a 'unifying legal concept' of unjust enrichment in the seminal Australian decision in *Pavey and Matthews Pty Ltd v Paul* (1987) 162 CLR 221, pp 256–67.

21   Eg, the availability of a 'change of position' defence: *Lipkin Gorman v Karpnale Ltd* [1991] 2 AC 548 and below, Chapter 13.

22   Eg, recovery of overpaid taxes: see below, Chapter 12. Cf *More (James) Ltd v University of Ottawa* (1974) 49 DLR (3d) 666, p 676 ('The categories of restitution are never closed').

23   'As in so many other fields of English law, the occasions on which recovery is permitted have been built up on a case-by-case basis' – Lord Browne-Wilkinson in *Woolwich Building Society v Inland Revenue Comrs (No 2)* [1993] AC 70, p 197.

24   Australia: *Pavey and Matthews Pty Ltd v Paul* (1987) 162 CLR 221, p 256 *et seq*; *ANZ Banking Group Ltd v Westpac Ltd* (1988) 164 CLR 662, p 673. Canada: *Air Canada v British Columbia* [1989] 1 SCR 1133, p 1201, and cf *Deglman v Guaranty Trust Co of Canada* [1954] 3 DLR 785. New Zealand: *Auckland CC v Henderson District Court* [1998] 1 NZLR 253, p 255; *Equiticorp Industry Corp Ltd v The Crown* [1998] 2 NZLR 481, p 710.

through the use of the term 'quasi-contract' has now been authoritatively disowned in Ireland,[25] England[26] and elsewhere.[27] In particular, in *Westdeutsche Landesbank Girozentrale v Islington BC*[28] the holding in *Sinclair v Brougham*, referred to above, that there could be no recovery *in personam* against an *ultra vires* deposit taker on the sole basis that there could be no liability in contract was expressly discountenanced by two members of the House of Lords[29] and strongly doubted by a third.[30]

II THE ESSENTIALS OF A CLAIM FOR RESTITUTION[31] OF UNJUST ENRICHMENT

1-5   In order to obtain restitution for unjustified enrichment, the claimant has, on principle, to show three things. These are: (a) that the defendant has obtained an enrichment, or gain; (b) that there is some factor (an 'unjust factor') indicating that the enrichment is unjustified and ought to be reversed; and (c) that the gain was made at the claimant's expense, or for some reason that the claimant has title to sue for its return. A claimant who demonstrates that these requirements are met *prima facie* has a right to restitution, unless the defendant in turn can show some valid defence to the claim. These requirements are regarded as axiomatic in Anglo-Irish law,[32] and will dictate the structure of this book.

It should be noted, however, that this is not the only possible scheme for a law of unjust enrichment. Other intellectual bases are undoubtedly possible. One could argue, for example, that all transfers of wealth had to be justified by

---

25 See *East Cork Foods Ltd v O'Dwyer* [1978] IR 103 and *Re PMPA Garages (Longmile) Ltd* [1992] IR 332.

26 *Westdeutsche Landesbank Girozentrale v Islington BC* [1996] AC 669, p 710 (Lord Browne-Wilkinson); *Halifax Building Society v Thomas* [1996] Ch 217, p 227 (Peter Gibson LJ)

27 Canada: *Deglman v Guaranty Trust* [1954] 3 DLR 785. Australia: *Pavey and Matthews v Paul* (1987) 162 CLR 221, p 256.

28 [1996] AC 669.

29 See Lord Browne-Wilkinson's opinion at [1996] AC 669, p 709, with which Lord Slynn agreed.

30 Ie, Lord Goff [1996] AC 669, p 686. Of course, there may still be cases where contractual non-liability may bar restitution, as his Lordship recognised. But, he said, this should be done overtly on the basis of public policy (namely, not allowing a remedy in at the back door when it had been deliberately excluded at the front), rather on a pure doctrinal basis.

31 There is room for argument over whether 'restitution' and 'unjust enrichment' are two sides of the same coin. Birks has argued that they are not, on the basis that transfers of wealth may be reversed by other means, such as the terms of a contract, and that the law may on occasion deal with unjust enrichment not by reversing it, but by preventing it occurring in the first place. (See Cornish (ed), *Restitution: Past, Present and Future*, Chapters 1, 2.) But this is very much a matter of terminology. This book will not deal in detail with reversing transfers on grounds other than unjust enrichment: conversely, 'restitution' will be taken to cover prevention of, as well as the cure for, unjust enrichment. See generally, McInnes [1999] RLR 118 and Burrows [2000] RLR 257.

32 They are enunciated in, eg, *Portman Building Society v Hamlyn Taylor Neck* [1998] 4 All ER 202, p 206 (Millett LJ).

some legal reason or substratum, such as a valid contract, the discharge of an obligation, or an intent to make a gift; that the absence of such a substratum *prima facie* justified restitution of the value transferred; and that this was the true essence of restitutionary recovery.[33] Nevertheless, there is at present little, if any sign of English or Irish law adopting this approach, or abandoning the tripartite classification referred to above.

(a) The first requirement: enrichment

1-6   A proper definition of what counts as enrichment for the purposes of restitution is central to any rational account of restitution law. We will adopt the following (which is not uncontroversial) for the sake of argument. It is suggested that a defendant will be regarded as enriched if:

- he receives money; or
- he obtains property with a money value; or
- he is saved expense or loss he would otherwise have incurred; or
- property of his is improved so as to be worth more; or
- services are rendered to him.

We will now deal with each of these ideas in turn.

Receipt of money

1-7   The receipt of money is relatively easy in restitution terms. If and in so far as I have more cash in hand or my bank balance is augmented, I am wealthier on any reckoning. Furthermore, it is submitted that exactly the same argument must apply where money is paid not to me but to my order: if I have the ability to decide whether money goes into my bank or someone else's, this is as good as receipt by me even if I actually cause the money to go to the benefit of some third party. So if you think you owe me £100 and at my request pay that sum to X, it ought not to lie in my mouth to say that I never actually received it myself.[34]

One qualification must, however, be noted. The above reasoning assumes that in receiving the money, the recipient regarded himself as absolute owner, and hence free (at least as against the claimant) to use it as he thought fit. If he obtained the money on the basis of a valid trust, accepting that he had no power to deal with it except in accordance with the terms of that trust, he is not without

---

33   This is largely how German law handles the problem: for a perceptive comparative account, see Zimmerman (1995) 15 OJLS 403.

34   It is true that if you sue me for a refund at a later stage, I may well be able to resist your claim on the basis of change of position. But that is a matter not of enrichment but of defences, and does not alter the basic proposition.

more[35] regarded as enriched by its receipt. It follows that any claim in unjust enrichment falls at the first fence. The point arose neatly in *Portman Building Society v Hamlyn Taylor Neck*,[36] where solicitors who had received purchase moneys as stakeholders in connection with a conveyancing transaction later misapplied them. The Court of Appeal declined to allow the lenders to sue them on the basis of restitution;[37] as Millett LJ pointed out, there was, in the circumstances, simply no enrichment to be reversed. Although the decision is not uncontroversial, this reasoning seems impeccable.

Receipt of property

1-8   As with money, so generally with other assets. So, where I gain ownership of a piece of property, for example, where I invest trust moneys in a life insurance policy,[38] or where I am your agent and I use moneys received as a bribe to buy a house,[39] there is a gain equivalent to the value of the asset. On principle, this gain is susceptible to capture through the law of restitution. But the same qualification applies as with money: the property must have been received in circumstances where the recipient regarded himself as free to deal with it as owner. It is submitted that where the defendant receives an asset explicitly as trustee, or *a fortiori* where he receives mere possession without ownership, he cannot in logic be regarded as having been enriched by its value.[40]

Expense saved

1-9   Benefit through expense saved (or loss averted) is less immediately visible than actual receipt of money or property. Nevertheless, at least on the question whether there is a gain on which the law of restitution can bite, there can be no rational ground for distinguishing between them. Positive and negative enrichment both increase a defendant's net assets, and are effectively two sides of the same coin. Moreover, a great many restitution claims do indeed fall in the category of expense saved, notably those for contribution,[41] those arising from compulsion to pay the defendant's liabilities,[42] claims for mesne profits against a

---

35   It may, of course, be otherwise if the recipient later treats the moneys as his own, eg, by transferring them into his own account.

36   [1998] 4 All ER 202.

37   The action was brought in restitution because a simple action for misapplication would have been statute-barred.

38   Eg, *Foskett v McKeown* [2001] 1 AC 102.

39   As in cases such as *AG for Hong Kong v Reid* [1994] 1 AC 324.

40   Though if he uses it, there seems no reason why he should not be regarded as having been enriched by the value of the use he has made of it. So, if a prospective hirer gains possession of property on the basis that a hire contract will be concluded, but no contract is actually entered into, he should on principle be liable for a reasonable rate of hire.

41   Below, Chapter 8.

42   *Ibid.*

lessee unlawfully holding over,[43] or claims based on the release of someone else's property from an obligation charged on it (for example, where a co-owner pays off a mortgage).[44] No problem has ever arisen over the fact that the enrichment in all these cases is negative. True, in many such cases, the defendant may have some defence to restitutionary liability (he may argue, for example, that he did not want the claimant's intervention, or could have compromised his liability for a lesser sum): but whatever those defences may be, it makes no sense to say that there was no enrichment in the first place.

1-10   It is true that some doubts have been thrown on this general principle, notably by certain unguarded *dicta* by Bowen LJ in the notorious decision in *Phillips v Homfray*.[45] There, a landowner attempted unsuccessfully to claim a reasonable wayleave in respect of unlawful mining under his land by suing the defendant on the basis of waiver of tort. It was held that whereas the defendant would have been liable had he actually gained money through his trespass, no action would lie where all that could be shown was a negative enrichment or saving of expense. But, there are two answers to this. First, the actual decision itself is controversial, and a number of commentators have regarded it as plainly wrong.[46] Secondly, it is highly arguable that the case turned simply on the form of action: on principle, an action for damages for trespass in these circumstances will indeed include a sum for expense saved by the defendant,[47] but this was not, at the time,[48] open to the plaintiff because the rule *actio personalis moritur cum persona* barred any such relief against a defendant's estate. In either case there is no reason to regard *Phillips v Homfray* as a serious obstacle to an award based on negative enrichment.

Improvements to property

1-11   Where a defendant's property is improved, or work or money expended on it, there are two ways in which it can be argued that he has been enriched.

First, the property concerned may actually be made more valuable: for example, where a house is repaired by a necessitous intervener,[49] or where X's

---

43 See *Ministry of Defence v Ashman* [1993] 2 EGLR 102, where it was emphasised that mesne profits were reckoned by the full use value of the property – ie, the rent saved by the defendant – and not by the lower rent the plaintiffs would have got in the circumstances. See, too, *Inverugie Investments Ltd v Hackett* [1995] 1 WLR 713.

44 Eg, *Ker v Ker* (1869) 4 Ir R Eq 15; *Re Pride* [1891] 2 Ch 135; *Re Hunter* (1998) unreported, Ch D, NI, 3 March.

45 (1883) 24 Ch D 439, p 461.

46 Goff & Jones, p 532; Burrows, p 391.

47 *Whitwham v Westminster Brymbo Coal Co* [1892] 2 Ch 538. See also the result of earlier litigation in *Phillips v Homfray* itself: (1871) 6 Ch App 770.

48 Today, the claimant could sue in both jurisdictions: Law Reform (Miscellaneous Provisions) Act 1934, s 1(1) (England) and Civil Liability Act 1961, s 7 (Ireland). See, generally, Virgo, *Principles of the Law of Restitution*, p 481 *et seq*.

49 Below, Chapter 9.

moneys go to pay the premiums on Y's life insurance policy, the value of which is enhanced as a result.[50] Here, it is suggested, the position is clear. The defendant cannot deny that he is richer – at least potentially. He may, of course, have other arguments as to why he should not have to make restitution:[51] but, on principle, these should not include saying that he has not been enriched at all.

Secondly, and on a wider basis, it may be argued that in any case where services are rendered which have the effect of improving the property, those services may *ipso facto* count as a benefit to the defendant. On this argument, it is irrelevant whether or not the property actually appreciates as a result. Suppose, for example, the claimant contracts to re-lay the defendant's otherwise perfectly serviceable drive according to a different pattern and to do other work on his house. After the drive has been laid, the defendant wrongfully repudiates the contract. If the claimant is to succeed in a restitutionary claim, this can only be on the basis that the services as such fall to be regarded as a benefit to him. This is a much more controversial and awkward point. However, this topic is better dealt with below, § 1-12. The reason is this: once the financial 'end product' of the services is disregarded, the fact that those services happened to consist of work on the defendant's property (rather than, say, the provision of investment advice to the defendant where no property at all was involved) is, in a sense, tangential. Its only relevance is that it shows that the services were rendered to the defendant, rather than to someone else. The issue is simply whether, and if so how far, the rendering of services *tout court* ought to be regarded as enriching the recipient.

Receipt of services

1-12   The most intractable problems with regard to benefit arise with alleged 'enrichments' not involving transfers of property or money, or payment of debts. Can a 'pure' service of this sort amount to an enrichment of the person receiving it?

In so far as the services directly cause an accretion to the defendant's net assets, there is little difficulty. If, for example, a builder agrees to carry out improvements to my property and I repudiate the contract when he has done part of the job, there can be no doubt that I am enriched at least to the extent that the property's market value is increased. Similarly, if you do work on my house wrongly thinking that I have contracted for it, and this is work which I would have had carried out in any event, it is suggested that I am plainly enriched by the amount of expense saved.

---

50 As in *Foskett v McKeown* [2001] 1 AC 102. An analogous case is *Re Diplock* [1948] Ch 465, where the claimant's moneys go to improve buildings or pay off a mortgage on them.

51 Eg, because he did not want the improvement, or because he would have to sell the property in order to make restitution.

More difficult is the case where there is no actual accretion to the defendant's wealth. An author starts to write a book under contract with a publisher: after he has done the research and written two chapters, the contract is cancelled. During negotiations for a lease of property, the would-be lessor at the request of the lessee carries out alterations: the negotiations break down and the lease is never signed. An exploration company prospects for oil: the contract is terminated before it finds any. Can the publisher, lessee or prospector be regarded as enriched? In short, can 'pure services' be regarded as enriching the recipient independently on any financial 'end product'?

The thesis advanced here (which largely follows Professor Birks's argument on the subject,[52] though for different reasons) is that they can, provided that it is possible to say that the services were indeed rendered to the defendant. In particular, this will be the case if, and in so far as the services concerned were requested or freely accepted by the recipient. The reason can be simply expressed: if I request you to do something for my benefit, or freely accept a service provided by you despite having had an opportunity to reject it, it should not lie in my mouth to allege later that what you did was of no benefit to me. The fact that I said I wanted the service should of itself be sufficient to show that I regarded it as a benefit.

1-13   The point is illustrated by the old (and notorious) case of *Planché v Colburn*,[53] where an author was commissioned to write a book, but the project was cancelled when he had produced part of it. He was held entitled, apparently on the basis of *quantum meruit*, to a sum in respect of the work he had done, despite the fact that *ex hypothesi* this had not enured to the benefit of the publishers. Although this case has been regarded with some scepticism,[54] it is suggested that it is perfectly defensible. Having asked for the work to be done, and indeed contracted for it, the defendants could quite rightly be told that they were disentitled from arguing that the work done was not a benefit to them.

Now, it is true that this view of services as a benefit is not universally accepted. At least two other views must be briefly mentioned.

The first is that of Birks, who reaches a similar conclusion, but by a different route. He argues[55] that a requested service indeed benefits the defendant, but on the ground that in such a case, it prevents the defendant pleading 'subjective devaluation': that is, it precludes a plea that the value of the services *to him* was less than their objective value in the market. In so far as the end result is much

---

52 Birks, *An Introduction to the Law of Restitution*, p 109 *et seq* (hereafter, 'Birks').

53 (1831) 8 Bing 14. Compare *Easat Ltd v Racal plc* (2000) unreported, 28 March. But cf, in this connection, *Marston Construction Ltd v Kigass Ltd* (1989) 46 Build LR 109, where in the context of services rendered in anticipation of a contract it was apparently regarded as important to show the presence of an end product in the defendant's hands in order to obtain recovery. *Sed quaere*.

54 Birks, p 109 *et seq*.

55 *Ibid*.

the same, this probably does not matter too much. Analytically, however, it is suggested that 'subjective devaluation' is more plausibly regarded as a matter going to whether the defendant is enriched unjustly, rather than whether he is enriched at all. If so, the necessity of keeping these two inquiries separate militates in favour of the view just expressed.

Much more important is Beatson's counter-argument.[56] He has trenchantly argued that, even if services are freely accepted, they cannot in the absence of some tangible financial benefit to the defendant be regarded as enriching him at all. His ground is essentially simple. The fact that a defendant has freely accepted, or even requested, a benefit may well be good grounds for making him pay for it: but this assumes that there is a benefit in the first place. The question whether the defendant has been benefited is logically prior to the issue whether he ought to be liable in restitution: to say that services are benefits because they have been requested or accepted by the defendant simply begs that question. It follows that, in respect of services, the only basis on which they can be said to enrich the defendant is actual accretion to his assets.

1-14 There are, it is submitted, two answers to this.

First, while it is true that request or free acceptance may be grounds for holding an enrichment unjust, it does not beg the question to say that there may also be grounds for deciding that there has been an enrichment. However intellectually untidy, there is no reason why, in a suitable case, the same factor should not denote both that the defendant has gained a benefit, and that it is unjust for him to retain it without paying.

The second point is that, if Beatson's argument is right, services which produce an end product must willy-nilly be valued according to that end product, rather than their reasonable value. For example, building works done under an uncompleted contract would have to be valued according to the actual value added to the defendant's premises, and so on. Although Burrows has argued that such services can only be regarded as 'objectively beneficial' in so far as the end product, or part of it, is actually received,[57] it is suggested that such a result is likely to be both arbitrary and counter-intuitive. And, indeed, its application has caused some judicial disquiet. In *BP v Hunt (No 2)*,[58] dealing with a claim under the English Law Reform (Frustrated Contracts) Act 1943,[59] Goff J felt constrained to hold that where services rendered under a frustrated contract contemplated a particular end product, the Act only permitted recovery for the value of that end product: nevertheless, he opined that this result was productive of a good deal of unfairness.

---

56 Beatson, *The Use and Abuse of Unjust Enrichment*, Chapter 2.

57 Burrows, p 9.

58 [1983] 2 AC 352.

59 This Act has no equivalent in the Republic, where frustration questions are governed by the common law.

Enrichment: measuring the defendant's gain

1-15   In many cases, once it is shown that the defendant has obtained a benefit, measuring the amount of that benefit causes little difficulty. Money is self-explanatory in this context: receipt of £x enriches me by £x. Goods and services have a market value, and in general this represents the amount of the gain to the recipient (though not necessarily the amount of recovery). But a few points are worth making.

First, a point about property. Where the defendant is unjustly enriched by becoming the owner of something (for example, where my purchasing manager is bribed with a case of whisky), his enrichment is clearly its value. It is submitted that this is not so, however, where the asset received was at all times owned, at law or in equity, by someone else. Suppose a thief steals your car and gives it to me. As pointed out above,[60] it seems absurd to say I am enriched by the value of something which is not mine, merely because I have received possession or control of it. Nevertheless, this does not necessarily mean I am not enriched at all. In the case of the car, indeed, it seems clear that I am: namely, by the value of the use of the car, or by what I got if I sold it or hired it out to somebody else.

The second point concerns the value of services or payment of debts. Suppose you paint my house (which I was about to paint anyway) thinking it is yours: a reasonable charge would be £1,000, but I would have had the job done for £400. Assuming I am liable to you at all,[61] I may well be able to avoid paying you more than £400 on the basis of what Birks has referred to as 'subjective devaluation': but, consistently with the view expressed elsewhere that subjective devaluation goes to whether the enrichment is unjust and not to its valuation, it is submitted that my gain remains at £1,000. Similarly, it is suggested that if you discharge a debt of £2,000 which I owe to X, my gain is £2,000. The fact that I might have been able to persuade X to accept £1,500 in full settlement may be an argument for limiting my liability, but it should not affect the amount of my enrichment as such.[62]

1-16   Thirdly, the question of timing. It is suggested that, for the purposes of restitution, it is normally the time of receipt that ought to matter rather than any other date (such as the time when restitution is requested, or when proceedings are taken to obtain it). Thus, if I pay you £1,000 which I later reclaim after the contract under which it was paid has been frustrated, no account is taken as a matter of the law of restitution of the fact that you have had the use of the money: your gain remains £1,000.[63] Conversely, if I pay you £1,000 by mistake and you some days later spend £800 as a result, your gain is still £1,000, no more,

---

60   See § 1-8.
61   See below, § 3-27 *et seq.*
62   See below, § 1-33 *et seq.*
63   See *BP (Exploration) v Hunt* [1983] 2 AC 352.

no less. Of course, this does not mean that my *claim* is necessarily for the amount of your gain. In the first case, your use of the money can be partly offset by an award of statutory interest:[64] in the second, if you had spent the £800 in all innocence, you would have a defence of change of position except as to £200.[65] But this is on the basis that it is unjust to make you repay the full £1,000, not that your enrichment has in some way diminished. Your enrichment would be the same even if you could not plead change of position (for example, if you had known of my claim all along): what would change would be the justice of making you refund what you got.[66]

There is one vital qualification to this. Certain restitutionary claims take effect as claims to a proprietary interest in an asset in the defendant's hands. Suppose my trustee steals trust shares, sells them for £10,000 and gives you the proceeds, whereupon you spend £4,000 of them; or suppose you, being my agent, are bribed with a case of whisky out of which you drink four bottles.[67] I have an equitable proprietary claim[68] against you to the money or the whisky: but in the nature of things, it must be limited to what you have still got when I bring it, namely, £6,000 or eight bottles, as the case may be.[69]

(b) The second requirement: a gain which is 'unjustified'

Unjust factors

1-17 Assuming a gain by the defendant, the second matter to be shown by the claimant is that the gain is 'unjustified', so as to call for action to reverse it. In Anglo-Irish law, this means that he must show some specific 'unjust factor' which calls for the gain to be reversed. Indeed, most of this book will be devoted to the discussion of the various 'unjust factors' involved.

What, then, are the factors which can form the basis of a claim for restitution? Logically, any such factor must be based on the position of either the claimant, or the defendant, or both. In fact it is suggested that unjust factors fall into six groups: three claimant-centred exclusively, one based on the common assumptions of both claimant and defendant, and two defendant-centred. These are, in order: (a) factors qualifying voluntariness; (b) a few miscellaneous cases of voluntary, but meritorious conduct by the claimant; (c) claims reflecting

---

64 See the Supreme Court Act 1981 (England), s 35A; Courts Act 1981 (Ireland), s 22(1). That the Irish legislation applies to restitutionary claims is clear from its terms: as for the English, see *BP (Exploration) v Hunt* [1982] 1 All ER 925 and *Woolwich Building Society v Inland Revenue Comrs (No 2)* [1993] AC 70.

65 See below, Chapter 13; and cf Birks, p 76.

66 *Contra*, however, Nolan in Birks (ed), *Laundering and Tracing*, p 135 et seq.

67 Cf *AG for Hong Kong v Reid* [1994] 1 AC 324.

68 Birks has argued that there is much to be said in certain cases for allowing a non-proprietary claim limited to what the defendant still has: see Birks, p 394 et seq.

69 Birks usefully calls this measure of restitution 'value surviving': see Birks, Chapter 3.

property or other rights of the claimant; (d) failure of assumptions; (e) free acceptance; and (f) wrongs by the defendant.

Factors qualifying voluntariness

1-18   Unjust factors of this sort principally involve benefits conferred by mistake or duress, or payments made under legal compulsion from a third party. It should be noted that the neutral word 'qualifying' is carefully chosen here. Particularly where property is transferred, some examples of mistake and duress nullify the consent, and hence the transfer, *ab initio* (for example, where a gold watch is handed to a robber, or A despatches goods to B, but they are intercepted by an impostor C).[70] Others leave the transfer *prima facie* intact, but nevertheless give restitutionary rights on the ground that the apparent consent is vitiated (for example, where I pay you money or give you a car under a non-fundamental mistake such as forgetfulness). Both types qualify under this heading.

Voluntary but meritorious conduct by the claimant

1-19   These include mainly miscellaneous cases of necessitous intervention, such as medical services rendered in an emergency and (possibly) maritime salvage. Peculiar in that the claimant acted voluntarily and no free acceptance need be shown by the defendant, this category is admittedly a ragbag of arguably restitutionary claims which do not fit comfortably anywhere else.[71]

Claims reflecting property or other rights of the claimant

1-20   This category concerns three types of case. One is where A obtains assets referable to something which belongs, or has belonged, to B: for example, where a trustee misappropriates trust property and transmutes it into another form; or where B's property is stolen by X who sells it and gives the proceeds to A; or where a bank computer goes haywire and makes an unauthorised transfer of £1,000 from B's account to A's.[72] Burrows[73] characterises the unjust factor in situations of this sort under the portmanteau title 'ignorance': but, while the idea is clearly right, the name is not entirely satisfactory. What is really at stake is whether B's property or other rights have been infringed with a resulting benefit to A. The only relevance of B's ignorance is that it clearly shows he did not consent to what was done: but lack of knowledge as such is obviously not crucial. A claimant does not lose his claim under this head merely because he knew someone was taking his property (imagine he is robbed of it at gunpoint),

---

70   As in the well known contract case of *Cundy v Lindsay* (1878) 3 App Cas 459.

71   This category is christened by Birks, a little uninformatively, 'policy-motivated restitution': see Birks, Chapter 9.

72   Cf *Re PMPA Insurance Co Ltd* [1986] ILRM 524 (restitution granted to intended payees in respect of cheques and contra-entries mistakenly posted to wrong account).

73   Burrows, p 139 *et seq*.

or even because he did not choose at that time to take any steps to stop it. If I see someone stealing my car, but fail to intervene because I am in a hurry to go out to dinner, there is no reason why I should lose my right to sue a subsequent handler of the car for the proceeds of its sale.

The second instance is situations referred to by Birks as 'interceptive subtraction'.[74] For example, A receives money from C for transmission to B, attorns to B but does not pay it over; or A usurps B's office and receives the perquisites of it; or A, the receiver of an insolvent company, receives payment of a debt which the company has previously assigned to B. Or again, suppose personal representatives mistakenly transfer assets to the wrong beneficiary (or, for that matter, a non-beneficiary).[75] Cases of this sort are a bit like those in the previous paragraph; but, there is one essential difference, namely, the futurity of B's interest. B's complaint is not that any existing property of his has been interfered with, but that some asset or advantage to which he had a right[76] has been diverted to A instead.

Failure of assumptions

1-21   The first three cases discussed above all have one common feature: they concern money or other benefits which the defendant ought never to have got at all. This category, by contrast, deals with benefits which the defendant would have been entitled to, but only *sub modo*, on the basis of some assumption which is now shown to have been unfounded. It includes, for example, the situation where payment is made for goods or services not forthcoming, or under a contract ineffective because of *ultra vires* or inability of one party to contract;[77] and where a person pays for an extension to someone else's house on the understanding that he will be allowed to live there for life, but the relationship later turns sour. In these cases, the assumption concerned – that goods or services will be provided, that the underlying transaction is valid, that the 'granny flat arrangement' will work out – fails, and by doing so removes the justification that would otherwise exist for the defendant retaining what he has got. The same reasoning, slightly less obviously, also applies to services rendered and goods supplied under a contract later terminated for breach or other reasons. Here, the parties contemplate that payment will become due according to the terms of the contract, but as events turn out, it does not: the original basis justifying the receipt therefore falls away. The 'consideration' for the services, in a wide sense, has failed.

---

74 Birks, p 33 *et seq*.

75 As in *Ministry of Health v Simpson* [1951] AC 251.

76 It must be an asset to which B had a legal right: *Official Custodian of Charities v Mackey (No 2)* [1985] 2 All ER 1016.

77 *Rover International Ltd v Cannon Film Sales Ltd (No 3)* [1989] 3 All ER 423; *Westdeutsche Landesbank Girozentrale v Islington BC* [1996] AC 669.

1-22   It is suggested that 'failure of assumptions' also explains another troublesome head of restitution, that of recovery of money paid for services which the claimant is entitled as of right to have free of charge, or (in Ireland,[78] and to a lesser extent in England[79]) of tax not in fact exigible, or of moneys paid under a judgment later reversed.[80] Although it is possible to regard these as *sui generis* heads of restitution, they can, without too much difficulty, be brought within straightforward private law principle by postulating a failure of assumption. Payment made to those with taxing or similar powers[81] is made on the basis that such payment is in fact due: similarly, with payment under a judgment. If that basis ceases to apply, the justification for allowing the payee to keep what he has received disappears.[82]

Free acceptance

1-23   Suppose that, while A and B are negotiating a lease, A, who urgently needs the premises, asks B to do work on them, whereupon B does so: but, in the event, no agreement eventuates. Or imagine that B does minor work on A's property, making it clear that he intends to be paid, and A knowingly allows him to do so in circumstances where it would be reasonable to expect him to say so if he does not want it. In both cases it seems that A is bound to pay B a reasonable sum. But why?

The correct answer, it is suggested, is that suggested by Birks. He argues, following Goff & Jones,[83] that the basis of this liability is simply that A has freely accepted the goods or services concerned in the knowledge that they were not being provided *gratis*: as mentioned above, in these circumstances, the acceptance establishes both that there is a benefit, and that its retention is unjust.[84]

It is true that there is a contrary view, powerfully put by Burrows. He bottoms B's right to restitution in this sort of case (assuming it exists at all) on the fact that even if there is no contract between A and B, A *bargains* for the services. The basis of the bargain is payment: if payment is not forthcoming, there is therefore a failure of consideration (or, applying the term used in this book, failure in a basic assumption), and it is this that justifies making A pay.

---

78 *Murphy v AG* [1982] IR 241.

79 *Woolwich Building Society v Inland Revenue Comrs (No 2)* [1993] AC 70; below, Chapter 12.

80 See particularly *East Cork Foods Ltd v O'Dwyer* [1978] IR 103, pp 110–11 (Henchy J).

81 Including, where appropriate, private defendants (eg, privatised water companies with the power to levy water rates).

82 Cf *Woolwich Building Society v Inland Revenue Comrs (No 2)* [1993] AC 70, p 197, where Lord Browne-Wilkinson refers to a payment of undue tax as having been made without consideration. If 'consideration' is taken in its wide sense as referring to the assumption or basis on which the payment was made, this supports the position in the text.

83 Goff & Jones, pp 18–22.

84 See Birks, Chapter 8. See, also, *Pavey and Matthews Pty Ltd v Paul* (1987) 162 CLR 221, p 227 where Mason CJ and Wilson J seem to accept this point of view.

Thus, Burrows denies the need for, or the existence of, an independent doctrine of 'free acceptance' and subsumes those cases that would otherwise come within it in 'Failure of assumptions', above.[85]

1-24 However, it is suggested, with respect, that Burrows's view is unsustainable. This is for two reasons. First, Burrows's argument that A 'bargained' for the benefit in the above situation seems, with respect, a little specious. *Ex hypothesi*, A did not contract for it: nor did he explicitly agree to pay for it. If he had done so, there would be no difficulty. The 'bargain' involved is thus reduced to a fiction: A must be treated *as though* he had agreed to pay, even if he did not. But this begs the question of why he is so treated: and the only sensible reason, it is submitted, is the acceptance itself – which, of course, brings us back to traditional free acceptance.

Secondly, in talking of B's disappointed expectation of payment as a failure of consideration, this assumes the very point in issue, that is, that payment of a reasonable sum was due in the first place. Unless it was, the whole argument falls away. It is true that the question whether B expected to be paid (or, perhaps more accurately, whether he behaved as if he did) is highly relevant in such cases. But its proper significance, it is suggested, is simply that it goes to show whether the benefit concerned was accepted on the understanding that it would be paid for; since, if it was not, everyone agrees that restitution falls to be denied anyway.

Wrongs as unjust factors

1-25 Like free acceptance, the idea of a wrong as a basis for restitution is defendant-centred: the essence of the claim is that where the defendant has committed a wrong against the claimant and has gained a benefit, whether in money or otherwise, it is unjust as against the claimant that he should be allowed to retain it. Two further preliminary points ought to be noted. One is that the discussion of 'wrongs' for this purpose will be on a general level, covering torts, breaches of contract or trust, and any act giving rise to legal liability. And, secondly, although the essence of the claimant's claim is that the defendant ought not to be allowed to profit from wrongdoing, by no means all wrongs give rise to such liability: indeed, Chapter 11 will, to a large extent, be concerned with how 'restitution-yielding wrongs' are, and ought to be, distinguished from wrongs in general.

(c) The third requirement: enrichment 'at the claimant's expense'

1-26 The third requirement for a claim in unjustified enrichment is traditionally stated thus: the defendant's gain must not only be unjustified, but it must also have been made 'at the expense of the claimant'. This can be a puzzling

---

85 See Burrows, p 315 *et seq*.

requirement: but (to anticipate argument that will appear below), it is suggested that it is best understood as dealing with the question of who, out of a number of possible claimants, has title to sue the defendant in respect of a given unjust enrichment. In other words, in restitution as in tort, the claimant must show not only that a potential cause of action arises, but that he personally has title to sue on the basis of it.

In the majority of cases, the question of 'at the expense of' raises few difficulties in practice. Save in the case of restitution for wrongs (of which more below), the defendant's gain can only have been made at the expense of someone else who has suffered a loss directly corresponding to it – whether by paying money, transferring property or rendering services, being defrauded or robbed of something, or otherwise. Take, for instance, the important decision in *Warman v Southern Counties Hire and Finance Co.*[86] A hired a car to B; it later transpired that they had no right to do so, since the car had been stolen from X. Against B's demand for return of the rent paid (as on a consideration that had totally failed), A claimed to deduct by way of counter-restitution the reasonable value of B's use of the car. They were unsuccessful: the car had never been theirs, and when B was allowed to use it, any corresponding loss was suffered not by them, but by the true owner X. Again, imagine I think – in error – that I owe you £1,000. To save trouble, I mention the supposed debt to X, a friend of mine who happens to owe me £1,000, and ask him to pay you direct, which he does. Now, I can clearly recover £1,000 from you: but what is to stop X doing so as well? After all, your enrichment is clearly unjustified (you have got £1,000 in respect of a bogus debt), and X indubitably paid you under a mistake (had he – and I – known the true facts, the payment would never have been made). Nevertheless, any claim by X is doomed to failure. His payment made to my order discharged his own debt to me; hence, any enrichment you have gained has been at my expense, not X's. I am the person to claim: X is not.

So far, so good: but a number of comments remain to be made.

1-27   First, although the idea of 'at the claimant's expense' comports the idea of a loss of some sort suffered by the claimant, 'loss' it seems is construed pretty widely in this context. In particular, he does not need to show he is ultimately out of pocket. So, a bank paying out on a forged letter of credit can sue the payee[87] even though it is entitled, if it wishes, simply to debit its customer's[88] account. Similarly, a party who has paid out moneys under a void interest swap arrangement is not prevented from recovering them merely because he has recouped his loss elsewhere by concluding a 'back to back' hedging operation. The claimant has suffered a loss in his own right, albeit one made good from

---

86   [1949] 2 KB 576.

87   At least at common law – see, eg, *Edward Owen Ltd v Barclays Bank Ltd* [1978] QB 159, pp 169–70, *per* Lord Denning MR. But cf, now, the Uniform Customs and Practice relating to Documentary Credits (1993 rev), § 14(e), which may complicate matters.

88   See *Uniform Customs and Practice relating to Documentary Credits* (1993 rev), § 15.

other sources:[89] for the purposes of restitution, the authority has been enriched at his expense and no one else's.

Indeed, this idea appears to be taken even further in one type of case, namely, where a payment which should have gone to A is in fact made to B, and A then seeks to recover it from B. Typically, this point has arisen in two types of situation: where B receives payment of a debt in fact owed to A,[90] and in a series of venerable authorities where B has usurped A's office together with its perquisites.[91] Here, it is submitted that 'at the expense of' also has an extended meaning: in so far as the claimant has not received what he ought to have got, the defendant's enrichment is invariably regarded as having been at his expense.[92] To put it another way, the existence of the claimant's right to the payment concerned here does double duty, satisfying both the 'unjust factor' and the 'at the expense of' requirements. This may matter. Suppose a company, having validly assigned its book debts to A, goes into receivership: the receiver B then receives payment from a customer C.[93] There seems no doubt that A can claim the money from B where C's liability to A is discharged.[94] But, what if this is not the case, for example, where A had previously given notice to C of the assignment?[95] Here, A technically suffers no loss, since he can still sue the customer direct; but it has never been judicially suggested[96] that this precludes his recovery from B on the basis that B's enrichment was not at his expense. Indeed, what authority there is suggests the contrary: the fact that a debt paid to the wrong person remains payable to the right one does not preclude a restitutionary claim by the latter.[97]

1-28   Secondly, there is no logical impossibility in the same gain having been made at the expense of two different persons. Assume a trustee, appointed as such to the board of a company in which the trust owns shares, uses corporate information

---

89   *Kleinwort Benson Ltd v Birmingham CC* [1997] QB 380. See, also, the important Australian decision in *Comr of Revenue v Royal Insurance Ltd* (1994) 69 ALJR 51, to the effect that the recovery of inexigible tax is not barred merely because the claimant has passed on the burden to his own customers. The point is discussed below, at § 12-18 *et seq.*

90   Eg, where B has previously assigned the debt to A.

91   *Arris v Stukeley* (1677) 2 Mod 260; *Jacob v Allen* (1703) 1 Salk 27. These cases are obsolete, but important from the point of view of principle.

92   Though note the contrary argument in Smith (1991) 11 OJLS 481.

93   We disregard, for simplicity's sake, any prospect of attacking the assignment under the insolvency legislation (eg, as a preference).

94   So assumed in, eg, *Aluminium Industrie BV v Romalpa Ltd* [1976] 2 All ER 552; *Pfeiffer Weinkellerei v Arbuthnot Factors Ltd* [1991] BCC 484 (though there, the claim failed for other reasons).

95   See, eg, *William Brandt's Sons v Dunlop Rubber Co* [1905] AC 454.

96   But see Smith (1991) 11 OJLS 481.

97   See *Official Custodian for Charities v Mackey* [1985] 2 All ER 1016, p 1021; cf *Tailby v Official Receiver* (1887) 18 QBD 25 (reversed on other grounds (1888) 13 App Cas 523). And see the judgment of Kelly CB in *Rusden v Pope* (1868) LR 3 Ex 269, pp 278–79 (freight paid to mortgagor of ship when owed to the mortgagee recoverable from mortgagor despite debtor having had notice of assignment).

to make a secret profit for himself. As trustee, he must on principle pay that profit to the trust: as director, to the company. Again, take the difficult case of *Reading v AG*,[98] where a venal British soldier in Egypt took bribes to transport contraband goods by making use of his position. The Crown successfully claimed to retain these in its capacity of employer: but there seems no reason why the Egyptian Government should not equally have maintained a claim on the basis that Reading had accepted payments rightfully due to them.

This, of course, gives rise to one obvious problem. There is nothing wrong, as such, with the trustee or the corrupt soldier being potentially liable to two claimants: on the other hand, it would be objectionable if he actually had to pay both. The best way to avoid double liability in such a case seems to be through the developing defence of change of position: payment of one claimant should bar action by the other.[99]

Finally, there is one case where the idea of 'at the expense of' ceases to have independent significance: namely, where the claim is for restitution for a wrong done to the victim. Here, the question whether the claimant has suffered a loss is irrelevant: indeed, as often as not, he will claim despite not being out of pocket at all. Thus, the trustee who profits from his office, or the agent who takes a bribe,[100] must account for any receipts to the beneficiary or principal, whether or not there is any evidence that the latter has suffered loss or would, but for the fiduciary's wrongdoing, have received the gain concerned. Similarly, if I unlawfully borrow your car while you are away and use it as a minicab, you are entitled to my profits even though you have suffered no loss, and had no intention to use or profit from the car while away.[101] The only way to rescue the 'at the expense of the claimant' requirement in cases of this sort is to say, here, any enrichment is *deemed* to have been at the expense of the victim. But, this is the land of fiction, and it does no good to anyone to linger there: it is simpler to admit that the requirement just does not apply.

III FACTORS JUSTIFYING RETENTION

1-29   The combination of enrichment at the claimant's expense and an 'unjust factor' constitutes a *prima facie* case for restitution. But, it is not conclusive. There may be a specific defence available to the defendant, such as *bona fide* purchase or change of position: these are discussed in detail below, Chapter 13. More importantly, however, it is suggested that there are a number of factors which go to show that, even where a *prima facie* case for restitution would seem to have

---

98   [1951] AC 507.
99   Below, § 13-14.
100 Discussed below, Chapter 11.
101 Cf *Strand Electric Ltd v Brisford Entertainments Ltd* [1952] 2 QB 246, discussed below, § 11-12

been made out, on the facts of the case, the defendant's enrichment is justified. Six will be dealt with here: (a) forced exchange; (b) *bona fide* purchase; (c) lawful receipt from a third party; (d) incidental benefit; (e) receipt under a subsisting valid contract; and (f) donative intent.

(a) Forced exchange, subjective devaluation and 'incontrovertible benefit'

1-30   The difficulty with benefits other than straightforward money receipts is that the defendant immediately has two plausible arguments as to why it would be unjust to force him to make restitution, despite the existence of what would otherwise be an 'unjust factor'.

Forced exchange: 'incontrovertible benefit'

1-31   The idea lying behind 'forced exchange' is easy to comprehend. It applies to any benefit which the defendant has not either accepted or at least acquiesced in. I pave your driveway mistaking it for your neighbour's; or I misdeliver cement to your house and builders working there use it. Given that you cannot undo what has been done, the decision to give me restitution here amounts to compulsory purchase in reverse. However much you may be benefited in financial terms, it *ipso facto* forces you to pay for something you never agreed to have.

It is true that previous writers have not referred to 'forced exchange' by name. Nevertheless, it is suggested that a reluctance to impose it by law forms the backdrop of a good deal of the law of restitution. In particular, with the possible exception of necessitous intervention[102] it is clear law, and uncontroversial, that the provision unasked of goods or services that leave no financial gain or marketable residuum in the hands of the recipient cannot, without more, give rise to restitution. To this extent at least, whatever the present status of the decision in *Falcke v Scottish Imperial Insurance Co*,[103] Bowen LJ's statement in that case that liabilities 'are not to be forced on people behind their backs any more than you can confer a benefit bestowed on him against his will' is clearly right as a matter of principle.

The difficulty arises where there is some such gain or residuum; how do we reconcile reluctance to make people pay for what they never chose to have, with the principle that uncovenanted benefits ought to be paid for? The answer often given is this: the defendant must pay if, and only if, he has received an 'incontrovertible benefit'.[104] Take the case where I pave your driveway, but change it slightly. Imagine, for instance, that you intended to have the work

---

102 On which see below, Chapter 9.
103 (1881) 34 Ch D 234, p 238. For further discussion, see below, Chapter 9.
104 Eg, Goff & Jones, p 22 *et seq*.

done anyway: indeed, it may have been necessary for you to do it to avoid damaging your car. Then, my work would have saved you actual expenditure. There is no doubt that this is a benefit: why should you not have to account for it? Similarly, too, with an actual or prospective conversion of a benefit into cash. I improve your house by mistake, increasing its value by £5,000. If (Birks) you have already sold the house and hence realised the £5,000,[105] or (Burrows) you intend to do so within a short time,[106] or even (Goff & Jones) if you could be expected to do so as a reasonable person,[107] then – the suggestion goes – the matter is different: you ought to have to make restitution to the extent of the added value.

Isolated *dicta* in England provide some support for the view that 'incontrovertible benefit' may indeed qualify the principle of forced exchange.[108] Furthermore, by statute in England,[109] a *bona fide* possessor who improves another's property does not have to give it back unless paid for his improvements – a rule possibly explicable on a similar basis.[110] Nevertheless, there is no clear authority in favour of the concept,[111] and (it is suggested) good reasons for caution before adopting the doctrine anyway, since the justice of it is not quite as obvious as it seems at first sight.

1-32   The first awkwardness is conceptual. Whichever form of argument based on incontrovertible benefit one accepts, the justice or otherwise of making the defendant pay is being reckoned by reference to events – whether actual or hypothetical – taking place *after* receipt of it. But, why should these be in account at all? If restitution is about the receipt of unjust benefits, the time for reckoning whether the defendant's enrichment is unjust is surely the time of receipt.

Secondly, the 'incontrovertible benefit' point as argued tends to confuse two distinct issues. It is effectively based on prejudice to the defendant: if he has turned the benefit into money or would have paid for it anyway, etc, then (the

---

105 Birks, p 121.

106 Burrows, p 10. This prevents a canny defendant from delaying realisation until after litigation.

107 Goff & Jones, p 22.

108 *The Manila* [1988] 3 All ER 843, p 855 (Hirst J); *Marston Construction Ltd v Kigass Ltd* (1989) 46 BLR 109, p 125 (Judge Bowsher QC); *Becerra v Close Bros Ltd* (1999) unreported, 25 June (*dicta* of Thomas J). Irish authority seems less friendly to the doctrine: eg, *O'Callaghan v Ballincollig Holdings Ltd* (1993) unreported, 31 March (Blayney J) (no recovery against landlord for repairs carried out by tenant after fire, despite apparent presence of clear incontrovertible benefit).

109 Torts (Interference with Goods) Act 1977, s 6 (in force in England and NI). This replaced a similar common law rule (*Greenwood v Bennett* [1973] QB 195) which presumably remains good law in the Republic.

110 See Birks, p 122. Burrows, p 120 *et seq*, is more doubtful whether the statutory liability under s 6 has much to do with unjust enrichment at all.

111 Cf *Bookmakers' Afternoon Greyhound Services Ltd v Gilbert* [1994] FSR 723, where a bookmaker who knowingly took advantage of an information service he had not asked for in order to increase his own profits nevertheless escaped any restitutionary liability to repay. See below, § 5-11.

proponents of 'incontrovertible benefit' will doubtless say) he ought to have to make restitution because he will suffer no prejudice. But, whether somebody would be prejudiced by having to pay for a benefit is not the same question as whether it is just to make him do so; the latter does not follow from the former. In this case, the point hinted at by Mead[112] remains good; the law of contract does not allow people to be forced to make payment for what they do not want, for the very good reason that they should, in justice, be allowed to do as they like with their own property, and to decide who they will contract with. There is, it is suggested, no reason in this respect why the claimant should be able to sidestep this rule by suing in restitution.

'Subjective devaluation'

1-33   Quite apart from the argument from forced exchange, a defendant may say that a supposed enrichment was not beneficial to him, or if it was, only beneficial to a limited extent. For this, Birks coined the useful term 'subjective devaluation'.[113] I lay tarmac on your driveway, thinking I have a contract to do so: had I not intervened, you would have had the job done for half the price by a friend. The law of restitution could say that your actual wants and idiosyncrasies were irrelevant; in fact, we shall see that, to a greater or lesser extent, it is prepared to take them into account.

First, a point of principle. Assuming that subjective devaluation may be relevant to a restitution claim, where does it belong in the scheme of the law? Does it, in fact, go to the question whether it is just to force the defendant to make restitution (as suggested here): or should it be in the section on valuation of the benefit?

Rather surprisingly, most writers take the latter view. In so far as you can invoke the doctrine of subjective devaluation, you are simply not enriched at all.[114] But it is, with respect, hard to see why this should be so. To begin with, the view just referred to assumes a strained view of the idea of enrichment. Suppose a paving contractor, owing to a mistake as to addresses, tars the drives of three identical adjoining houses owned by A, B and C respectively, increasing the value of each by £1,000. Suppose further that Owner A asked for the job to be done, Owner B did not and had no intention of having it done at all, and Owner C was going to get a similar service from a third party for £600. Whatever the equities as to demanding payment, it seems perverse to say that A is enriched by £1,000, B not at all, and C by £600. In financial terms they all gain £1,000. Secondly, the 'no enrichment' view of subjective devaluation overlooks the question why we take into account the defendant's wishes and intentions at all. In the case of the tarred drives, the reason we think B and C ought to pay less

---

112 Mead, 'Free acceptance: some further considerations' (1989) 105 LQR 460.

113 Birks, p 109 *et seq*.

114 Eg, Birks, Chapter 5.

than A is, it is suggested, essentially one of justice. Our instinctive feeling that it is hard to make B raise money to pay for what he did not want, or to make C pay £1,000 for a job he could have had for £600, is that it is unfair: not that there is no enrichment at all.[115]

1-34　This might look like an arid exercise in classification for its own sake, but it is not. There may be cases where, exceptionally, a defendant ought not in justice to be able to invoke his own subjective wishes or idiosyncrasies. One example is medical attention – even unsuccessful – to those temporarily incapacitated: another is where urgent repairs are carried out to joint property by one co-owner even though the other was happy to let the property fall down.[116] A statutory case is the right of a party to a dissolved marriage to recognition of improvements to matrimonial property when questions arise as to the division of the parties' assets.[117] If subjective devaluation goes to whether the enrichment is unjust, there is no problem here: but if we say there is simply no benefit in such cases, it is hard to see how a claim could even get off the ground at common law, or find any plausible justification if a statutory one.

How far does the idea of subjective devaluation extend? Apart from the examples already cited, it is not difficult to think of other potential instances. Suppose all the windows in my street are shattered in a gale: I telephone A and arrange for him to replace mine for £250. Another glazier, B, then arrives, having mistaken my address for my neighbour's. Thinking he is A, I allow him to deal with my windows. Even if the reasonable value of B's work is £300, any claim he has against me (based, say, on free acceptance) ought to be limited to £250. My previous arrangement with A is ample evidence that that was the value I put on the service concerned. Or again, take the case where you are compelled to pay off my debt of £1,000: if I can show that I could have persuaded the creditor to accept only £900 in full satisfaction, that figure should, it is suggested, represent my benefit. Similarly, too, in the case of breach of contract: where a person renders services under a contract later rescinded for breach, the contractual rate agreed for the services clearly represents the amount they were valued at by the other party, and (it is suggested) the latter ought to be entitled to take advantage of that factor in limiting any restitutionary award.[118]

---

115 Cf Aldous J in *Bookmakers' Afternoon Greyhound Services Ltd v Gilbert* [1994] FSR 723, p 743: 'When a party makes it clear to the provider of a service that he will not pay for it or does not want it, then it cannot be against the conscience of that man that he should refuse to pay for the service.' See, too, *Easat v Racal plc* (2000) unreported, 28 March.

116 A possible third is maritime salvage, where an award is technically possible even against a non-consenting shipowner: see *The Kangaroo* [1918] P 327. But this is not as significant as it might seem, since it is argued below (§ 9-26) that the connection between salvage and restitution law is problematical in any case.

117 Eg, under the (English) Matrimonial Causes Act 1973, s 25.

118 See Birks in Burrows, *Essays on Restitution*, Chapter 5, p 135 *et seq*.

1-35 Actual authority supporting the idea of 'subjective devaluation' *eo nomine* is admittedly somewhat difficult to find. But the idea lying behind it can, it is suggested, be seen in action in a number of instances.

One example is statutory, and arises where a seller of goods short delivers, but the buyer accepts what he does get. The buyer must pay, and since the seller cannot claim the full contract price, this liability is clearly restitutionary. But the buyer need only pay the contract rate.[119] Why the limitation? The answer is surely this: the contract price of the goods shows what they were worth to this recipient. Or again, take the difficult case of *Boulton v Jones*.[120] Jones ordered piping from one Brocklehurst, who at the time owed him a sum greater than the agreed price. In fact, unknown to Jones, the piping was supplied by Boulton, who owed Jones nothing, but who had since bought Brocklehurst's business. It was held – pretty uncontroversially – that Boulton could have no contractual claim against Jones, since Jones had clearly not intended to deal with him at all.[121] But, should he have had a restitutionary claim based on the fact that Jones accepted, and no doubt used or sold, the piping? The best answer would seem to be no, on the basis that while there might well have been an acceptance by Jones, the value of the goods *to him* – the amount he expected to have to pay for them – fell to be reduced by the amount of the set off against Brocklehurst, in this case to nil.[122]

(b) *Bona fide* purchase

1-36 It is a feature running through most of restitution law that a person receiving money or other benefits *bona fide* and for value is normally immune to restitutionary liability. The only major exception is restitution for wrongs,[123] where, owing to the strict liability attaching to the property torts of conversion and detinue,[124] an innocent purchaser who subsequently disposes of goods may find himself liable to a restitutionary action for the price received, together with any other benefits.

Despite the tendency to treat *bona fide* purchase as an autonomous defence to a restitutionary claim,[125] it is suggested that this is not very helpful. A more straightforward explanation for the good faith purchaser's immunity is simply

---

119 See s 30(3) of the Sale of Goods Act 1979 (England) and the Sale of Goods Act 1893 (Ireland).

120 (1857) 27 LJ Ex 117.

121 To this extent the case is analogous to *Cundy v Lindsay* (1878) 3 App Cas 459.

122 It seems to follow that had Jones's set off been less than the price of the goods, Boulton ought to have received restitution based on the difference. Cf *Greer v Downs Supply Co Ltd* [1927] 2 KB 28.

123 Below, Chapter 11.

124 Detinue in the Republic only: it was abolished as a cause of action in England and NI by the Torts (Interference with Goods) Act 1977, s 2(1).

125 Eg, Burrows, p 472. Cf Barker [1999] RLR 75.

that it amounts to a justification for retaining a benefit that would otherwise be impermissible. Certain property claims aside, freedom of commerce demands that one ought to be able to keep what one has paid for in all innocence, even if the result is a gain at someone else's expense.[126]

Sometimes, indeed, the good faith purchaser's immunity follows from ordinary principles of property law. Thus, it is well established that the right to regain a chattel transferred under a voidable contract, which is a proprietary restitutionary right, yields to a *bona fide* purchaser of it.[127] Again, where the claimant's right is given effect to by awarding him some equitable proprietary interest or lien, arising (say) from a constructive trust or a right to trace in equity, or (in Ireland) from the doctrine of salvage,[128] orthodox equitable doctrines apply. Equitable rights here, as elsewhere, give way to a *bona fide* purchaser of a legal, and sometimes even an equitable,[129] interest.[130]

But, while general equitable principles may well be relevant, and indeed decisive in a number of cases, the principle of *bona fide* purchase in restitution goes much further than that. In *Lipkin Gorman v Karpnale Ltd*,[131] for instance, where a dishonest solicitor stole the plaintiff firm's moneys and gambled them away at the defendants' casino, it was plainly accepted by the House of Lords that even though the firm's claim lay at law for money had and received, the defendants would have escaped liability had they given value. Again, in the old case of *Aiken v Short*,[132] a bank, having obtained a second mortgage over landed property in the hands of X, paid off the first chargees. Discovering later that X had no title to the land, the bank sued the chargees for money paid by mistake. Although there had indubitably been a mistake, the bank failed on the basis that the chargees had taken the money for value, that is, in payment of X's liability to them.

---

126 There will be such a gain if the amount paid was less than the value of what was received.

127 See, eg, *Anderson v Ryan* [1967] IR 34; *Lewis v Averay* [1972] 1 QB 198.

128 See below, § 9-16.

129 'Mere equities' give way to a good faith purchaser of a mere equitable interest. Arguably, a right to claim proceeds by virtue of the doctrine of equitable tracing should come in this category: cf *Re ffrench's Estate* (1887) 21 LR Ir 283, p 300 (Porter MR) (but compare less favourable *dicta* by Lord Browne-Wilkinson in *Westdeutsche Landesbankgirozentrale v Islington BC* [1996] 2 All ER 986, p 987). Another example of a restitutionary interest classified as a mere equity is a right to recover land on rescission of a contract relating to it. See *Phillips v Phillips* (1862) 4 De G, F and J 208, p 218 (Lord Westbury), and generally cf *Latec Investments Ltd v Hotal Terrigal Pty Ltd* (1965) 113 CLR 265.

130 But cf *Re Irish Shipping Ltd* [1986] ILRM 518, where moneys impressed with a constructive trust were paid into an overdrawn bank account and the bank, though ignorant of the trust, was not allowed to appropriate them to its customer's indebtedness. It is respectfully submitted that the decision is wrong on this point.

131 [1991] 2 AC 548.

132 (1856) 1 H and N 210. See, too, *Watson v Russell* (1862) 5 B and S 968. In *ANZ Bank Ltd v Westpac Ltd* (1988) 164 CLR 662, where moneys were mistakenly credited to an overdrawn bank account, the bank – oddly – does not seem to have taken the point that it might have had a defence of bona fide purchase.

1-37 One case, however, causes difficulty here. In *Jones (RE) Ltd v Waring and Gillow Ltd*,[133] a fraudster, B, owed W £5,000 secured on certain furniture. He induced J to send a cheque for that sum to W by saying, falsely, that he wanted to borrow the money from J to finance the purchase of a number of cars from W. W accepted the cheque in payment of B's actual debt to themselves and cashed it. One would have thought the case was on all fours with *Aiken v Short*,[134] above; yet the House of Lords, not citing that case, held that J could recover the £5,000 as money paid by mistake. Today, no doubt, W would have a defence based on change of position,[135] so the actual decision is in a sense academic; but the reasoning in it is difficult to justify.[136] It should be regarded as open to reconsideration in the House of Lords; in Ireland, where it is of course not binding, it is submitted that it ought not to be followed on this point.[137]

For these purposes, *bona fide* purchase means acceptance of the benefit in payment of a debt or under a valid contract. A mere change of position does not count, however[138] (though it may itself provide a defence *pro tanto*):[139] nor does receipt under a contract void under, say, the (English) Gaming Act 1845.[140] There is authority that, at least as regards rights to restitution founded on equitable doctrines such as undue influence, the defence is not available unless the recipient shows not only that he took in good faith but that he had no means of knowledge of the claimant's right.[141] It remains to be seen whether this rule of constructive notice will be extended to other rights.

(c) Lawful receipt from a third party[142]

1-38 Suppose A pays B £1,000 by mistake; B thereupon gives a different £1,000 to his son C. Or suppose B intends to give £1,000 to A, but in a fit of forgetfulness makes out a cheque to C instead, which C cashes. In either case, can A claim

---

133 [1926] AC 670.

134 (1856) 1 H and N 210.

135 See *Lipkin Gorman v Karpnale Ltd* [1991] 2 AC 548.

136 Particularly since there is authority that W could have sued J on the cheque had J countermanded it: *Hasan v Willson* [1977] 1 Lloyd's Rep 431. See Tettenborn [1998] RLR 63.

137 *Jones's* case was cited with approval by Budd J in *National Bank v O'Connor* (1966) 103 ILTR 73, p 96, but not on this issue.

138 See *Jones (RE) Ltd v Waring and Gillow Ltd* [1926] AC 670, above: where B fraudulently induced J to draw a cheque in favour of W, and W having received it released certain furniture to B, this was held not to be a purchase sufficient to bar J's action against them.

139 Since *Lipkin Gorman v Karpnale Ltd* [1991] 2 AC 548.

140 *Lipkin Gorman v Karpnale Ltd* [1991] 2 AC 548. In Ireland, for the Gaming Act 1845, s 18, read the (identical) Betting and Lotteries Act 1956, s 36.

141 *Barclays Bank plc v O'Brien* [1994] 1 AC 180.

142 Tettenborn [1997] RLR 1. Cf Jaffey, *The Nature and Scope of Restitution*, Chapter 8.

£1,000 from C? It is generally accepted that he cannot, at least in England:[143] but why? He can show an unjust factor (mistake): he can also (let it be assumed) show that, but for that unjust factor, C would not have been enriched.

One way to deal with this problem is to seek an explanation based on the concept of enrichment *at the claimant's expense*: C's enrichment, it can be argued, is irrecoverable by A in such a situation because it was at B's expense, not A's.[144] But, this is not entirely convincing. A has indubitably suffered a diminution of his assets corresponding to the augmentation of C's. To say that, nevertheless, C's enrichment is not at A's expense must therefore involve giving a technically restricted meaning of some sort to enrichment 'at the claimant's expense', for instance, by subjecting it to some arbitrary limitation, such as 'privity'.[145]

1-39   A better answer, it is suggested, is that in both cases C can show an independent justification for his enrichment: namely, that he received the £1,000 from B, and that B was entitled to do as he wished with his own property. Moreover, it is submitted that (startling though this may seem at first sight) it follows that it ought not to matter for these purposes whether C gave value, or even that he had notice of the situation as between A and B.[146] No doubt *bona fide* purchase is necessary to defeat a claim based on a pre-existing property right, or where benefits are received direct from the claimant; but there is no reason why the mere fact that X receives payment from Y knowing that it would not have been made but for the fact that Y had been unjustly enriched at Z's expense should impeach X's own title to keep what he has got. Property claims aside, it should not be incumbent on a person receiving money or other benefits to investigate the state of accounts between the person providing them and third parties.

1-40   Is there any authority supporting this proposition? It is respectfully suggested that there is. A neat example is the controversial case of Re Byfield.[147] B went bankrupt. Not knowing that this had happened, B's bank honoured a cheque drawn by her in favour of her mother. The latter paid it to the credit of her own account and used part of the proceeds to pay some of B's creditors. Having had to repay the amount of the cheque to B's trustee in bankruptcy (in whom B's assets were vested at the time), the bank argued that it had a restitutionary claim

---

143 But see *Khan v Permayer* (2000) unreported, 22 June, CA, for a suggestion, *obiter*, that there may be recovery here. In Ireland, the situation is also not quite clear: cf *M'Mehan v Warburton* [1896] 1 IR 435, p 441 and *Shanahan v Redmond*, (1994) unreported, 21 June, HC. But, the matter has never been discussed as a matter of principle.

144 Cf Smith (1991) 11 OJLS 481 *et seq* and also Burrows, p 42.

145 Cf Burrows, p 45 *et seq*; cf Hayton in Birks (ed), *Laundering and Tracing*, 'Equity's Identification Rules'.

146 Cf the thinking behind the Irish Law Reform Committee's *Report on Minors' Contracts* (1985 LRC No 15): although a minor receiving property under a contract not binding on him should be liable to an order requiring him to return it, this should not apply to any subsequent recipient, whether or not that recipient was a *bona fide* purchaser.

147 [1982] 1 All ER 249. Carney J in Ireland approved this decision in *Re Towey, A Bankrupt* (1994) unreported, 24 March, HC.

against B, provable in the bankruptcy, on the basis that it had mistakenly paid her creditors. The claim failed. Although the creditors would not have been paid but for the bank's mistaken honouring of the cheque, they had nevertheless been paid not by the bank but by the mother out of her moneys: even if the bank had a claim against the mother, there was, as Goulding J put it, no adequate nexus between its action and the payment of the creditors.[148] Again, this principle forms the assumption behind most of the law on tracing: it is the obverse of the rule that in order to trace, one must show both a proprietary base, and that the defendant received something representing that erstwhile property. *Agip (Africa) Ltd v Jackson*[149] makes the point straightforwardly. Money was siphoned from the claimants' account by one Z and passed through the banking system to, *inter alia*, the defendant accountants. Even though an unjust factor (interference with the claimants' property) was shown, and it was also clear that the defendants: (a) were not in good faith; and (b) would not have received the money but for the theft, the claimants' action for money had and received failed. Owing to the intricacies of the banking system, the moneys received could not at common law be regarded as the product of the claimants' property; they represented a disbursement by an intermediary bank of its own money, and the defendants had title at law to retain them.

A similar principle, it is suggested, also applies to goods and services. Assume A Ltd negotiates with builders B for urgent improvements to factory premises owned by its subsidiary C Ltd. Speed being vital, B begin work immediately at A's request; but negotiations eventually fail. Whatever B's claim against A,[150] it is suggested they have none against C. The services were being provided, in effect, by A to C: by virtue of that supply, C ought to have an indefeasible title to any enrichment gained thereby. And the same should follow where what was ordered by A was not improvements to C's property, but goods to be supplied direct to C. Nor, for the reasons given above, should it make any difference whether intra-group accounting practice required C to credit A for the goods or services provided.

1-41   We have already hinted at the major exception to this principle. It cannot apply where the claimant's claim is based on an allegation that the defendant received the proceeds of *property* or some analogous right vested in him. If A pays B £1,000 by mistake, thus arguably rendering B a constructive trustee of the £1,000,[151] and B gives that very money to C, C will be bound by the constructive trust, and will have to make restitution. Again, in *Lipkin Gorman v Karpnale*

---

148 See [1982] 1 All ER 249, p 256.

149 [1991] Ch 547.

150 *British Steel Corp v Cleveland Bridge and Engineering Co Ltd* [1984] 1 All ER 504.

151 See *Chase Manhattan NA v Israel-British Bank Ltd* [1981] Ch 105 (England); *Re Irish Shipping Ltd* [1986] ILRM 518 (Ireland). Note, however, that there has more recently been some scepticism as to whether a trust is appropriate in such cases: eg, *Westdeutsche Landesbank Girozentrale v Islington BC* [1996] AC 669, pp 690, 706.

Ltd[152] it was irrelevant to the defendants' liability that they received cash from an intermediary, Cass: the basis of the solicitors' claim was that the moneys received directly represented their assets wrongfully filched.

This may also explain the difficult case of *Shanahan v Redmond*.[153] A took out a life assurance policy in favour of B: he then had second thoughts and instructed the insurance company to cancel the policy and replace it with one in favour of himself. The company failed to heed these instructions and paid B notwithstanding. Carroll J held that B held the payment on trust for A, apparently on the basis that A's lawful but unfulfilled instruction to the company created a trust in his favour affecting the original policy.[154] The difficulty with this holding, however, is that it is difficult to see on what basis such a trust could have arisen. A better view, it is submitted, is that A's remedies against the company were merely contractual, and that for that reason no restitutionary remedy ought to have lain.

(d) Incidental benefit

1-42   Take the facts of a well known American case, *Ulmer v Farnsworth*.[155] A and B owned neighbouring quarries. A pumped out his own, since otherwise he would not be able to work it; as a necessary result the water level in B's fell, and B was saved expense he would otherwise have incurred. The decision in that case was that A had no claim against B, and this is clearly right: there was no unjust factor here, and in addition A had a plausible plea of 'no forced exchange'. But now, change the facts: suppose a public authority had ordered A to act as he did (say for health and safety reasons), and further that it had done so as a result of pressure from B. There is now an unjust feature (compulsion, or lack of voluntariness): furthermore B, having instigated the whole process, can hardly plead non-acceptance of it. Nevertheless, although there is no authority, it is suggested that B should still be immune to a restitutionary claim. But why? The argument that A acted in his own self-interest in discharging his liability will not do, since it would apply equally to a co-debtor who is compelled to pay the whole debt – and who clearly does have a claim. The least unsatisfactory explanation seems to be that just as one takes the risk that others' actions may incidentally cause one uncompensatable loss, one ought to be entitled to keep any benefits incidentally incurred. The difference between cases of this sort and that of the co-debtor is, it is submitted, the admittedly imprecise one of directness: where there is no nexus between the parties and the relation between

---

152 [1991] 2 AC 548.
153 (1994) unreported, 21 June, HC (Ireland).
154 On the basis (so it was said) that equity regards as done that which ought to be done.
155 16 Atl 65 (1888) (Supreme Court of Maine).

the claimant's act and the defendant's benefit is entirely contingent, the benefit should be regarded as 'incidental' and irrecoverable.

(e) Receipt under contract with the claimant

1-43   Benefits conferred under a valid contract between the claimant and the defendant cannot form the subject of restitutionary relief so long as the contract remains enforceable against the claimant.[156] Although no authority directly states this, it is clearly assumed by cases such as *Bell v Lever Bros*[157] dealt with below, Chapter 3. Employers paid substantial severance pay to two directors in exchange for a promise by the latter to give up any rights they might have had to sue for wrongful dismissal. Discovering later that they could have dismissed the directors summarily without any payment, they then sought to recover what they had misguidedly disbursed. Although the case turned on whether the contract under which the money had been paid could be impugned for mistake, it was clearly fundamental to the decision that, unless it could, the payments would be irrecoverable.

(f) Donative intent

1-44   A person who genuinely intends to benefit someone else and waive any claim to restitution should obviously be able to do so: it cannot be unjust to retain a benefit one was intended to have all along. Normally, this will cause no difficulty. With ordinary gifts, there is no unjust factor anyway. In the slightly more complex case where A pays money to B in circumstances of error, but makes it clear that he is happy for B to keep it even if he was mistaken, there is equally no difficulty in denying restitution on causation grounds: the mistake, even if it existed, did not cause the payment. But, one cannot always argue thus. Suppose a contractor is faced with a demand for money he does not owe, backed by a threat of an unlawful breach of contract; in order to preserve good relations in future, he pays up. Here, there is an unjust factor (duress) and causation (but for the threat, payment would not have been made). Nevertheless, restitution ought to be refused: the payer's donative intent here acts as an independent factor justifying retention of the payment.[158]

---

156 Burrows, p 250.

157 [1932] AC 761. See, too, *Re Richmond Gate Property Ltd* [1964] 3 All ER 936, where the plaintiff acted as informal managing director of a company. Even though the company accepted his services, he was denied recovery on the basis that there was a subsisting contract with him and the company that he would receive only such salary as the directors, and that the directors had never resolved to pay him anything.

158 See below, § 4-16 *et seq.*

(g) A questionable factor: 'officiousness'

1-45   Goff & Jones[159] posit an independent doctrine whereby, even where the requirements for restitution are otherwise satisfied, an 'officious' claimant should be denied recovery: in other words, where a benefit is officiously conferred, there is nothing unjust about the defendant retaining the benefit of it. The point is particularly relevant in the case of necessitous intervention: indeed, Goff & Jones cite as a classic example the case of a rescuer acting without good reason where others could have done the job better.[160] But, it is not limited to such cases: another plausible example is the person who, unasked, stands surety for another and then, having paid the debt, seeks recoupment from the debtor.[161]

With respect, however, it is open to a little doubt whether the doctrine does any work that cannot be done using other techniques.[162] Taking first the necessitous intervener, the only 'unjust factor' triggering his claim in the first place is the rather vague one of meritorious conduct: an officious intervener is surely unmeritorious, and so falls at the first fence anyway. As for the voluntary surety, it is suggested below[163] that the job supposedly done by 'officiousness' can equally well be done by a flexible interpretation of the concept of compulsion: a surety who agrees to pay another's debt voluntarily and with no other sound business or other reason to do so can hardly claim that he has been compelled to pay it when called on to do so.

IV THE RELATION BETWEEN UNJUST ENRICHMENT AND OTHER SOURCES OF LIABILITY

1-46   The idea of unjust enrichment as a separate source of liability being a recent invention, it is not surprising that there is no absolute distinction between unjust enrichment and other causes of action. Resulting and constructive trusts on occasion are applied with a view to remedying unjustified enrichment,[164] as, for that matter, are the general principles of the law of property.[165] Similarly, the measure of damages in tort and contract may sometimes be aimed in practice at

---

159 Goff & Jones, pp 63–65.

160 See *ibid*, pp 64–65.

161 See *ibid*, pp 128–29. Cf *Petro-Canada Ltd v Capot-Blanc* (1992) 95 DLR (4th) 69 (voluntary payment of another's tax held on this basis to give no right of recoupment).

162 As argued by Birks, pp 102–03.

163 Below, 8-7.

164 Eg, in cases of mistake under the rule in *Chase Manhattan Bank NA v Israel-British Bank Ltd* [1981] Ch 105 (assuming that case to have been rightly decided in the light of later *dicta* in *Westdeutsche Landesbank Girozentrale v Islington BC* [1996] AC 669: see below, § 3-20).

165 Eg, the rule that on rescission of a contract for fraud, property transferred automatically revests in the transferor.

removing gain, rather than their 'official' purpose of compensating loss. The possibility of punitive damages for torts aimed at making a profit,[166] the liability of a wrongful user of goods to pay a reasonable hire charge,[167] and the residuary category of damages based on the defendant's profit adumbrated in *AG v Blake*[168] are cases in point. But, arid questions of legal taxonomy need not worry us here: provided the restitutionary foundations of such claims are recognised, and where appropriate, suitable restitutionary rules applied to them,[169] the technical source of the liability is comparatively unimportant.

Nevertheless, there are a number of important matters which are worth mentioning in this connection.

1-47 First, there remain cases where restitutionary liability must be clearly separated from liability based on other factors. A neat and instructive instance is *The Batis*.[170] The charterers of a ship ordered her owners to call at a certain port in circumstances where, on the proper interpretation of the charter, the latter were not bound to do so. The owners, having complied, sued to recover all the loss and expenses incurred by them as a result; the charterers retorted that the owners could only claim in so far as they could show they had conferred a benefit on the charterers. The answer to this question clearly turned on whether the owners' claim was properly characterised as one for breach of contract (when the loss would be recoverable) or for restitution (when it would not). Hobhouse J, after some argument, decided that the claim was contractual.

1-48 Secondly, rules applicable to other heads of liability may, of course, affect restitutionary recovery. An elementary example is the rule that the right to restitution may be excluded by contract. Again, where benefits are rendered under a contract terminated for breach, the agreed contract price may, it seems, affect the measure of recovery.[171] So, also, for obvious reasons, where the claimant is forced to rely on restitution for wrongs, he must be defeated if he cannot show any wrong at all. This is particularly important – and can be somewhat unfortunate – where the defendant has gained from dealings with the claimant's chattel. Restitutionary liability here is based on waiver of the tort of trespass or conversion, which means that if the claimant has no action in tort (for example, because he has no immediate right to possession), he has no right to restitution either.

---

166 As in, eg, *Broome v Cassell and Co Ltd* [1972] AC 1027.

167 Cf *Strand Electric Ltd v Brisford Entertainments Ltd* [1952] 2 QB 246.

168 [2001] 1 AC 268.

169 This is an important point. It is not clear how far matters such as the defence of change of position now accepted as a general defence in restitution cases apply to forms of recovery which are in effect restitutionary, but in form appear under some other legal category.

170 [1990] 1 Lloyd's Rep 345.

171 Below, § 6-30 *et seq*.

1-49   Thirdly, whereas it is axiomatic that mere lack of contractual or tortious liability cannot bar restitution, the case may well be different where that lack is due to matters of important policy: for example, rules relating to form, capacity, or public policy in the law of contract. In so far as the grant of restitution would circumvent the policy behind such requirements, it should be denied. If a minor cannot be sued on a loan,[172] for example, that equally bars an action based on his unjust enrichment in keeping the money;[173] if a moneylender cannot enforce a mortgage because his action is out of time, he cannot save himself by claiming subrogation to the original vendor's lien.[174] But, any such principle must be applied sensitively. The question in all cases is whether the rule or statute concerned ought, or is intended, to apply to restitutionary as well as to other recovery. This was made clear by the High Court of Australia in *Pavey and Matthews Pty Ltd v Paul*.[175] There, having considered New South Wales legislation barring enforcement of building contracts not in a given form, the court decided that this did not bar an action for the reasonable price of services rendered under the defective contract. A topical English example is s 234(4) of the Insolvency Act 1986, exonerating a company liquidator from liability for loss or damage if he seizes or sells property which seems to belong to the company, but does not. It seems clear that this section is intended to leave intact any restitutionary liability he may be under to account for the proceeds of sale.

Restitution and the law of property

1-50   As appears below, restitution often takes the form of causing property obtained by the defendant to vest in, or be treated as beneficially owned by, the claimant. Claims to proceeds of misapplied property invoking the 'tracing' rule are one example;[176] another is the employer's claim to recover bribes *in specie* in the hands of his agent.[177] The form of the action may be for the enforcement of a property right vested in the claimant; its substance, by contrast, is undoubtedly restitutionary.

On principle, however, it is submitted that the use of the term 'restitution' in this connection ought to be limited to property the ownership of which is obtained by the defendant so as to represent an unjust enrichment in his hands. In particular, it should not cover claims for the return of property that has belonged to the claimant all along, which should be discussed as part of the law of property. Admittedly, in one sense, if you borrow my car and refuse to give it

---

172 In England because of the common law: in Ireland, because of the effect of the Infants' Relief Act 1874, s 1.
173 *Leslie (R) Ltd v Shiell* [1914] 3 KB 607.
174 *Orakpo v Manson Investments Ltd* [1978] AC 95.
175 (1987) 162 CLR 221.
176 See below, Chapter 10.
177 See *AG for Hong Kong v Reid* [1994] 1 AC 324, discussed below, § 11-33 *et seq*.

back, or if you wrongfully decline to admit that you hold Blackacre on trust for me and recognise my rights in it, you are unjustifiably enriched by the value of the car or Blackacre: you have something you ought not to have.[178] (True, also, that in Ireland the language of the Civil Liability Act 1961 seems to assume that an action in conversion to recover property in the hands of the defendant may be regarded as based on unjust enrichment.)[179] Nevertheless, there seems little point in subsuming the whole of the law of property in this book as a result. Indeed, there are good reasons not to. No one has seriously suggested that actions to recover one's property should be subject to restitutionary defences such as change of position; furthermore, as mentioned above, it is a little odd to say that if a person is in possession or control of something that is not his, he is thereby enriched by its value. Therefore, claims to recover one's property in the hands of another, whether in conversion or its equitable equivalent, will not be covered.

1-51　Two important points about the ambit of restitution follow from this. First, if we exclude from the law of restitution my claim that something in your hands has been mine all along, by parity of reasoning we must do the same where the item in question is no longer in your possession because you have lost or disposed of it. Thus, restitution ought not to embrace claims for conversion at common law, or for 'knowing receipt' in equity, where all that is alleged against the defendant is that he has handled something stolen from the claimant in the past, but no longer has it. Admittedly, a number of writers[180] disagree. They say that these liabilities are based on unjust enrichment, adding that where the property has been innocently sold, there should to avoid injustice be a defence of change of position. But this is unconvincing. The point already made, that one is not enriched by the mere possession of something belonging to somebody else, applies with equal or greater force to cases of this sort. Their natural place is in the category of claims for compensation for a wrong, legal or equitable as the case may be.

Secondly, cases of presumed resulting trusts arising out of certain gifts without consideration, and resulting trusts occurring where a gift is made that does not exhaust the beneficial interest, should equally not count as restitutionary. Admittedly, there is authority that in such cases, there is in strict law a grant of the whole property and an immediate grant back of equitable

---

178 Grantham & Rickett [1998] LM & CLQ 514. Cf, however, Burrows (2001) 117 LQR 412; Fox [2000] RLR 465; Jaffey, *The Nature and Scope of Restitution*, Chapter 9. See, too, *Macmillan Inc v Bishopsgate Investment Trust Ltd* [1995] 3 All ER 747, p 757, where Millett LJ referred to an action to recover trust property as 'restitutionary'.

179 See s 34(2)(d), allowing a defence of contributory negligence in an action for conversion except where the defendant is unjustly enriched. The problem does not arise in England, where s 10 of the Torts (Interference with Goods) Act 1977 excludes contributory negligence from all contribution claims *tout court*.

180 See, eg, McKendrick (ed), *Commercial Aspects of Trusts and Fiduciary Obligations*, Chapter 8; Millett, in Goldstein (ed), *Equity and Contemporary Legal Developments*, p 407 *et seq*; and Harpum in Birks (ed), *Frontiers of Liability*, Chapter 1.

title;[181] nevertheless, the essence of these rights is the same as that of straightforward property claims, namely, property retained by the claimant. If I have something and have not disposed of it, I must in the nature of things still be entitled to it. Again, the facts of *Quistclose Investments v Barclays Bank*[182] are another example. If a financier lends a company £5,000 to be used to pay a given debt and for no other purpose, the court may infer an intention to create a trust so that the financier retains equitable ownership so long as the purpose remains unfulfilled. Although this has affinities with a restitutionary claim based on failure of consideration, it is suggested that it is, and ought to remain, conceptually distinct.[183]

But, the logic of this cannot be taken too far. If I hand my car over to you under a mistake fundamental enough to prevent property passing, I recover it by saying it remained mine all along. If I pay you £100 by mistake, I am arguably entitled to claim beneficial ownership of the £100 as long as it is in your hands, on the basis that I never intended to dispose of it.[184] Strictly, claims such as this should lie outside restitution: nevertheless, they all involve 'unjust factors' such as mistake or failure of assumptions, and are so close to restitution that it would be pedantic not to cover them.

V   RESTITUTION: A COHERENT LEGAL CATEGORY?

1-52   The account of the basic rules of restitution just described is vital, and will dictate the scheme of this book. Before going on to deal with the law in detail, however, it is worth noting that it rests on at least three fundamental assumptions, none of which is universally accepted, and all of which could do with at least a brief defence. These assumptions are: (a) that the idea of 'unjustified enrichment' is a coherent concept, rather than an interesting, but ultimately uninformative, collection of single instances; (b) that the concept of a 'gain', or enrichment – a fundamental idea without which a supposed 'law of restitution' would have nothing to bite on in the first place – is similarly defensible; and (c) that, if the idea of a law of unjust enrichment is indeed a coherent one, it is one worth writing about in its own right, separately from, and parallel to, the law of (say) the law of contract, tort and property.

---

181 Eg, *Stroud Architectural Systems Ltd v John Laing Construction Ltd* [1994] 2 BCLC 276.
182 [1970] AC 567.
183 Cf Swadling (1996) 16 LS 110.
184 *Chase Manhattan Bank NA v Israel-British Bank Ltd* [1981] Ch 105 (assuming that case to have been rightly decided in the light of later *dicta* in *Westdeutsche Landesbank Girozentrale v Islington BC* [1996] AC 669).

(a) 'Unjust enrichment': a coherent idea?

1-53   Today, as is mentioned above, there is no doubt that courts do in fact recognise the existence of the principle of unjust enrichment.

Although the idea of a general liability to return unjust enrichment is not universally accepted by commentators,[185] it is suggested that this must be right. Assuming that the concept of 'enrichment' is sound in this respect (a matter we deal with below), it is difficult to argue with the proposition that the various heads of liability now collected under the title 'unjust enrichment' have a great deal in common, and that differences between them, while they may exist, ought to have to be justified. Like cases should be decided alike; and this should apply to cases of unjust benefit as it applies anywhere else. This is not, of course, to say that different treatment can never be defended. To take one example: where the State is a defendant to a claim for the return of taxes wrongfully demanded, there may well be good grounds for limiting recovery in order to prevent disaster to public finances.[186] But, where there are differences or discrepancies, they should have to be justified.

Indeed, one useful by-product of a unified law of restitution is precisely to point out inconsistencies and anomalies between different kinds of recovery and attempt to remove or reconcile them: witness, for example, the differences between liability to restore profits resulting from tort and breach of trust,[187] or between the rules applied to identify substitute property in 'tracing' cases at common law and in equity.[188] A prime example of just such a process in action has been the gradual assimilation of errors of fact with those of law for the purposes of recovery of money paid by mistake.[189]

1-54   It is also sometimes suggested that the concept 'unjust' is inherently too vague to be of use here. But a moment's thought shows that there is little substantial in this point. In connection with restitution, it is obvious that when we refer to enrichment that is 'unjust' or 'unjustified', we mean more than that it is simply 'unfair' or 'unjust' in the wide sense. There is no more a right to recover gains from someone else whenever it is fair and reasonable, than there is a right of recovery in tort merely on the ground that one has suffered a loss and that it is fair and reasonable that someone else should pay for it: nor has any restitution lawyer ever said there should be.[190] If I wish to use the law to take a given gain

---

185 Hedley [1995] CLJ 578.

186 Compare *Murphy v AG* [1982] IR 241 with *O'Rourke v Revenue Comrs* [1996] 2 IR 1 (remedy for overpaid taxes may vary according to amount of receipts affected).

187 Below, Chapter 11.

188 Below, Chapter 10.

189 See *Kleinwort Benson Ltd v Lincoln CC* [1999] 2 AC 349; below, Chapter 3.

190 'The recovery of money in restitution is not, as a general rule, a matter of discretion for the court' – Tuckey LJ in *Amoco (UK) Exploration Co v Teesside Gas Transportation Ltd* (1999) unreported, 30 July, CA (reversed on unconnected grounds: [2001] UKHL 18).

from you, I must show some specifically legal ground to attack it, such as that you have profited from wrongfully selling my car, or I paid you £100 by mistake, or have done work for you under a contract which for some reason turned out not to be effective. If I cannot do this, I lose.

(b) The coherence of the concept of 'gain'

1-55   Just as there could be no law of tort without some concept of what is to count as loss or damage, the idea of restitution presupposes a coherent conception of gain, or enrichment, on which the law can and ought to operate. Without this, it would be unworkable. Nevertheless, the notion that there is such a conception has been attacked on two bases.

The first runs as follows. Restitution is not simply about benefit, but about enrichment – financial gain, if you like, or gain that can, at least potentially, be measured in money terms. No one has ever argued that mere pleasure, such as the appreciation of an elegant façade erected opposite one's house, should be in account for the purposes of the law of restitution. But outside cases of money actually paid to a defendant, or property transferred to him, which constitute a gain on any reckoning, a large number – perhaps the majority – of so called restitutionary claims concern less tangible benefits, such as services rendered (for example, a haircut, or the writing of a book), or work on property (such as building operations). And these, however much appreciated by the recipient, either do not make him richer at all,[191] or if they do (as in the case of a stockbroker's advice, or work such as double glazing which may or may not enhance a house's value), they do so in an entirely arbitrary amount unrelated to the 'value' of the service concerned. It follows that if we allow recovery for services of this sort on the basis of unjust enrichment, we are simply begging the question of what counts as enrichment: we are merely pretending that an enrichment exists in order to give recovery on some other, unexplained, ground.[192]

1-56   One riposte to this contention is to point to the fact that services, as much as things, have a market value, and to argue that therefore, by getting them, one must be enriched. But this alone will not do. Market value merely reflects the fact that people are prepared to contract to pay for something. It does not show that where someone who has not so contracted, or who for some reason (such as non-completion of the work by the claimant) cannot be sued for the contract price, he is independently enriched by virtue of mere receipt of it.

---

191 Leaving aside cases where the defendant would have purchased the service elsewhere if the claimant had not provided it, and hence has been saved the expense of doing do. This is dealt with elsewhere.

192 Cf Hedley (1985) 5 LS 556, p 562.

The proper answer is, it is suggested, that of Birks. To anticipate argument that will appear later, it is suggested that there is no reason why, in suitable cases, the same factor should not determine *both* that there is a benefit of the kind contemplated by the law of restitution, *and* that the recipient ought to pay for it. Certain cases of services, notably those which do not directly augment anyone's wealth, are a prime example. Suppose I erect a fence on my land between my house and yours. You may like the fence and the privacy it produces, but (assuming it does not enhance the value of your house) it surely cannot count as an enrichment on your part.[193] On the other hand, if I make it clear that I will not put it up unless you ask me, and that I expect to be paid for my trouble, and you do request me to do so, then you must pay me: the fact of your request goes to show both that you are enriched, and that you ought to have to pay me.[194] Admittedly, Burrows argues[195] that this conflation of enrichment and injustice detracts from clarity of thought; logically, one has to see whether there is an enrichment at all before one can ask whether it is unjust. But to this, one can only respond that, even if the two questions are distinct, there is no reason why the same factor should not be relevant in answering both of them.

1-57   The second argument the restitution lawyer has to meet is this. Even assuming enrichment is a feature in all so called restitution cases, it is very often not the vital or deciding factor. Forcing all restitution claims into the 'unjust gain' model, therefore (it is said) assumes the very point to be established. For example, barring restitution for wrongs, virtually all other cases of restitution (in Birks's phrase, claims to reverse 'enrichment by subtraction')[196] involve loss as well as gain. If I pay you £100 by mistake, we can ground recovery just as easily on the fact that I have lost it as that you have got it. Indeed, if we change the example and assume I render you some service such as painting your house, my loss through expenditure of time and money is a good deal less controversial than your benefit from having it painted. Why not regard these as cases of liability for loss suffered, the event triggering it being receipt by the defendant?[197] Again, if I do work for you in the expectation of a contract that never materialises, the reason why we are sympathetic to my claim is not so

---

193 Cf *Ruabon SS Co v London Assurance* [1900] AC 6, p 10, where Lord Halsbury pooh-poohed the idea that: 'if a man were to cut down a wood that obscured his neighbour's prospect and gave him a better view, he ought upon this principle [ie, enrichment] to be compelled to contribute to cutting down the wood.'

194 Compare Deane J's classification of requested services as constituting a kind of 'constructive' enrichment: *Foran v Wright* (1989) 64 ALJR 1, p 24. The idea is clear, even if its expression is (with respect) clumsy.

195 'The benefit issue can be, *and, for the sake of clarity, should be,* cleanly isolated from the question of whether the enrichment is unjust.' Burrows, p 16 (my italics).

196 Birks, p 132 *et seq.*

197 Or, to take Stoljar's phrase, cases of 'unjust sacrifice': see (1987) 50 MLR 603.

much that you are richer (indeed, you may not be),[198] but that I have lost out through acting in reliance on you.[199]

1-58 While initially attractive, it is nevertheless suggested that this view is implausible for three reasons. First, it leaves out of account the fact that in restitution cases, courts concentrate very largely on the defendant's position: witness their unwillingness to make him pay for something he did not ask for, the defence of change of position and the limitation in tracing cases to property still in his hands. If restitution is based on loss, this extreme concern for the situation of the defendant becomes, to say the least, difficult to explain.

Secondly, liability for loss, while of course it need not involve the defendant's *fault*, normally predicates at least some *action* by him but for which the loss would not have happened. But, many cases of restitution cannot be analysed thus. Suppose, for instance, A steals money from B and gives it to C: C is liable to repay B because he has received it,[200] even though that receipt postdated B's initial loss and in no way was causative of it.

And lastly, it should be noted that an action may lie even for 'enrichment by subtraction' even where the claimant has lost nothing. For example, recovery may be possible where a bank has paid out money under a void transaction, but has successfully hedged against any loss,[201] or (arguably) where a taxpayer sues for the return of tax wrongly paid, but whose burden has since been passed on to someone else.[202] Each of these cases is hard to reconcile with the contention that cases we know as restitutionary are really concerned with loss rather than gain.

(c) Unjust enrichment: worth discussing separately?

1-59 There is no doubt that even if there is a general principle of recovery in respect of unjust enrichment, it is closely related to, and overlaps with, existing established areas of law. Most cases of so called restitution do arise in the context of contracts, or wrongs, or trusts, or the recovery of assets that have got into the wrong hands. For example, the doctrine of waiver of tort, whereby at least some tortfeasors are liable to disgorge the profits of their wrongdoing, is

---

198 To make this point clearer, suppose that I did work on your son's house in the expectation of a contract under which you would pay me.

199 For further examples, see Hedley (1985) 5 LS 56, p 61.

200 *Lipkin Gorman v Karpnale Ltd* [1991] 2 AC 458 is a straightforward example.

201 See *Kleinwort Benson Ltd v South Tyneside MBC* [1994] 4 All ER 972.

202 This raises the controversial question of 'passing on'. In *Kleinwort Benson Ltd v Birmingham CC* [1997] QB 380 it was held that restitution was on principle available even if the claimant has passed on his 'loss' to another. See, too, the Australian tax recovery case of *Comr for Revenue v Royal Insurance Australia Ltd* (1994) 69 ALJR 51, p 57. The point is dealt with below, in Chapter 12.

normally discussed as part of the law of restitution.[203] But it could equally plausibly be regarded as a remedy in tort;[204] indeed, there is little of substance to distinguish it from exemplary damages for, say, libel, or the rule allowing the owner of property to claim as his loss a reasonable rate of hire from a wrongful possessor.[205] Again, take the case where A contracts to do building work for B, but after he has done some of it, B wrongfully cancels the contract. We tend to say nowadays that B must pay A for what he has done because he would be unjustly enriched were he to obtain A's services for nothing;[206] but there would be nothing very peculiar in saying that his liability arose from an implied term in the contract. Again, if you request goods or services from me in the understanding that I am not acting gratuitously, there would be nothing particularly outlandish in saying that you have to pay for them on the basis of an inferred contract between us.

1-60   This is an important point, and it has led some commentators[207] to suggest that the arguments in favour of a separate principle of restitutionary liability are much weaker than they appear at first sight. It is suggested, however, that the case for a separate treatment of unjust enrichment law remains basically sound, for at least two reasons.

First, although many cases of restitution can, with a little ingenuity, be fitted into existing areas of law, not all can. If I pay you money by mistake, you have to repay an equivalent sum. It is difficult to see how this can be rationalised except by reference to the fact that you have been unjustly enriched by the receipt.[208] Even if we say that your enrichment exactly matches a loss suffered by me, the problem remains: why, in the absence of any fault or other wrong on your part, should you have to compensate me for that loss? Similarly, if I am forced by legal process to pay off a debt owed by you,[209] I am entitled to claim the amount I have paid from you. Here again, it is hard to see any other ground for allowing recovery than the fact that you would otherwise be unjustifiably enriched.

Secondly, even where restitutionary liability does arise in connection with (say) a contract or a wrong, there remains the difficult question of why recovery

---

203 See below, Chapter 11.

204 As Birks puts it, '[the claimant] may show that for this kind of wrong the money award of damages to which he is entitled can be calculated in the restitutionary, instead of the compensatory, measure'. Birks, p 316.

205 As in *Strand Electric Co Ltd v Brisford Entertainments Ltd* [1952] 2 QB 246. See, generally, O'Sullivan, in Rose (ed), *Failure of Contracts*, Chapter 1.

206 See below, Chapter 6.

207 A good example is Hedley, 'Restitution: contract's twin?', in Rose (ed), *Failure of Contracts*, Chapter 18.

208 True, it has been argued here that recovery of a mistaken payment bears some resemblance to a claim for lost property: see Stoljar, *Law of Quasi-Contract* (2nd edn, 1989), Chapter 1, and cf Watts [1995] RLR 49. But while this might justify giving me a proprietary claim, it does not justify affording me a personal claim to recovery.

209 Eg, by seizure of my property: *Exall v Partridge* (1799) 8 TR 308.

is allowed. Why should the law of tort, which is normally concerned with making good losses, allow recovery of benefits gained instead? Why should a contracting party who has partly performed be entitled to anything? What justifies giving a remedy to a mistaken payer who has divested himself of ownership of the sum paid? It is suggested that if we can find a common explanation for recovery here we should; and further that, subject to certain variations, that explanation can only be a broad principle allowing recovery for unjust enrichment.

CHAPTER 2

REMEDIES

I INTRODUCTION

2-1   A book on contract or tort can be broken quite neatly into sections on liability and remedies. By contrast, the chapter on remedies in a book on restitution is a good deal less simple, for a number of reasons.

To begin with, the subject of restitution is itself fragmented. The old actions for *quantum meruit*, money had and received, money paid for a consideration that totally fails, and account of profits, for instance, all constitute pecuniary relief for unjust enrichment; but, at least as yet, they have not been regarded as anything other than separate remedies. And the same goes for proprietary relief. Rescission, constructive trusts and equitable liens all potentially provide restitutionary relief in some shape or other; but they do so in different ways and subject to different rules. Unification of the remedies available, and the application, where possible, of common rules applicable to all, would clearly add a great deal to the consistency of the law, and indeed ought to be one object of a consistent theory of restitution. But this stage is a long way off, and for the moment the different forms of action must continue to be treated separately.

2-2   Secondly, a large number of remedies sit awkwardly between unjust enrichment and other heads of liability. While effectively restitutionary, they nevertheless traditionally appear under different rubrics. Damages for breach of contract and tort, for instance, on occasion cover not loss caused, but gains illegitimately made, and hence spill over into restitution. Similarly, the constructive trust and equitable lien are traditionally discussed in books on equity: nevertheless, they are not infrequently used to reverse unjust enrichment.

Thirdly, the distinction between rights and remedies is more difficult to draw in unjust enrichment cases than, for instance, in contract, where there is a clear analytical bar between the (primary) right to have a contract performed and the (secondary or remedial) right to a payment of money or other order if it is not. As an example, take the trust imposed in *Chase Manhattan Bank NA v Israel-British Bank Ltd*[1] to allow the claimants to recoup $2m paid by mistake to the defendants. Burrows observes the difficulty in classifying this as a remedy at all.[2] On the reasoning in *Chase Manhattan*, the claimants' right in equity arose by operation of law, on the simple ground that they never intended to divest

---

1   [1981] Ch 105; see, too, *Re Irish Shipping Ltd* [1986] ILRM 518.
2   Burrows, pp 37–38.

themselves of beneficial title in what they paid. But this is the mark of a substantive right (in this case property), not a remedy, which we normally regard as being the result of judicial intervention, or of at least some election by the claimant to invoke it. Similar reasoning applies also to certain cases of subrogation. If someone borrows £1,000 from me in your name, but without your authority, and then uses it to discharge your debt to X, I stand in the shoes of X *ipso facto*, and not as a result of any election or judgment.[3] Nevertheless, there is no doubt that, as a matter of practice rather than strict law, the reason claimants get the benefit of the rules just described is that otherwise defendants would be unjustly enriched, and we take the view that it would be over-technical to exclude them from the subject of restitutionary remedies on doctrinal grounds.

2-3   Bearing these points in mind, however, remedies for unjust enrichment can be broadly split into two categories: pecuniary (the award of a sum of money) and proprietary (whereby the claimant obtains a proprietary interest of some sort in an asset in the defendant's hands). Of these, the first is invariably judicial. The second may or may not be, since the claimant in certain cases obtains rights to property in the defendant's hands either by his own act, or by operation of law, rather than by judicial decision. Nevertheless, even here, in practice the claimant is likely to need the aid of the law in recovering the property concerned. There is also a third form of remedy, subrogation, which lies awkwardly between pecuniary and proprietary remedies, but this requires separate (and fairly extensive) treatment.

II PECUNIARY RESTITUTION

2-4   The vast majority of restitutionary claims concern pecuniary liability. Indeed, in the case of services, and assets which are alleged to have unjustly enriched the defendant, but which he no longer has or are no longer in existence, it is the only possible remedy.

The main instances of common law pecuniary remedies are the following:

(a) The remedies of *quantum valebat* and *quantum meruit*. These deal in the restitutionary context with the case where I supply goods (*quantum valebat*) or services (*quantum meruit*) to you without a contract at all, or under a contract which is either ineffective *ab initio* or subsequently avoided.

(b) Money had and received. This is a protean remedy, applying where the claimant's money finds its way into the defendant's hands, where a third party has paid money to the defendant to be passed on to the claimant,

---

3   Eg, *Reversion Fund and Insurance Co Ltd v Maison Cosway Ltd* [1913] 1 KB 364; below, § 2-31.

where the defendant has usurped the claimant's office or received payment otherwise due to the claimant, where money is paid by mistake, compulsion or for a consideration that has totally failed, or where the claimant claims on the basis of what is known as waiver of tort.

(c) Damages in tort or for breach of contract. As we pointed out above, where such damages are awarded in order to reverse unjust enrichment rather than as simple reparation for loss, these are in effect pecuniary restitutionary remedies.

2-5 Equity is also a player in this market.[4] The action for profits made out of his position by a fiduciary, such as an agent or trustee, is one example: in addition to and independently of any constructive trust over the proceeds in the hands of the defendant, it creates a kind of 'equitable debt'.[5] Another is the right to underpaid beneficiaries or creditors of an estate to recover *in personam* against anyone overpaid out of the same estate under the rule in *Ministry of Health v Simpson*;[6] yet another is a trustee's right in certain cases to sue the beneficiaries personally for necessary services rendered to the trust estate.[7] Finally, there is no reason why at least some claims normally referred to as 'proprietary' should not give rise to this liability. If a trustee steals trust funds and buys shares which he gives to X, who acts in bad faith, X must give up the shares if he has them: but, if he has sold them, he will nevertheless have to account for their value.

III PROPRIETARY CLAIMS[8]

2-6 Claims of this sort invariably involve enrichment of one of two kinds: receipt of an asset by the defendant, or improvement of something already belonging to him. In so far as (a) the receipt or improvement represents an unjust enrichment at the claimant's expense, and (b) the property concerned remains in his hands, the claimant may have a claim to legal or equitable ownership of it, or of an interest in it. Straightforward examples are property received by a fiduciary or agent as a bribe, the proceeds of trust property wrongfully appropriated by a trustee, chattels transferred under a contract subsequently rescinded for fraud or mistake, and (in England, though not in Ireland) property transferred to a minor where the latter is not bound by the contract.[9] Whatever other restitution is

---

4   Cf the statement in *Murphy v AG* [1982] IR 241, p 316, that the constructive trust is a simple equitable equivalent of the action for money had and received.

5   *Lister v Stubbs* (1890) 45 Ch D 1; *Boston Deep Sea Fishing Co v Ansell* (1888) 39 Ch D 339; *Iran Shipping Co v Denby* [1987] 1 Lloyd's Rep 367.

6   [1951] AC 251. See, too, *Gray v Richards Butler and Co* (1996) *The Times*, 23 July.

7   Eg, *Hardoon v Belilios* [1901] AC 118.

8   Goode, in Cornish *et al* (eds), *Restitution – Past, Present and Future*, Chapter 5.

9   This is because of the effect of the Minors' Contracts Act 1987, s 3(1) (England). A similar rule applies in Northern Ireland: Minors' Contracts (NI) Order 1988, SI 1988/930.

available to the claimant, he can claim equitable ownership in the first two cases, and legal ownership in the third. Similarly, too, someone who has spent money on land so as to enhance its value with the express or tacit encouragement of the true owner may obtain restitution by receiving an interest in it.[10]

2-7 Proprietary restitutionary rights of the sort discussed here are different from pecuniary ones in a number of important respects. To begin with, they are *ex hypothesi* limited to assets remaining in the defendant's hands at the time he sues: in Birks's terms,[11] they lie for 'value surviving'. You cannot claim an interest in property where that property does not exist, or against a defendant who has not got it.

Secondly, since the law of insolvency excludes general creditors from all assets in so far as they belong at law or in equity to third parties, whatever the reason, proprietary restitutionary claims take precedence where the defendant is not solvent.[12] For obvious reasons, this is one of the most important consequences of establishing a proprietary claim: it is also the reason why considerable care needs to be taken when deciding whether to extend the list of those accorded proprietary status.

Thirdly, a claim to property in the defendant's hands may sometimes allow a claimant to circumvent a bar which would apply were he to bring a personal action. Suppose goods are delivered to a minor, who is not liable to pay for them by reason of his age. To allow a personal claim based on his unjust enrichment by having kept them is unacceptable, since it amounts to enforcing the contract by the back door.[13] But, in England, statute allows a claim against such property as remains in the minor's hands at the time the action is brought, on the basis that there is nothing wrong in forcing him to give back something he still has and is not prepared to pay for.[14] Again, perhaps less defensibly, the House of Lords in *Sinclair v Brougham*[15] allowed an *ultra vires* depositor with an insolvent bank to exercise a proprietary remedy against its assets to get round the lack – at least as the law then stood[16] – of any personal remedy.

2-8 Fourthly, in the case of claims to equitable or legal ownership (though not in the case of an equitable lien), the principle that an owner of something is entitled to it *in specie* means that the claimant gets the benefit of any rise in value. If my

---

10 See *Unity Joint Stock Banking Co v King* (1858) 25 Beav 72 and the cases following it; below, § 2-18.

11 Birks, p 77 *et seq.*

12 See, generally, Rose (ed), *Restitution and Insolvency*, Chapter 4.

13 Cf *Leslie (R) Ltd v Shiell* [1914] 3 KB 607 (similar reasoning applied to loan to minor).

14 Minors' Contracts Act 1987, s 3(1).

15 [1914] AC 398.

16 In *Westdeutsche Landesbank Girozentrale v Islington BC* [1996] AC 669, p 711, Lord Browne-Wilkinson (with whom Lord Slynn agreed) thought an action *in personam* would now lie in this situation; Lord Goff thought it probably would: *ibid*, p 686 *et seq*. Hence, *Sinclair v Brougham* is now of historical interest only.

agent accepts a bribe of shares worth £1,000 and they subsequently appreciate to £1,500, I am entitled to that gain.

Fifthly, the claimant's right, once established, survives against any third party transferee of the property concerned unless he can defeat that right, for instance, by pleading *bona fide* purchase.[17]

Sixthly, the proprietary claimant has the benefit of procedural rules aimed at preserving property over which there is a dispute.[18] It is true that since the rise of the Mareva injunction (in England, the freezing order),[19] this is less important than it was; nevertheless, it still has a good deal of significance.[20]

2-9 Seventhly, restitutionary proprietary remedies differ from pecuniary ones in that they may or may not be judicial. The trust arising where an agent takes a bribe, for instance,[21] or where an insurer recovers funds for the benefit of his insured,[22] is regarded as arising by operation of law: however important a judicial decision may be to establish the existence of the claimant's right, it is not essential to create it. Other such rights arise from a mere act of the parties, again without the need for judicial intervention. One instance arises where a trustee misdeals with trust property, as by selling it to a purchaser who does not take in good faith. The beneficiary can claim the proceeds in the trustee's hands as an alternative to following his property in specie: all he needs to do to constitute his claim is to elect accordingly. Another instance is rescission of a contract for fraud after it has been executed: a remedy that may be granted judicially, but is normally effected by mere notice to the other side.[23] The result of a successful rescission is that legal title to any chattels transferred revests *ipso facto* in the transferor,[24] subject to a duty in the latter to make counter-restitution by returning the price. In the case of other property not transferable by mere delivery, such as land or securities, and possibly in the case of all property where rescission is for mistake or misrepresentation not amounting to fraud, it seems that there is no automatic retransfer at law, but the transferee from the moment of rescission holds them on bare trust for the transferor.[25] Although

---

17 A matter which caused Lord Browne-Wilkinson to balk at imposing a proprietary remedy in respect of payments under an *ultra vires* contract: *Westdeutsche Landesbank Girozentrale v Islington BC* [1996] AC 669, p 703.

18 See (England) CPR Pt 25 r 1(1)(c)(i); (Ireland) RSC Ord 50 r 4.

19 See CPR Pt 25 r 1(1)(f).

20 Thus a freezing order or Mareva injunction will not protect a claimant against an insolvent defendant's creditors, but an injunction to protect property in dispute will: compare *The Angel Bell* [1980] 1 All ER 480 with *Bekhor (AJ) Ltd v Bilton Ltd* [1981] 2 All ER 564, p 577.

21 *AG for Hong Kong v Reid* [1994] 1 AC 324.

22 See *Lonrho Exports Ltd v Export Credit Guarantee Dept* [1999] Ch 158, p 180 *et seq*.

23 Or, occasionally, even less: *Car and Universal Finance Co Ltd v Caldwell* [1965] 1 QB 525.

24 *Car and Universal Finance Co Ltd v Caldwell* [1965] 1 QB 525.

25 See Meagher, Gummow and Lehane, *Equity – Doctrines and Remedies*, 3rd edn, § 2418; and cf *Re French's Wine Bar Ltd* [1987] BCLC 499 (effect of rescission where transaction open to attack under the (English) Insolvency Act 1986).

there is no clear authority, presumably the same is true where a gift of property is made by reason of fraud or mistake.

Nevertheless, there is no reason on principle why proprietary remedies should not be judicial in the same way as pecuniary ones. Rectification of a deed of gift is one example: it does not take effect unless and until ordered by a court. Again, it seems that some kinds of rescission, such as for undue influence, can only be effected by the court and not by the parties; unless and until the court acts, no property is revested in the claimant, and he has at best a mere equity.[26]

2-10　　One further point is worth making. There is no reason why, in a suitable case, a claimant should not have both a proprietary and a personal claim arising out of the same circumstances. Thus, if I pay you £1,000 by mistake, I can make a personal claim for £1,000 from you as money had and received to your use; further and alternatively, if you still have the £1,000 in your bank, I can claim a constructive trust over that part of your balance. If you do not still have the original money, but you do have gilt-edged stock that you bought using it, I can claim the stock (or at least a proportionate interest in it).

The boundary between personal and proprietary restitution[27]

2-11　　The receipt or improvement of property may give rise to a proprietary claim: it is vital to remember, however, that it will not necessarily do so. Suppose I agree to sell you goods by instalments, but the contract is frustrated after I have delivered some of them. There is no doubt that your receipt of those goods represents an unjust enrichment at my expense; nevertheless, even if you still have them, I have no right against them. Again, if I pay you money for goods that you do not deliver, I cease to have any claim against that money even if it remains in your hands.[28] My only claim in such cases is to pecuniary relief.[29]

26　Cf *Lonrho plc v Fayed (No 2)* [1992] 1 WLR 1, pp 11–12 (Millett J). See, too, *Latec Investments Ltd v Hotel Terrigal Pty Ltd* (1965) 113 CLR 265, p 277 (Kitto J), dealing with rescission of a transaction against a mortgagee who abused his powers.

27　See, generally, Rose (ed), *Restitution and Insolvency*, Chapter 5.

28　*Re Goldcorp Exchange Ltd* [1995] 1 AC 74. *Quaere*, however, where the defendant obtained the money by actual fraud. Millett J suggested in *El Ajou v Dollar Land Holdings plc* [1993] 3 All ER 717, p 734 that there would be a proprietary remedy by way of trust: see, too, *Neste OY v Lloyds Bank plc* [1983] 2 Lloyd's Rep 658. But this was doubted by Ferris J, at least in cases where no steps had been taken to avoid the transaction, in *Box v Barclays Bank plc* (1998) *The Times*, 30 April. It is suggested that the issue turns on the correctness of the holding in *Chase Manhattan Bank NA v Israel-British Bank Ltd* [1981] Ch 105 that payment of money by mistake (which, of course, includes fraud) automatically gives rise to a proprietary remedy in favour of the payer. See below, § 3-20.

29　Oddly enough, the position is different with would-be purchasers of land, who have a lien over the land for the return of the purchase moneys: see, eg, *Middleton v Magnay* (1864) 2 H and M 233; *Lee-Parker v Izzett* [1971] 1 WLR 1688; *Tempany v Hynes* [1976] IR 101. A principled justification for this preference is hard to fathom.

How, then, should we decide whether a proprietary claim is available? This is obviously a very important question in practice, particularly where property has increased in value or the defendant is insolvent.

2-12 A radical solution, sometimes called the 'swollen assets theory',[30] would be to say that in so far as the defendant is unjustly enriched at all, the claimant should have a proprietary charge over his assets unless he deliberately gave credit to him: the claimant has lost, the defendant – or through him his creditors – is richer than he should be, and that should be an end of the matter. Indeed, on an extreme version of this view, there should not even be a need to show that the defendant still has the asset gained or its proceeds, provided he is in a global sense enriched by its receipt. But, this theory presents considerable difficulties, if only because it effectively requires the complete rewriting of the insolvency laws in favour of the restitution claimant. There is little sign, at least at present, of its being accepted in Anglo-Irish law.[31]

2-13 Another possible answer is that the matter should effectively be left to the discretion of the court, taking into account factors such as whether the defendant is insolvent, or whether the defendant's conduct has been so egregious that he should be made to give up not only what he received, but any increase in value as well. But, this is likely to lead at the very least to considerable uncertainty and difficulty in settling litigation, and may in any case involve the introduction of the 'swollen assets' theory by the back door. Moreover, in the case of the insolvent defendant, the English Court of Appeal has implicitly rejected it. In *Re Polly Peck Ltd (No 2)*,[32] plaintiffs sought the imposition of a remedial constructive trust over the assets of an insolvent company, arguing that the company had previously enriched itself with assets misappropriated from them. They failed, the Court of Appeal pointing out that the insolvency legislation required unsecured creditors to share assets *pari passu*, and that to allow a remedy of this sort would effectively bypass that scheme and set at nought the statutory provisions concerned.

2-14 When, then, should a proprietary remedy be available? As long as we continue to apply the insolvency laws to restitution claimants as a whole, and to say that (except for restitution for wrongs) restitution from the defendant should be no greater than the loss suffered by the claimant, it is difficult to avoid the conclusion that only two factors justify allowing a claim against property held by the defendant. One is some strong public policy militating in favour of an exception to the general rule: the protection of vulnerable parties such as cohabitees, or the need to assure remuneration to successful maritime salvors,

---

30 Summarised in Smith, *The Law of Tracing*, p 310 *et seq*. See too Taft (1939) 39 Col LR 172.

31 In England, *dicta* of Lord Templeman in *Space Investments Ltd v CIBC* [1986] 3 All ER 75, pp 76–77, which arguably countenanced some such theory, were rejected by Lord Mustill in delivering the opinion of the Privy Council in *Re Goldcorp Exchange Ltd* [1995] 1 AC 74, p 108 *et seq*.

32 [1998] 3 All ER 812.

are possible instances. The other, much more important, is where the 'unjust factor' relied on involves some asset which the claimant has been deprived of, and the defendant is in possession of either its direct or indirect proceeds, or its fruits.[33] The reason is not hard to see; if claims to one's property in specie naturally give priority, it requires very little imagination to extend this rule to cases where one is claiming not that property itself, but its exchange product in the defendant's hands, or its fruits which one would have thought should belong to the claimant anyway.

Having said this, the solution in fact adopted by Anglo-Irish law to the problem of when to allow a proprietary claim is, admittedly, haphazard.[34] The categories of case where a proprietary remedy is available have grown *ad hoc*, with little thought given to what the justification for granting it may be. Indeed, it is difficult as the law stands to do more than list the categories concerned and discuss briefly how far, if at all, each instance can be justified.

When is a proprietary remedy available?

(a) Rescission

2-15 The first case where restitutionary relief is clearly proprietary in effect is where property revests as a result of rescission of a contract or gift;[35] indeed, this follows from the very nature of rescission, as an undoing of an executed transaction so as to return the parties to their original position.[36] As the law stands, this is clearly unexceptionable. Nevertheless, even here it is not immediately apparent why the transferor *should* get the benefit of secured status. In particular, it should be noted that the transferee has no reciprocal privilege: if I pay for goods under a contract voidable for mistake and avoid the contract before delivery, I am limited to a personal claim against the seller.[37]

---

33 See, in particular, Goode, in Cornish *et al* (eds), *Restitution, Past, Present and Future*, Chapter 5. For a slightly different view, see Rotherham, in Rose (ed), *Restitution and Insolvency*, Chapter 6.

34 But note *Re Goldcorp Exchange Ltd* [1995] 1 AC 74, p 109, where Lord Mustill said that the law on the creation and tracing of equitable proprietary remedies was 'still in a state of development'.

35 Eg, where a contract is rescinded for fraud: *Car and Universal Finance Co Ltd v Caldwell* [1965] 1 QB 525.

36 See Burrows, p 40.

37 Even, apparently, where the seller still has the money *in specie* or its direct proceeds. Cf *Re Goldcorp Exchange Ltd* [1995] 1 AC 74, where would-be buyers of gold under a contract allegedly voidable for fraud were held to have no possible claim against bullion bought with their money. The conclusion is attacked in Birks [1995] RLR 83, p 88.

(b) Claim in respect of claimant's property or its proceeds

2-16 The second situation, clearly justified on the above reasoning, is where an asset in the defendant's hands represents property of which the claimant has been deprived. Claims to property using the process of tracing are the prime example:[38] another arises where a bankrupt purports to alienate money or property with which he has no power to deal.[39] But, there may well be others, such as certain subrogation rights (of which more below).

(c) Mistake

2-17 Thirdly, there is the situation where money or assets are transferred by mistake. This is more troublesome. The leading authority is *Chase Manhattan Bank NA v Israel-British Bank Ltd*.[40] Goulding J held that where the plaintiff bank mistakenly paid the same debt of $2 m twice over, the payee held the second payment on constructive trust, so protecting the plaintiff from its subsequent insolvency. But, with respect, it is not easy to see why this should be. Goulding J's arguments that the defendant's receipt of the money made it a fiduciary, and that the claimant should be deemed never to have intended to part with equitable title to it, beg the question and rather assume the point in issue.[41] True, it can be argued that the claimant in such cases, not having intentionally extended credit to the defendant, should not suffer in his insolvency:[42] but, as observed above, the same could be said of many others, who do not have the benefit of proprietary remedies. No doubt for this reason, some scepticism has been expressed about *Chase Manhattan* in subsequent cases. Although it has been followed by the English Court of Appeal in a criminal case,[43] Lord Mustill, delivering the opinion of the Privy Council in *Re Goldcorp Exchange Ltd*,[44] pointedly declined to say whether he thought it had been correctly decided.[45] In *Westdeutsche Landesbank Girozentrale v Islington BC*,[46] Lord Goff followed suit.[47] Lord Browne-Wilkinson, in the same case, specifically rejected Goulding's reasoning, and thought *Chase Manhattan* could be supported, if at all, only on the basis that the defendant bank was guilty of unconscionable conduct in retaining the money

---

38 Below, Chapter 10.

39 *Jones (FC) and Co (Trustee) v Jones* [1997] Ch 159.

40 [1979] Ch 105. A similar conclusion has been reached in Ireland: *Re Irish Shipping Ltd* [1986] ILRM 518.

41 Cf Lord Mustill's comments in *Re Goldcorp Exchange Ltd* [1995] 1 AC 74, p 98. See too Rose (ed), *Restitution and Insolvency*, Chapter 9, p 178 *et seq*.

42 See Jones [1981] CLJ 275, p 276.

43 *R v Shadrokh-Cigari* [1988] Crim LR 465 (mistaken payee guilty of theft in giving the money away).

44 [1995] 1 AC 74.

45 *Ibid*, p 103.

46 [1996] AC 669.

47 *Ibid*, p 690.

with knowledge of the circumstances.[48] As a result, it is suggested that *Chase Manhattan* remains, and should remain, open to some question in the future.

(d) Land improvement cases

2-18   Fourthly, there is authority that where A contributes to the improvement of B's land under a mistake as to ownership,[49] or on the basis of some assumption (such as being able to live there rent-free for life)[50] which goes unfulfilled, A will have the benefit of a lien over that land for the value of the improvements. Why a proprietary, rather than a personal, remedy should be available here is not entirely clear. The former case may possibly be justified by analogy with payment by mistake: if cash transferred in error directly to the defendant is held on constructive trust, it seems odd not to treat similarly cash injected into property of his.[51] As for the latter, it is difficult to see any rational explanation, save possibly an inclination to protect relatives and cohabitees who are likely to be in a vulnerable position.

(e) Gains in breach of duty[52]

2-19   It now seems clear, at least in England, that any gain made in breach of duty by a person in a fiduciary position, such as a trustee or agent, will have a constructive trust imposed on it. In the case of a trustee making a profit from the use of trust assets, this is understandable: the claimant is claiming the fruits of his own property, and hence, the case is covered by the previous category. But, where there is no question of use of the claimant's property, as with a bribe, it had previously been held by the English Court of Appeal in *Lister and Co v Stubbs*[53] that no proprietary remedy ought to be given; hence the recipient was merely held personally liable to account for the amount of the bribe, and not for any profits made on its successful investment. However, in *AG for Hong Kong v Reid*,[54] the Privy Council declined to follow *Lister's* case and held that a constructive trust would be imposed in the case of any gain made in breach of fiduciary duty, whether or not derived from the claimant's property. Thus, a Hong Kong prosecutor who had accepted large scale bribes from alleged

---

48   *Ibid*, p 714. See, too, *Bank of America v Arnell* [1999] Lloyd's Rep Bank 399, Aikens J; Millett (1998) 114 LQR 399.

49   As in *Unity Joint Stock Banking Co v King* (1858) 25 Beav 72.

50   As in *Hussey v Palmer* [1972] 3 All ER 744. Cf *Re Sharpe (A Bankrupt)* [1980] 1 All ER 198 (though the latter is arguably not a restitution case) and *NAD v TD* [1985] ILRM 153.

51   But note that this may become awkward if *Chase Manhattan Bank NA v Israel-British Bank Ltd* [1981] Ch 105 is overruled. Another possible justification is by analogy to the trust that may arise where money filched from the claimant is used by the defendant to buy an asset for himself: cf *El Ajou v Dollar Land plc* [1993] 3 All ER 717, p 734 (Millett J).

52   Oakley [1994] CLJ 31.

53   (1890) 45 Ch D 1.

54   [1994] 1 AC 324.

wrongdoers held the proceeds, in the form of New Zealand real estate, on trust for the government which had employed him.

Again, with respect, this is a little difficult to justify on principle. The reason given, that the fiduciary is, admittedly, bound to account for improper profits and that equity regards as done that which ought to be done, is a little unconvincing. It assumes the very point at issue – namely, that the agent is under a duty to account for bribes *in specie*[55] – despite the existence of clear authority that fiduciary obligations to account, such as that of an agent to pay over sums received on his principal's behalf, do not normally engender any trust relationship at all.[56] Indeed, apart from a vague feeling that disloyal fiduciaries ought to receive very short shrift, it is hard to see any positive reason for giving anything more than a personal liability to account: particularly since here, we are concerned with restitution for wrongs, where recovery is likely to result in a pure windfall for the claimant.[57] For this reason, it is respectfully submitted that Irish courts should reject *Reid's* case and continue to apply *Lister v Stubbs*.

(f) Payments and transfers made ultra vires

2-20   There is little doubt that where a corporation or public authority makes an *ultra vires* payment, a right to restitution arises in its favour against the payee in the absence of some principle protecting the latter.[58] There is some authority that this will carry with it a proprietary remedy, notably in the judgment of Lord Goff in *Woolwich Building Society v Inland Revenue Comrs (No 2)*.[59] Presumably, this is on the basis that the payer is simply incapable of divesting itself of its own proprietary rights, in the same way that a bankrupt is unable without his trustee's concurrence to pass a good title to property otherwise vested in him.[60] Nevertheless, if this rule is correct, it sits somewhat curiously with the established principle that money paid to a body under a contract *ultra vires* the latter cannot be subject to a proprietary remedy.[61]

---

55   [1994] 1 AC 324, p 336.

56   See, eg, *Henry v Hammond* [1913] 2 KB 515, esp p 521.

57   A point nicely made in Rose (ed), *Restitution and Insolvency*, Chapter 1, p 13 *et seq*.

58   Which, in the case of companies, will normally be the case. In England, see Companies Act 1985, s 35, providing that in most situations third parties dealing with a company need not concern themselves with whether the transaction was within the company's powers. In Ireland, see Companies Act 1963, s 8, where there is a similar, though more cautious, attempt to draw the sting of the *ultra vires* doctrine.

59   [1993] AC 70, p 177: see, too, *Auckland Harbour Board v R* [1924] AC 318. In *Allied Carpets plc v Nethercott* (2000) unreported, 28 January, Colman J, an *ultra vires* dividend payment was held to be subject to a constructive trust in the recipient's hands: but here, the defendant was also a director who had himself acted in breach of fiduciary duty.

60   Cf *Jones (FC) and Co (Trustee) v Jones* [1997] Ch 159.

61   *Westdeutsche Landesbank Girozentrale v Islington BC* [1996] AC 669.

(g) Miscellaneous

2-21   Sixthly, there are miscellaneous cases such as that of the maritime salvor and the general average claimant, who it is well established have a lien over any property salved or protected as a result. It is difficult to fit these into the general scheme of restitution at all: the justification for affording a proprietary claim can be found, if at all, in considerations of policy peculiar to the areas of law concerned.

IV SUBROGATION[62]

Definition

2-22   Subrogation is a doctrine whereby in certain cases A obtains an entitlement by operation of law to enforce for his own benefit rights enjoyed by B against C. Its significance to restitution law is that in many cases, A's right arises by virtue of the fact that he has conferred a benefit on C in circumstances amounting to unjust enrichment on C's part. For instance, where A has lent money to C under an *ultra vires* contract which C has then used to pay off a genuine creditor B, A may be entitled to exercise B's *quondam* rights against C. To that extent, there is no doubt that it counts as a restitutionary remedy. Furthermore, since the rights enforceable by A may be either simple pecuniary obligations or secured rights, such as a mortgage or charge over C's property, subrogation is best classified as a separate remedy straddling pecuniary and proprietary relief.

2-23   It is sometimes suggested that subrogation in its true nature is a form of equitable assignment, or the transfer of a right by operation of law.[63] Again, A is often said compendiously said to 'stand in the shoes' of B.[64] But analogies of this sort are unhelpful and potentially deceptive. For one thing, it is not clear whether certain rules of assignment, such as that an assignee takes subject to equities,[65] apply to a subrogation claimant. For another, as often as not, A's ability to enforce C's obligations vis à vis B arise from the fact that he has *discharged* those very obligations, and it does not make much sense to talk of a transfer of a right that no longer exists.[66] Furthermore, although subrogation by

---

62 See, generally, the excellent Mitchell, *The Law of Subrogation*.

63 '[Subrogation] is a convenient way of describing a transfer of rights from one person to another, without assignment or assent of the person from whom the rights are transferred and which takes place by operation of law in a whole variety of widely different circumstances.' *Orakpo v Manson Investments Ltd* [1978] AC 95, p 104 (Lord Diplock).

64 See, eg, *Re Wrexham, Mold and Connah's Quay Rly Co* [1899] 1 Ch 440, p 459 (Vaughan Williams LJ); *Highland Finance Ltd v Sacred Heart College of Agriculture* [1992] 1 IR 472, p 476 (Murphy J).

65 Derham, *Set-Off*, 2nd edn, Chapter 13.

66 Birks, pp 93–97.

definition involves A exercising B's rights (or erstwhile rights) for his own benefit, it by no means follows that he takes over those rights complete or unmodified. On the contrary: A is normally entitled only to such rights as will effectively reverse the defendant's unjust enrichment and not provide him with a windfall in addition. Thus, a claimant discharging a secured obligation may be entitled to exercise only the underlying personal claim:[67] alternatively, he may be entitled to exercise those rights only as against a given person and not *erga omnes*.[68]

2-24 The best analysis of subrogation today is undoubtedly that of Mitchell,[69] which takes account of these and other points and runs as follows. Subrogation takes two rather different forms, 'simple' and 'reviving'.

The former does not involve the discharge of any obligation or liability: it simply permits A to exercise for his own benefit an existing cause of action available to B against C in certain cases where he has himself paid B. The cause of action remains B's, and proceedings will be in his name: but A has the right to direct them, and to take part or all of any recoveries that may result. A straightforward example is the right of an underwriter (A) in an indemnity insurance contract to take over for his own benefit any cause of action vested in the assured (B) against a third party (C).[70]

In reviving subrogation, by contrast, A actually discharges the liability of C so that it ceases to exist. Nevertheless, A may be allowed to resuscitate and exercise for his own benefit, in whole or in part, the rights once enjoyed by B against C.[71] The object is generally to prevent C's unjust enrichment (that is, to prevent him being undeservedly and gratuitously relieved from the liability concerned). For instance, a surety (A) who discharges the principal debt *ipso facto* discharges any security given in respect of that debt: but having done so, he is entitled to exercise as against the principal debtor (C) any rights, including security, that the creditor (B) once enjoyed.

It must be noted, however, that subrogation of this type is not limited to cases where the person unjustly enriched is C. As the vital decision in *Banque Financière de la Cité v Parc (Battersea) Ltd*[72] makes clear, it may equally be

---

67 *Re Wrexham, Mold and Connah's Quay Rly Co* [1899] 1 Ch 440.

68 *Banque Financière de la Cité v Parc (Battersea) Ltd* [1999] 1 AC 221 (subrogation of lender to secured creditor's rights, but only as against one named creditor: re other creditors, claimant unsecured).

69 See Mitchell, *The Law of Subrogation*, esp Chapter 1.

70 This is by far the most significant example, but not the only one. Another arises where a bill of exchange is paid by someone secondarily liable on the instrument: Bills of Exchange Act 1882, s 59(2) (in force in all jurisdictions), and see Mitchell, *The Law of Subrogation*, p 86 *et seq* and *Duncan Fox and Co v North and South Wales Bank* (1880) 6 App Cas 1.

71 As Lord Hoffmann put it: '[The plaintiff's] legal relations with a defendant who would otherwise be unjustly enriched are regulated *as if* the benefit of the charge had been assigned to him.' (*Banque Financière de la Cité v Parc (Battersea) Ltd* [1999] 1 AC 221, p 236) (italics in the original).

72 [1999] 1 AC 221.

available where the effect of A's payment is to benefit not C, but some other party, D.

2-25 Like any other restitutionary right, the right (or remedy) of subrogation can be excluded by express or implied agreement between the parties (that is, A and B).[73] It has been suggested that the court has in addition a more general discretion to disallow it in any case where it feels it is not just and equitable,[74] but with respect, this seems contrary to principle. If it is a remedy available to reverse unjust enrichment, it ought to be available as of right if the conditions for its grant are made out.

When will the right to subrogation arise?

2-26 Subrogation is not invariably a restitutionary remedy: it may equally arise by contract.[75] Nevertheless, in the restitution context it is now clear it will generally be available where: (a) A discharges C's obligation to B;[76] (b) as a result of this discharge, C or a third party, D, is benefited; and (c) some unjust factor is present making that benefit *prima facie* subject to restitution.[77] Apart from occasional statutory provisions specifically granting it,[78] five paradigm cases need discussion: claims based on: (a) dispositions of the claimant's property; (b) invalid loans; (c) unauthorised debits; (d) payments under compulsion; and (e) more general applications in the unjust enrichment context.

It should be noted that a number of other miscellaneous cases traditionally grouped under this head of restitution – including, most importantly, insurers, and also others, such as creditors of a business operated by insolvent trustees – will be dealt with later.

---

73 Eg, it was held to have been excluded (in the insurance context) in *Morris v Ford Motor Co Ltd* [1973] 2 All ER 1084.

74 *Morris v Ford Motor Co Ltd* [1973] 2 All ER 1084, p 1090 (Lord Denning MR).

75 See *Orakpo v Manson Investments Ltd* [1978] AC 95, p 119 (Lord Keith); *Banque Financière de la Cité v Parc (Battersea) Ltd* [1999] 1 AC 221, pp 213–32 (Lord Hoffmann). Examples of contractual subrogation include, it is suggested, the right of an insurer to take over third party claims (below, § 2-41 *et seq*) and also the *prima facie* right (if it exists) of one lending money for the express purpose of discharging a secured obligation to exercise for his own benefit the security concerned (below, § 2-32 *et seq*).

76 'Discharge' seems to involve actual payment, so that a mere guarantee to a third party creditor will not do. See *Bankers Trust v Namdar* (1997) unreported, 14 February, CA. Cf *Ex p Turquand* (1876) 3 Ch D 445; *Re 19th Ltd* [1989] ILRM 652 (no subrogation of surety till actual payment).

77 *Banque Financière de la Cité v Parc (Battersea) Ltd* [1999] 1 AC 221, p 234.

78 Eg, the right of one lending money to a company in order to pay wages to be subrogated to the workers' preferential treatment in insolvency: Insolvency Act 1986, Sched 6, § 11 (England), Companies Act 1963, s 285(6) (Ireland). Another example in Ireland is the right of the Law Society when making good a solicitor's defalcations to take over all the rights of the person defrauded: Solicitors (Amendment) Act 1960, s 21(8) and *Re Reilly (orse O'Reilly)* (1989) unreported, 11 January, HC (Ireland).

(a) Property claims and analogous cases

2-27   First, property claims. Here, subrogation in effect allows a form of 'negative tracing': tracing, that is, into a negative asset. For example, suppose a company director steals £10,000 from the company and gives it to his girlfriend. If she buys a picture with the £10,000, the company can claim the picture. But what if, knowing the money's provenance,[79] she uses it to pay off her mortgage? In this case, where there is otherwise nothing to show for the money but the disappearance of a debt, the company can revive the mortgage for its own benefit. It has effectively paid off the girlfriend's debt: and the fact that its money was used without its consent provides the necessary 'unjust factor'. A neat example is *Boscawen v Bajwa*.[80] A prospective house buyer put his solicitor in funds to complete a purchase. The solicitor, assuming the transaction would go ahead in due course, used those funds prematurely to pay off an existing mortgage of the vendor. In the event, the transaction was aborted: nevertheless, the would-be purchaser was held entitled to the mortgagee's security in priority to a judgment debtor of the vendor who had meanwhile obtained a charging order against the premises.

Similarly, too, with claims analogous to property. In *Re Diplock*,[81] executors wrongly paid moneys to various charities on the basis of an invalid will. The real beneficiaries claimed to be subrogated to mortgages paid off by certain recipients with the moneys received. Their claim failed, but only because the recipients' innocence was held to make such negative tracing inequitable:[82] had this not been so, it seems to have been assumed that subrogation would lie.

(b) Defective loan cases

2-28   The defective loan cases split into a number of groups.

First, a series of authorities holds that where a corporation borrows *ultra vires*, but spends the money on discharging valid obligations, the lender (who, of course, cannot enforce the loan itself) can nevertheless enforce the rights of the creditors thus paid off.[83] It does not seem to matter whether the borrower was bound by contract to use the sum advanced to pay off the other obligation concerned:[84] what matters, it is said, is simply the actual use to which the money

---

79 This is to avoid any possible plea of change of position on the basis of *Re Diplock* [1948] Ch 465 and *Lipkin Gorman v Karpnale Ltd* [1991] 2 AC 548: on which, see below, Chapter 13.

80 [1995] 4 All ER 769.

81 [1948] Ch 465.

82 See [1948] Ch 465, pp 521, 549.

83 The cases are legion. See, eg, *Re Cork and Youghal Rly Co* (1869) LR 4 Ch App 748; *Wenlock (Baroness) v River Dee Co* (1887) 19 QBD 155: cf *Re Wrexham, Mold and Connah's Quay Rly Co* [1899] 1 Ch 440. The problem is unlikely to arise much today: see Companies Act 1963, s 8(1) (Ireland) and Companies Act 1985, s 35 as amended (England).

84 Cf *Wenlock (Baroness) v River Dee Co* (1887) 19 QBD 155, where the money advanced was used to pay off liabilities incurred after the loan was made: yet subrogation was allowed.

was put.[85] To that extent, the law seems happy to give a windfall to the lucky would-be creditor.

Secondly, the same kind of reasoning has been applied where a minor borrows money which he does not have to repay, but then uses to discharge an obligation or security which is enforceable against him. Thus, in *Thurstan v Nottingham Permanent Building Society*,[86] where a minor took out a mortgage to buy a house, neither loan nor security was enforceable against her: nevertheless, the lender was held able to enforce the unpaid vendors' lien, which had been valid, and which its loan had gone to discharge. Again, a line of authority allows recovery of loans to minors in so far as the moneys are used to pay for necessaries supplied[87] (though such cases are of little importance in England since the enactment there of the Minors' Contracts Act 1987).

Thirdly, much the same result has followed where a loan is unenforceable against the borrower not for incapacity, but for lack of authorisation. If X's agent purports to borrow money on his behalf but without his authority, the loan may nevertheless be enforceable against X in so far as it is in fact used to pay off X's existing liabilities.[88] Although there is no authority, there seems no reason on principle why subrogation should not also be allowed where the loan is unenforceable for some other reason, such as undue influence.[89]

2-29 Apart from the cases where the claimant's loan is entirely unenforceable against the borrower, an analogous principle has been held to obtain where there is no question as to the validity of the loan itself, but for some reason, the security taken for it is ineffective. If the moneys advanced are used to pay off some existing (and valid) security, the lender may be permitted instead to exercise the rights of that secured creditor. Thus, in *Butler v Rice*,[90] a borrower obtained a loan of £450 in order to redeem a previous mortgage over a house and used it for that purpose. The loan was supposedly secured on the house, but it then transpired that the borrower had no title to it. The lender, who would otherwise have been left with a worthless unsecured claim, was held entitled to exercise the rights of the previous mortgagee.

---

85 *Blackburn Benefit Building Society v Cunliffe Brooks and Co* (1882) 22 Ch D 61, p 71 (Lord Selborne).

86 [1902] 1 Ch 1; [1903] AC 6.

87 Eg, *Marlow v Pitfeild* (1719) 1 P Wms 558: see, too, *Re National Permanent Benefit Building Society* (1869) LR 5 Ch App 309, p 313.

88 As in *Bannatyne v MacIver* [1906] 1 KB 103 and *Reversion Fund and Insurance Ltd v Maison Cosway Ltd* [1913] 1 KB 364. Similarly, too, with forgery: see *Halifax Building Society v Muirhead* (1998) 76 P&CR 418 (wife's signature forged on refinancing agreement re matrimonial home: although charge unenforceable against wife's interest, lender subrogated to previous lender's valid rights against her).

89 Eg, where a lender refinances a mortgage over a matrimonial home, but the wife's consent is obtained by undue influence which is held to affect the lender. Cf *National Westminster Bank Ltd v Morgan* [1985] AC 686.

90 [1910] 2 KB 277. See, too, *Chetwynd v Allen* [1899] 1 Ch 353; *Ghana Commercial Bank Ltd v Chandiram* [1960] AC 732.

2-30   Describing the defective loan cases is easy. Fitting them into the restitutionary scheme of things is less so. As regards the *ultra vires* loan cases, they have been justified on the basis that since granting restitution merely substitutes one creditor (the lender) for another (the original creditors paid off), the defendant does not, in the event, lose out:[91] but, this merely says that granting restitution is unlikely to be unjust, rather than giving a good reason for giving it in the first place. Similarly, the proposition permeating many of the 'invalid security' cases, that the lender presumptively intends to keep alive securities discharged with his funds,[92] is a blatant and disingenuous fiction.[93] The best explanation, it is suggested, is that in nearly all of them the lender has acted under a mistake (he believed, wrongly, that the loan and/or the security were enforceable against the borrower) or, possibly as a necessitous intervener (where money is lent to a minor for the purchase of necessaries): and that this provides the necessary 'unjust factor'.[94]

2-31   If this is right, it must follow that where the loan is invalid, but there is no unjust factor such as mistake, restitution ought to be denied. In *Burston Finance Ltd v Speirway Ltd,*[95] moneys were lent to buy land, security being taken over the land. As the lender knew, the security had to be registered in order to be effective, but in the event it was not. Walton J refused to succour the lender by subrogating him to the unpaid vendor's lien. The reason given was unsatisfactory and fictional – namely, that the lender must be regarded as having given up any intent to preserve the unpaid vendor's lien – but the result can be equally justified on the basis that the lender there made no mistake in any event. Although there are other cases where restitution has been made available despite the absence of any unjust factor, it is submitted that they should be open to reconsideration.[96]

    A fortiori, it must also follow that where all that is shown is that A lent money unsecured to C, which, in fact, was used to discharge C's secured obligation to B, A cannot be entitled to restitutionary relief by way of subrogation to B's rights. Thus, where members of the Junior Carlton Club lent it

---

91   As Lord Selborne put it in *Blackburn Benefit Building Society v Cunliffe Brooks and Co* (1882) 22 Ch D 61, p 71, 'has the transaction really added to the liabilities of the company?'.

92   Mitchell, *The Law of Subrogation,* p 12 *et seq,* p 124 *et seq.*

93   'Such an analysis has inevitably to be propped up by presumptions which verge upon outright fictions' – *Banque Financière de la Cité v Parc (Battersea) Ltd* [1999] 1 AC 221, p 234 (Lord Hoffmann); and see p 241 (Lord Hutton). See too, Mitchell, *The Law of Subrogation,* p 12 *et seq.*

94   See *Banque Financière de la Cité v Parc (Battersea) Ltd* [1999] 1 AC 221, p 234 (Lord Hoffmann), insisting that these cases ought to be regarded as restitutionary in nature.

95   [1974] 3 All ER 735.

96   In particular, *Reversion Fund and Insurance Ltd v Maison Cosway Ltd* [1913] 1 KB 364 would seem to have been wrongly decided in so far as it allowed recovery even where the claimant knew of the lack of authority. In such a situation it is submitted that there is no unjust factor, and should be no restitution. See Mitchell, *The Law of Subrogation,* pp 134–35.

money to discharge a mortgage over its premises, they were rightly denied any interest in the premises thus released.[97]

2-32 Nevertheless, there is authority in both England[98] and Ireland[99] suggesting a possible extension of the lender's subrogation right to cover cases where neither the loan nor the security is defective, but where money has been advanced specifically to pay off a given secured obligation, so that the borrower has no discretion as to its use. Thus, Murphy J has said:[100]

> *prima facie*, a lender who advances money for the express purpose of those moneys being applied in payment of the purchase price of property is entitled to the lien to which the vendor would have been entitled if the purchase price of the balance thereof had not been paid unless there is a bargain between the lender and the borrower which is inconsistent with an intention of the parties that the lender should acquire that right.

But, even if this authority is correct, which is open to some doubt,[101] it is not really something that need concern the restitution lawyer. The essence of the grant of subrogation here seems to be giving the lender what he (presumably impliedly) bargained for, rather than preventing anyone's unjust enrichment: particularly since it is difficult to see any unjust factor which would justify awarding restitution in the first place.

2-33 The grant of subrogation in the 'invalid loan' cases is subject to a number of restrictions. In particular, subrogation will not be available if it would allow *de facto* enforcement of contracts which are unenforceable by statute.[102] Moreover, even where granted, it will only apply to the extent necessary to prevent unjust enrichment: the claimant cannot use it to gain an uncovenanted windfall. Thus, an unsecured lender whose moneys are used to pay off a secured obligation will normally succeed only to a personal claim against the debtor.[103]

(c) Unauthorised debits

2-34 A venerable line of authority, closely related to the 'invalid loan' cases, indicates that where a bank debits its customer's account without authority (for example, on an improperly signed cheque), but in so doing directly or indirectly causes a

---

97 *Wylie v Carlyon* [1922] 1 Ch 51. Cf *Paul v Speirway Ltd* [1976] Ch 220.

98 *Patten v Bond* (1889) 60 LT 583, pp 584–85 (Kay J); *Orakpo v Manson Investments Ltd* [1978] AC 95, p 104 (Lord Diplock); *Paul v Speirway Ltd* [1976] Ch 220, p 232; *Boodle Hatfield v British Films Ltd* [1986] BCC 99. Criticised in Mitchell, *The Law of Subrogation*, p 12 *et seq*.

99 *Highland Finance (Ireland) Ltd v Sacred Heart College of Agriculture* [1998] 2 IR 180. See, too, *Bank of Ireland Finance Ltd v Daly* [1978] IR 79.

100 In the *Highland Finance* case at first instance: [1992] 1 IR 472, p 478.

101 It is convincingly criticised by Mitchell, *The Law of Subrogation*, p 145 *et seq*.

102 *Orakpo v Manson Investments Ltd* [1978] AC 95 (loan irrecoverable under English moneylenders' legislation).

103 *Re Wrexham, Mold and Connah's Quay Rly Co* [1899] 1 Ch 440.

creditor with a valid claim against the customer to be paid off, the bank is entitled to be subrogated to the rights of the creditor paid off. Thus, in *Liggett v Barclays Bank Ltd*,[104] Wright J held that the bank, while liable to the customer for wrongfully debiting its account, could offset any debt so discharged against this liability. In modern restitutionary terms, the unjust factor at work here is mistake: the bank, by paying its customer's creditor in the belief that it was authorised to do so, has unjustly enriched the customer and is entitled to credit for having done so.

One awkwardness needs noting, however. The bank's right to credit depends on the assumption that the bank's payment did indeed discharge the customer's debt, since otherwise there will be no benefit to the customer. Normally, a payment without a debtor's authority will not have this effect,[105] a point regarded as vital in *Crantrave Ltd v Lloyds Bank plc*,[106] where subrogation was held unavailable to a bank which paid a judgment creditor on the basis of an invalid garnishee order. The debt had not, in fact, been discharged,[107] a matter fatal to the bank's claim.

(d) Sureties

2-35   A surety who pays the principal debt has a clear personal right to recoupment against the principal.[108] In addition he is entitled by statute[109] on payment of the debt[110] to exercise for his own benefit all rights vested in the creditor, together (significantly) with any security available.[111] Perhaps oddly, it has been held that the surety remains entitled to these securities even if he did not know of them, and hence regarded himself as having no more than a mere personal claim against the principal debtor: to this extent, he may obtain a substantial windfall. Indeed, in Ireland this principle has been taken even further. In *Re Chipboard Products Ltd*,[112] the Government guaranteed a company's debt, which was secured by a general charge over its entire assets. On payment of the debt, it

---

104 [1928] 1 KB 48.

105 See below, § 8-5 *et seq*, and Burrows, pp 90–91. Cf *Barclays Bank Ltd v WJ Simms Ltd* [1979] 3 All ER 522, where in a slightly different context it was held that a bank paying a countermanded cheque in respect of a customer's debt had not in fact discharged the debt.

106 [2000] 4 All ER 273.

107 But cf Goode (1981) 97 LQR 254, p 258, suggesting that the bank might have had ostensible authority to pay the cheque.

108 Below, § 8-11.

109 Mercantile Law Amendment Act 1856, s 5 (in force in both jurisdictions). The right to subrogation at common law was far more limited: reviving subrogation did not apply, with the result that in so far as any security was extinguished by discharge of the principal debt, there was nothing for the surety to take over. See *Copis v Middleton* (1823) Turn & R 224, p 229; Mitchell, *The Law of Subrogation*, p 57 et seq.

110 But not before: eg, *Ex p Turquand* (1876) 3 Ch D 445; *Re 19th Ltd* [1989] ILRM 652.

111 *Craythorne v Swinburne* (1807) 14 Ves 160; *Re Chipboard Products Ltd* [1994] 3 IR 164.

112 (1994) unreported, 20 October, HC (Ireland), Barr J.

was held entitled to subrogation to that general security despite the fact that it had stipulated for a much more limited charge from the company itself to cover the latter's liability for recoupment.

The surety's right to restitution has been extended to those in an analogous position to sureties, such as secondary parties to bills of exchange who paid them,[113] thus releasing the person primarily liable.[114]

(e) More general applications

2-36   The above situations are well established: but, consistently with the recognition of subrogation as a general 'equitable remedy to reverse or prevent unjust enrichment',[115] they cannot be exhaustive. On principle, it would seem that whenever the discharge of an obligation gives rise to potential unjust enrichment, subrogation is on principle available. The nature of the unjust factor should be immaterial. The seminal decision in *Banque Financière de la Cité v Parc (Battersea) Ltd*[116] neatly illustrates the point. Lenders provided funds unsecured to a company, P, in order to allow P to pay off part of its secured debt to R. They thought that a junior secured creditor, O, had agreed to subordinate its claim to their own. In fact, O had not so agreed;[117] it followed that, as a result of the payment to R, O's debt was not postponed, but actually promoted. The House of Lords held that O would thereby be unjustly enriched, and that this enrichment arose as a result of the lenders' mistake. To correct the imbalance, the lenders were held entitled to exercise R's rights as against O, though not as against any other creditors of P.

Other 'unjust factors' may also give rise to subrogation in a similar way. *Re Downer Enterprises Ltd*,[118] for example, concerned not mistake, but compulsion. A lease was assigned to D Ltd, which later collapsed with rent unpaid: a prior assignor was forced to pay the landlord. In fact, the right to the rent had, by the law of insolvency, the status of a preferential debt in D's insolvency: having paid it, the prior assignor was held entitled to obtain by subrogation the benefit of that preferential status. Similarly, it is well established that a joint owner of property who is compelled to pay off an obligation secured on it may be subrogated, as regards the other joint owner, to the incumbrancer's rights.[119] No

---

113 *Duncan, Fox and Co v North and South Wales Bank* (1880) 6 App Cas 1.

114 Ie, the acceptor, or if none, the drawer.

115 [1999] 1 AC 221, pp 231–32 (Lord Hoffmann).

116 [1999] 1 AC 221.

117 An agent of O had purported to agree on their behalf, but was held to have acted without authority.

118 [1974] 2 All ER 1074.

119 See, eg, *Ker v Ker* (1869) 4 Ir R Eq 15; and below, § 8-14 *et seq*.

doubt there is room for analogous treatment of other cases of compulsion,[120] or, for that matter, other unjust factors.[121]

Is the concept of subrogation worth keeping as a restitutionary remedy?

2-37   At this point, however, an understandable puzzle arises. As Birks has pointed out,[122] when subrogation is used as a remedy for unjust enrichment, the claimant *ex hypothesi* has a right to restitution anyway. The unjust factor is deprivation of property, mistake, compulsion or whatever: the corresponding enrichment consists in discharge of an obligation. But, if this is so, why continue to treat subrogation as though it were a separate doctrine, and why continue the fiction that the claimant is taking over someone else's rights when, in reality, he is being given an independent restitutionary remedy?

The answer, it is submitted, is as follows, though it is not entirely satisfactory. Subrogation may well provide an answer to what might otherwise develop into an awkward remedial puzzle. Take the case where the claimant wants to get the benefit of a secured obligation which his property has been instrumental in discharging, as in the case already mentioned of *Boscawen v Bajwa*,[123] or alternatively complex relief such as that made available in *Banque Financière de la Cité v Parc (Battersea) Ltd*[124] (that is, an order allowing the claimant to prevail over some, but not all, creditors). A simple action for pecuniary restitution can clearly not do duty here: nor, without a good deal of adjustment, can the traditional proprietary remedies such as an interest in, or lien over, a given asset. Subrogation provides at least an understandable framework for a remedial scheme in cases of this sort.

2-38   This said, however, it must be added that Birks is right on a deeper level. If the law were entirely rational, and had a more adaptable system of remedies for unjust enrichment, there would be no need for subrogation as a separate doctrine. A restitutionary hermaphrodite of this type, awkwardly straddling personal liability and proprietary remedies, would simply be redundant and

---

120 Eg, where an insurer discharges a tortfeasor's liability and thereby also discharges one who would have been liable to indemnify the tortfeasor had he himself paid the victim. In the Scottish case of *Elf Enterprises (Caledonia) Ltd v London Bridge Engineering Ltd* (1997) *The Times*, 28 November, it seems to have been accepted that a reviving subrogation claim might have been apposite.

121 A possible case of subrogation for failure of assumptions might arise thus. A lends C money to discharge a mortgage over Blackacre in favour of B, C agreeing in return to grant A a mortgage over Whiteacre. If the mortgage from C is not forthcoming, eg, because C later sells the land to an innocent purchaser, there seems no reason why A should not be subrogated to the rights of the original mortgagee B.

122 Birks, p 93 *et seq*.

123 [1995] 4 All ER 769.

124 [1999] 1 AC 221.

confusing. Take the invalid cases. In this context, the only issues ought logically to be (a) whether the defendant has been unjustly enriched, and (b) if he has, whether an unjust enrichment claim should be allowed despite the policy behind defences such as *ultra vires* or lack of authority. If the answer to both these questions is 'Yes', the claimant should be entitled to restitution: the fact that the defendant's enrichment takes the form of an obligation discharged rather than some other kind of enrichment should not affect the matter.

2-39   Moreover, keeping subrogation as a separate doctrine has, at times, had the effect of skewing the substantive law. This is notably so in the rule already mentioned that a surety can take over any security given by the principal debtor, and indeed can do so whether or not he knew it existed in the first place, and even if he plainly intended to take no security or a lesser one.[125] It is difficult to see why he should have what is, in effect, a proprietary claim: were he forced to exercise non-subrogation rights he would probably not get one. Unfortunately, it has always been assumed in this context that if he takes over the creditor's rights, he takes them over in their entirety. This is odd, since in the invalid loan situation the courts have so far qualified subrogation so as to hold that the lender cannot invoke it to put himself into a better situation than he would have been in had his loan been enforceable in the ordinary way. Hence, if he intended to make an unsecured loan, but the moneys were used to discharge a secured obligation, the lender cannot take over the security:[126] he merely takes over a personal claim against the borrower.

Nevertheless, it must be admitted that sureties are not the only claimants who seem to be unusually well treated by the law of subrogation. There are undoubtedly other claimants who get a similarly uncovenanted proprietary benefit granted. A financier advancing money to pay the crew of a ship is apparently entitled to be subrogated to the latter's maritime lien without regard to whether he intended to lend secured;[127] and by statute, a person advancing money, even unsecured, to a company to pay wages is subrogated to the rights of the workers so paid ahead of other creditors in the event of the company going into liquidation.[128]

Other cases of 'subrogation'

2-40   It is now time to turn to a number of other cases which are normally referred to as cases of subrogation, which we deliberately left on one side at an earlier stage.

---

125 Above, § 2-35.

126 *Re Wrexham, Mold and Connah's Quay Rly Co* [1899] 1 Ch 440.

127 Eg, *The Tagus* [1903] P 44.

128 Insolvency Act 1986, Sched 6, s 11 (England); Companies Act 1963, s 285(6) (Ireland).

(a) Insurance

2-41   It is a fundamental assumption behind an indemnity insurance contract that the assured ought not to recover more than he has lost. For that reason, an underwriter who pays a claim in full has two rights. The first is to exercise for his own benefit any right of action available to the assured against a third party in respect of the loss covered.[129] Secondly, if, having been paid by the underwriter, the assured recovers compensation, he must account to the former[130] up to the amount of the payment.[131]

2-42   Now, the first of these rights is clearly a form of simple subrogation (the defendant's liability not being discharged by the underwriter's payment, and the right being invariably exercised in the assured's name).[132] A more difficult question, however, is whether it has anything to do with unjust enrichment, and hence any place in a book on restitution. It is often treated as self-evident that it must have: on this view, the assured's right of action is transferred because, if he were allowed to keep both it and his payment, he would be unjustly enriched vis à vis the underwriter.[133]

2-43   There is, however, a minority view that the underwriter's remedy is not restitutionary at all, but essentially contractual;[134] and, with respect, it is suggested that this is the more realistic approach. The basis of subrogation is the structure of the insurance contract; more particularly, it derives from the universal understanding that an entitlement to indemnity for a loss is an entitlement to this and no more. Hence, for instance, the rule that if the insurance contract concerned is not construed as containing this limitation – as happens in the case of life and insurance and other policies paying out a fixed sum irrespective of loss – then, even though exactly the same issues may be raised, subrogation is unavailable.

---

129 Including not only tortious, but also contractual and other rights: eg, *Andrews v Patriotic Insurance Co of Ireland* (1886) LR Ir 335; *Castellain v Preston* (1883) 11 QBD 380. But note that the underwriter takes the rights warts and all, so that (eg) the defendant is not deprived of a set off: *Re Casey (A Bankrupt)* (1993) unreported, 1 March, HC (Ireland), 1993.

130 Eg, *Castellain v Preston* (1883) 11 QBD 380; *Napier and Ettrick (Lord) v Hunter* [1993] AC 713. Similarly, where the assured himself owes money to the defendant, but has a set off against him, he must make this set off available to the underwriter: *National Oilwell v Davy Offshore Ltd* [1993] 2 Lloyd's Rep 582, p 624.

131 But no further: *Yorkshire Insurance Co v Nisbet Shipping Ltd* [1962] 2 QB 330.

132 Mitchell, *The Law of Subrogation*, p 36 et seq.

133 See, eg, Mitchell, *The Law of Subrogation*, p 9 et seq; Derham, *Subrogation in Insurance Law*, p 8 et seq. To the same effect, Brett J in *Castellain v Preston* (1883) 11 QBD 380 insists that the underwriter's right is based in the general law, and denies that its origin is merely contractual.

134 See *Yorkshire Insurance Co v Nisbet Shipping Ltd* [1962] 2 QB 330, pp 339–40; *Hobbs v Marlowe* [1978] AC 16, p 39; also dicta of Lord Goff in *Napier and Ettrick (Lord) v Hunter* [1993] AC 713, p 743 and Lord Hoffmann in *Banque Financière de la Cité v Parc (Battersea) Ltd* [1999] 1 AC 221, p 231.

Not only is insurers' subrogation at bottom dependent on the terms – express or implied – of the relevant contract, its connection with unjust enrichment can be, to say the least, tenuous: indeed, there are cases where it applies notwithstanding the lack of any plausible unjust enrichment. Take the underwriter who pays out on a valued policy: he is entitled to subrogation to the assured's claims even where the agreed value is less than the assured's actual loss, and hence recovery by the latter cannot be said to enrich him at all.[135]

Furthermore, apart from contract, it is in any case unclear why an assured would be unjustly enriched by retaining both his indemnity and his right of action. If I choose to insure my property, any recovery from my underwriters has been paid for by me; absent an express or implied contract to the contrary, why should I not be allowed to keep it in addition to any other recovery I am lucky enough to get from third parties?[136]

2-44 As for the insurer's second right, to collect from the assured any recoveries the latter may actually have made, although this is universally called 'subrogation', it clearly cannot be based on subrogation in the normal sense. The underwriter exercises no rights against any third party, but merely has a right to force the assured to account for moneys recovered from a third party. It is probably right to regard it as based on unjust enrichment, but on a different basis: namely, that the right to recover from the third party was, as from the time the underwriter paid out, vested in the latter. The assured, having received a payment in respect of a debt he is no longer entitled to, should have to account to the person who is entitled to it. This solution also has the great advantage of justifying the suggestion in *Lord Napier and Ettrick (Lord) v Hunter*[137] and *Lonrho Exports Ltd v Export Credits Guarantee Dept*[138] that this right can, where necessary, be enforced by a proprietary remedy in the shape of an equitable lien.

In short, it is respectfully submitted that the rules as to insurers' subrogation have no place in a coverage of subrogation as a restitutionary remedy. The underwriter's right to take over the assured's rights of action is subrogatory, but has nothing to do with unjust enrichment: conversely, his rights in respect of moneys received by the assured may be restitutionary, but are nothing to do with subrogation.

(b) Two oddities: businesses operated by insolvent trustees, and the Third Parties (Rights against Insurers) Act 1930

2-45 In two cases, subrogation is used to relieve parties against the insolvency of an intermediary. Creditors of a business run by trustees are, in the event of the

---

135 Eg, *Goole and Hull Steam Towing Ltd v Ocean Marine* [1928] 1 KB 589.

136 Cf the treatment of collateral benefits, such as pensions, in personal injury cases: *Parry v Cleaver* [1970] AC 1. See too, *England v Guardian Insurance Ltd* [1999] 2 All ER (Comm) 481 (underwriter collects assured's recovery in preference to Legal Aid Board charge).

137 [1993] AC 713.

138 [1996] 4 All ER 673, p 690.

trustees' insolvency, entitled to take over the right of the trustees to an indemnity in respect of trust obligations.[139] And, by a statutory scheme along the same lines, in England, s 1 of the Third Parties (Rights against Insurers) Act 1930 provides that, where a person covered by liability insurance is insolvent, a claimant is entitled to take over his right to indemnity and enforce it for his own benefit.

It has been said that both these rights are based on unjust enrichment, though there is some difficulty as to whose enrichment is involved. In the former case, it is said to be that of the *cestui que trust* who otherwise gets the benefit of the business without paying its debts;[140] in the latter, that of the insured's general creditors.[141] In reality, it is suggested that the connection with unjust enrichment is tenuous. The business creditor's claim against the *cestui que trust* is not conditional on proof of actual benefit by the latter, but only on a sort of nebulous presumption of it. Moreover, in both cases it is a little difficult to see any unjust factor; we all take the risk of the insolvency of a contractor or tortfeasor with whom we come into contact, and the admittedly draconian operation of the insolvency laws in this context can hardly be enough of itself to render unjust any benefit obtained under them. It is suggested that these cases are better seen simply as attempts to reform particular procedural defects in the law: in the first case, to give a *de facto* action to third parties against the trust estate as such, and in the second to give accident victims a direct claim against liability insurers.[142]

---

139 Eg, *Dowse v Gorton* [1891] AC 190; *Re Johnson* (1880) 15 Ch D 548, p 552. Executors are similarly treated (*Ex p Edmonds* (1862) 4 De G F and J 488, 498), as are court-appointed receivers (*Re London United Breweries Ltd* [1907] 2 Ch 511).

140 *Re Johnson* (1880) 15 Ch D 548, p 552 (Jessel MR); Burrows, p 84; Mitchell, *The Law of Subrogation*, pp 155–56.

141 Mitchell, *The Law of Subrogation*, p 8.

142 In the Republic, the Civil Liability Act 1961, s 62 very sensibly does just this.

CHAPTER 3

MISTAKE

3-1   However strong the feeling that one should not be allowed to repent of voluntary largesse, there is no doubt that mistaken assent deserves less weight in this context. If I claim to be allowed to retain a benefit which you only provided to me because, at the time, you were labouring under some error, this requires, at the very least, some justification. Hence the fact that mistake is a well established 'unjust factor' justifying restitutionary recovery. On the other hand, the subject of mistake is a broad one, and different mistakes may well need different treatment according to the circumstances and the type of benefit involved. Services rendered under a mistake, for example, cannot necessarily be treated in the same way as property erroneously transferred or simple mistaken payments of money. In addition, issues may arise as to the appropriate remedy – different mistakes may give rise to pecuniary restitution, a proprietary remedy, subrogation, or a combination of these. As a result, the topic of mistake can be unexpectedly complex at times.

I WHAT MISTAKES SHOULD GROUND RESTITUTION?

3-2   For obvious reasons, the definition of what should count as an operative mistake is a vital starting point. Four points in particular call for treatment:

(a) the distinction between mistakes as to the present and future mistakes;

(b) the question of how far mistake of law should ground recovery;

(c) whether some limit, such as a requirement that a mistake be substantial or fundamental, ought to be imposed; and

(d) how far it is relevant that the benefit was rendered pursuant to a contract between the relevant parties.

(a) Present and future mistakes

3-3   As in the law of contract, restitution *for mistake* is limited to mistakes as to matters of present fact. Mispredictions as to the future do not count.[1] This is not, of course, to say that failure of future expectations cannot give rise to restitution. On the contrary, it clearly can: if I pay you in advance for goods which I think you will deliver, but the goods are not forthcoming, I can recover my money.

---

1   See generally Birks, p 147 *et seq*.

But this is under the different rubric of failure of assumptions[2] (even though this may be closely related to mistake proper).[3] Nevertheless, the law of restitution is (understandably) slower to compensate for disappointed hopes than for presently blighted intentions, if only because a person rendering a benefit in the expectation of a future return is more likely to be taking a risk, either as to whether he will be paid at all,[4] or as to the solvency of the payee. *Re Goldcorp Exchange Ltd*[5] nicely illustrates the point. Investors paid Goldcorp for gold on the basis that Goldcorp would buy and hold the necessary bullion on their behalf. Goldcorp, however, did no such thing, and instead went into receivership. The investors claimed restitution on the basis that their money had been paid by mistake, a claim which, if good, would have arguably given them a constructive trust over any of their moneys in Goldcorp's hands.[6] But the Privy Council refused this relief, holding that their claim was for failure of expectations, which gave no such remedy.

Presumably, the rules applicable elsewhere as to what counts as a present mistake, such as the contractual rule that mistake as to a person's present intentions counts as mistake as to present facts[7] apply equally here.

(b) Mistake of fact and mistake of law

3-4 Assuming mistake is a plausible ground of restitution, it is difficult to see why it should make any difference of principle whether it is an error of fact or law. In both cases, the intention of the claimant providing the benefit is equally vitiated. For many years, however, a long line of authority in both jurisdictions insisted that mistake of law would not, without more, found restitutionary recovery[8] (though there were exceptions).[9] The origin of the rule was, it seems, *Bilbie v Lumley* in 1801,[10] where an underwriter who satisfied a claim that was voidable for non-disclosure in the (remarkable) ignorance of the rule entitling him to refuse to do so, failed to get back what he had paid. Although that decision was

---

2 Below, Chapter 6.

3 Below, § 3-10 *et seq*.

4 Cf Birks, p 277 *et seq*.

5 [1995] 1 AC 74.

6 Because of *Chase Manhattan Bank NA v Israel-British Bank Ltd* [1981] Ch 105.

7 Eg, *Edgington v Fitzmaurice* (1885) 29 Ch D 459.

8 Typical were cases such as *Bilbie v Lumley* (1801) 2 East 469; *Brisbane v Dacres* (1813) 5 Taunt 143; *O'Loghlen v O'Callaghan* (1874) IR 8 Ch 116; *National Pari-Mutuel Ltd v R* (1930) 47 TLR 110.

9 The most important were: (a) if the mistake of law was due to the payee's deliberate (or conceivably negligent) misrepresentation of law (*Harse v Pearl Life Assurance Co* [1904] 1 KB 558; *Byrne v Rudd* [1920] 2 IR 12); (b) where the duty to ascertain and observe the law was placed on the recipient, so the parties are not *in pari delicto* (*Re Cavalier Insurance Ltd* [1989] 2 Lloyd's Rep 450; *Dolan v Neligan* [1967] IR 247; *Rogers v Louth County Council* [1981] ILRM 144); (c) moneys received by officers of the court (*Ex p James* (1874) LR 9 Ch App 609).

10 (1801) 2 East 469.

hardly supported by rigorous reasoning, the bar on recovery was long thought too well rooted to be abolished except at the highest level.[11]

3-5 In the past, the denial of recovery may not have been indefensible. It was very often the payer's own fault if he did not trouble to ascertain his legal position.[12] Furthermore, there was an understandable fear that excessive liabilities would be placed on recipients after they had changed their position in reliance, or that *bona fide* disbursements or settlements would be vulnerable to subsequent judicial development of the law.[13] But, the first point lost all force once it was established that a payer's negligence did not bar recovery for mistake of fact:[14] there is no sensible reason for distinguishing between mistakes of fact and law here. The growth of a generalised defence of change of position[15] undermines the second; and, as for the third objection, this was not necessarily insuperable.

3-6 As a consequence, a rule which had lost its *raison d'être* was vigorously and convincingly criticised by academics,[16] the English Law Commission,[17] and judges[18] alike. It was progressively sidestepped[19] and, in a number of other common law jurisdictions, simply abolished.[20] In *Kleinwort Benson Ltd v Lincoln*

---

11 See, eg, the Court of Appeal's decision in *Woolwich Building Society v Inland Revenue Comrs (No 2)* [1991] 4 All ER 577, pp 601, 631. (The point was left open on the appeal to the House of Lords: [1993] AC 70.)

12 Eg, it is hard to resist the conclusion that the payer was seriously at fault in *Bilbie v Lumley* (1801) 2 East 469.

13 As would have been the case had recovery been allowed in *Henderson v Folkestone Waterworks Co* (1885) 1 TLR 329. See, also, *Casey v Irish Sailors Land Trust* [1937] IR 208 (no recovery of rent paid by tenants of almshouses whom subsequent court decision held entitled to reside rent free). But now cf *Kleinwort Benson Ltd v Lincoln CC* [1999] 2 AC 349, below, § 3-6.

14 Established beyond doubt by *Kelly v Solari* (1841) 9 M and W 54.

15 In *Lipkin Gorman v Karpnale Ltd* [1991] 2 AC 548. See below, Chapter 13.

16 Eg, Goff & Jones, 5th edn, Chapter 4; Burrows, p 109 *et seq*.

17 Report No 227, *Restitution: Mistakes of Law* (1994).

18 In Ireland, see *Dublin Corp v Trinity College* [1985] ILRM 283, p 286 (Hamilton J); *Pine Valley Ltd v Minister of the Environment* [1987] IR 23, p 42 (Henchy J). In England, see, eg, *Woolwich Building Society v Inland Revenue Comrs (No 2)* [1993] AC 70, p 199 (Lord Slynn) and p 164 (Lord Goff).

19 Eg, in *Woolwich Building Society v IRC (No 2)* [1993] AC 70, the House of Lords held that taxes paid where they were not in fact exigible could be recovered on other grounds, namely, high constitutional principle. In Ireland, the Supreme Court did much the same thing in *Dolan v Neligan* [1967] IR 247, this time on the basis that taxing authorities ought to be expected to understand their own law. Again, *ultra vires* payments made by the Crown or any other corporation are recoverable as such: eg, *Auckland Harbour Board v R* [1924] AC 318. In all these, arguments over whether mistake of law would allow recovery were simply avoided.

20 By judicial action in Scotland (*Morgan Guaranty Trust v Lothian Regional Council* 1995 SC 151), Australia (*David Securities Pty Ltd v Commonwealth Bank of Australia* (1992) 175 CLR 353) and Canada (*Air Canada v British Columbia* (1989) 59 DLR (4th) 161). By statute in New Zealand (Judicature Act 1908 (NZ), s 94A(2)) and some States in Australia (eg, Law Reform (Property, Perpetuities and Succession) Act 1962 (WA), s 23).

CC[21] the House of Lords, without opposition,[22] administered the *coup de grâce*. The facts arose out of a completed *ultra vires* interest rate swap. Normally, there would be no difficulty over recovery here on the basis of failure of assumptions;[23] but in this case, the events had occurred some time ago, and a claim under that rubric would be statute-barred. The plaintiffs, therefore, claimed on the alternative basis that they had parted with their money over under a mistake of law (payment having been made before the House of Lords declared such swaps illegal),[24] and that time had not run against them until they were aware of the mistake.[25] The House of Lords held unanimously that recovery was not barred by the fact that the mistake was one of law, and by a majority that the claim was indeed not statute-barred.

The mistake of law rule has not been abrogated as such in Ireland: indeed, there remain a number of pre-*Kleinwort Benson* authorities accepting its existence, albeit grudgingly.[26] However, there is already at least one *dictum* in the Supreme Court that mistake of fact *or law* will allow recovery,[27] and it is suggested that the courts in Ireland will almost certainly follow the lead of the House of Lords in *Kleinwort Benson* and hold that the rule has ceased to apply on either side of the Irish Sea.[28]

Mistake of law – definition

3-7   Although the distinction between mistake of law and error of fact is of greatly reduced importance since the removal of the mistake of law bar,[29] it is not yet clear that the two forms of liability are on precisely the same footing.[30] Therefore, it is worth noting briefly where the line between them is drawn. In particular, it is noteworthy that mistake of law is relatively narrowly defined.

---

21 [1999] 2 AC 349.

22 Both parties to the appeal accepted that the 'mistake of law' rule had to be abolished.

23 *Guinness Mahon and Co Ltd v Kensington BC* [1999] QB 215.

24 In *Hazell v Hammersmith & Fulham LBC* [1992] 2 AC 1.

25 Because of the (English) Limitation Act 1980, s 32(1)(c). The same would, it seems, apply in the Republic: Statute of Limitations 1957, s 72.

26 Eg, *Dolan v Neligan* [1967] IR 247; *Dublin Corp v Trinity College* [1985] ILRM 84.

27 *Dublin Corp v Building & Allied Trades Union* [1996] 1 IR 468, p 484 (Keane J).

28 In any case, Irish judges had long shown commendable adroitness in avoiding application of the rule, eg, by categorising the mistake as one of fact rather than law, or invoking the exception referred to below where the parties are not *in pari delicto*: eg, *Byrne v Rudd* [1920] 2 IR 12; *Dolan v Neligan* [1967] IR 247; *Dublin Corp v Trinity College* [1985] ILRM 84.

29 In particular, the House of Lords in *Kleinwort Benson* declined to introduce restrictions on recovery for mistake of law where the claimant had acted in reliance on a commonly accepted view, or where the defendant had accepted the benefit in all innocence: see *Kleinwort Benson Ltd v Lincoln CC* [1999] 2 AC 349, pp 359, 376, 381.

30 Lord Goff in *Kleinwort Benson Ltd v Lincoln CC* [1999] 2 AC 349, p 385, accepted that recovery for mistake of law should develop pragmatically, and that there might be 'circumstances which, as a matter of principle or policy, may lead to the conclusion that recovery should not be allowed'.

For instance, while misconstruction of a deed,[31] statute,[32] or rule of the common law[33] is a mistake of law, misguided belief as to ownership of property or other matters of private rights apparently counts as a mistake of fact for these purposes even though founded on a legal misapprehension.[34] The same is true of the misapplication of the law to particular facts (for example, whether premises are so configured as to come within rent control legislation).[35] Also classified as a mistake of fact is the case where moneys are paid automatically because the payer has neglected to stop payment, even if he would have acted otherwise had he realised that the payments were not legally due.[36]

Yet again, as a matter of both English and Irish private international law, foreign law is regarded as a matter of fact to be proved: from which, by a process of reasoning that is logical, if a little unreal, it has been held that mistakes about it equally count as factual rather than legal.[37]

The effect of changes in the law

3-8 If a payment or other benefit is provided because of ignorance of a statute, there is clearly a mistake of law. More awkward is the case where payment is made under the belief that it is due, but where that belief is later shown by judicial decision to have been erroneous. Was there a mistake *at the time of payment* if, at that time, the prevailing opinion was that the payment was indeed due? This was the issue that divided the House of Lords in *Kleinwort Benson Ltd v Lincoln CC*.[38] By a majority, their Lordships decided to accept the logic of the declaratory theory of judicial decision, and determined that where an accepted view of the law was reversed by a court ruling, this event should be given full retrospective effect. It followed that a person who had relied on the previously accepted view of the law should be deemed to have acted in error, even though at the time, any lawyer not endowed with prescience would have advised him that his belief was correct.[39] Consonant with this ruling, their Lordships also

---

31 *Re Hatch* [1919] 1 Ch 351.

32 *O'Loghlen v O'Callaghan* (1874) IR 8 CL 116. Indeed, the *Kleinwort Benson* case itself involved legislative misconstruction, namely, of the statutory borrowing powers of public authorities.

33 *Nurdin and Peacock plc v Ramsden & Co Ltd* [1999] 1 All ER 941 (mistake as to legal recoverability of money paid by way of disputed rent).

34 Cf *Cooper v Phibbs* (1865) 17 Ir R Ch 73, (1867) LR 2 HL 149 (a contract case, but one where the same distinction fell to be drawn).

35 Cf *Solle v Butcher* [1950] 1 KB 671; and see, too, *Platt v Casey's Drogheda Brewery Ltd* [1912] 1 IR 271.

36 *Nurdin and Peacock plc v DB Ramsden & Co Ltd* [1999] 1 All ER 941.

37 *Lazard Bros v Midland Bank Ltd* [1933] AC 289.

38 [1999] 2 AC 349.

39 What where the law was changed by retrospective legislation? Lord Goff was sceptical as to whether a previous payment could be regarded as having been made under a mistake of law (p 381). The point divided the High Court of Australia in *Comr of State Revenue v Royal Insurance Australia Ltd* (1994) 126 ALR 1.

declined to recognise a defence, which would have been peculiar to mistakes of law,[40] that the benefit was conferred according to a generally accepted (if erroneous) legal view.[41]

Limitations on recovery for mistake of law

3-9   Although, in theory, the abolition of the mistake of law bar has been a revolutionary development, in practice, its effects may not be as drastic as expected. In particular, recovery for mistake of law is subject to a number of self-correcting limitations. For example, even where there is a mistake of law, there is often another, independent, reason to refuse recovery, such as where payments are made in submission to actual or threatened legal proceedings,[42] or to compromise an honest claim,[43] in which case there can be no recovery anyway. Yet others involve overpayments of taxes or duties, where recovery is normally governed by specific statutory provisions and not by the common law.[44] Moreover, it must always be remembered that there must be an actual mistake. If there is a dispute over A's liability to pay B a given sum of money, for example, A cannot recover any sums paid on the basis of mistake of law even if his interpretation of the law was correct. He was not mistaken as to the law: on the contrary, he was right about it.[45]

(c) The nature of the mistake

3-10   There is no doubt that the kinds of mistake capable of giving rise to restitution are widely drawn. Most of the cases concern money paid by mistake. They include mistakes due to the claimant's own fault,[46] and rightly so: although the point could be controversial, it is suggested that there is no reason why one man's negligence should be another man's windfall. Furthermore, despite certain antique authority the other way,[47] it is clear that recovery goes beyond

---

40 And which had been advocated by the English Law Commission: Report No 272, *Restitution: Mistakes of Law*, 1994, 5.13.

41 See [1999] 2 AC 349, p 359 *et seq* (Lord Browne-Wilkinson), p 376 *et seq* and p 381 *et seq* (Lord Goff).

42 Eg, *William Whiteley Ltd v R* (1909) 101 LT 741; and indeed (arguably) *Bilbie v Lumley* (1802) 2 East 469 itself.

43 *Bullingdon v Oxford Corp* [1936] 3 All ER 875.

44 Below, Chapter 12.

45 Cf *Nurdin and Peacock plc v Ramsden and Co Ltd* [1999] 1 All ER 941.

46 *Kelly v Solari* (1841) 9 M and W 54, p 59 (where the point was first established): *Rover International Ltd v Cannon Film Sales Ltd (No 3)* [1989] 3 All ER 423, p 431 (Kerr LJ); *Scottish Equitable plc v Derby* [2001] 3 All ER 818, pp 824–25 (Robert Walker LJ).

47 Notably, *dicta* in *Aiken v Short* (1856) 1 H and N 210, p 215.

cases where the claimant believed himself legally obliged to the recipient.[48] Thus, a gift made in error may be recovered,[49] as may a payment inadvertently made by a bank on a countermanded cheque,[50] even though in neither case was there a question of the payer being under any obligation whatever to the payee. And, it seems, it makes no difference for these purposes whether the mistake be of fact or law.[51]

3-11 Can any limitation be put on what mistakes will trigger restitution? Older authorities suggested a discrete requirement that the error be, in some sense, 'fundamental'. Typical was Lord Wright in *Norwich Union Fire Insurance v Price*:[52]

> It is, however, essential that the mistake relied on should be of such a nature that it can properly be described as a mistake in respect of the underlying assumption of the contract or transaction or as being fundamental or basic.

And in 1966, Budd J, discussing recovery of money paid by mistake, reviewed the authorities exhaustively and then said laconically: 'It must be a fundamental mistake'[53] (without, however, expatiating on how one identified such an error).

3-12 But, this approach is somewhat discredited, if only because the criterion of what ought to count as 'fundamental' is irredeemably uncertain.[54] As a result, academic writers[55] and a number of recent *dicta*[56] have sought to abandon the effort to distinguish between different sorts of mistake, some being operative and some not, as undesirable and a waste of time. They argue, with engaging simplicity, that the claimant should merely have to show (a) that he was mistaken, and (b) that this, in fact, caused him to pay money or provide the benefit. Any necessary protection for the payee (it is argued) should come from defences such as *bona fide* purchase or change of position.[57] From this, of course,

---

48 Unless, perhaps, statute provides otherwise. This possibly explains *Morgan v Ashcroft* [1938] 1 KB 49, which otherwise seems wrongly decided (no recovery in respect of overpayment of gambling debt).

49 Eg, *Larner v London CC* [1949] 2 KB 683. Cf *Hood of Avalon (Lady) v Mackinnon* [1909] 1 Ch 476 (revocation of deed of gift executed in error).

50 *National Bank v O'Connor* (1966) 103 ILTR 73; *Barclays Bank Ltd v WJ Simms Ltd* [1979] 3 All ER 522. See, too, *Lloyds Bank plc v Independent Insurance Co Ltd* [2000] QB 110 (payment of cheque where bank mistaken re available balance: recovery assumed available). *Sed quaere*: is this not a risk that ought to be borne by the bank rather than the payee?

51 *Kleinwort Benson Ltd v Lincoln CC* [1999] 2 AC 349.

52 [1934] AC 455. The point of 'fundamentality' was left open by the High Court of Australia in *ANZ Bank Ltd v Westpac Ltd* (1988) 164 CLR 662, pp 671–72.

53 *National Bank v O'Connor* (1966) 103 ILTR 73, p 94.

54 Finn, *Essays in Restitution*, Chapter 4, p 98.

55 Eg, Burrows, p 95 *et seq*; Goff & Jones, p 177 *et seq*; Virgo, *Principles of the Law of Restitution*, p 148 *et seq*.

56 *Barclays Bank Ltd v WJ Simms Ltd* [1979] 3 All ER 522, pp 532–35, approved by Dillon LJ in *Rover International Ltd v Cannon Film Sales Ltd (No 3)* [1989] 3 All ER 423, pp 440–41; *Lloyds Bank plc v Independent Insurance Co Ltd* [2000] QB 110.

57 See Goff & Jones, p 177 *et seq*.

it follows that, however small or idiosyncratic the mistake, a mere volunteer who had not relied on the gift would deserve and receive no indulgence at all.

With respect, however, this view may go too far the other way. Assume I give £1,000 to my niece as a birthday present, not realising that she has just married a man I privately detest. It seems instinctively odd that a footling or idiosyncratic error like that should entitle me to repent of my generosity and recover my money, even if I can prove by impeccable evidence that had I known the relevant facts, I would not have made the gift in the first place.

3-13   Is there any way in which non-recovery can be justified as a matter of principle in situations of this sort?[58] It is suggested that there is. The 'pure causation' theory of recovery is based on one vital assumption: namely, that mistake is an entirely claimant-sided ground of restitution based somehow on the metaphysics of the will. In other words, a person doing something as a result of mistake does not 'really' intend to do so, and hence should be allowed to retract. It is submitted, however, that this theory of recovery for mistake is a fallacy. A better view of mistake is (it is suggested) as a variant of failure of assumptions,[59] looking to the intentions of both claimant and defendant as understood by a reasonable person: the only thing which marks off mistake from the rest of failure of assumptions being that it deals with present assumptions rather than future contingencies. Indeed, it is worth pointing out that the two doctrines not infrequently co-exist on the same facts, as in cases such as *Rover International v Cannon Film Sales (No 3)*,[60] where money was paid for benefits to be rendered under a contract which was, unknown to either party, void.

3-14   Now, with failure of assumptions, it is incontrovertible that a mere disappointment will not do, however causative of the defendant's benefit. Suppose I give you £500, secretly hoping you will invite me to your estate for a shooting weekend. No one suggests I can (or should) recover it if the invitation is not forthcoming, even if I can prove that had I known you would not invite me, I would not have given you anything. My only chance of restitution is by showing that you ought to have known, from the circumstances or otherwise, that my gift was made on that assumption. In other words, my right of recovery is based not on any supposed vitiation of my intent to give you £500, but on the assumption shared by both of us, as shown by agreement or the objective circumstances surrounding my action. But, if so, it is difficult to see why it ought to make any difference if my payment was made in the erroneous belief that you

---

58   A supporter of the 'simple causation' theory could argue that in such a case I intended to pay 'in any event' and deny recovery on that basis. But this will not do. I had no such intent in fact. Arguably, I ought to be treated as if I had: but this simply begs the question of why recovery ought to be denied in the first place.

59   This view is not without support: see Finn, *Essays in Restitution*, Chapter 4, p 111. And cf the Australian decision in *York Air Conditioning Ltd v Commonwealth* (1949) 80 CLR 11, pp 63–64, where just this parallel is drawn.

60   [1989] 3 All ER 423.

had already posted an invitation to me. Yet, on the pure 'causation' approach, this is precisely what happens. This surely cannot be right.

3-15   It is therefore suggested that in cases of mistake, as with failure of assumptions, what matters is not the metaphysical question of whether the claimant acted voluntarily, but the circumstances surrounding the payment or other benefit as they would have been understood by the reasonable person. If such a person, knowing the facts behind the rendering of the benefit, but not the individual characteristics of the parties, would have regarded the mistake as immaterial, then restitution is not available: otherwise, *prima facie*, it ought to be.

3-16   One further point is of considerable practical significance: does a claimant lose his right to restitution if he had some doubt as to the true facts? Suppose an insurer believes that a claim is a good one, but is aware that there is a chance that it is not; he chooses to pay now and, if necessary, argue later. Does this count as a payment by mistake? It is suggested that it should, and that if it later appears that he did have a defence, he should be able to recover:[61] it would be unfortunate were the law to penalise those who sought to be reasonable and accommodating in their disputes with others.

II THE RELEVANCE OF CONTRACT

3-17   There can generally be no restitution for benefits rendered under a contract if, at the time relief is claimed, that contract remains binding.[62] This is a vital point in connection with restitution for mistake, since the class of errors capable of impugning a contract is much narrower than that of mistakes giving rise to restitution in the absence of a contractual nexus. It follows that where a claimant has rendered a *contractual* benefit to another,[63] however mistakenly, his claim for restitution falls at the first fence unless he can first get rid of the contract by showing that his mistake falls into the narrower category. The decision in *Bell v Lever Bros Ltd*[64] provides a cast-iron example. Employers paid two senior employees considerable sums by way of severance pay under a contract by which the latter gave up their rights to sue for wrongful dismissal. They later discovered that the employees had been guilty of misconduct which would have justified their summary dismissal. There is no doubt that these payments were made as a result of a mistake, and a pretty serious mistake at that. But, because the mistake was regarded as not fundamental enough to set aside the contract,

---

61 Cf the Australian decision in *York Air Conditioning Ltd v Commonwealth* (1949) 80 CLR 11. *Contra*, though, Arrowsmith in Burrows (ed), *Essays in the Law of Restitution*, Chapter 2.

62 Burrows, p 126 *et seq*.

63 This means, of course, a benefit actually due under a contract. A benefit which the claimant thinks is due, but which in fact is not, is recoverable in any case.

64 [1932] AC 161.

no relief was available. Equally instructive is the Irish case of *Cooper v Phibbs*,[65] where the buyer of certain fishing rights sued for return of the price when he discovered that they had been his own all along. He recovered, but had to give credit for improvements wrought by the seller, since these were the only terms on which the court was prepared to set aside the contract of sale.

3-18   Not only may contract restrict the right of restitutionary recovery: it may also supplement or, indeed, replace it. In particular, there is nothing to prevent the recipient of money actually contracting to return it if it should turn out not to have been due.[66] This was, indeed, found to have happened in *Nurdin & Peacock plc v Ramsden and Co Ltd*.[67] In a situation of uncertainty and litigation as to the rent payable under a lease, the lessee paid the larger sum under a covering letter stating: 'Obviously, the payment will be refundable if [the lessee] is successful at trial.' Neuberger J held that by accepting the payment, the lessor had accepted a contractual liability to return any excess. On the other hand, such a duty will not lightly be inferred: in particular, the mere acceptance of money paid 'under protest' will not do.[68]

III MONEY PAID BY MISTAKE

(a) The principle of recovery

3-19   Ever since the English decision in *Kelly v Solari*[69] in 1841, it has been accepted that money paid by mistake of fact is *prima facie* recoverable as money had and received.[70] It does not matter whether the recipient knew of the mistake at the

---

65 (1865) Ir Ch Rep 73; (1867) LR 2 HL 149. See also *Lecky v Walter* [1914] IR 326, where a buyer of worthless shares failed to recover the price despite a misrepresentation by the seller (and hence despite a mistake on his own part), on the ground that the rule in *Seddon v North Eastern Salt Co Ltd* [1905] 1 Ch 326 precluded the setting aside of the contract. (This would no longer happen in England or NI: Misrepresentation Act 1967, s 1 and the equivalent Misrepresentation (NI) Act 1967.)

66 'A payment may be made on such terms as it has been agreed, expressly or impliedly, by the recipient that, if it shall prove not to have been due, it will be repaid by him': Lord Goff in *Woolwich Building Society v Inland Revenue Comrs (No 2)* [1993] AC 70, p 165–66. See, too, *Sebel Products Ltd v Comrs of Customs and Excise* [1949] Ch 409.

67 [1999] 1 All ER 941.

68 *Woolwich Building Society v Inland Revenue Comrs (No 2)* [1993] AC 70, pp 165–66 (Lord Goff). See, too, *Roxborough v Rothmans Australia Ltd* (1999) 161 ALR 253. The actual decision in *Sebel Products Ltd v Comrs of Customs and Excise* [1949] Ch 409, holding that moneys had been received under an implied contractual obligation to return them if not due, may be doubtful on the facts: see *Nurdin & Peacock plc v Ramsden and Co Ltd* [1999] 1 All ER 941, p 959.

69 (1841) 9 M & W 54.

70 See, too, *National Bank v O'Connor* (1966) 103 ILTR 73; *Norwich Union Fire Insurance Society Ltd v Price* [1934] AC 455; *Rover International Ltd v Cannon Film Sales Ltd (No 3)* [1989] 3 All ER 423.

time he received the payment,[71] nor that he himself did not induce it,[72] nor what the nature of the payment was. Gifts of money are recoverable in the same way as payments supposedly made under a valid contract (as where I inadvertently pay your bill twice) or payments made pursuant to a contract which, unknown to either party thereto, is entirely ineffective.[73] Money paid to the payee's order counts as money paid to the payee. Nor does it matter that the payee was acting as agent for another (as with a payment to a bank),[74] though here, the agent has a defence of change of position once he has accounted to his principal.

(b) Mistaken payments: the availability of a proprietary remedy

3-20 We have seen that money paid by mistake is recoverable at common law as money had and received. But, this may not be the only remedy. In *Chase Munhattan NA v Israel British Bank Ltd*,[75] it was held by Goulding J that an alternative means of recovery was available by way of constructive trust. Hence, where the plaintiffs inadvertently credited $2 m twice to a payee who subsequently became insolvent, they were able to claim the second payment from the liquidator (who still held it), on the basis that it was subject to a constructive trust in their favour.

The reasoning behind this is not entirely clear, but the best justification for it is that, whatever the position with regard to legal title in the second payment, the claimants should be regarded as never having intended to confer any equitable ownership on the defendants.[76] It has also been argued academically – though not accepted judicially – that *Chase Manhattan* is really an application of resulting trust principles: in the absence of informed intent to give the defendant beneficial ownership of the payment, the equitable interest should result back to the payer.[77] But, all this has an air of fiction about it. If anything, the claimant's intention was to transfer a beneficial interest to the defendant, albeit misguidedly. Nor does there seem any other good reason for preferring his

---

71 The insured in *Norwich Union Fire Insurance v Price* [1934] AC 455 and the defendant in *Jones (RE) Ltd v Waring & Gillow Ltd* [1926] AC 696 both acted entirely innocently.

72 Eg, *Barclays Bank Ltd v WJ Simms Ltd* [1979] 3 All ER 522. But note *Sybron Corp v Rochem Ltd* [1983] 2 All ER 707, where the English Court of Appeal, oddly, seem to have assumed the contrary. This assumption (which did not affect the outcome of the case) seems plainly wrong.

73 *Rover International Ltd v Cannon Film Sales Ltd (No 3)* [1989] 3 All ER 423.

74 *Re Irish Shipping Ltd* [1986] ILRM 518.

75 [1981] Ch 105.

76 Cf *Eldan Services Ltd v Chandag Motors Ltd* [1990] 3 All ER 459, pp 461–62 (Millett J).

77 Birks, *Restitution and Resulting Trusts*, in Goldstein (ed), *Equity and Contemporary Legal Developments*; Chambers, *Resulting Trusts*, pp 2–3 and Chapter 4. But this view, rejected by Swadling (see (1996) 16 LS 110), was discountenanced by Lord Browne-Wilkinson in *Westdeutsche Landesbank Girozentrale v Islington BC*: see [1996] AC 669, pp 702–03.

interests to those of the defendant's general creditors. For these and other reasons, the case has, as has already been pointed out above,[78] met with a mixed reception.[79] There must remain some doubt as to whether it will be followed in future in either jurisdiction.

In any case, the practical effect of the *Chase Manhattan* principle may well be limited. The availability of a proprietary remedy is chiefly relevant where the defendant is insolvent: but, in the majority of cases of mistaken payment, the moneys concerned will have been credited to the payee's overdrawn bank account.[80] Where this happens, the bank will be treated as a *bona fide* purchaser,[81] and there will simply be nothing for a proprietary claim to bite on.

IV PROPERTY TRANSFERRED BY MISTAKE

(a) General

3-21   There are few authorities directly dealing with property transferred by mistake. Nevertheless, all other things being equal, it ought logically be treated on the same footing as for money paid. If my mistake in paying you £100 *prima facie* makes it unjustifiable for you to keep the money, so too should my error in giving you a cow (or a house) equally oblige you to make restitution, whether in money or otherwise.

A declaration of trust, for instance, may be set aside for mistake, as happened in *Sybron Corp v Rochem Ltd*.[82] Employers took out certain life policies in respect of an employee who resigned, and declared a trust of them in favour of the employee and his wife. On discovering that the employee had been systematically defrauding them when the trust was declared, the employers successfully sued to have the trust revoked. The Sale of Goods Act,[83] reproducing the common law position, provides another example. Where a

---

78   § 2-17.

79   In the Republic, it was followed by the High Court in *Re Irish Shipping Ltd* [1986] ILRM 518. Mummery LJ referred to it without disapproval in *Re Polly Peck Ltd (No 2)* [1998] 3 All ER 812, p 827. But, its correctness was left open by Lords Browne-Wilkinson and Goff in *Westdeutsche Landesbank Girozentrale v Islington BC* [1999] AC 669, pp 690, 714. Aiken J in *Bank of America v Arnell* [1999] Lloyd's Rep Bank 399, said that, had the question of its correctness arisen, he would not have been prepared to follow it.

80   It is noteworthy that in *Chase Manhattan*, the payee was itself a bank.

81   See above, § 1-36. *Contra*, admittedly, Barr J's judgment in *Re Irish Shipping Ltd* [1986] ILRM 518. But, it is submitted that it cannot stand on this point.

82   [1983] 2 All ER 707. See, too, *Hood (Lady) v Mackinnon* [1909] 1 Ch 476, and cf *Re Butlin's Settlement Trusts* [1976] 2 All ER 483.

83   1893 (Ireland); 1979 (England).

seller of goods over-delivers, the buyer, assuming he accepts the increased quantity (which he need not), must pay for the excess at the contract rate.[84]

Property claims, nevertheless, merit separate treatment for two reasons: remedies, and the problems connected with forced exchange.

(b) Property transferred by mistake: remedies

3-22 Where property is transferred by mistake, there are two restitutionary remedies theoretically open to the law. It could accept that the defendant now owns the asset, allow him to keep it and order a money payment to correct the unjust enrichment. It could alternatively hold that the claimant still owns the asset, either outright or through the medium of a trust imposed in his favour, and give him all the remedies associated with that ownership.[85]

The easiest remedy, because it neatly parallels the action for money had and received in the case of money payments, is the pecuniary one, known as *quantum valebat*. Subject to questions of forced exchange and subjective devaluation, since *Rover International v Cannon Film Sales (No 3)*,[86] there seems no reason why a mistaken transferor of goods as much as services should not have a claim for their value. True, there is a possible difficulty over gifts, since the remedy of *quantum valebat* is traditionally limited to goods accepted in circumstances suggesting an intention to charge, which *ex hypothesi* a gift is not. But, it is suggested that mistake on the part of the donor ought to be sufficient to overcome any argument based on gratuitous intent. The moral case for the donor is undeniable: furthermore, the recent acceptance of a general defence of change of position[87] suggests that adequate protection can be given to the donee who may have passed the gift on, or sold it and frittered away the proceeds.

However, questions of title complicate the question of restitution for property transferred. We have already mentioned the possibility of revoking a trust declared in error. Again, in certain cases the claimant can in effect claim to be compensated by receiving (or retaining) legal ownership of the thing concerned. Although the latter example is not strictly a restitutionary remedy, but an ordinary claim to one's own property, it is covered here for the sake of completeness.

3-23 We now turn to the possibility of a proprietary remedy in mistaken transfers of property.

---

84 Section 30(2) (Ireland); s 30(3) (England). Compare *Rover International v Cannon Film Sales Ltd (No 3)* [1989] 3 All ER 423, where precisely this point was accepted in respect of the analogous case of services rendered and accepted under a mistake, namely, under a contract which both parties thought binding, but was in fact void.

85 Including claims to any proceeds.

86 [1989] 3 All ER 423, esp p 431 (though this case was actually about services rather than goods).

87 See Chapter 13, below.

In the case of contractual transfers, such a remedy is afforded *de facto* by application of the rule that the validity of any transfer of title to chattels depends on the validity of the underlying contract. If, owing to mistake, there is no contract at all, no title passes, and hence the claimant can simply rely on his continuing property right. *Cundy v Lindsay*[88] illustrates the point. A, masquerading as B, induced C to send him goods on credit, which A then sold to D. C was held able to recover the goods by an action in conversion, not only against A,[89] but against D. And similarly, no doubt, with a gift of a chattel under an equally fundamental mistake. Suppose you live in the same house as a hard-up friend of mine and telephone me in his name asking me to give you my old car; I leave it outside your gate, and you take it. It is suggested that legal title to the car would remain in me; I never intended to give anything to you at all, and I could recover it from you or any subsequent transferee – however innocent – simply by suing in conversion.[90]

3-24   Analogous rules apply to chattels transferred under transactions voidable for mistake, such as contracts entered into as a result of error or misrepresentation. Gifts of chattels induced by misrepresentation also seem to be subject to similar reasoning.[91] If a transaction is subsequently avoided, any chattels transferred pursuant to it revest automatically in the transferor, who thus, once again, gets a de facto right to restitution against the transferee[92] (though not against a *bona fide* purchaser from him, since rescission cannot be had where it would affect his rights).[93] Indeed, there seems no reason why this remedy should not be combined with a pecuniary claim. Suppose I agree to sell you 100 cases of champagne very cheaply as a result of an innocent misrepresentation by you. After I have delivered it and you have drunk one case, I successfully avoid the contract. It is suggested that I can recover the remaining 99 cases *in specie* and sue you for the value of the odd case.

3-25   Most of the cases concern chattels, which have the peculiarity of being transferable at law by contract or by mere delivery. What of other property, such as land, shares or book debts, which need further formality such as a deed or written instrument? The position here appears to be that, in contrast to chattels, revesting at law is impossible. However, it seems that the transferor will obtain

---

88   (1878) 3 App Cas 459.

89   Note, however, that if A is innocent (eg, if both A and C have been duped by a third party X) and A has disposed of the chattels without negligence, he escapes liability in conversion: *Elvin and Powell Ltd v Plummer Roddis Ltd* (1933) 50 TLR 158. But this is due to the vagaries of the law of conversion rather than to any deep-seated restitutionary principle.

90   This would seem to be *a fortiori* to the facts in *Cundy v Lindsay* (1878) 3 App Cas 459.

91   See *Re Glubb* [1900] 1 Ch 354.

92   See, eg, *Car and Universal Finance Ltd v Caldwell* [1965] 1 QB 525 (contract voidable for fraud: transfer after contract avoided).

93   Eg, *Lewis v Averay* [1972] 1 QB 198.

an equitable claim to have them reconveyed to him,[94] good as against anyone but a *bona fide* purchaser.[95]

Finally, it should be noted that in some cases, the mistaken transferor of property may possibly have the benefit of a constructive trust, with its concomitant advantage in insolvency. Suppose a seller of oil mistakenly makes two deliveries of the amount ordered instead of one. If the decision in *Chase Manhattan NA v Israel-British Bank*[96] is right (which is, admittedly, open to some doubt),[97] there seems no reason not to apply it to property as to money,[98] and to say that the recipient holds the excess on trust for the seller.

(c) Forced exchange and subjective devaluation: property cases

3-26   Telling a transferee of money to refund it, or an equivalent sum, simply reverses the original transaction. By contrast, to order a mistaken recipient of goods or services to make pecuniary restitution goes further: its effect is to force on the defendant not simply a refund, but an exchange. As such, it is immediately open to the potential objection from the defendant that he ought not to be forced, in effect, to buy something he never agreed to purchase and which he might well not have wanted. In practice, however, this is of little importance in property cases. In most such situations, the transferee can decide to reject the thing concerned. If you mistakenly deliver wine to my house or building materials to my site, I can either use them or tell you to take them away.[99] If I use them, I have freely accepted them, and this normally disables me from taking the point of forced exchange; if I reject them, no question of restitution arises.

Nevertheless, this is not invariably so. Take the facts of *Boulton v Jones*.[100] Jones ordered piping from one Brocklehurst. Boulton, who had meanwhile taken over Brocklehurst's business, supplied it, and Jones (who had hoped to set off the price against money owed him by Brocklehurst) used it. Boulton's action in contract for the price was unsuccessful. It is suggested that an action by

---

94   See *Hood (Lady) v Mackinnon* [1909] 1 Ch 476; *Ellis v Ellis* (1909) 26 TLR 166. And cf the analogous position where a transfer valid at common law is avoided by provisions of the insolvency legislation (eg, preferences): *Re French's Wine Bar Ltd* [1987] BCLC 499.

95   Including, it is suggested, a purchaser of a mere equitable interest, since the right to avoid a transfer is normally reckoned as a mere equity. See *Phillips v Phillips* (1861) 4 De G F and J 208; and cf *Allied Irish Banks Ltd v Glynn* [1973] IR 188.

96   [1979] Ch 105.

97   Above, § 3-20.

98   As Goulding J seems to have accepted in *Chase Manhattan*: see [1981] Ch 105, p 118, where he cited the American authority of *Scott on Trusts*, 3d edn, Vol 5, p 3428, to that effect.

99   This is true even in the case where title to property automatically vests in the recipient without the need for any action on his part, as with a declaration of trust or transfer by deed. The recipient has an indefeasible right to disclaim it, in which case it will retrospectively vest in the transferee: see, eg, *Re Paradise Motor Co Ltd* [1968] 2 All ER 625.

100 (1857) 2 H and N 564.

Boulton in *quantum valebat* equally would (and should) have failed. True, Jones had accepted the piping: but his expectation that he would be able to set off the entire price against Brocklehurst's debt meant that its value *to him* was nil. He could, in other words, subjectively devalue any alleged benefit to nothing.[101]

V SERVICES AND MISTAKE

(a) Generally

3-27   There is no doubt that services rendered by mistake to, and accepted by, another give rise to a *prima facie* right to restitution. Normally, this takes the form of an action in *quantum meruit*. Thus, in *Rover International Ltd v Cannon Film Sales Ltd (No 3)*,[102] the plaintiffs rendered services to the defendants by arranging the dubbing and distribution in Italy of certain films belonging to the latter. This was done under a contract which both parties assumed to be valid and enforceable, but which, in fact, was entirely ineffective, having been made before the plaintiffs were incorporated. The Court of Appeal had no difficulty in accepting that the plaintiffs were entitled to a *quantum meruit* for what they had done.

The difficulty arises from the fact that in many cases, no prior acceptance as in the *Rover* decision can be shown. And, whereas property transferred can normally be accepted or declined after the event, the same does not necessarily go for other benefits in kind. True, some services can be meaningfully accepted or rejected *ex post facto*. If you owe X £1,000 and I pay X off in your name, but without your authority, you can choose whether to ratify the payment and take the discharge. If you do, then I can claim £1,000[103] from you as a benefit freely accepted. If you do not, the debt remains undischarged,[104] and there is therefore no benefit to pay for. But, in most cases, there is no such choice. If I do something for you, such as servicing your van, that is it. If you did not ask me to do it,[105] there is nothing that can be done about it now: it is a *fait accompli*.[106] Hence, in the absence of a valid acceptance, it has been held that no claim lies for

---

101 See above, § 1-33.

102 [1989] 3 All ER 423, esp p 431.

103 But *quaere* what happens if you could have settled with X for £900? Does this sum represent the amount of your benefit, and hence limit my recovery? Or are you, by your acceptance, precluded from denying that you have benefited by £1,000?

104 See, eg, *Walter v James* (1871) LR 6 Ex 124, and cf, more recently, *Crantrave Ltd v Lloyds Bank plc* [2000] 4 All ER 273. See generally, Birks and Beatson (1976) 92 LQR 188; Friedmann (1983) 99 LQR 534.

105 Or, possibly, acquiesce in my doing so: see below, § 3-30 *et seq*.

106 As Pollock CB notoriously put it in *Taylor v Laird* (1856) 25 LJ Ex 329, p 332: 'One cleans another's shoes; what can the other do but put them on?'

paying off a third party's debt,[107] or providing professional services to a dead person's estate.[108] Again, assume you buy a house subject to a mortgage to a bank, and I, thinking the house is mine, discharge the mortgage. The house is *ipso facto* released, whether you like it or not: for this reason, I have no claim against you.[109] In other words, most cases of services rendered under mistake raise in acute form the issue of forced exchange; the only way to recompense the recipient is effectively to force him to buy something from the claimant which you never agreed to pay him for in the first place.

3-28   Hence, in stark contrast to payments of money, the general assumption is that a person providing services does so at his own risk, even if he should turn out to have been mistaken. It is the view epitomised, for instance, by *Falcke v Scottish Imperial Assurance Co*.[110] The claimant paid premiums to keep alive an insurance policy, wrongly thinking he was entitled to the benefit of it (in fact, he had mortgaged it). When the true facts came out, he failed to obtain any sort of relief against the person in fact entitled, who had bought it from the mortgagee. Although it is arguable that the decision is right quite independently of restitutionary considerations since, at least in England,[111] a mortgagor cannot set up his own interest against that of a mortgagee, Bowen LJ put the position much more generally:

> work or labour done or money expended by one man to preserve or benefit the property of another do not according to English law create any lien upon the property saved or benefited ... Liabilities are not to be forced on people behind their backs any more than you can confer a benefit upon a man against his will.[112]

3-29   What, then, are the cases where restitution is available for services rendered under a mistake? We have already mentioned prior acceptance: it should be noted, however, that this may on occasion be defeated by subjective devaluation or some similar doctrine. *Boulton v Jones*,[113] already mentioned in connection with property, is a case in point. The plaintiff there was denied a remedy in contract: it is suggested that he equally ought to be denied restitution, since

---

107 *Re Cleadon Trust Ltd* [1939] Ch 286 (payer wrongly believed company had agreed to refund payment to subsidiary: no restitution, since meeting purporting to accept benefit inquorate and ineffective).

108 *Gray v Richards Butler* (1996) *The Times*, 23 July (professional services by executor appointed under ineffective will).

109 This seems the best explanation for *Owen v Tate* [1976] QB 402, where restitution was denied for the discharge of a mortgage debt.

110 (1886) 34 Ch D 234. It is true that the case is hardly impregnable authority. The plaintiff failed to establish his mistake on the facts: the defendant had no chance to reject the benefit: and the plaintiff was claiming, not recompense, but a lien on the property. But, the statement of principle is unequivocal.

111 The position may well be different in Ireland: see *Re Power* [1899] 1 IR 6 and the doctrine of salvage: below, § 9-16.

112 (1886) 34 Ch D 234, pp 248–49.

113 (1857) 2 H and N 564.

although the defendant no doubt accepted the piping delivered, he did so under a fundamental misapprehension as to who was delivering it and hence did not do so freely.

A similar case, which has caused some difficulty, is *Upton-on-Severn RDC v Powell*.[114] A Worcestershire farmer saw a fire in his barn and telephoned the police. The police alerted the Upton fire brigade, who came and put it out. Unfortunately, no one realised that the farmer lived outside the area where he was entitled to the services of the brigade free of charge. The local authority, the body responsible for fire services, successfully sued him for the value of services rendered. It is difficult to defend the ground on which the action ostensibly succeeded, namely that the farmer had contracted for the brigade's services.[115] But why not regard the case as one of restitutionary recovery, based not on any supposed contract, but on benefit to the defendant? Nevertheless, even this runs into difficulties. Even if the defendant accepted the services, they did not in fact benefit him because he was entitled to the services of his own fire brigade for nothing. It follows, it is suggested, that the *Upton-on-Severn* case should be regarded as a highly doubtful decision.

(b) Services, mistake and acquiescence

3-30   Acquiescence is a sort of halfway house between free acceptance and outright refusal. If you watch me doing something for you, knowing of my mistake and saying nothing, the equity against you becomes stronger than if you did not know what was happening, albeit still a good deal weaker than if you asked me to do it, or took positive steps to appropriate the benefit of what I had done. Nevertheless, there is some indication that, for the purposes of recovery for mistaken benefits, acquiescence may be equiparated to acceptance.[116]

3-31   Most of the relevant authorities concern improvements to land (though there is no reason why the principle should not apply to chattels as well).[117] Thus, in *Unity Joint Stock Banking Co v King*,[118] a farmer's two sons, thinking they owned certain land which in fact belonged to their father, improved a piece of it to the extent of some £200 by building on it. Their father stood by and let them. The sons were held entitled as against him to a lien for their improvements. Again, in *Lee-Parker v Izzett (No 2)*,[119] the plaintiff, as a result of a confusing series of transactions, wrongly thought she was the purchaser of a house. In this belief,

---

114 [1942] 1 All ER 220.

115 The farmer clearly had no idea that he was agreeing to pay for anything: nor is it clear that the local authority believed that he was. This is unpromising material for constructing onerous contracts of any kind.

116 For possible reasons, see Chapter 5.

117 Cf *Greenwood v Bennett* [1973] QB 195.

118 (1825) 245 Beav 72. See, too, *Willmott v Barber* (12880) 15 Ch D 96.

119 [1972] 2 All ER 800, esp pp 804–05.

she wrought certain improvements to it. When the true situation transpired, she was held entitled on principle to a lien on it to the extent of those improvements.[120]

3-32   In fact, however, claims of this sort are of comparatively little importance, owing to the existence of the related doctrine of equitable estoppel.[121] Assume you wrongly believe you have, or will have, an interest in my property, and as a result of that belief you improve that property or otherwise alter your position; and assume, further, that I acquiesce in your doing so. (A typical modern example is where you are my cohabitee, and believing you have an interest in our joint home, you pay for an extension to it.)[122] An equity arises in your favour, which according to the facts may entitle you to the full interest you hoped for or thought you had, or such lesser interest (such as a lien for expenditure) as amounts to the minimum necessary to do justice between you and me.[123] In practice, this covers much the same ground as the previous head of recovery; indeed, it is rather wider, since it covers disappointment as to what may happen in the future as well as traditional mistake.[124] However, it is not really a restitutionary claim, since (a) it does not depend on benefit to the other party – indeed, mere expenditure may trigger it, whether or not it benefits anyone[125] – and (b) while, on the facts, the equitable remedy may be equal to the benefit received, there is no requirement that it must be: it may be either greater or less according to the circumstances.

In any case, it is arguable that these cases of acquiescence are not really an exception to the general rule. In them, the claimant gets a remedy not because he was mistaken, but because the defendant accepted what he had done (indeed, the claimant need not have been mistaken at all, though he often will have been). If so, they really belong below, in Chapter 5 on 'Free acceptance'.

---

120 In fact, her claim was defeated because of countervailing benefits she herself had received. It is also doubtful whether there was genuine acquiescence, since it was arguable that the true owner of the house in fact shared the claimant's mistake. If so, then arguably her acquiescence should not have been effective.

121 Ie, the doctrine stemming from such cases as *Dillwyn v Llewellyn* (1862) 4 De G F and J 517 and *Ramsden v Dyson* (1866) LR 1 HL 129 (on which, see Birks, pp 290–92). A more modern example of the invocation of this doctrine by an innocent improver is *Cullen v Cullen* [1962] IR 268, where, however, the claim failed in the absence of proof of any relevant mistake.

122 As in, eg, *Pascoe v Turner* [1979] 2 All ER 945: see, too, *Re R(J) (A Ward of Court)* [1993] ILRM 657.

123 *Pascoe v Turner* [1979] 2 All ER 945.

124 As in *Ramsden v Dyson* itself. The plaintiffs improved properties belonging to the defendants in the belief, not that they were the owners, but that if they did so they would be granted long leases. See Birks, p 277 et seq.

125 *Crabb v Arun DC* [1976] Ch 179 and *Re R(J) (A Ward of Court)* [1993] ILRM 657 are good examples of estoppel where no benefit to the other party was shown.

(c) Services: non-pecuniary remedies

3-33   It will be seen that the acquiescence cases mentioned above[126] resulted not in a pecuniary award as such, but in a lien being created against the defendant's property. The solution of applying a non-pecuniary remedy, which avoids many of the problems of forced exchange,[127] is not, however, limited to such cases. For example, in *Banque Financière de la Cité v Parc (Battersea) Ltd*,[128] the claimants discharged certain obligations of X vis à vis a preferred creditor Y in the belief that the defendants had agreed to subordinate their own secured debt to the claimants. In fact, this belief was unfounded, and the effect of the claimants' payment was to promote, rather than subordinate, the defendants' debt. It was held by the House of Lords that the claimants were entitled, as against the defendants, to be subrogated to Y's rights in order to prevent what would otherwise be unjust enrichment on the defendants' part.

VI RESTITUTION FOR MISTAKE WHERE NEITHER ACCEPTANCE NOR ACQUIESCENCE

3-34   As mentioned in Chapter 1, the principle against forced exchange that lies behind cases like *Falcke v Scottish Imperial Assurance Co*[129] loses a good deal of moral authority where the exchange is one that the defendant would have had to make, or would have made anyway, even if it had not been forced on him by the claimant. This is the situation referred to by Goff & Jones[130] as 'incontrovertible benefit'. At present, however, despite the advocacy of a number of writers,[131] there is no clear authority in England or Ireland that a showing of 'incontrovertible benefit' will generally defeat a defence based on forced exchange in a mistake case. It should be noted, however, that in one situation[132] a tort defendant is allowed a set off which is difficult to explain except on this basis. A series of early cases[133] establishes that the *bona fide* miner

---

126 § 3-30 *et seq.*

127 If the lien is stated not to be enforceable unless and until the defendant sells the property, the 'forced exchange' objection drops away entirely.

128 [1999] 1 AC 221.

129 (1886) 34 Ch D 234.

130 Goff & Jones, p 23.

131 Besides Goff & Jones, see Birks, p 116; Virgo, *Principles of the Law of Restitution*, p 72 *et seq.* A few judicial *dicta* are not unfriendly towards the idea: see above, § 1-31.

132 Another possible situation arises where a trustee renders services in administering property subject to a trust or settlement later set aside. Assuming the putative trust instrument allows him to charge for his services, he has a lien over the assets for his charges which is enforceable against those actually entitled. See, eg, *Bullock v Lloyds Bank Ltd* [1955] Ch 317.

133 *Martin v Porter* (1839) 5 M & W 351; *Wood v Morewood* (1841) 3 QB 440n; see, too, the Scottish case of *Livingstone v Rawyards Coal Co Ltd* (1880) 5 App Cas 25.

of minerals which in fact belong to another (for example, because his excavations inadvertently cross his neighbour's boundary), while he must pay for what he has taken, can, if sued for conversion, claim credit for the cost of extraction. And, in the difficult case of *Greenwood v Bennett*,[134] the principle was taken rather further, so as to cover not only services relating to the getting of the chattel, but subsequent improvements as well. A bought a wrecked car from a thief, and in good faith repaired it. The car was then seized by the police: in interpleader proceedings between A and the owner C, it was held by the Court of Appeal that A was entitled to refuse to surrender the car except against repayment of his expenditure. This principle is, indeed, now statutory in England.[135] Lord Denning MR, in a minority, suggested that if C had already recovered the car independently, he would in addition have had a monetary claim against A: but this suggestion, which would amount to giving a generalised right of restitution for incontrovertible benefit rendered by mistake, has never been followed up in England or Ireland.[136]

VII EXCEPTIONS TO RECOVERY FOR MISTAKE

3-35   Besides the general defences to restitutionary claims, such as change of position and *bona fide* purchase, there are a number of specific points arising particularly in connection with mistake.

(a) Risk

3-36   It must be possible for a potential claimant to take the risk of a given mistake, thus effectively waiving any claim to recovery. Imagine, for instance, that, having heard that you have got a place at university, I give you £1,000; but I say at the same time that even if my information is wrong, you can keep the money. Even if I would not have made the gift but for the information received (and hence, you cannot show lack of causation) a successful claim for restitution must be inconceivable. A more topical example would be where a contract between a buyer and seller provides that no claim in respect of overpayment of an invoice will lie unless made within three days: clearly the buyer takes the risk of any mistake coming to light after that time.

3-37   Agreement to accept the risk may presumably also be implied: and, it is suggested that, in practice, there will be many cases where the only reasonable interpretation of a transaction will be that the person rendering the benefit took

---

134 [1973] QB 195.
135 Torts (Interference with Goods) Act 1977, s 6, also in force in NI (there is no equivalent in the Republic, where the situation remains governed by the common law).
136 But it has in Canada: eg, *Gidney v Shark* [1995] 5 WWR 385.

the risk of a given mistake. You see a book of negligible market value on my shelf and ask me if I am prepared to give it to you; I do so, not knowing that you have found an eccentric collector willing to pay £1,000 for it. It is submitted that I have (and should have) no claim against you: this is one of the risks that a donor takes. Again, suppose a bank honours a cheque having forgotten, not that it has been stopped, but that the drawer has insufficient funds to cover it. Can the bank recover the amount from the payee? On the preponderance of the authorities, the answer is 'No'.[137] Although the reason given in the cases is the now untenable theory that the mistake must go to liability vis à vis the payee, it is suggested that this is still the law: on a proper interpretation, the bank should be regarded as taking the risk of this sort of mistake.

(b) Compromise

3-38   Most payments to compromise claims involve no mistake anyway. You claim I owe you £1,000; I think your claim is bad, but pay you £500 to get rid of it. I cannot claim I was mistaken about anything. But, this is not always so. Suppose I think your claim is in fact good: even so, I may in practice be able to induce you to compromise it for, say, 90% of its value. Nevertheless, it seems clear that I cannot recover my payment even if I later discover that I had a good defence after all.[138]

(c) Benefits rendered in the face of litigation

3-39   There is a rule, grounded in public policy, that payment made (or other benefit rendered) in the face of litigation cannot form the subject of restitutionary recovery even though the claim later turns out to have been ill founded: the defendant cannot, as it were, have two bites at the cherry.[139]

---

137 See *Pollard v Bank of England* (1871) LR 6 QB 623, and *National Westminster Bank Ltd v Barclays Bank Ltd* [1974] 3 All ER 834, p 841 (Kerr J). *Contra*, however, *Lloyds Bank plc v Independent Insurance Co Ltd* [2000] QB 110.

138 Cf *Cooke v Wright* (1861) 1 B and S 559; *The Ypatia Halcaussi* [1985] 2 Lloyd's Rep 364.

139 Eg, *Moore v Fulham Vestry* [1895] 1 QB 399; *William Whiteley Ltd v R* (1909) 101 LT 741 (the latter apparently accepted as good on this point in *Woolwich Building Society v Inland Revenue Comrs (No 2)* [1993] AC 70, p 165 *et seq*).

CHAPTER 4

DURESS AND UNCONSCIENTIOUS DEALING

4-1 Some means of persuading others to do what one wants are entirely justifiable. Others are not. This is a point that any legal system has to recognise. Extracting a princely sum from your neighbour in exchange for a ransom strip which will let him develop his own land at great profit, or accepting a high figure in settlement of a *bona fide* but doubtful legal claim you have against him, are at one end of the scale. Extorting a benefit by threatening to beat him up, or buying up his property at a knock-down price by acting as a self-appointed business adviser and then abusing his trust, are at the other. And there are more equivocal cases, for example, where you persuade him to pay more for work you have already agreed to do by saying (truthfully) that you cannot afford to perform it at the stipulated price. Not surprisingly, the drawing of the line between acceptable and unacceptable pressure, and the question of recovery of benefits rendered as a result of the latter, form a well established subject within the law of restitution.

4-2 This chapter is divided into two parts. English law draws a fairly clear distinction between (a) duress proper, which deals with the effect of pressure which is actually unlawful, and (b) other, more fluid forms of protection against unfair pressure – most importantly, equitable relief in respect of undue influence, and a few other exceptional cases of protection against blatantly unconscionable exploitation.[1] This chapter will largely reflect that division

One feature makes relief under this head a good deal simpler than for mistake. In mistake, the person seeking to impugn a contract faces a much higher threshold than someone merely seeking to recover a non-contractual benefit.[2] In duress, by contrast, it is invariably assumed that there is no difference between the degree of duress (or other exploitation) necessary to attack a contract and that required to trigger restitution for a non-contractual benefit.[3] It follows that benefits rendered pursuant to a contract fall to be treated in virtually the same way as those provided where there is no contractual relation between the parties.

---

1   See generally, Cartwright, *Unequal Bargaining*, Chapters 7–9.
2   Above, § 3-17.
3   But cf Burrows, p 167, suggesting that the introduction of some such distinction might be helpful.

I BENEFITS RENDERED UNDER DURESS

Forms of duress

4-3   As a concept, duress can be divided into two categories. These are: (a) direct unlawful violence to the person; (b) other unlawful pressure falling short of actual personal violence. This does not, of course, mean that relief is unavailable for forms of pressure which are not themselves unlawful: however, cases of this sort are dealt with not as duress, but under the separate doctrines covered in the second part of this chapter.

(a) Direct violence

4-4   There are, understandably, few decided cases on this subject. Nevertheless, there is no doubt that money paid as a result of violence or the threat of it is recoverable as money had and received.[4] It is, moreover, enough for these purposes if the threat was a cause of the payment: it does not have to have been the sole cause.[5] There is little, if any, authority on chattels transferred as a result of the threat of personal violence: but, they can doubtless be recovered by suing in conversion, on the basis that no property at all passes.[6] And, it is suggested, if restitution is available for chattels, parallel recovery must be possible in respect of other property, such as land or shares, which are not transferable by mere delivery, and in respect of services rendered.

All the decided cases seem to deal with threats to the claimant himself and not to a third party. Nevertheless, there is no reason to think that any different result would follow in the case of threats to others. It would be extremely odd if a bank could not recover money paid to a robber who threatened to shoot an innocent and unconnected hostage.

(b) Other unlawful pressure ('economic duress')

The general principle

4-5   This is less straightforward than violence, if only because those threatening violence invariably know they are acting unlawfully and hence deserve no

---

4   See the old Irish case of *Blackwood's Lessee v Gregg* (1831) Hayes 277, and the Privy Council's decision (on appeal from New South Wales) in *Barton v Armstrong* [1976] AC 104.

5   *Barton v Armstrong* [1976] AC 104, above. This was the reason why this case was appealed to the Privy Council.

6   See *ibid*, p 120, where Lord Cross said that a contract induced by a threat of violence would be void. It seems to follow from this that no property would pass in chattels transferred pursuant to it. By contrast, it may well be that less egregious forms of duress make a contract (and hence any underlying transfers of property) merely voidable: see *Pao On v Lau Yiu Long* [1980] AC 614, pp 635–36.

indulgence, whereas other threats, while wrongful, may well be made in perfect good faith. For example, in a contractual dispute, one party may well threaten a course of action which in fact amounts to a breach of contract, but nevertheless believe that he is acting entirely in accordance with his rights.

Notwithstanding this, it is now clear that any threat to commit a tort or breach of contract *prima facie* amounts to duress, and hence potentially allows recovery of any benefits thereby obtained. This was originally established in the case of money paid to obtain the release of goods wrongfully detained, where old authority confirmed that such payments could be recovered as money had and received. So, in *Astley v Reynolds*,[7] the English Court of Queen's Bench had no difficulty in allowing recovery where a pawnbroker demanded a sum in excess of what was in fact owing before he would release plate pledged to him. And, more recently, in *The Alev*,[8] shipowners who wrongfully refused to deliver goods to the owners unless the latter paid freight due from the charterers (but not from them) were ordered to repay it.

4-6   Since *Astley v Reynolds*, the rule has been generalised. Today, money is *prima facie* recoverable – and no doubt similar relief is available in respect of benefits in kind – if provided to avert[9] the threat of any act wrongful vis à vis the payer, such as a tort or breach of contract. Furthermore, it does not seem to matter whether or not the person making the threat believed it was lawful or otherwise acted in good faith.[10] Thus, in *The Universe Sentinel*,[11] money paid to a trade union to induce it to lift the tortious 'blacking' of a vessel in a Welsh port was held recoverable even though it seems that the union thought itself entitled in law to act as it did.

Tort cases, apart from threats to withhold goods (which technically amounts to conversion,[12] and in Ireland detinue as well), tend in practice to involve industrial disputes and the threat of unlawful industrial action. Typical is *The Universe Sentinel*[13] itself, where shipowners successfully recovered sums paid to a trade union organisation against the threat of tortious action against the vessel.

---

7   (1731) 2 Str 915. See, too, *Maskell v Horner* [1915] 3 KB 106 (threatened seizure of goods by market franchisee to enforce payment of tolls not owing).

8   [1989] 1 Lloyd's Rep 138.

9   Or, no doubt, partly to avert: compare *Barton v Armstrong* [1976] AC 104, above, § 4-4.

10 But honest belief may be relevant where the defendant alleges that any payment was irrecoverable as money paid to compromise an honest claim, since this defence will not apply if the payee knew his claim was bad. Cf the New Zealand decision in *Moyes and Groves Ltd v Radiation (NZ) Ltd* [1982] 1 NZLR 368.

11 [1983] AC 366. Cf *Atlas Express Ltd v Kafco Ltd* [1989] 1 All ER 641, where the carriers seem all along to have been acting on their own honest (though, as it turned out, erroneous) interpretation of the contract.

12 As in *Astley v Reynolds* (1731) 2 Str 915, above.

13 [1983] AC 366.

4-7   Cases where restitution has been given in respect of threats to break a contract have been more varied. In the classic contract case of *D & C Builders Ltd v Rees*[14] the partial release of a debt in face of a refusal to pay which would have tipped the creditor into insolvency was held by Lord Denning MR to have been tainted by duress. More recent cases have involved threats by a parent company to withdraw support from a subsidiary leaving the other contracting party with a worthless claim for damages,[15] and (more commonly) refusal to perform contractual obligations at a time when it is impossible or impracticable to find alternative sources of supply. Thus in *The Atlantic Baron*,[16] shipbuilders in breach of contract refused to deliver a vessel unless paid an extra 10% over the agreed price to cover a devaluation in the US dollar. The buyers complied: having safely got the ship, they then sought their money back. Mocatta J held that they would have been able to recover the extra sum had they not subsequently affirmed the transaction. And in *Atlas Express Ltd v Kafco Ltd*,[17] a contract case where carriers wrongfully declined to transport an urgent consignment of goods unless the consignors agreed to a surcharge, the consignors successfully resisted an action for the surcharge on the basis that they had agreed under duress.

A further line of authority ought to be mentioned here, holding that office-holders, or semi-public utilities such as railway companies, who demanded fees for services over and above those permitted by statute, had to repay the excess. A number of old cases justified recovery on the basis of an unlawful threat that otherwise, the services would not be forthcoming.[18] But this raises difficulties. First, the presence of a threat, which is essential to a claim in duress,[19] is by no means clear in all the cases. Secondly, even where it is present, it is not clear whether non-provision of such services is necessarily wrongful in the sense of giving rise to liability in damages. At least since the decision in the *Woolwich* case[20] in England, it is (it is suggested) better to regard these as a form of recovery on the basis of public law.

4-8   It is not clear whether duress will apply to benefits rendered as a result of other wrongful acts not amounting to breaches of contract or torts. It must be at least arguable, however, that an analogous result would be reached where a threat of a breach of trust was used to extort money. In practice, the point may not be very important, since most such wrongs involve breach of fiduciary duty, and

---

14 [1966] 2 QB 617.
15 As in *The Siboen and The Sibotre* [1976] 1 Lloyd's Rep 293 (where, however, the claim failed on the facts).
16 See also *Pao On v Lau Yiu Long* [1980] AC 614.
17 [1989] QB 833.
18 Eg, *GW Rly v Sutton* (1869) LR 4 HL 226, p 249 (England); *GS and W Rly v Robertson* (1878) 2 LR Ir 548 (Ireland).
19 *Nurdin v Peacock plc v Ramsden & Co Ltd* [1999] 1 All ER 941, p 950.
20 *Woolwich Building Society v Inland Revenue Comrs (No 2)* [1993] AC 70.

recovery from a fiduciary who threatens to breach that duty can just as well be had on the basis of the rule prohibiting untoward profits by fiduciaries.

The need for unlawfulness

4-9   Hitherto, there has been little if any sign of the idea of duress being extended beyond unlawful conduct, or of recovery being allowed where it is absent. Thus, although the claimants succeeded in *The Universe Sentinel*,[21] discussed above, it was made clear that they would have failed had the industrial action been protected from tortious liability under the industrial relations legislation then in force. Again, a similar point fell directly for decision in *CTN Cash & Carry Ltd v Gallagher Ltd*.[22] There, money was paid by a customer to its supplier over and above what was owed, the reason being a threat by the supplier that, unless the disputed payment was forthcoming, it would withdraw future credit facilities and effectively paralyse that customer's business. The Court of Appeal had little difficulty in holding the payment irrecoverable, on the basis that the supplier had no obligation to advance credit to anyone and hence was entitled to act as he had. The fact that in practice, such credit might be vital to the claimant's business, was irrelevant.[23]

There is no direct authority on whether a threat of this sort must be unlawful *as against the payer*, in the sense that if it was carried out, the latter would have a cause of action for damages in respect of it. There are, however, good reasons not to insist strictly on such a requirement. Suppose you contract to supply goods not to me, but to a private company in which I own all the shares: you then threaten to break that contract unless I personally pay you £1,000. It would seem excessively technical to deny my claim to restitution merely because your contractual duty was owed to the company and not to me. This view receives some support from *Pao On v Lau Yiu Long*.[24] A agreed to sell B Ltd a building in exchange for shares to be issued by B Ltd: A then refused to perform unless C, the majority shareholder in B Ltd, unilaterally guaranteed the value of the shares by giving a 'put option' over them. The Privy Council certainly assumed that this could amount to duress, even though the threat was not against C personally (the claim, in the event, failed on the facts).

4-10   Of course, this should not mean that any threat to commit a wrongful act against anybody will give rise to restitutionary recovery: there must presumably be some close connection between the payer and the victim of the threat such that

---

21 [1983] AC 366.

22 [1994] 4 All ER 714.

23 But note Steyn LJ, p 719, refusing absolutely to rule out the possibility of an action based on 'lawful act duress'. 'In this complex and changing branch of the law,' he said, 'I deliberately refrain from saying "never".'

24 [1980] AC 614. See too *Fell v Whitaker* (1871) LR 7 QB 120, where a husband recovered payments made in order to obtain release of his wife's goods. And cf *Mutual Finance Ltd v Wetton and Sons Ltd* [1937] 2 KB 389, setting aside a guarantee executed by a family company in the face of a threat to prosecute the major shareholder's son.

the payer is likely to be directly affected by it. If my payment of £1,000 to you resulted from your threat to withhold property from some entirely unconnected third party, my action would fail, either because my act would count as voluntary, or because of the principle of reasonableness (on which, see below).

One further point on unlawfulness. It is suggested that the mere fact that an act is criminal does not, as such, make it unlawful: there is no generalised right of restitution for criminal gains, any more than there is a generalised right of action in tort where crime causes loss. The point arises in particular in connection with blackmail, where the threat to reveal the victim's past is criminal but not tortious; can the victim seek to reclaim moneys paid to the blackmailer? Presumably he can:[25] but, despite certain unguarded *dicta* that blackmail amounts to duress,[26] in no reported case has such an action succeeded on that basis: and (it is suggested) it is better to regard any right of recovery, if it exists, as based on undue influence or some similar doctrine in equity.[27]

Causation, coercion and reasonableness in duress cases

4-11   In *Barton v Armstrong*,[28] the Privy Council held that the prospect of violence sufficed to give relief provided it was a cause of the victim's action: as in the law of tort, it did not have to be the sole, or even the predominant, causal factor. Although it could be argued that violence is more egregious than other unlawful threats and hence more in need of penalising, it is suggested that a similar rule ought to apply to all cases of duress. Admittedly, this might cause problems in the commercial context, where the victim of a threatened breach of contract succumbed with the intent to close the transaction, but (it is suggested) cases of that sort could be dealt with under the rubric of waiver or donative intent (discussed below).

4-12   More awkward is the suggestion in *Pao On v Lau Yiu Long*[29] that the metaphysics of the will are somehow in account in cases of this sort, even where all the other ingredients of a duress claim are otherwise present. In that case, the buyers of a property company executed a guarantee in favour of the sellers, which had not been a feature of the original contract, as a result of a threat by the

---

25   Cf *Davies v London & Provincial Marine Insurance Co* (1878) 8 Ch D 469. Presumably, however, recovery might in certain cases be barred by the maxim *ex turpi causa non oritur actio*: cf the Irish decision in *Brady v Flood* (1841) 6 Circuit Cases 309.

26   *Thorne v Motor Trade Ass'n* [1937] AC 797, p 821 *et seq* (Lord Wright). See, too, *Hardie and Lane Ltd v Chiltern* [1928] 1 KB 663, where the same seems to have been assumed.

27   Cf the cases exemplified by *Williams v Bayley* (1866) LR 1 HL 200, discussed below, § 4-22 *et seq*.

28   [1976] AC 104.

29   [1980] AC 614, p 635. Strictly, this case concerned a claim to set aside a contract rather than a claim for the return of money paid: but nothing seems to turn on this. See too *The Siboen and The Sibotre* [1976] 1 Lloyd's Rep 293, p 336 (Kerr J); *The Proodos C* [1980] 2 Lloyd's Rep 390.

sellers to break that contract. They later sought to escape from the arrangement on the basis of duress, but the Privy Council, speaking through Lord Scarman, denied relief. Despite the undoubted wrongfulness of the sellers' threat, it was said, duress required in addition a 'coercion of the will', and that was not present. The buyer, it was said, had merely taken a hard-headed commercial decision as to what was in his best interests; and, having done so, he should be expected to abide by it.

This alleged principle must, however, be regarded with some scepticism. Any decision to succumb to a wrongful threat is, in one sense, a commercial decision, since few people give in to menaces unless they feel it is in their immediate interest to do so. But, if this barred recovery as such, a great deal of the law of duress would simply disappear. In practice, it is submitted that this does not really amount to a separate requirement for restitution at all,[30] and that all 'no coercion' cases are better read as cases where recovery is denied for other reasons such as waiver or disproportionality. As more recent authority suggests,[31] the fundamental question is, and should remain, whether the pressure used was of the sort regarded by the law as legitimate. Indeed, what seems to have swayed the court in *Pao On* itself was evidence that the buyers thought it most unlikely that the guarantee would, in the event, 'bite', and hence that they were happy to give it; that is, that there was in fact an intent to give the guarantee 'in any event'.[32]

4-13 This said, the fact remains that an unlawful threat and a causal relation, while necessary conditions of relief, are not necessarily sufficient.

First, it seems that relief will be denied if the victim's response is unreasonable or disproportionate; by way of a loose analogy to the rule on mitigation of loss in tort or contract, if some other course of action is reasonably open to the victim, he is expected to take it. For example, suppose a seller of goods states, some weeks before delivery is due, that he will not deliver unless paid an extra 10% there and then. Whether the buyer can reclaim his payment ought to depend on whether he can reasonably be expected to find alternative supplies, if he can, he should be denied recovery. *Atlas Express Ltd v Kafco Ltd*,[33] already mentioned above, is instructive in this context. There, Tucker J clearly regarded it as relevant to the defendants' claim for relief that at the time of the threatened breach of contract, time was too short to give them any opportunity to make arrangements for alternative transport. Again, in *The Atlantic Baron*,[34] Mocatta J clearly thought that had it been reasonable to expect the owners to

---

30 Cf the Australian case of *Crescendo v Westpac* (1988) 19 NSWLR 40, pp 45–46, where McHugh JA trenchantly rejected the 'coercion' test in *Pao On* as misconceived.

31 Cf the remarks of Lord Diplock in *The Universe Sentinel* [1983] AC 366, p 384.

32 See, especially, *Pao On's* case [1980] AC 614, p 635.

33 [1989] QB 833.

34 [1979] QB 705.

take other steps, such as suing the yard for breach of contract, restitution could have been denied on that ground.

In commercial disputes, moreover, this may well be a highly significant limitation on relief. Assume a building dispute: the site owner threatens to throw the builder off the site unless the latter does certain work which the site owner asserts, but he denies, is due under the contract. If there is a quick and easy means to settle the dispute, for example, by an immediate arbitration, the builder might well be expected to use it, rather than doing the work and then attempting to claim the cost.[35]

Nevertheless, one suspects the courts will follow the practice in cases concerning mitigation of damage, and allow reasonable latitude to victims. Especially where business decisions have to be taken quickly, they should get the benefit of the doubt, and only in the case of clearly unreasonable conduct should relief be refused. Furthermore, it is suggested that – again mirroring the law on mitigation – what is reasonable should be seen from the point of view of the victim, taking account where necessary of his own financial position and vulnerability. Thus, in the face of threatened non-payment, it clearly ought to be relevant whether the victim faced the risk of insolvency or other substantial loss, as in *D & C Builders v Rees*;[36] if he did not, and could be expected to absorb any temporary cash flow difficulties, then relief should be less forthcoming. Such a position also has the advantage of meeting the point made by Burrows[37] that however unsympathetic one feels towards the victim who acts unreasonably, the mere fact that he is weak or foolish should not, as such, bar his claim.

4-14   It has been suggested elsewhere[38] that relief for economic duress ought to be further limited. In particular, it has been said that the rules of duress should not apply where the threatener acts to preserve his own cash flow or solvency (rather than simply to exploit the other party's weakness),[39] or alternatively, where he acts in order to relieve himself of a bargain that was clearly bad – either from the outset, or as a result of some unexpected supervening event falling short of frustration. But this proposal raises difficulties, and on balance it is suggested that it is misconceived. First, motives, especially those of corporate parties in commercial disputes (which the majority of economic duress cases are about) are difficult to fathom at best, and where discernible are unlikely to appear without expensive litigation. Secondly, while re-negotiation of losing contracts ought not to be discouraged, there are dangers in providing an incentive to contractors to force this by self-help: to do this is profoundly subversive of the rationale of commercial contracts. Thirdly, contractors who

---

35   Cf the instructive Canadian decision in *Peter Kiewit's Sons v Eakins Construction Ltd* [1960] SCR 361.

36   [1966] 2 QB 617.

37   Burrows, p 178.

38   *Ibid*, p 179 *et seq*.

39   Or, to put it another way, where the coercer acts 'in good faith': cf Birks, p 183.

wish to re-negotiate ought to be encouraged to do so timeously, while alternative sources of supply are open to their co-contractors. And, lastly, situations of economic duress frequently require quick action by victims acting on clear advice: to introduce fluid criteria such as whether a bargain is clearly bad can only frustrate this purpose.

'Defences' to duress claims

Waiver and ratification

4-15 The law must recognise that in the nature of things, one can make a donation, even to a coercer. Even in the extreme case of threatened violence, it is perfectly possible (though no doubt unlikely) for the victim of a street robbery to turn the other cheek and make a gift of his wallet to the robber: if he genuinely intended to do so, then even though the gift would not have been made but for the robber's threat (thus disposing of any argument on causation), there is no reason why he should thereafter be able to recover it. Indeed, there is an important principle running through the law of duress that the restitutionary action is barred if the recipient of the benefit can show[40] that the victim intended to waive any right of recovery.[41] As Lord Reading CJ put it in *Maskell v Horner*:[42]

> If a person with knowledge of the facts pays money, which he is not in law bound to pay, and in circumstances implying that he is paying it voluntarily to close the transaction, he cannot recover it. Such a payment is in law like a gift, and the transaction cannot thereafter be reopened.

4-16 The otherwise awkward contract case of *The Siboen and The Sibotre*[43] is perhaps best interpreted in this way. A company chartered a ship at a rate that proved improvidently high. The charterer's parent corporation (on which it was entirely reliant for funds) contacted the shipowners and threatened to put the charterer into liquidation unless they agreed to reduce the amount of hire. The owners did so: later they argued that the reduction in hire was unenforceable against them since it had been obtained by duress. This plea was rejected on the ostensible basis that there had been no 'coercion of their will';[44] but a better view, hinted at by Kerr J,[45] was that the alteration had, in any event, been voluntarily made. This is likely to be highly significant in practice: one suspects that a plea of this kind will often succeed where commercial contracts are renegotiated in order to ensure the future co-operation of one party or to cement future relations.

---

40 This, it is suggested, ought to be the position. But cf the Australian decision in *Mason v New South Wales* (1959) 102 CLR 108, where Windeyer J suggested that it was for the claimant to prove that his payment was not voluntary.

41 Or (which amounts to the same thing) 'close the transaction'.

42 [1915] 3 KB 106, p 118.

43 [1976] 1 Lloyd's Rep 293.

44 Criticised above, § 4-12.

45 See [1976] 1 Lloyd's Rep 293, p 336.

It is suggested that the question whether such a donative intention, or intent to close the transaction, is present is viewed objectively.[46] Its existence is simply a matter of evidence. The presence of a protest is neither necessary[47] nor sufficient[48] to negative it (though victims are well advised to make one since, in practice, cases will be rare where a person who has done so will be held to have acted voluntarily).[49] A declaration by the claimant that he acted voluntarily is of evidential force, but for obvious reasons cannot be conclusive: if extorted in the same way as the payment, it is, not surprisingly, just as ineffectual.

4-17   Restitution may apparently be negatived by subsequent ratification or affirmation, as much as by an *animus donandi* at the time. This is neatly illustrated by the facts of *The Atlantic Baron*,[50] already mentioned. There, it will be remembered, some months before a ship was due for delivery to buyers, the builders said they would not hand it over unless the buyers increased their subsequent stage payments by 10%. The buyers gave in and did so, but made no subsequent protest, even after it had become apparent that they would get the ship in any event. Mocatta J held that although the extra payments would originally have been recoverable, the owners' later inaction amounted to a ratification of the renegotiated transaction and negatived any restitutionary right of recovery.

Benefits rendered under the threat of litigation

4-18   Benefits rendered in response to a demand backed by litigation, or the express or implied threat of it, are irrecoverable.[51] The rule is traditionally explained on the basis that such benefits are deemed to be 'voluntary': but any voluntariness here is likely to be largely fictional, and it is submitted that the rule is better regarded as a matter of public policy. Settlements should be upheld; those who use the court's processes in good faith ought generally to be able to retain the fruits of their action unless deprived of them by the ordinary process of litigation.

As a principle of public policy, this rule is subject to exceptions. In particular, it is limited to litigation conducted in good faith; there is no reason to protect those who abuse the legal process by bringing claims they know to be bad.[52]

---

46   Thus, in *The Atlantic Baron* [1979] QB 705, the buyers were held to have ratified their payment despite a finding that they had never subjectively intended to do any such thing.

47   See *Maskell v Horner* [1915] 3 KB 106.

48   Eg, *Twyford v Manchester Corp* [1946] Ch 236.

49   *Twyford v Manchester Corp* [1946] Ch 236, where this happened, was regarded with some little scepticism by Glidewell LJ in the Court of Appeal in *Woolwich Building Society v Inland Revenue Comrs (No 2)* [1993] AC 70.

50   [1979] QB 705. See, too, *The Siboen and The Sibotre* [1976] 1 Lloyd's Rep 293.

51   See, eg, *Moore v Fulham Vestry* [1995] 1 QB 399.

52   See, eg, the old case of *Cadaval (Duke) v Collins* (1836) 4 A and E 858.

And, for constitutional reasons, it applies with less vigour to actions at common law for recovery of taxes and other inputs paid to public authorities.[53]

Remedies for benefits rendered under duress

4-19   Most cases of duress concern payments of money, in which case the action for money had and received provides the obvious pecuniary remedy. In addition, in so far as a proprietary remedy is available in the case of payments by mistake,[54] there seems no reason why a parallel remedy by way of trust should not be available in addition in duress cases. Some support for this comes from the Supreme Court of Ireland in *Murphy v AG*,[55] where it was held that such a trust arose in the case of payments of tax unconstitutionally levied.

As for property transferred, in the absence of unequivocal authority it is suggested that such transfers are voidable in the case of economic duress,[56] though it is arguable that no title at all passes in chattels transferred under the threat of immediate violence.[57]

There is little authority respecting services rendered. But, it seems obvious that payment should be due, either on the basis of *quantum meruit* or free acceptance. To adapt the facts of *D and C Builders v Rees*,[58] suppose that in that case, Mr Rees had demanded, not that the builder release part of the price, but that he should carry out further work not required by the contract. It would be very odd if the builder did not have a restitutionary claim for the extra work done in such circumstances. Clearly, it should not lie in the mouth of a coercer to say that he did not want, or agree to pay for, the services he got.[59]

II OTHER FORMS OF PRESSURE

4-20   As we mentioned above, our use of the word 'duress' will, for clarity's sake, be limited to threats to commit *unlawful* acts. It would be possible for a legal system wedded to an extreme version of *laissez-faire* to limit relief to such cases: but neither English nor Irish law has ever done this. On the contrary: there is no

---

53   *Murphy v AG* [1982] IR 241; *Woolwich Building Society v Inland Revenue Comrs (No 2)* [1993] AC 70. See below, Chapter 12.

54   On the basis of *Chase Manhattan Bank NA v Israel-British Bank Ltd* [1981] Ch 105. For the correctness or otherwise of this decision, see above, § 3-20.

55   [1982] IR 241.

56   Cf *Pao On v Lau Yiu Long* [1980] AC 614, pp 635–36.

57   Cf *Barton v Armstrong* [1976] AC 104, p 120, where Lord Cross said that a contract entered into in such circumstances was void. If this is right, it would seem to follow *a fortiori* that a purported transfer of property would be similarly ineffective.

58   [1966] 2 QB 617.

59   Cf Burrows's concept of 'reprehensible seeking-out' (Burrows, p 15) and the discussion of the same issue in this book below, § 5-13 *et seq*.

doubt that there are other forms of unacceptable, if not actually unlawful, pressure which are equally capable of grounding restitution. To these we now turn.

(a) Undue influence

Generally

4-21 Undue influence is an equitable doctrine of protean characteristics, providing not only a head of restitutionary recovery, but also (like duress) a means of attacking a contract, trust or will.[60] It is a wide and flexible principle, and encompasses a large number of different sorts of coercion and exploitation.

Nevertheless, for the purposes of the law of restitution, it can profitably be rationalised as involving the giving of a benefit under two sorts of pressure. These are:

- threats to commit certain acts that, although not themselves unlawful, are frowned on by the law; and

- the use or abuse of moral authority or a relationship of trust or dependence, whether such relationship be actual or perceived.

Threats and undue influence

4-22 The *prima facie* position taken by Anglo-Irish law is that if you have a right to do something, you are equally entitled to keep any gains made by threatening to do it:[61] in other words, your motives for exercising an established right will not be scrutinised for the purposes of the law of restitution, any more than for the law of tort.[62] But, this is far from an absolute rule. Certain kinds of conduct, while not in themselves wrongful, are nevertheless not permitted to be used for the collateral purpose of extorting a gain, and if they are so used, any money paid or other benefits conferred will be recoverable. To this extent, undue influence acts as a sort of 'quasi-duress'.

4-23 Two kinds of action in particular come under this head. One is threats to divulge information, and similar menaces covered by the law of blackmail. It is generally assumed that money paid to avert this threat can be recovered,[63] despite the fact that there may well be nothing unlawful in a blackmailer's disclosing unpalatable facts about his victim.

---

60 As a result, many authorities referred to in this part will be concerned with the validity of contracts rather than restitutionary liability proper.

61 See *CTN Cash and Carry Ltd v Gallagher Ltd* [1994] 4 All ER 714, and above, § 4-9.

62 Cf *Bradford Corp v Pickles* [1895] AC 587.

63 Assumed in cases such as *Thorne v Motor Trade Ass'n* [1937] AC 797, p 821 *et seq*. See too *Hardie and Lane Ltd v Chiltern* [1928] 1 KB 663.

The other head involves threats to invoke the criminal process. If you have stolen my money, I am of course free to prosecute you, and indeed to demand reasonable compensation from you by threatening to do so.[64] Presumably such compensation, once paid, is irrecoverable. But, I cannot use this threat to obtain more than reasonable compensation, nor to obtain reparation from anyone else. Thus, in *Williams v Bayley*,[65] a father gave security to his son's employers to cover certain defalcations by his son, having been informed that unless he did so, the son would be faced with prosecution and the prospect of a stiff sentence for forgery. He successfully sued to have the security cancelled.

It is unclear whether other rights in private law, such as the right to terminate a long standing contractual relationship, will be thus characterised so as to give rise to restitutionary recovery in cases of abuse, but the possibility must remain open.[66]

4-24 In addition, however, it is important to remember that unlike private persons and bodies, public authorities are, in exercising their rights, almost invariably bound to do so for adequate and relevant reasons. What if an authority demands a sum in circumstances where its decision can be challenged as having been made for illegitimate reasons?[67] Although there is no clear authority on the matter, it seems right on principle that moneys paid to, or other benefits conferred on, a public authority in such circumstances should be recoverable[68] – as indeed they are where the demand is wholly *ultra vires*.[69]

Undue influence: moral authority and reliance

4-25 The typical situation covered here is the improper taking advantage of a position of confidence or ascendancy, but in a way falling short of outright misrepresentation. Suppose, for example, a husband bullies his wife into mortgaging her share of the matrimonial home to support his business;[70] or a son, knowing his elderly parents rely entirely on his advice in such matters, causes them to guarantee a loan to him.[71] In either case, the transaction will be

---

64 A principle now enshrined by statute in England and NI: Criminal Law Act 1967, s 5 and Criminal Law (NI) Act 1967, s 5.

65 (1866) LR 1 HL 200. Also *Mutual Finance Ltd v Wetton & Sons Ltd* [1937] 2 KB 389.

66 Note that in *CTN Cash & Carry Ltd v Gallagher Ltd* [1994] 4 All ER 714, Steyn and Nicholls LJJ both pointedly refused to rule out such a possibility.

67 Cf *R v Richmond LBC ex p McCarthy & Stone Ltd* [1992] 2 AC 48, where a successful challenge was made to the practice of a local authority in charging for services that had to be provided gratis, namely, preliminary consideration of planning proposals. *Quaere* what would have happened had the applicants sought to recover any fees already paid.

68 As was indeed suggested by Goff LJ in *Wandsworth LBC v Winder* [1985] AC 461, p 480 (the point was not mentioned in the HL).

69 As in *Woolwich Building Society v Inland Revenue Comrs (No 2)* [1993] AC 70.

70 As in *CIBC Mortgages Ltd v Pitt* [1994] 1 AC 200; and cf *Langton v Langton* [1995] 2 FLR 890.

71 *Coldunell Ltd v Gallon* [1986] 1 All ER 429.

set aside, and restitution will be available on principle for any benefits transferred.

4-26   These are cases of actual influence: when it is proved, the transaction concerned may be avoided as a matter of course. But, undue influence goes a great deal further than this. Even where actual bullying or unconscientious persuasion cannot be shown, two presumptions aid the claimant.

First, where it is shown that the recipient was in a position of *de facto* influence, for instance, where the claimant was known to rely implicitly on him for protection of his interests, any benefit rendered is *prima facie* recoverable, or the arrangement liable to be set aside, as the case may be. Typical of the 19th century authorities is *Tate v Williamson*,[72] setting aside a sale of land by a bibulous and improvident youth at a considerable undervalue to a confidant of his. But, the principle retains its vigour today. More recently, it has found its *métier* in dealing with unfair advantage taken of aged relatives by younger members of the family[73] (and, indeed, of relatives generally),[74] of elderly farmers by over-astute neighbouring landowners,[75] of accident victims by insurers' representatives,[76] and of musicians by their publishers.[77] But, the categories are not closed, and any benefit proved to have been rendered as a result of overbearing influence or pressure may give rise to restitution.[78] It should be noted, moreover, that unfairness is viewed objectively: conscious wrongdoing is not necessary, still less dishonesty. All that is required is some kind of unconscionable pressure or influence.[79]

4-27   Secondly, and more importantly, certain specified relationships are presumed as a matter of law, until the contrary is shown, to put one party in a position of de facto reliance on the other.[80] Transactions between such parties are thus

---

72   (1866) LR 2 Ch App 55. Cf *Hargreave v Everard* (1856) 6 Ir Ch R 678 (gift by cohabitee: claim failed on the facts).

73   *Gregg v Kidd* [1956] IR 183 (nephew); cf *Coldunell Ltd v Gallon* [1986] 1 All ER 429 (though in the latter case, actual influence was proved).

74   Eg, *Gregg v Kidd* [1956] IR 183.

75   See *Goldsworthy v Brickell* [1987] 1 All ER 853; and cf *McGonigle v Black* (1988) unreported, Ir HC, referred to in Clark and Clarke, *Contract Cases and Materials*, p 576.

76   *Arrale v Costain Ltd* [1976] 1 Lloyd's Rep 98.

77   Eg, *O'Sullivan v Management Agency Ltd* [1985] 3 All ER 351 (finding unchallenged on appeal); *John v James* [1991] FSR 397.

78   Cf *CIBC Mortgages Ltd v Pitt* [1994] 1 AC 200 (husband's pressure on wife). See, too, *O'Flanagan v Ray-Ger* (1983) unreported, 28 April, Costello J and the Northern Irish decision in *McCrystal v O'Kane* [1986] NI 123.

79   '... the court interferes, not on the ground that any wrongful act has in fact been committed by the donee, but on the ground of public policy, and to prevent the relations between the parties and the influence arising therefrom being abused': Cotton LJ in *Allcard v Skinner* (1887) 36 Ch D 145, p 171. See, too, *John v James* [1991] FSR 397, where relief was given in the teeth of a clear finding of good faith.

80   The distinction between these cases and those found in the previous paragraph is well described by Slade LJ in *Bank of Credit and Commerce International Ltd v Aboody* [1990] 1 QB 923, p 953, and by Jones LJ in *Re Founds Estate* [1970] NI 139.

presumptively tainted with abuse of moral authority without the need to prove actual reliance or overbearing influence. Examples include solicitor and client,[81] doctor and patient,[82] religious enthusiast and acolyte,[83] trustee and beneficiary,[84] and parent and child;[85] though not employer and employee[86] or (perhaps oddly) husband and wife).[87] In such cases, benefits rendered by one to the other can be recovered unless they are proved to have been rendered voluntarily and independently. But, even here, the rule is not absolute: the inference of reliance is itself rebuttable where the facts are sufficiently out of the ordinary to indicate that the presumption ought not to apply.[88]

Where the exercise of undue influence is proved, or the inference that it has been exercised is not rebutted, any benefit is *prima facie* returnable: to prevent this conclusion, the recipient must in turn prove that the benefit was voluntarily conferred on him as a result of the independent judgment of the other party. Traditionally, this burden is discharged by showing that the latter had the benefit of, or at least had been offered access to, independent advice.[89] Nevertheless, the essential matter is voluntariness;[90] the fact of independent advice is evidentiary only, and of itself is neither necessary[91] nor sufficient.[92]

One further qualification needs to be mentioned. Although benefits proved to have resulted from actual misuse of a superior position are recoverable without more ado[93] (subject, where appropriate, to counter-restitution),[94] the claimant who cannot prove this and hence has to rely on either of the

---

81   *Wright v Carter* [1903] 1 Ch 27.

82   *Radcliffe v Price* (1902) 18 TLR 466.

83   *White v Meade* (1840) 2 Ir R Eq 420; *Allcard v Skinner* (1887) 36 Ch D 145. Cf *Roche v Sherrington* [1982] 1 WLR 599.

84   Eg, *Ellis v Barker* (1871) LR 7 Ch App 104.

85   Eg, *Croker v Croker* (1874) 4 ILT 181; *Lancashire Loans Ltd v Black* [1934] 1 KB 380. The same goes for guardian and ward: *Mulhallen v Marum* (1843) 3 Dr and W 317.

86   Cf *Crédit Lyonnais Nederland NV v Burch* [1997] 1 All ER 144, p 154 (Lord Millett) (though actual undue influence was there proved).

87   *Northern Banking Co v Carpenter* [1931] IR 268; *Midland Bank plc v Shepherd* [1908] 3 All ER 17. But see *Barclays Bank plc v O'Brien* [1994] 1 AC 180, below. The same goes, *a fortiori*, for unmarried cohabitees: *Hargreave v Everard* (1856) 6 Ir Ch R 678.

88   A clear, if recondite, example would be were a prominent Chancery silk to make a gift to his family solicitor. See, too, the decision in *Kirwan v Cullen* (1854) 2 Ir Ch R 322, where a gift to a religious superior was found to be untainted on the facts, since the relationship had been defunct for two years before the relevant time.

89   *Wright v Carter* [1903] 1 Ch 27.

90   It must be shown that the benefit was a 'spontaneous act of the donor' amounting to a 'free exercise of the donor's will': *Allcard v Skinner* (1887) 36 Ch D 145, p 171 (Cotton LJ).

91   See *Inche Noriah v Shaik Allie Bin Omar* [1929] AC 127, p 133 *et seq, per* Lord Hailsham, and *McCormack v Bennett* (1973) unreported, 2 July, Finlay P.

92   Eg, where the independent adviser himself acts on inadequate information: *Wright v Carter* [1903] 1 Ch 27, or (more controversially) in certain cases where the advice is not taken: *Royal Bank of Scotland plc v Etridge (No 2)* [1998] 4 All ER 705.

93   *CIBC Mortgages v Pitt* [1994] 1 AC 200.

94   Eg, *Mulhallen v Marum* (1843) 3 Dr and W 317.

presumptions referred to above is in a different position. Even if willing to return what he himself has got, he must show in addition that the transaction he seeks to attack left him substantially worse off as a result. This is the result of the House of Lords' decision in *National Westminster Bank plc v Morgan*,[95] where a wife mortgaged her share in the matrimonial home to a bank at her husband's insistence in circumstances where her relations with her husband raised a presumption of undue influence. She nevertheless failed to set aside the transaction because her interest was already subject to an existing charge, which was admitted to be perfectly valid; this charge was to be refinanced by the new one. She had, therefore, in Lord Scarman's words, suffered no 'manifest detriment'. This result is understandable: but the limits of the 'manifest detriment' principle are nevertheless unclear. In particular, there is no authority on whether the detriment must be financial. Suppose an elderly person, while under the influence of her solicitor, agrees to sell him at market value an *objet d'art* of large sentimental, but small pecuniary, value. There is much to be said for allowing her to undo this transaction, despite the decision in *Morgan*.[96]

'Defences' to undue influence claims

4-28   No doubt conduct such as subsequent acquiescence, which would bar a duress claim, will have the same effect in a case of undue influence; though in practice, this will tend to be subsumed under general equitable defences, such as the doctrine of *laches*.[97] Equally, the threat of litigation can no more amount to undue influence than to duress, and for the same reasons. This does not mean, however, that one party to litigation cannot come under the undue influence of the other on some independent ground: for example, if the defendant to a claim asks the claimant's advice what to do about it and makes it clear that he relies implicitly on his advice. In such a case, any money paid in settlement would, it is suggested, be recoverable.[98]

The so called 'defence' of *bona fide* purchase is also available, but is dealt with below, under Remedies.

(b) An extension of undue influence: the 'poor and ignorant' cases

4-29   Undue influence depends in the last resort on some abuse, conscious or not, of a position of trust. A perceptible line of authority, however, has extended equity's

---

95   [1985] AC 686.

96   And note that *Morgan's* case itself was regarded with some unease by Lord Browne-Wilkinson in *CIBC Mortgages Ltd v Pitt*: see [1994] 1 AC 200, p 207 *et seq*.

97   Which defeated the claim in, eg, *Allcard v Skinner* (1887) 36 Ch D 145, above. But claimants are fairly benignly treated in this respect: cf *O'Kelly v Glenny* (1846) 9 Ir Eq R 25 (12 years' delay not fatal).

98   Cf *Horry v Tate and Lyle Ltd* [1982] 2 Lloyd's Rep 417, setting aside a wholly inadequate settlement by a plaintiff in such circumstances.

interference further than this, by allowing a transaction to be set aside simply on the basis that:

- the exchange was objectively unequal;[99]

- the party attacking the transaction was 'poor or ignorant', so as to be seriously unable to look after his own interests, and in such a relation to the other that the latter can take an undue advantage of him;[100] and

- that party received no independent advice. Actual overreaching or sharp practice does not seem to be a prerequisite: it is probably sufficient that it would be obvious to a reasonable person that the transaction was one which the other party could not have consented to in a properly considered way.[101]

Typically, the cases have involved sales of land by youthful, elderly or incapable owners in need of ready cash, as in the leading case of *Fry v Lane*[102] in England and *Garvey v McMinn*[103] in Ireland. Another fruitful source of authority concerns transactions with improvident would-be heirs, as in the well known Irish decision in *Slator v Nolan*,[104] where a sale of a prospective inheritance in grossly unequal circumstances by a youth in need of ready cash was set aside.

4-30   Viewed simply as a source of contractual invalidity, this doctrine is of no direct restitutionary interest.[105] But, can it be extended more generally, to attack (for instance) gifts where, despite the lack of undue influence, the donee is seeking unconscionably to retain the fruits of the donor's improvidence? At first sight, the answer would seem to be yes, on the basis that a donee should not be in any better position than a purchaser: and, indeed, this seems to have been accepted in Ireland.[106] But this, if right, leads to one odd consequence: since it is in the nature of any gift worth having that it leaves the donor substantially worse off, all gifts by 'poor and ignorant' persons would be presumptively open to attack unless made under independent advice. Furthermore, it can be argued that the essence of the *Fry v Lane* doctrine is abuse of the bargaining process (the point being that the enforcement of unequal exchanges presupposes a degree of commercial awareness, and in its absence ought not to be readily available): if so, there is no reason to apply it to benefits rendered other than in a commercial

---

99   See *Smyth v Smyth* (1919) 53 ILTR 145.

100 See *Slator v Nolan* (1876) IR 11 Eq 367, p 409 (Sullivan MR).

101 Thus, in *Lydon v Coyne* (1946) 12 Ir JR 64 and *Cresswell v Potter* (1968) [1978] 1 WLR 255n, relief was given despite the seeming absence of any conscious overreaching.

102 (1888) 40 Ch D 312. See, too (England): *Evans v Llewellin* (1787) 1 Cox Eq Cas 333; (Ireland): *Grealish v Murphy* [1946] IR 35 and *Lydon v Coyne* (1946) 12 Ir Jur R 64 (both the latter involving transfers of land in exchange for support or labour).

103 (1846) 9 Ir Eq R 526. See, too, *Rae v Joyce* (1892) 29 LR Ir 500.

104 (1876) IR 11 Eq 367. See, too, eg, *Aylesford (Earl) v Morris* (1873) LR 8 Ch App 473.

105 Though once a contract is set aside, restitutionary issues will obviously arise.

106 See *Gregg v Kidd* [1956] IR 183, p 205 *et seq*. This was admittedly obiter, since the gift concerned had already been successfully attacked on the basis of undue influence.

situation, such as gifts. This latter view has since been taken by the English Family Division in *Langton v Langton*.[107]

To the extent that *Fry v Lane* does apply, it should be noted that 'poor and ignorant' is fairly indulgently interpreted. Anyone obviously deficient in commercial acumen may qualify as 'ignorant'.[108] Furthermore, despite the supposed requirement of poverty, some surprisingly well endowed claimants have in fact brought successful claims.[109] Indeed, we are coming close to a position where it extends to almost anyone who is asset rich but cash poor.

(c) Demands contrary to legislative provisions

4-31   The subject of public authority demands for more than is owing by way of taxes or levies, or for services rendered under statutory powers,[110] is dealt with in Chapter 12. However, in certain cases, private suppliers of goods and services (for example, landlords and suppliers of electricity, gas or water) are affected by legislation limiting the price they can lawfully charge. Such limitations may take effect by imposing overall maxima, or introducing 'anti-discrimination' provisions, or by way of outlawing certain kinds of charges entirely. Normally, the relevant legislation will provide for the recovery of overcharges; if it does, it no doubt pre-empts any right that may exist at common law. But, in the absence of specific provision, then *prima facie* it seems there is a common law right to reclaim any amounts paid in excess of those allowed.[111] This right is a little difficult to classify, but seems best treated as a form of statutory duress. The overcharging organisation is, as it were, deemed by operation of law to be in a position to exercise undue pressure on the citizen so as to justify recovery by the latter.

---

107 [1995] 2 FLR 890. But cf *Cresswell v Potter* (1968) [1978] 1 WLR 255n, where the gratuitous disposal of a house was set aside, the only thing received in exchange being an indemnity in respect of mortgage instalments. To regard this as an exchange, rather than a gift, requires some mental agility.

108 See, in particular, *Cresswell v Potter* (1968) [1978] 1 WLR 255n, 257 and *Butlin-Sanders v Butlin* (1985) 15 Fam Law 126.

109 In *Boustany v Pigott* (1993) 69 P and CR 298 (noted (1993) 109 LQR 530) the landlady of a not insubstantial commercial property in Antigua was held to qualify under this head. And it is noteworthy that in *Grealish v Murphy* [1946] IR 35, the successful claimant owned outright a 180 acre farm in Co Galway, together with large cash deposits. Cf *Stronge v Johnston* (1997) unreported, Ch D (NI), 16 April.

110 The so called *colore officii* cases.

111 Eg, *Gt Western Rly Co v Sutton* (1869) LR 4 HL 226; *Gt Southern and Western Rly Co v Robertson* (1878) 2 LR Ir 548. Cf *South of Scotland Electricity Board v BOC Ltd (No 2)* [1959] 2 All ER 225.

III REMEDIES

(a) Money paid

4-32   Money paid under duress proper, whether physical or economic, is recoverable at common law as money had and received;[112] as is money paid under a demand contrary to law[113] (assuming such recovery is available at all). This remedy is not, of course, available in respect of undue influence, this being an equitable head of relief: nevertheless, it would seem that there is an analogous personal right to reimbursement arising here too.[114]

Apart from personal rights, there is the question of proprietary remedies. In the case of undue influence, there is (it is suggested) no doubt that any sums transferred are subject to a constructive trust in the hands of the recipient.[115] There is no direct English or Irish authority on whether duress (of either type), or a demand contrary to statute, also gives rise to a constructive trust.[116] But there seems no reason not to extend the analogy of *Chase Manhattan NV v Israel-British Bank*[117] to cover such payments: if transfers rendered involuntary by mistake give rise to such a remedy, so, also, *a fortiori* should those affected by duress.

(b) Property transferred

4-33   We can begin with physical duress. A chattel obtained by force remains the property of the victim; he can therefore recover it (or its value) by suing in conversion, and there is no need for a separate restitutionary action.[118] With other property (such as land or things in action), it is suggested that a formal

---

112 The leading case is *Astley v Reynolds* (1731) 2 Str 915.

113 See the authorities in fn 111 above.

114 Cf the Canadian decision in *Dusik v Martin* (1985) 62 BCLR 1. If this were not so, the consequence would be bizarre; it would mean that if I made a gift of £100 to you as a result of your undue influence and you immediately spent it on ordinary living expenses, I would be left without remedy. See too *Mahoney v Purnell* [1996] 3 All ER 61.

115 Cf *Dickinson v Burrell* (1866) LR 1 Eq 337 (right to set aside proprietary so as to pass under will). The right may also bind third parties: cf *Bainbrigge v Browne* (1881) 18 Ch D 188, p 197, and *Lancashire Loans Ltd v Black* [1934] 1 KB 380, p 417 *et seq.*

116 See, however, *Murphy v AG* [1982] IR 241, where Kenny and Henchy JJ clearly assumed that the State, having collected unconstitutional taxes from its citizens, would hold any moneys so paid on constructive trust. In the equivalent English case of *Woolwich Building Society v Inland Revenue Comrs (No 2)* [1993] AC 70 it was tentatively argued before the Court of Appeal that the same result should follow. But the question did not have to be decided, and no answer was given.

117 [1981] Ch 105.

118 Though one may coincidentally be available: eg, if a robber sells his booty and his victim chooses to waive the tort of conversion and sue him for the proceeds.

transfer obtained by force will again be simply void,[119] and hence that similarly, no title passes.

What of economic duress? It is submitted that at common law, this probably makes a transfer of property not void, but voidable at the election of the transferor.[120] In addition, it would seem that a constructive trust, if available in cases of money payments, should also be available here. Apart from this, it is suggested that there is no reason why a personal claim in *quantum valebat* should not equally lie. If you coerce me into transferring my car to you, it hardly lies in your mouth to allege that you thought you would receive it free of charge, or that you have any reason not to be forced to pay for it.

Undue influence gives rise in the orthodox way to a constructive trust, and possibly also to a money claim: see the previous paragraph.

(c) Services rendered

4-34　It is suggested that services rendered under duress ought to give rise to a claim in *quantum meruit*, for the same reason as property transferred should create a *quantum valebat*: the services have been requested, and the person who exercises duress should not be allowed to deny that they were rendered with the expectation of payment.[121] The question is slightly more awkward where services are rendered to a third party other than the person responsible for the duress: here, by analogy to what has been suggested to be the rule for mistake, the better rule is probably to deny any remedy except where the recipient had any choice whether to accept the benefit of the services concerned. In any case, one suspects this is an unlikely problem to arise in practice.

It is unclear whether, and if so how far, services that go to improve property ought to give the claimant an interest in the property. Assume you force me at gunpoint to improve your house: if you are insolvent, can I escape the consequences of your insolvency by claiming a lien on your house to the value of my improvements? Equity suggests I ought to be able to, by analogy either to the decisions on acquiesced-in improvements (for example, *Unity Joint Stock Banking Co v King*)[122] or to the position in relation to payments of money.

---

119 Under the doctrine of *non est factum*, or something similar.

120 Thus, there are *dicta* that contracts affected by economic duress are 'voidable' (eg, *Pao On v Lau Yiu Long* [1980] AC 614, pp 635–36 (Lord Scarman); *The Universe Sentinel* [1983] AC 366, pp 383–84 (Lord Diplock)). There seems no reason not to apply a similar rule by analogy to non-contractual transfers of property.

121 Thus differentiating the case from that of mistake. Mistake is not necessarily induced by the recipient of services; duress, by contrast, normally is.

122 (1858) 25 Beav 72.

(d) The position of third parties

4-35 We have hitherto assumed that relief is sought against the person exerting duress himself. But, how far is relief also available against third parties? As might be expected, the answer to this question depends on the nature of the claim, and in particular on what remedies are available in respect of it.

Where the claim is one for money had and received in respect of a payment made under duress – whether physical or economic – it is suggested that it should not matter whether the payee is the coercer or a third party. If I threaten to break my contract with you unless you pay me £1,000, you can recover the £1,000; it should make no difference in this connection if I demand that the money be paid to a company controlled by me, and you subsequently claim against that company.[123] The only exception, it is suggested, is where the payee is innocent[124] and gives value: for instance, where X coerces me into paying X's debts to you. In such a case, you as a *bona fide* purchaser ought to be able to hold on to what you got,[125] and my only claim should be against X.

Relief for benefits conferred under undue influence is similarly available against a third party where the latter is not a *bona fide* purchaser, so as to take free of equities: that is, where he is a volunteer, or has actual or constructive notice of the circumstances giving rise to undue influence,[126] or where the 'influencer' acted as his agent.[127] Where the recipient is indeed a *bona fide* purchaser he will prevail,[128] as where a bank takes a mortgage over a matrimonial home with no means of knowing that the husband has exercised undue influence over his wife.

4-36 But, in this connection, at least two important points fall to be made. First, it probably makes no difference whether the defendant was a *bona fide* purchaser of an equitable or legal interest in the property concerned: this being on the basis

---

123 Presumably, there would be a claim against me as well; the money was, after all, paid to my order, although not to me personally.

124 Assuming, of course, that no agency or similar relationship exists between the recipient and the coercer: the recipient will be bound by the acts of his agent, and in such circumstances can hardly claim to be innocent. The point has arisen in connection with undue influence: see below.

125 Cf *Barclays Bank Ltd v WJ Simms Ltd* [1979] 3 All ER 552, holding that where X paid Y's debts to Z by mistake, no action for restitution lay against Z.

126 See *Bainbrigge v Brown* (1881) 18 Ch D 188, p 197. See too *Lancashire Loans Ltd v Black* [1934] 1 KB 380, p 417 *et seq*.

127 Typically, where a would-be mortgagee of a matrimonial home entrusted the husband with the task of obtaining his wife's concurrence: see, eg, *Kingsnorth Trust Ltd v Bell* [1986] 1 All ER 423. But, while this avenue of relief remains open as a matter of law, the Court of Appeal has recently suggested that it will very rarely be established in practice: *Barclays Bank v O'Brien* [1993] 4 All ER 983, pp 1006–07, 1013 (CA).

128 *Bainbrigge v Brown* (1881) 18 Ch D 188; *CIBC Mortgages Ltd v Pitt* [1994] 1 AC 200.

that the right to set aside a transaction for undue influence counts as a mere equity, rather than a full equitable interest in it.[129]

Secondly, the decision in *Barclays Bank plc v O'Brien*[130] makes it clear that certain fact situations automatically, as it were, put recipients on notice that undue influence may have occurred. This is particularly so where one family member is known to be mortgaging his property to support some project in which another member is, but he himself is not, interested:[131] typically, where a wife[132] is asked to concur in the hypothecation of the matrimonial home to a bank in order to support her husband's ailing and chronically under-capitalised business. Here, assuming undue influence is in fact present, it is not enough for the bank to plead ignorance of it: it must show in addition that it took all reasonable precautions[133] to ensure proper advice for the party concerned.[134] If it cannot do this, it is in no better position than the husband (or whoever exercised the influence).

---

129 This is certainly true of the right to set aside a transfer to fraud: see *Phillips v Phillips* (1862) 4 de G F and J 208, p 218. The claimant relying on undue influence can hardly be in a better position.

130 [1994] 1 AC 180. The position is the same in Ireland: *Bank of Nova Scotia v Hogan* [1996] 3 IR 239 (Supreme Court).

131 This qualification is vital. If, on the face of the transaction, it appears that both family members are interested, the bank comes under no duty to look to the interests of either. See *CIBC Mortgages Ltd v Pitt* [1994] 1 AC 200, above.

132 But not only a wife. Similarly with a cohabitant (*Massey v Midland Bank plc* [1995] 1 All ER 929), and possibly an elderly parent too.

133 Though not necessarily successful ones: cf *Coldunell Ltd v Gallon* [1986] 1 All ER 429, where the creditor's letter of explanation to the surety was unforeseeably intercepted by the debtor, but the transaction nevertheless stood.

134 Eg, by specifically warning the wife to get a solicitor's advice (*Banco Exterior Internacional v Mann* [1995] 1 All ER 936), or actually referring her to a particular firm and confirming that she received advice (*Massey v Midland Bank plc* [1995] 1 All ER 929).

CHAPTER 5

FREE ACCEPTANCE

I THE FUNCTION OF FREE ACCEPTANCE

5-1   The concept of free acceptance has two functions in restitution, which have to be kept separate.

One is a limiting function, and it has already been dealt with in Chapter 1. It has to do with concepts like forced exchange and subjective devaluation, and the extent to which a claimant should escape liability to pay for a benefit on the basis that he has had no proper chance of rejecting it.[1]

But, quite apart from that, the fact that I have voluntarily taken the benefit of goods or services supplied by you may itself give you an independent right to restitution against me. In other words, free acceptance may act as an 'unjust factor' in its own right. That is what this chapter is about.

5-2   When will free acceptance act as a restitutionary sword in this way? It is suggested that it may do so in three situations. The *first* is where benefits are rendered at the request of the defendant in a non-contractual, but equally non-gratuitous context. A simple instance is where I ask you to pay my debt to X, or do work for me on a non-gratuitous basis, and you do so. The *second* is where a benefit, while unrequested, is taken up or acquiesced in by the recipient, whether at the time or after the event. And the *third* is where the defendant deliberately and unconscionably takes the advantage of something supplied or done by someone else. An example of this last would be where a businessman slipped unnoticed into a private educational conference fully knowing that entry was meant to be restricted to those who had paid for it. It would be odd, to say the least, if he did not by so doing come under a duty to the organisers concerned to pay for what he got (or rather, took).

5-3   Before any detailed discussion, however, one preliminary point of classification needs to be made. For the purposes of this chapter, free acceptance is a relatively narrow head of recovery, limited to the three heads mentioned above. As Burrows has rightly pointed out,[2] and Birks has now accepted,[3] a large number of other cases previously thought of as involving it ought to be excluded on the basis that they are better seen as concerned with failure of assumptions.

---

1   Nevertheless, cases on whether an otherwise good restitutionary claim is defeated by a lack of free acceptance may well be relevant in illustrating what does, and does not, amount to free acceptance sufficient to ground a claim in its own right.

2   See Burrows, 'Free acceptance and the law of restitution' (1988) 104 LQR 576.

3   In Chapter 5 of Burrows, *Essays on Restitution*, p 111.

Most importantly, this class of case – that is, the class of cases which do not, properly analysed, involve free acceptance – includes the situation where goods or services are supplied in performance, or part performance, of a contract between claimant and defendant. A straightforward example is goods or services supplied under a contract later terminated before completion, as where a builder fails to complete works owing to his own or the owner's breach of contract. The essence of the claimant's right to restitution here is not free acceptance by the other party (though the lack of such acceptance may be fatal to the claimant's claim): rather, it is the fact that the supplier did not – for whatever reason – get what he bargained for.

5-4   Slightly less obviously, there must also be excluded from the 'free acceptance' cases those decisions holding that a person providing benefits is entitled to restitution if he acted on the basis of a projected contract which is not in fact concluded,[4] or a contract which turns out ineffective,[5] or a belief that he would thereby get some other benefit, such as the freehold of tenanted land which he has improved.[6] In all these cases, the claimant's complaint is that the return he expected to receive – reimbursement under the hoped-for contract, the grant of the freehold, or whatever – will not now be forthcoming, and that for that reason he seeks the alternative remedy in unjust enrichment. Free acceptance strictly so called, in other words, does not apply to the claimant who says: 'I conferred a benefit hoping to receive x in return, but not having received x I now wish to fall back on my right to restitution.'

5-5   So far, so good. At this point, however, we must dispose of a more radical argument (strongly advanced by Burrows in particular). This is that even in the three cases which we have said are concerned with free acceptance as such, free acceptance is not the proper explanation. On this argument, free acceptance as an independent head of recovery is not necessary at all, and should be ditched on the basis that its work can be done just as well by other doctrines.

The reasoning goes as follows. In the case of requested benefits, the recipient's liability to pay can be put on the basis of simple contract, or perhaps (short of contract) on 'bargain'.[7] As for benefits not requested, but in fact accepted or acquiesced in (excluding those rendered under contracts or putative contracts), Burrows argues that even here, what lies behind the cases granting recovery is either some other ground such as mistake or necessity,[8] or alternatively failure of consideration. His argument is that, since in such cases the common understanding of the parties as reasonable people (that is, that

---

4   As in *William Lacey (Hounslow) v Davis* [1957] 1 WLR 932.

5   As in the vital Australian decision in *Pavey & Matthews Pty Ltd v Paul* (1986) 162 CLR 221.

6   As in (arguably) *Ramsden v Dyson* (1886) LR 1 HL 129. Cf *Cullen v Cullen* [1962] IR 268, and cases such as *Hussey v Palmer* [1972] 1 WLR 1286.

7   'Free acceptance and the law of restitution' (1988) 104 LQR 576, p 578; Burrows, p 14.

8   As in cases such as *Lamb v Bunce* (1815) 4 M & S 275, referred to below.

payment would be made) has been defeated, restitution ought to be available to fill the gap.[9]

5-6   But, this wholesale attack is, it is respectfully suggested, misconceived. Let us begin with requested benefits. Here, it is submitted, with great respect to Burrows, the idea of a 'bargain' to pay for them is fiction, not truth. No doubt the recipient is treated as if he had so bargained; but this answers nothing. The question remains: why should he be so treated? The only rational explanation, it is suggested, is that he freely accepted what he got knowing and acquiesced in an understanding that it would be paid for. Had he not done so, or had he made it clear that he would not pay, the case for inferring a bargain of any sort falls away.[10]

5-7   We can now turn to the 'non-request' cases, based on acquiescence or something similar. True, some of the cases on acquiescence can be regarded as based on other grounds such as mistake or necessity. But, there is no indication that they would – or should – have been decided differently if that factor had been absent. Take *Lamb v Bunce*,[11] where a doctor attending a pauper recovered from the parish authorities on the basis that the responsible officer had stood by and acquiesced in his doing so. True, this could be regarded as a case of necessitous intervention: but there is no indication that that fact mattered, or even should have. Change the facts slightly. What if the claimant had been a builder carrying out repairs to some building owned by the parish? There would then be no immediate necessity; but there is, it is suggested, no reason why the result should have been any different.

        Nor, it is suggested, is an explanation based on failure of consideration much more satisfactory. Such an explanation works perfectly well in the case of benefits rendered under a defunct, ineffective or putative contract, for there, the claimant is claiming restitution to *replace* the reimbursement he did not get by virtue of the contractual arrangements he had made (or thought he had). But with straightforward acquiescence, no such solid ground appears. The claimant here is suing for precisely the consideration that allegedly failed – namely, reasonable recompense for what he did. This is, it is submitted, an artificial and ultimately untenable notion of failure of consideration.

        Moreover, a further point is worth adding. Burrows's analysis offers no explanation of the third class of case mentioned above, namely, that of 'unconscientious advantage-taking'. This (it will be suggested below)[12] cannot be elucidated except on the basis of an independent doctrine of free acceptance.

5-8   Assuming the doctrine of free acceptance as an unjust factor exists, why do we have it? To say it satisfies the claimant's legitimate expectations begs the

9   Burrows, pp 318–19, accepted by Birks, *Essays on Restitution*, Chapter 5, p 115 *et seq*.

10 Cf *Becerra v Close Bros Ltd* (1999) unreported, 25 June, QBD (Thomas J) (agency services accepted, but on clear basis that they would not be paid for: no claim in *quantum meruit*).

11 (1815) 4 M & S 275.

12 See § 5-13 *et seq*.

question: if the law provided (as it logically might, but in fact does not) that you render benefits to me at your own risk unless you took the trouble to extract from me a contractual promise to pay for them, you would have no legitimate expectation to fulfil. The correct answer, it is suggested, is that of Birks:[13] it is a liability based on the defendant's conduct, grounded ultimately on whether he acts unjustifiably in seeking to retain a benefit willingly accepted without accepting a balancing liability to pay for it. If I have asked you to do something, or led you on to do it by failing to stop you, and at the time I knew you were acting in the expectation of having a right to reimbursement, it is presumptively unjust – or, if you will, unconscionable – for me to refuse to give you that reimbursement. I cannot justifiably take the benefit without accepting the obligation attaching to it. Moreover, the very fact that you have to show request or free acceptance protects you from any prejudice if you are made to pay.[14] And, similarly, at least in some cases, where I take the benefit of some service provided by you without even asking. Indeed, this must be *a fortiori*: someone grabbing a benefit willy-nilly can hardly be in a better position than the person who asked first. In practice, however, this – as we shall see – raises more tricky issues.

Note, however, the word 'presumptively', which is important. Quite apart from general restitutionary defences such as change of position, there will often be factors, such as the circumstances of my request or acceptance, or some other justification for my conduct, that ought to negative your right to recompense.

II FREE ACCEPTANCE IN OPERATION

(a) The idea of acceptance

Request

5-9   We suggested above that, in order to create a restitutionary liability, the relevant acceptance could take three forms: request, acquiescence and (for want of a better word) unconscionable advantage-taking.

Request is the least troublesome. Indeed, in many cases of requested benefits, there is no need to worry about restitutionary recovery at all; instead, the law simply implies a contract to pay. If I ask you to paint or sell my house without discussing the price,[15] the law has little difficulty in saying that I implicitly agree

---

13 Birks, p 276.

14 The argument over whether requested services benefit the recipient at all (Beatson, *Use and Abuse of Unjust Enrichment*, Chapter 2) seems, with respect, a sterile one. If they do, *cadit quaestio*; if they do not, the recipient, by accepting them, surely should be regarded as having disabled himself from taking the point.

15 For cases concerning requested services in this connection, see, eg, *Way v Latilla* [1937] 3 All ER 759; *British Bank for Foreign Trade v Novinex Ltd* [1949] 1 KB 623; *Henehan v Courtney* (1966) 101 ILTR 25; *Bergin v Farrell* (1999) unreported, 17 December, HC (Ireland).

to pay you a reasonable sum.[16] But, the contractual escape will not always work. If I request you to pay my debt to X, I have to reimburse you: if I request you to do work for me on a non-gratuitous basis, but never actually contract with you, you can claim the reasonable value of your performance. But, it is (as pointed out above) somewhat fictional to say I contracted to do so, and more in accordance with the realities of the situation to ground my liability on acceptance.

Admittedly, one might think this was a distinction without a difference – if I am bound to pay, I will not care whether my obligation arises from promise or free acceptance, contract or restitution. But, from your point of view, it may matter a great deal. If you want to sue me for doing work badly or late, or for loss suffered because goods supplied were defective, mere acceptance will not do: you will have to show an actual contract between us.[17]

Acquiescence

5-10   The second form of acceptance, it will be remembered, arises where a benefit is taken up or acquiesced in, even where there has been no prior request.

It is probably simpler to use the term 'taking up' to cover the case where the defendant takes the benefit of goods or services after the event. Obvious examples include the situation where you send me a crate of whisky, unasked, with a bill enclosed, and I drink it;[18] or where you take it on yourself to pay my debt to X and I subsequently adopt the payment by ratifying what you have done.[19] A nice example is the unreported decision of the Supreme Court of Ireland in *Chieb v Carter*.[20] The plaintiff forwarding agent made arrangements for shipment of the defendant's stock from Ireland to Egypt. The shipment never took place as contemplated, but the same stock was later shipped by the defendant, building on the work previously done by the plaintiffs. The defendant was held liable to pay the plaintiffs a reasonable sum for services rendered and later taken advantage of.

5-11   Acquiescence, which we will use to deal with the case where a benefit is accepted *at the time of provision*, is not quite so straightforward. To understand it better, suppose the following situation. A developer is planning two housing estates. A quantity surveyor employed to deal with one of them without any

---

16   Indeed, this is provided by statute in the sale of goods: Sale of Goods Act 1979, s 8(2) (England); Sale of Goods Act 1893, s 8(2) (Ireland).

17   For a neat illustration, see *British Steel Corporation v Cleveland Bridge & Engineering Co Ltd* [1984] 1 All ER 504 (a case concerning an anticipated contract and hence, strictly, failure of assumptions: but nothing turns on this).

18   Eg, *Weatherby v Banham* (1832) 5 C & P 228.

19   See Beatson in *The Use and Abuse of Unjust Enrichment*, Chapter 7, pp 190–91 and cf *Walter v James* (1871) LR 6 Ex 124, pp 126, 128; *Crantrave Ltd v Lloyds Bank plc* [2000] 4 All ER 473.

20   (1987) unreported, 3 June.

request carries out work on the other despite the lack of any request to do so. Nevertheless, the developer accepts and continues to accept this work as it is done. Should the surveyor have a claim for the extra work? Instinctively one feels he should be able to; and the better position appears to be that he can. There is indeed 19th century,[21] and more recent,[22] authority to the effect that acquiesced-in benefits, even if provided with no other basis of restitution, can give rise to recovery.[23] So, for example, where in the context of industrial action, an employer voluntarily accepts services provided by his employees in only partial performance of their contracts, it seems accepted that he may come under an obligation to pay pro rata for what he has acquiesced in.[24] Again, in a statutory context, it has been held by the Court of Appeal that a football club which acquiesces in a prophylactic police presence at its matches can be regarded as having 'requested' that presence so as to incur a liability to pay for it.[25]

5-12   But, it is worth thinking for a moment: why should this be? You cannot, after all, impose a contract on me by saying you will assume that silence means acceptance;[26] if so, why treat restitution any differently?[27] The answer, it is suggested, is twofold. First, your claim that I should pay for actual benefits conferred by you is normally more compelling than a claim to enforce a contract that may be wholly executory by suing me for non-acceptance: to that extent, it may be justifiable to relax the strict requirement of a positive acceptance. Secondly, injustice is unlikely in practice to result from such a relaxation, because in many cases – including most of the undeserving ones – an action for payment will fail for other reasons. Imagine, for instance, you decide to paint my house without any apparent reason at all while I look on. I may well act

---

21 See *Lamb v Bunce* (1815) 4 M & S 275 and *Paynter v Williams* (1833) 1 C & M 810, concerning medical attention to paupers acquiesced in by the parish officers responsible, together with other cases referred to by Birks (*Essays on Restitution*, pp 116–17). Burrows's dismissal of these cases as involving necessity or failure of consideration (Burrows, pp 318–19) is, with respect, unconvincing: see above, § 5-5 *et seq*.

22 Cf *Bookmakers' Afternoon Greyhound Services v Gilbert* [1994] FSR 723, where Aldous J seemingly accepted that bookmakers who used broadcast material in their betting shops in the knowledge that it was not provided free would have been liable to pay for it, but for the fact that they had consistently told the providers that they were not prepared to accept it on that basis. Furthermore, in *Becerra v Close Bros Ltd* (1999) unreported, 25 June, QBD, Thomas J seemed to accept that acquiescence of this sort could, on principle, give rise to liability (though it did not on the facts in front of him). And cf *Wiluczynski v Tower Hamlets LBC* [1989] ICR 493, below.

23 Eg, *Alexander v Vane* (1836) 1 M & W 511 (guarantee of debt acquiesced in by principal debtor).

24 *Wiluczynski v Tower Hamlets LBC* [1989] ICR 493. But such acceptance, for obvious reasons, will not be lightly inferred: *ibid*.

25 *Harris v Sheffield United Football Club Ltd* [1987] 2 All ER 838.

26 *Felthouse v Bindley* (1862) 11 CB (NS) 869.

27 Mead forcefully makes this point: see 'Free acceptance: some further considerations' (1989) 105 LQR 460.

reasonably in assuming that you are doing me a favour, in which case the requirement of lack of gratuitous intent will not be satisfied.

Advantage-taking

5-13   The third form of free acceptance is the rather more enigmatic one of unconscionable advantage-taking. Typified by the liability at common law of the fare-dodger,[28] or (no doubt) the theatre-goer who sneaks in without paying, it differs from the other two in that the claimant never intended to benefit the defendant at all. The complaint is rather that the defendant simply appropriated some advantage to himself in circumstances where it should have been obvious that he was not entitled.

Admittedly, it could be argued that this is really a branch of restitution for wrongs. One can, for instance, take the analogy of the fiduciary or company director who unjustifiably seizes a corporate opportunity for himself, or the misuser of confidential information,[29] who has long been regarded as guilty of a kind of interference with property. The fare-dodger and the gate-crasher do, after all, commit a trespass (even if only a technical one): why not say that they should not be allowed to profit from it,[30] and that this provides ample ground for restitution?

5-14   Unfortunately, the 'wrongs' explanation will not necessarily do. There are cases where the defendant should be liable even though the claimant cannot show a wrong, or cannot show a wrong to himself. Should a business competitor, for example, be entitled to abstract confidential information by using intrusive but non-trespassory surveillance techniques?[31] Again, suppose a conference organiser arranges a seminar, books a hall, and charges delegates a fee for attendance payable in advance to him: but, on the day of the conference, a mean but acquisitive entrepreneur creeps in without paying. The person who ought to be entitled to sue him for a reasonable fee is surely the organiser: but the defendant's wrongful act (if any) is committed against the owners of the hall. Again, to bring matters up to date, imagine a satellite television broadcaster who, for a fee, procures the issue of decoders to potential viewers on the basis

---

28   Cf *Rumsey v North Eastern Rly* (1863) 14 CB (NS) 641 (passenger carrying unauthorised luggage liable for reasonable carriage charge in respect of overplus).

29   Compare *Douglas v Hello!* [2001] 2 All ER 289, where the English Court of Appeal thought that the law of confidence might be extended to allow a claim for an account of profits against the publisher of unauthorised photographs taken at a society wedding.

30   Thus, in *Rumsey v North Eastern Rly* (1863) 14 CB (NS) 641, above, the passenger's liability was put, rather enigmatically, on the basis of 'fraud'. Similarly, in the English case of *Atlantic Shipping Ltd v Finagrain Ltd* (1999) unreported, 15 January, Toulson J thought that where a warehouseman's customer took advantage of storage facilities for more than the contractual period, he was liable to pay for the extra on the basis of restitution for wrongs (citing in this connection authorities on *mesne* profits, such as *Ministry of Defence v Ashman* (1993) 40 EG 144.

31   See the American decision in *Du Pont de Nemours v Christopher* 431 F 2d 1012 (1970).

that they are to pay further per programme watched. A person who dishonestly receives one of these broadcasts by stealing a decoder from a third party presumably ought to be liable to pay the broadcaster for what he has illicitly watched: but, once again, there is no guarantee that any unlawful act will have been committed by him against the broadcaster.[32] More recently still, the Court of Appeal has regarded as arguable a claim by a telecommunications provider against an entrepreneur who misuses his service to make an uncovenanted profit.[33] It is this kind of case that seems to point up the need for a separate restitutionary principle of advantage-taking, albeit a principle which needs to be sensitively dealt with in order to accommodate the needs of the law of restitution with a person's right to use his own property as he thinks fit. These issues are dealt with in greater detail below.

(b) The need for 'free' acceptance

5-15   What lies behind the principle of free acceptance is the defendant's *choice* to receive the benefit. It is unfair to decline to pay for something one chose voluntarily to have in the knowledge that it was not provided free. But the less genuine the choice, or the more affected by (for example) mistake, the weaker the argument.

What may make a choice unfree? Clearly, if the defendant continues to render services, or send goods, to the claimant over the latter's protest, any claim based on free acceptance must fail *in limine*. But, this is not the only case. Another significant example is, it is suggested, where the defendant does exercise a choice, but that choice itself is affected by error. Take the well known facts of *Boulton v Jones*.[34] Jones ordered piping from a dealer, Brocklehurst. Boulton, who had bought Brocklehurst's business, sent it, and Jones (who hoped to set off the price against money owed him by Brocklehurst) used it. Boulton's action in contract for the price was, predictably, unsuccessful. It is suggested that an action in *quantum valebat* for its value equally would (and should) have failed. True, Jones had accepted the piping: but he had done so as a result of a mistake, and his acceptance should not count for these purposes.

However, it is suggested that a mistake will not cause acceptance to be 'unfree' unless it caused the defendant to act as he did. The result in the difficult case of *Craven-Ellis v Canons Ltd*[35] may well be justifiable on this basis. The plaintiff acted as a director of the defendant company when, unknown to him, his appointment by the board of directors was technically invalid. The company

---

32 Assume, for instance, that the decoders are the property of some third party whom the broadcaster pays to make them available.

33 *ET Ltd v Fashion Gossip Ltd* (2000) unreported, 29 July, CA.

34 (1857) 2 H & N 564.

35 [1936] 2 KB 403. Strictly, this is a 'failure of consideration' case, since it concerns benefits rendered under a putative contract: but the issue of acceptance is the same.

was held, nevertheless, to have accepted the services rendered, and to be liable to pay a reasonable sum for them. Although this is not entirely clear from the judgments, the reason would seem to be that if the company had known the contract was void, it would no doubt still have employed the plaintiff.[36]

5-16 Rather more importantly, however, the idea of free acceptance must be balanced against the recipient's right to arrange his own affairs, and use his own property, as he wishes.[37] In so far as that is all he has done, it can hardly be unfair for him to decline to pay for some benefit incidentally received or realised as a result. The facts of the Australian decision in *Victoria Park Racing Ltd v Taylor*[38] illustrate the issue beautifully. The enterprising owner of a tall building next to a racecourse took advantage of his situation to overlook, and broadcast results from, races as they occurred, to his own considerable profit and the understandable annoyance of the course owners who were thus excluded from a lucrative source of revenue. The case turned on whether he had committed any enjoinable wrong as against the racecourse owner. It was decided he had not. It is suggested that an action in restitution brought on the same facts should equally fail: a person should be entitled to take for himself the natural advantages of his property without being called on to pay someone else. Another illustration comes in *Forman and Co Pty Ltd v The Liddesdale*.[39] Ship repairers carried out unauthorised work on a vessel, increasing her value. Afterwards, her owners took her back and sold her, thus realising the appreciation. The repairers were denied recovery, on the basis that in so far as the owners were benefited at all, the benefit was one they had had no reasonable opportunity to refuse. But the case can be put in another, and simpler, way: their acts in taking the ship and later turning her into money were simple exercises of their property rights.

5-17 Another case which could have been decided similarly was *Bookmakers' Afternoon Greyhound Services Ltd v Gilbert*.[40] Bookmakers received, and displayed in their shops, racing commentaries broadcast by X which incorporated material provided by the plaintiffs. The plaintiffs made it clear that they expected payment for this material from those bookmakers making use of it. The bookmakers made it equally clear that they had no intention to pay. The plaintiffs were denied recovery. Although Aldous J grounded his decision on

---

36 It can be argued that Craven-Ellis was necessarily not a 'free acceptance' case at all, because the invalidly appointed directors could no more accept Mr Craven-Ellis's services than they could contract for them. With respect, however, it is submitted that this would not prevent a claim against the company based on passive acquiescence. Note that the result in the *Craven-Ellis* case was mentioned, and not dissented from, by the House of Lords in *Guinness plc v Saunders* [1990] 2 AC 663.

37 Cf Pollock CB's laconic question in *Taylor v Laird* (1856) 25 LJ Ex 329, p 332: 'One cleans another's shoes. What can the other do but put them on?'

38 (1937) 58 CLR 479.

39 [1900] AC 190. But cf *The Manila* [1982] AC 939.

40 [1994] FSR 723.

the plaintiffs' knowledge of the bookmakers' refusal to pay,[41] a better ground seems to be that the latter had a perfect right to take broadcasts from X, and hence there was nothing unconscientious about their taking incidental advantage of the plaintiffs' information.

This is particularly important in the area of 'unconscientious advantage-taking'. In the area of information, it provides the essential background to intellectual property law. Unless guilty of a specific wrong such as infringement of patent or breach of confidence, or perhaps of particularly egregious conduct,[42] one is entitled to do as one wants with one's own property, as (for instance) by buying a product with a view to 'reverse engineering' and emulating it for one's own benefit, or using – without breach of copyright – information derived from that product for one's own advantage.[43] Similar principles would no doubt apply, for instance, to a legatee under a long-lost will who obtained his inheritance as a result of the efforts of a lawyer acting for another legatee.[44]

(c) Lack of gratuitous intent

5-18   However widely drafted, a principle of free acceptance cannot be allowed to turn gifts into sales: hence the requirement that, at least in cases of request and acquiescence, the benefit must have been provided on the basis that it was to be charged for. In *Gilbert v Knight*,[45] for instance, an architect was requested by a building owner to carry out certain extra work. He was nevertheless held to have no recovery, on the basis that the owner had no reason to know he intended to charge for it. Presumably, moreover, it must have been obvious to the recipient not only that the provider of the benefit intended to charge, but that such charge should be legally enforceable: however much I encourage a street musician to play outside my house, it is highly unlikely that this will give rise to any restitutionary liability. And, indeed, in practice this may well cut out many of the more outrageous claims based on acquiescence. If you clean my windows

---

41   Which seems doubtful. Could the unauthorised receiver of satellite broadcasts escape any obligation by telling the broadcaster that he was happy to receive the broadcasts on a stolen decoder but declined to pay for them? Surely not.

42   See the decision in *Du Pont de Nemours v Christopher* 431 F 2d 1012 (1970), above. Another example might arise in the case of a mean, but electronically sophisticated television viewer who used his own electronic expertise to decode satellite signals he was not meant to receive (this being in English law a criminal offence: Copyright, Designs and Patents Act 1988, s 297(1)).

43   It might be thought that these cases concerned implied consent. But it seems unlikely that any different result would follow even if consent were negatived – if, for instance, a manufacturer purported to stipulate by notice attached to his product that a royalty would become payable in the event of 'reverse engineering'.

44   Which has been the subject of extensive (and expensive) litigation in the US. For details, see Dawson (1974) 87 Harv LR 1597.

45   [1968] 2 All ER 248.

for me while I look on,[46] a court may well be astute to infer that I reasonably thought you were doing me a favour, or providing a free sample of work in order to drum up future business.

5-19   Deciding when I should be entitled to assume that a benefit rendered by you is gratuitous is clearly tricky; in practice, it will often depend on the court's assessment of who should bear the risks inherent in a particular transaction, and on any contractual or other arrangements between the parties. We have already mentioned *Craven-Ellis v Canons Ltd*,[47] where acceptance of services from an invalidly appointed director were held to give rise to a duty to pay. Contrast *Re Richmond Gate Property Co Ltd*,[48] where the plaintiff was employed by a company at such remuneration 'as the directors shall determine'. No rate was ever set, and his action in *quantum meruit* failed: his contract of employment excluded any right to be paid until the amount was set, and up to then he was regarded as acting gratuitously.

Again, often the real question is not whether benefits were to be paid for, but who should pay; it may well be that a benefit was intended to be gratuitous as against A but not as against B. A neat example is the situation where I take my car to your garage to be repaired at the instance of my insurers, but the insurers fail to pay. The repairs will be regarded as gratuitous vis-à-vis me, but not the insurers.[49]

---

46 The example is Birks's (Birks, pp 265–66). It is attacked for other reasons by Burrows (Burrows, p 316).

47 [1936] 2 KB 403.

48 [1965] 1 WLR 335. See, too, *Guinness plc v Saunders* [1990] 2 AC 663; where it would be unlawful for a director to be paid for reasons of conflict of duty and interest, no *quantum meruit* was permissible.

49 See *Brown and Davis Ltd v Galbraith* [1972] 1 WLR 997 (a contract case; but it is suggested that a claim in *quantum meruit* would yield the same result).

CHAPTER 6

FAILURE OF ASSUMPTIONS (1)

I INTRODUCTION

6-1 This chapter and the next are concerned with restitutionary recovery based on the fact that a benefit has been rendered on some assumption that later turns out to have been unjustified. The simplest example is where you pay me in advance for something you do not get. Your payment was made on the assumption that the return would be forthcoming, and once that assumption is negatived, my right to retain the payment disappears. Another is where you agree to build me a house for a given price, but I wrongfully eject you from the site before you have finished the job. You provided services on the assumption that on completion, you would be paid the contract price: that assumption cannot now be realised, and means must be found to allow you to claim something for what you have done. Yet another instance is the case where something is done in the expectation that a contract will materialise, but it does not. Imagine, for example, that you are an architect in negotiation with me over proposed works. Because I am in a hurry, you, at my request, prepare preliminary drawings. Then negotiations break down and no contract ensues. Yet again, suppose you pay for the construction of a 'granny flat' in my house with a view to your residing with me there for the rest of your life, but the relationship between us later sours. In all these cases, you are *prima facie* entitled to restitution from me, and for the same reason. The assumption on which you rendered, and I accepted, the benefit – that you would get what I promised, that I would employ you as my architect, that we would live together in harmony, and so on – is not satisfied. It is this disappointment which provides an unjust factor, and means that I am not justified in refusing you recompense.

6-2 To this extent, this head of recovery has a great deal in common – a good deal more, indeed, than most commentators allow[1] – with mistake. Indeed, as was suggested in Chapter 3,[2] it is arguable that mistake itself as a ground of restitution is arguably a sub-species of failure of assumptions. Not only does this have the effect of keeping the concept of operative mistake within reasonable bounds: more importantly, it preserves the essential symmetry of restitution law in this area. If I have given you a wedding present in respect of a wedding that did not come off, there is no reason for my remedy against you to vary radically

---

1 Cf Birks, p 219, where mistake is said to be about vitiation of the will, whereas failure of consideration about its qualification. Burrows, pp 108–09, is even more emphatic in distinguishing them.

2 § 3-10 *et seq.*

according to whether I sent it to you before the putative ceremony (failure of assumption) or afterwards in ignorance of the cancellation (mistake).

(a) Free acceptance and failure of assumptions

6-3   Restitution for failure of assumptions is largely, though not exclusively, a substitutionary remedy. In the case of services, or property which the defendant has consumed or disposed of, it can only be substitutionary: there is simply nothing to return *in specie*, so the remedy must needs be pecuniary.

In such cases, recovery for failure of assumptions begins to look a little like free acceptance, which is dealt with in Chapter 5.[3] Nevertheless, it is suggested that the concepts are analytically distinct. The thinking behind failure of assumptions is that if the claimant fails to receive what he hoped to get, he should, at the very least, be able as an alternative to recover the value of the benefit he provided. Free acceptance proper, by contrast, is premised on a simpler idea: namely, that one should not be able to accept a benefit provided at a price, and at the same time deny an obligation to pay for it.[4] Moreover, there are cases on failure of assumptions that cannot convincingly be regarded as free acceptance situations. In the case of part performance of a contract, for example (the case of the builder ejected from the site), the part performance was never knowingly accepted at all. The defendant did not want a partly done job: the claimant, for his part, never envisaged charging for anything other than a complete one. Some other basis for liability must therefore be found.

6-4   Nevertheless, although failure of assumptions as a cause of action is different from free acceptance, nevertheless there are issues that are common to both. For example, the problem of forced exchange, or making people pay for benefits in kind which they have not actually asked for or accepted, may arise here in a particularly acute form in the case of failure of assumptions. Again, the fact that a benefit is rendered gratuitously will bar a claim based on failure of assumptions as much as one based on free acceptance. It follows that the issue of whether the claimant could reasonably have been thought to have an intent to charge will often be relevant in these cases – particularly in situations where benefits are rendered in anticipation of a contract that does not materialise.[5]

(b) Contractual and non-contractual expectations

6-5   It will be apparent that one of the most important sides of failure of assumptions concerns benefits rendered under a contract – payment to a seller who

---

3   And in many earlier works was, indeed, treated as a species of free acceptance: eg, Goff & Jones, 1st edn, 1966, pp 30–31.

4   Above, § 5-8.

5   *William Lacey (Hounslow) Ltd v Davis* [1957] 1 WLR 932.

wrongfully fails to supply goods or services, part performance of contractual obligations, and so on. Nevertheless, there is no necessary connection between this head of recovery and the law of contract. Failure of assumptions can apply just as much in a non-contractual context.[6] One example is benefits rendered in anticipation of a contract that never materialises. Others are where a buyer of land pays a pre-contractual deposit in the expectation that contracts will be exchanged, but for some reason they never are,[7] or where money is paid in the expectation of a contract eventuating between the payer and a third party other than the payee.[8] Indeed, similar considerations can apply where the expected return was not, and was never intended to be, anything to do with contract at all. A good instance concerns the recipient of a wedding present: he does not contract to get married, but nevertheless is *prima facie* liable to refund anything received if the nuptials never take place.[9] Again, those paying for improvements to others' property have a presumptive right to restitution, whether or not they ever stipulated for any contractual right against the building owner.[10]

Indeed, the assumption (or 'consideration') which fails need not even relate to anything to be supplied by the recipient at all. Suppose a father gives his son £300 to reimburse the latter for a dental bill that he expects to have to pay in a week's time. If the son's toothache miraculously disappears two days later, it is suggested that he will, on principle, be liable to repay the £300 to his father. All that matters is that the purpose for which the money was paid has not been fulfilled.[11]

(c) Forms of benefit covered by failure of assumptions

6-6 Not only is there no necessary tie between failure of assumptions and contract: equally, there is no reason arbitrarily to limit discussion of the subject to particular types or classifications of benefit. This is an important point of principle. Traditionally, discussions of failure of assumptions have often tended to concentrate on claims for recovery of money paid, to the exclusion of almost everything else (witness the fact that the common law has always recognised an action for 'money paid for a consideration which has totally failed', but never, at least in so many words, one for other benefits provided in similar

---

6   For this reason, this chapter – indeed, this book – do their best to avoid referring to the loaded phrase 'failure of consideration' except where specifically contractual matters are being discussed.

7   *Chillingworth v Esche* [1924] 1 Ch 97; *Lowis v Wilson* [1949] IR 347.

8   *Hayes v Stirling* (1863) 14 Ir CLR 277 (payment to promoter of stillborn company for shares to be issued by it).

9   As in *P v P* [1916] 2 IR 400.

10 Eg, *Hussey v Palmer* [1972] 3 All ER 744.

11 But note that this reasoning does not seem to apply where money is paid to an assignee of contractual rights, since here the only remedy is against the assignor: *The Trident Beauty* [1994] 1 All ER 470. *Sed quaere*: cf Tettenborn [1993] CLJ 220.

circumstances). Nevertheless, analytically, the subject must cover all benefits, including services rendered and goods supplied:[12] and this is the approach taken in this chapter.

To discuss all kinds of benefit in the context of failure of assumptions is not to say that they must always be treated in the same way, of course. On the contrary, in particular cases there may well be highly relevant differences between them. For instance, in the case of services (but not money), the defendant may well be able to plead that he did not freely accept them, so that the 'no forced exchange' principle[13] applies. Furthermore, there is no doubt that the law does *in fact* discriminate between payments of money and other benefits. For example, whereas a person who has paid in full for something he has not got can claim failure of consideration, the better view seems to be that a person who has fully performed a contract in kind cannot: he is limited to claiming the contract price.[14] Again, in actions for the recovery of money paid, but not elsewhere, the rule remains (albeit much criticised) that the claimant must have received nothing of what he contracted for: the failure of consideration, in other words, must be total. But, this does not alter the fact that the fundamental restitutionary issues affecting both are the same, and that any differences in treatment should have to be justified.

(d) The problem of counter-restitution

6-7   If I complain that I have provided money, goods or services to someone else, but not got the expected return, my right to restitution must be subject to one major condition. Before I can recover for my own performance, I can be expected to return, or at the very least give credit for, what I myself have received in return for it. In other words, I cannot in the same breath seek both to impugn a transaction and to keep what I have received under it. Birks[15] and others,[16] indeed, postulate the existence of a general restitutionary 'defence' entitled 'counter-restitution impossible'. In practice, however, this is overwhelmingly a feature of claims based on failure of assumptions.

This is obviously an important point: why, then, does it arise so rarely? The reason is that most cases of failure of assumption are contract cases, and here, two specific rules pre-empt any discussion of the general position. One is the

---

12 Cf *Key v Harwood* (1846) 2 CB 905 (contract to exchange services for services: restitution where defendant's services were not forthcoming).

13 See above, § 1-30 *et seq*.

14 Unless, perhaps, something subsequently happens to make the contact unenforceable: see the Privy Council's decision in *Goss v Chilcott* [1996] AC 788 (loan advanced: contract then avoided because of alteration of mortgage deed: restitution granted).

15 Birks, p 415.

16 Eg, Virgo, *Principles of the Law of Restitution*, p 690 *et seq*.

'total failure' rule, discussed below, § 6-15. By peremptorily cutting off all restitution once the claimant has got anything at all in return, this prevents the question of counter-restitution arising in the first place. The other is the fact that where benefits are rendered under voidable contracts (for example, where mistake, misrepresentation or undue influence are in issue), the question of counter-restitution is regarded not as restitutionary but contractual. It is subsumed in the rule that rescission cannot be had unless *restitutio in integrum* is possible: and, of course, if the contract cannot be validly rescinded, restitution is equally barred.

6-8 Nevertheless, there seems little doubt that counter-restitution is generally required of all 'failure of assumptions' claimants outside this area. Thus, in the void contract case of *Rover International Ltd v Cannon Film Sales Ltd (No 3)*,[17] where the plaintiff sought to recover the value of services provided under a void contract, it was accepted that in order to do so he had to give credit for what he had himself received. And again, in *Cheese v Thomas*[18] a great-uncle was persuaded by his great-nephew's undue influence to contribute £43,000 towards buying a house for himself and his great-nephew to share. The relationship did not prosper; and on later setting aside the arrangement, the Court of Appeal regarded it as axiomatic that in seeking to extricate his investment, the uncle had to give credit for accommodation actually enjoyed in the house.

(e) Proprietary claims and failure of consideration

6-9 Although we have suggested that there is a good deal in common between claims for mistake and for failure of consideration, one difference is that claims of the latter sort should not, without more, give rise to a proprietary remedy. A straightforward illustration is *Re Goldcorp Exchange Ltd*.[19] Gullible members of the New Zealand public paid Goldcorp in advance for gold bullion to be bought for them, sold to them and stored on their behalf. None was; nevertheless, the Privy Council had little difficulty in holding that the customers had no right against the moneys paid or their proceeds in Goldcorp's hands. They merely had unsecured claims in Goldcorp's liquidation.

Why should this be? The answer, it is suggested, is that a person paying in advance for goods or services – or, for that matter, providing goods in expectation of payment – presumptively relies on the other party's credit, and takes the risk that it may fail. To put him in a better position by superadding a

---

17 [1989] 3 All ER 723. Strictly, this involved payment under a void contract, but the principle is the same.

18 [1994] 1 All ER 35.

19 [1995] 1 AC 74, p 100 *et seq*. See, too, *Box v Barclays Bank plc* (1998) unreported, 24 March, Ch D. Earlier authorities include, eg, *Moseley v Cressey's Co* (1865) LR 1 Eq 405.

claim to the money itself would therefore subvert the assumption underlying the contract.[20]

6-10   It should be remembered, however, that this exclusion of proprietary relief is only a *prima facie* rule. It is always open to the parties to stipulate for a prepayment to be made in trust, on the basis that if they are not used for the stated purpose, they are recoverable *in specie*.[21] And, indeed, where A pays money to B for a given purpose and stipulates for the moneys to be held separately pending their application to that purpose, such an arrangement will often be inferred.[22] Moreover, as will be made clear in Chapter 7, where property is transferred under a contract which is void or voidable, a proprietary remedy may be much easier to establish.[23]

Furthermore, it should be remembered that claims for failure of consideration may often overlap with claims for mistake.[24] In such cases, assuming the decision in *Chase Manhattan Bank NV v Israel-British Bank Ltd*[25] to be correct,[26] there will always be a possibility of a proprietary remedy being made. This is the best explanation for the decision in *Neste Oy v Lloyds Bank Ltd*,[27] where a principal who put his agent in funds to meet certain obligations not knowing that the agent had recently become insolvent was held able to trace the payment. If the decision is correct at all, the remedy there can only have been justified on the basis of the principal's mistake of fact.

---

20   See, too, *Westdeutsche Landesbank Girozentrale v Islington BC* [1996] AC 669, p 683 *et seq* (Lord Goff). Oddly enough, the position is different with would-be purchasers or lessees of land, who have a lien over the land for the return of the purchase price or premium: see eg, *Lee-Parker v Izzett* [1971] 1 WLR 1688 and *Middleton v Magnay* (1864) 2 H & M 233. While the rule is well established, a principled justification for it is hard to fathom.

21   Eg, *Barclays Bank Ltd v Quistclose Investments Ltd* [1970] AC 567; *Re Kayford Ltd* [1975] 1 All ER 604.

22   Eg, *Quistclose Investments Ltd v Rolls-Razor Ltd* [1970] AC 567; see, too, *Shansal v Al-Kishtaini* (1999) unreported, 9 June (Richards J). Similarly, where moneys are supplied on the basis that they are to be used for a given purpose and none other: cf *Twinsectra Ltd v Yardley* [1999] Lloyd's Rep Banking 438.

23   As in, eg, *Cundy v Lindsay* (1878) 3 App Cas 459 (void contract); or *El Ajou v Dollar Land Holdings plc* [1993] 3 All ER 717 (voidable contract).

24   Eg, in *Kleinwort Benson Ltd v Lincoln CC* [1999] 2 AC 349 it was held that a claim for return of moneys paid under a void interest rate swap could be characterised as one for mistake as much as one for failure of assumptions.

25   [1981] Ch 105.

26   Which is open to some doubt: above, § 3-20.

27   [1983] 2 Lloyd's Rep 658.

II BENEFITS RENDERED UNDER VALID CONTRACTS[28]

(a) Contract cases: 'failure of consideration'

Generally

6-11   It is worth treating contractual restitution separately in this connection for several reasons.

First, a number of rules have grown up which are specific to restitutionary recovery between contracting parties. The most obvious examples are the working out of the common law rules relating to *quantum meruit* and *quantum valebat* in the context of partial performance, and (in England and Northern Ireland) the statutory provisions on frustration contained in the Law Reform (Frustrated Contracts) Act 1943.

Secondly, where a restitutionary claim is made against a contractual background, there may be a need to tailor relief so as to prevent it subverting the terms of the contract itself. For instance, if I perform services at your request without a contract, I should obviously be able to claim their reasonable value.[29] Subject to arguments based on 'subjective devaluation' and such-like, there is no other way to quantify the recovery. But, if the services amounted to partial performance of a contract between us, then arguably I should be limited to a *pro rata* proportion of the agreed price for the whole, on the basis that I should not be able to do better by performing in part than I would have done had I performed in full. This is discussed more fully below.[30]

before a contractor can sue for restitution in respect of benefits provided under the contract, he must show that the contract itself is ineffective.[31] As pointed out in Chapter 1, there is nothing unjust about your retaining benefits rendered in performance of a valid and subsisting contract. This explains why the contractor who performs in full by providing goods or services and has nothing left to do but claim the price cannot choose instead to claim the reasonable value of what he has done.[32] Unlike the person who pays in advance and gets nothing, such a person has no grounds for regarding the contract as terminated merely by the other's failure to pay: he is therefore limited to his action on the contract. It also explains why, if I do work for you under a contract that provides a means for payment to be assessed, I cannot bypass that contractual provision by claiming on a *quantum meruit*.[33]

---

28 See Rose (ed), *Failure of Contracts*, Chapter 5.
29 As in *British Steel Corp v Cleveland Bridge and Engineering Co Ltd* [1984] 1 All ER 504.
30 See below, § 6-30.
31 A proposition which, as Burrows points out, is so obvious that it is invariably assumed rather than expressed: see Burrows, p 250.
32 *Pace* Birks: see Birks, p 226 *et seq*.
33 As in *Cotter v Minister of Agriculture* (1991) unreported, 31 July, HC (Ire). Cf the analogous English decision in *Re Richmond Gate Property Co Ltd* [1965] 1 WLR 335.

'Consideration'

6-12   One important point needs to be made on the meaning of 'failure of consideration' in the contractual context. The 'consideration' that must fail is the actual return expected by the claimant under the contract – that is, the performance which it was wrongly assumed would be forthcoming.[34] The concept of consideration here does not mean the abstract promise to provide that return (even though, in the law of contract generally, the promise may itself be regarded as 'consideration' for the purpose of deciding whether the contract is enforceable). So a claimant who gets the benefit of the defendant's obligation to counter-perform, but nothing else, can nevertheless show failure of assumptions (or failure of consideration) and hence obtain restitution.

This explains why a claimant who pre-pays for goods under a contract later terminated, for example, by frustration, recovers his money: the fact that for a time, he had the benefit of the payee's contractual obligation is irrelevant.[35] Conversely, it is suggested that a claimant who pays for and receives goods under a contract which, unknown to him, is unenforceable has no claim to get his money back. What he paid for was the goods themselves, not the promise to provide them, and those goods he has now got.

6-13   The above reasoning applies to the vast majority of ordinary contracts. But it is not invariable. It may be that the claimant is specifically concerned to obtain the benefit of the defendant's legal duty to counter-perform. If so, then the remedy for failure of assumptions will be tailored accordingly. One example is contracts of insurance. Here, the assured is buying not a thing or a service, but a right: indeed, in most cases he fervently hopes that that it is a right he will not have to exercise. Hence, once the underwriter has been on risk (that is, contractually bound to indemnify the assured), for however short a time, the right to recover premiums on cancellation is lost, whether or not the assured has actually claimed.[36] Another example is a contract for the loan of money, or for the placing of money on deposit. The lender or depositor is effectively buying a legally enforceable obligation to repay. If he gets it, he gets what he paid for and

---

34   The test of whether consideration has failed is 'whether the promisor has performed any part of the contractual duties in respect of which the payment is due': Lord Goff in *Stocznia Gdanska SA v Latvian Shipping Co* [1998] 1 All ER 883, pp 895–86.

35   An important point of principle cemented in *Fibrosa Spolka Akcyjna v Fairbairn Lawson Combe Barbour Ltd* [1943] AC 32, p 48 (Lord Simon LC), overruling the decision to the contrary in *Chandler v Webster* [1904] 1 KB 493.

36   Eg, *Wolenberg v Royal Co-operative Collecting Society* (1915) 83 LJ KB 1316; *Stapleton v Prudential Assurance Co* (1928) 62 ILTR 56. Contrariwise, if the underwriter was never at risk, the premium is repayable: *Tyrie v Fletcher* (1777) 2 Cowp 666.

the consideration does not fail. If he does not, then even if in fact he receives repayment, there is a failure of consideration.[37]

Valid contracts: money paid

6-14　At first sight, one might have thought that where I pay for something which I do not get under a valid contract, there was no need for a restitutionary claim at all. After all, if I pay you for a car which you do not deliver, I can simply claim damages for breach of contract. But a moment's thought shows matters are not as simple as this. There may be no claim for damages at all. For instance, you may be protected by an exemption clause, or the contract may have been frustrated or otherwise become unenforceable;[38] nevertheless, I will still want my money back. Furthermore, a claim for damages may give me less than I want. If the undelivered car is worth less than the price agreed, this must be taken into account in reckoning damages, but I may wish to recover the whole amount I paid.

Hence, the common law action for return of money paid for a consideration which has totally failed. This allows a person paying money to recover it in full if he can show that he has received no part of what was promised in return. Three points in particular need discussing.

(1) Need for total failure

6-15　In pre-payment cases, restitutionary recovery is limited to where there has been a *total* failure of consideration: that is, to cases where the claimant has got no part of the expected return. If he has received any part of what he paid for, it is said that restitution is barred. So, if you pay me £1,000 to paint your house and I only do half the job, you are limited to your claim – if any – in damages, and have no separate remedy for a proportion of the sum paid.[39]

This is a bizarre and unprepossessing limitation, which today attracts little or no academic support;[40] and in England, at least, there have been increasing hints

---

37　*Goss v Chilcott* [1996] AC 788 (contractual duty to repay loan abrogated because of alteration of mortgage deed: restitution for lender nevertheless granted). Cf *Westdeutsche Landesbank Girozentrale v Islington BC* [1996] AC 669, p 710 (Lord Browne-Wilkinson) (fact that counterparty to void swap agreement under no duty to pay means failure of consideration). But void contracts are, in any case, treated rather differently: see below, Chapter 7.

38　Eg, where a loan is made, but subsequently avoided by the unauthorised alteration of the loan documents: see *Goss v Chilcott* [1996] AC 788, granting restitution of the amount lent.

39　Eg *Hunt v Silk* (1804) 5 East 449: *Lecky v Walter* [1914] IR 378. See, too, *Rover International Ltd v Cannon Film Sales Ltd (No 3)* [1989] 3 All ER 723; *The Trident Beauty* [1994] 1 All ER 470.

40　Burrows, p 253 *et seq*; Goff & Jones, p 516 *et seq*. Birks, p 242 *et seq*, is, admittedly, slightly more equivocal. See, too, Watts (1998) 114 LQR 341.

that it may be judicially reconsidered.[41] The arguments in its favour are pretty unconvincing. One is that a person who has received (say) services cannot give them back so as to effect counter-restitution and return the parties to their original position. But this is hardly a knock-out point: there is no reason why the impossibility of counter-restitution *in specie* should prevent the provision of a cash equivalent or set off.[42]

Slightly more plausible is the argument that quantifying claims to a proportionate return – or, to put it another way, the amount of counter-restitution to be allowed to the defendant – might be difficult. If a builder fails to complete a house for which his client has pre-paid, how much is a part-built structure worth to the latter for the purpose of deciding how much to deduct from his claim to recover his money? The answer is not necessarily 50% of the value of a complete house. But, this is not an insuperable difficulty either. The courts have little difficulty in making such valuations elsewhere,[43] and if the claimant is prepared to submit to counter-restitution, he should not be prevented from doing so.

6-16   No doubt because of the unattractiveness of the rule, its ambit is narrow. It does not apply to claims other than for money,[44] nor (it seems) to sale of goods cases. A builder wrongfully prevented from completing a job[45] is not disabled from recovering a *quantum meruit* for what he has done, merely by having received part of the price: what he has already been paid is merely deducted from any recovery. Again, where a pre-paid seller of goods delivers short, the buyer is, on the authorities, entitled to recover the price *pro rata* in respect of what he did not get.[46] Furthermore, there are *dicta* in the Privy Council that total failure is not required in the case of contracts for the loan of money. In *Goss v Chilcott*,[47] the plaintiffs made an advance to the defendant on mortgage, but the contract of loan was later avoided because of an unauthorised alteration in the

---

41 See *Goss v Chilcott* [1996] AC 788, p 798; *Stocznia Gdanska SA v Latvian Shipping Co* [1998] 1 All ER 883, p 895–96. Cf *Ferguson (DO) Associates Ltd v Soh* (1992) 62 Build LR 95, where the requirement was simply ignored and a builder who part performed was ordered to return a proportionate part of the price; and see *Roxborough v Rothmans of Pall Mall (Australia) Ltd* (1999) 167 ALR 326.

42 As is done in a number of cases where it is sought to rescind a contract: see, eg, *Erlanger v New Sombrero Phosphate Co* (1878) 3 App Cas 1218 (contract for sale of phosphate mine rescinded on payment for guano extracted), or *O'Sullivan v Management Agency and Music Ltd* [1985] QB 428 (pop star able to rescind management agreement by paying in cash for non-returnable services received).

43 And see *Goss v Chilcott* [1996] AC 788, p 798.

44 Save, perhaps, in one maverick case. In *Pearce v Brain* [1929] 2 KB 310 it was held that where a contract to exchange two chattels was successfully impugned on account of minority, the plaintiff could not in the absence of total failure have restitution for the chattel he had provided.

45 On which, see below, § 6-23 *et seq*.

46 *Behrend v Produce Brokers Ltd* [1920] 3 KB 530.

47 [1996] AC 788.

documentation.[48] The plaintiffs sought, and got, restitution of the amount lent on the basis of failure of consideration. In fact, no repayments of principal had been made at the time the contract became unenforceable, so the 'total failure' requirement was satisfied in any case. Nevertheless, it was clearly Lord Goff's view that restitution *pro rata* would have been ordered even if there had been one or more repayments: 'for,' he said, 'at least in those cases in which apportionment can be carried out without difficulty, the law will allow partial recovery on this ground.'[49] Whether these words will be read in future as heralding the end of the total failure requirement generally remains to be seen.

It is arguable, indeed, that the only reason the requirement of total failure survives at all is that the exceptions to it are so extensive, and the interpretation of it so generous to claimants, that it does not matter except in a small minority of cases. A good deal of its sting is, in any case, removed by the existence of the exceptions to it.

(2) Total failure: what is the 'consideration'?

6-17   It is not always easy to determine what counts as the 'consideration' which has to be shown to have totally failed. Fundamentally, this depends on what was promised by the defendant: it is the contractual performance that matters, and not (for instance) acts preparatory to it. This, in turn, can depend on a nice construction of the terms of the contract itself. The point came up neatly in *Hyundai Heavy Industries Co Ltd v Papadopoulos*.[50] Buyers of a ship in the course of construction agreed to pay by five instalments as her building proceeded; the defendant guaranteed these instalments. The buyers failed to pay one instalment; the builders cancelled the contract (as they were entitled to do) and sued the defendants for that instalment. One argument of the defendants was based on circuity of action. On the assumption that their liability was co-extensive with that of the buyers, they contended that had the instalment been paid by the buyers, it would have been recoverable by them on the basis that the consideration – provision of the ship – had totally failed. Although the case eventually turned on other matters, two members of the House of Lords[51] rejected this plea, saying that the contract here was not simply one of sale, but for construction and sale: construction having started, consideration had not totally failed.

---

48   Under the rule in *Pigot's* Case (1614) 11 Co Rep 26b.
49   See [1996] AC 788, p 798.
50   [1980] 2 All ER 29. See too *Stocznia Gdanska v Latvian Shipping Co* [1995] 2 Lloyd's Rep 592; *Clowes Developments Ltd v Mulchinock* (2001) unreported, 24 May, Ch D.
51   Viscount Dilhorne and Lord Fraser.

(3) Total failure: the problem of collateral benefits

6-18   The authorities strictly limit the benefits to the claimant that will prevent the failure being total and hence defeat an action for restitution of the price. Only receipt of something *actually promised* by the defendant as part of the exchange will do: the fact that the claimant may have received some other incidental or collateral benefit will not.[52] Take the facts of the English case of *Rowland v Divall*.[53] A bought a car from B; some months later, he had to give it up to the true owner when it transpired that B had had no title to it in the first place. He recovered the price in full, even though he had had the incidental use of the car meanwhile: he had paid for a good title and not got it. And the same result was reached on very similar facts in Ireland in *Chartered Trust (Ireland) Ltd v Healy*.[54] Again, in *Rover International Ltd v Cannon Film Sales Ltd (No 3)*,[55] film distributors paid sums in advance to C under an agreement whereby they would be given possession of certain films with a view to distributing them at a profit. After delivery of the films, but before their distribution *en masse*, C terminated the arrangements. The distributors successfully claimed their money back, despite the fact that they had had possession of the films for some time. These results are logically tendentious, since it seems indubitable that under their contracts, possession of car and films were something to which Rowland and Rover respectively were entitled.[56] They are best explained as resulting from a dislike of the total failure requirement and a desire to limit it as far as possible: were claims for partial failure to be admitted, the courts might well be more willing to allow the defendant credit for such benefits.[57]

6-19   It is also worth noting that where a contract of sale is rightfully terminated after the buyer has received the subject matter of it (for example, where goods are

---

52 Cf *P v P* [1916] 2 IR 400 (money paid in pursuance of void marriage recoverable: receipt of benefit of putative marriage irrelevant).

53 [1923] 2 KB 500. And similarly with hire purchase: *Warman v Southern Counties Car Finance Ltd* [1949] 2 KB 576. See, too, *Butterworth v Kingsway Motors Ltd* [1954] 1 WLR 1286.

54 (1985) unreported, 10 December, HC. The only difference was that the plaintiff was a hire-purchaser and not a buyer, as in *Warman v Southern Counties Car Finance Ltd* [1949] 2 KB 576. See too *UDT (Ireland) Ltd v Shannon Caravans Ltd* [1976] IR 225.

55 [1989] 3 All ER 723. Strictly, this involved payment under a void contract, but the principle is the same. See too *South West Water Services Ltd v International Computers Ltd* (1999) unreported, 26 June, QBD (recovery of price paid for useless computer system despite receipt of a great deal of technical advice).

56 This is because, however good the title he may pass, a seller must be in breach of contract if he fails to provide the buyer with possession of the goods themselves. It must follow that possession is a part of the promised consideration. See, too, the intriguing Privy Council decision in *Goss v Chilcott* [1996] AC 788, that receipt of instalments of interest, as against capital repayments, on a loan which later became unenforceable, did not prevent the lender claiming on the basis of total failure of consideration.

57 In fact, the court's refusal to do this in *Rowland's* case is more defensible than it looks. The seller did not have a strong claim to receive credit for a benefit to the buyer (use of the car) which he himself had no right to give. Furthermore, the buyer faced a theoretical liability to the true owner in conversion. True, he might well not sue in practice: but, if so, should this enure to his benefit or that of the seller? Surely the former.

sub-standard, or where the contract was induced by the seller's misrepresentation), the effect of this is to revest title in the seller and give rise to a total failure of consideration, with a concomitant right in the buyer to recover the price in full.[58] This is despite the fact that the latter has incontrovertibly received, if only for a time, what he was entitled to.

One complication in connection with Irish law must be noted here. Essentially, the position is as stated above, but matters may be obscured by the remnants of the rule in *Legge v Croker*[59] and *Seddon v North Eastern Salt Co Ltd*[60] that an executed contract (other than one for the sale of goods)[61] cannot be rescinded at all for misrepresentation. This explains, for example, the decision in *Lecky v Walter*[62] that a person induced to buy worthless bonds by a misrepresentation could not sue to recover the price once she had received the bonds.

(4) Effect of a losing bargain

6-20   On the authorities,[63] it does not matter whether or not the claimant seeking to recover his money also has an action in breach of contract which would yield him less. If I pay you £10,000 for a car worth £8,000, I can recover the full £10,000 if you do not deliver it, despite the fact that the contract was a losing one and had you fulfilled it I would have lost £2,000. This rule has been attacked,[64] but it is suggested that, on balance, it is entirely justifiable. However odd it may seem that I should be saved from a bad bargain willingly contracted with you, it is clearly unjust that you should be allowed to keep the profit (£2,000) that you would have made on the deal if you did not in fact perform your part of it.

The relationship of this principle with the question whether a supplier of goods or services can similarly escape from a bad bargain is discussed below.

(5) Recovery of money by claimant who is himself in breach of contract

6-21   Most cases of payment of money for something that is not forthcoming will involve a breach of contract by the defendant (or possibly some form of excused

---

58   And similarly, it seems, where what is delivered is entirely worthless, eg, where the plaintiff buys an annuity on the life of an annuitant who has in fact died: cf *Strickland v Turner* (1852) 7 Ex 208.

59   (1811) 1 Ball & B 506.

60   [1905] 1 Ch 326.

61   Section 44(b) of the Sale of Goods and Supply of Services Act 1980 (Ire) now allows rescission of an executed contract for the sale of goods. But this provision does not affect other types of contract. Contrast the English Misrepresentation Act 1967, s 1(b) (and its NI equivalent, the Misrepresentation (NI) Act 1967), which has removed the whole difficulty by simply abolishing the rule in *Seddon's* case.

62   [1914] IR 378.

63   The leading authority is *Wilkinson v Lloyd* (1845) 7 QB 27. *Rowland v Divall* [1923] 2 KB 500, discussed above, is another example.

64   Eg, McKendrick in Birks (ed), *Laundering and Tracing*, p 227 et seq. It is, however, defended by Virgo: *Principles of the Law of Restitution*, pp 351–52.

non-performance, as where a contract is frustrated). But not necessarily: what if I pay you in advance for a car and then break the contract myself by refusing delivery? In such a case, the fact that I am in breach is, it would seem, no bar to recovery. Thus, in *Dies v British International Mining and Finance Corp*,[65] a plaintiff who paid £100,000 in advance for a shipment of arms was held able to recover it when, albeit in breach of contract, he failed to take delivery. This is clearly right: the defendant not having provided the consideration involved, there is no reason to allow him to keep the price, particularly since he is adequately protected by his right to set off against the claimant any claim he may have for damages for breach of contract. Furthermore, it is, of course, always possible for the parties to stipulate that a prepayment is a deposit to be forfeited in the event of breach. Subject to statutory[66] and possible equitable[67] intervention, such an agreement will be upheld and will oust any putative right to restitution.

6-22   One difficulty arises in this connection, however. It is sometimes said that there can never be recovery for failure of consideration while the underlying contract subsists.[68] In *Dies's* case, this did not matter, since it was apparently assumed that the seller had accepted the plaintiff's repudiation and hence the contract was at an end. But, what if this had not happened, and the seller had continued to insist on keeping the contract alive, relying on the principle that one contracting party cannot *ipso facto* terminate a contract by repudiation? It seems incredible that a seller should be able thus indefinitely to bar the buyer's right to restitution: yet this seems to follow from the view just outlined.

The answer, it is suggested, is that the supposed rule against restitution where the contract remains in force is itself misconceived. The authorities said to support it are *Thomas v Brown*[69] and *Fitt v Cassanet*.[70] In the former case, a purchaser of land paid a deposit under a contract which turned out to be unenforceable because of the Statute of Frauds. He failed to recover it back on the basis that the vendor remained at all times ready and willing to convey the land concerned. In the latter, a buyer who paid in advance for goods, accepted some of them, but wrongfully rejected the rest was refused recovery.

However, *Thomas v Brown* is hardly strong authority, since the gist of the decision was that the parties clearly intended the deposit to be irrecoverable in the event of default by the buyer: indeed, this was the point on which most of the discussion turned. It is true that *Fitt v Cassanet* was supposedly decided on the basis that the seller remained willing to deliver the balance,[71] but there, the

---

65   [1939] 1 KB 724. Cf *Stevenson v Snow* (1761) 3 Burr 1237 (premium recoverable on insurance policy cancelled by assured before risk has attached).

66   Eg, the (English) Law of Property Act 1925, s 49(2).

67   Eg, *Workers Trust Ltd v Dojap* [1993] AC 573: but cf *The Scaptrade* [1983] 2 AC 694, p 700.

68   Birks, p 235 *et seq*; Burrows, p 257.

69   (1876) 1 QBD 714, followed in *Monnickendam v Leanse* (1923) 39 TLR 445.

70   (1852) 4 M & G 898.

71   See (1852) 4 M & G 898, 903–04.

buyer had already received more than he had paid for, so it is difficult to see any basis for his claim anyway. The true principle, it is submitted, is more limited: namely, that recovery is barred if and so long as the sum paid remains due under the contract.[72] If it is not so payable or ceases to be due, it is recoverable whether or not the contract subsists for other purposes. And where a buyer refuses, even wrongfully, to accept goods, no part of the price is, or ever can be, payable: his sole liability is in damages.[73] It follows, it is submitted, that despite the interpretation placed by some authors on cases such as *Thomas v Brown*, in such cases the subsistence of the contract is no bar to recovery.

Valid contracts: goods provided and services rendered

(1) Generally

6-23   Parallel to the right to recover money for failure of consideration, the common law remedies of *quantum meruit* (for services) or *quantum valebat* (for goods) allow a claimant to recover the reasonable value of benefits in kind rendered under a contract which for some reason is not fully performed. The basis of this, as with money paid, is failure of consideration: since a contractor who performs only in part, for whatever reason, cannot claim the contract price,[74] the return he hoped to get is unavailable to him. Nevertheless, whatever logic might be seen to demand,[75] the two rights are not necessarily mirror images of one another, and there are a number of important differences between them.

6-24   The first difference is that restitution will normally be limited to the contractor whose performance is incomplete: the contractor who has rendered full performance in kind is restricted to his action on the contract for the price.[76] Despite the apparent discrepancy with the claimant who has paid the full price for something he has not got (who is permitted restitution as an alternative to an action on the contract, and on occasion a more profitable one), it is suggested that this is quite right. Contract, it must be remembered, ousts restitution; and the person who contracts to do something for a given price agrees to receive that price, no more and no less.[77]

---

72 Cf *Hyundai Heavy Industries Co Ltd v Papadopoulos* [1980] 2 All ER 29.

73 Sale of Goods Act 1979 (England) and Sale of Goods Act 1893 (Ireland), s 49(1); *Colley v Overseas Exporters Ltd* [1921] 3 KB 302.

74 Unless the failure is very small so as to trigger the doctrine of 'substantial performance': eg, *Hoenig v Isaacs* [1952] 1 All ER 176.

75 Cf Birks, p 266 *et seq*.

76 This is normally regarded as so obvious that there is little authority: but frustration cases such as *Davis and Co (Contractors) Ltd v Fareham UDC* [1956] AC 696 or *Tsakiroglou & Co Ltd v Noblee Thorl GmbH* [1962] AC 93 are straightforward examples.

77 Birks, p 226 *et seq*, agrees with this outcome but not the reasoning. He grounds the result on the basis that there ought to be a restitutionary action, but that the recipient of the goods or services can plead 'subjective devaluation' in order to avoid paying more than the contract price. With respect, this seems a somewhat roundabout way of reaching the same result.

What is the position where the expected return is itself in kind and not in cash? This point may arise in counter-trade, for instance, or out of an agreement for exchange of services. Suppose A supplies wheat to B in exchange for a shipment of oil that never materialises: if the price of oil has collapsed, can A claim the value of the wheat, or is he limited to claiming damages set at the value of the undelivered oil? Although there is no direct authority, the analogy of the land improvement cases (for example, where X pays to extend Y's house in exchange for Y's promise, later broken, to let him live in it rent-free for life)[78] suggests that he should be able to. The reason for this contrast with the ordinary case of the fully performing contractor is not immediately obvious: but arguably, it lies in the idea that it is not open to a contractor who has performed and merely needs to claim the price to rescind the contract for non-payment and thus get rid of his own obligation to perform.

6-25   The second difference between actions for the value of goods and services and those for the return of money is that it has never been suggested that the much-criticised requirement of total failure should apply here. If I agree to build you a house and you wrongfully terminate the contract, I can claim the reasonable value of what I have done. It is nothing to the point that you may have already paid me a sum on account under the contract: that sum will merely be deducted from my total claim.

Thirdly, as will appear, issues will arise here which are irrelevant to money payments: namely, what amounts to a benefit, how it should be valued, and whether it has been freely accepted.

Fourthly, in certain cases statute has intervened. Under s 2 of the Apportionment Act 1870:[79]

> all rents, annuities, dividends, and other periodical payments in the nature of income ... shall ... be considered as accruing from day to day, and shall be apportionable in respect of time accordingly.

In a number of particular situations, particularly in the employment context where services are rendered under a contract terminated other than by the defendant's breach, this provision will override the rules that would otherwise apply.

(2) Contracts terminated by defendant's breach

6-26   Restitution is clearly available where the claimant's failure to render full performance is due to breach of contract by the other side. If I agree to build you a house, but you wrongfully throw me off the site while I am building it, I can claim the reasonable value of the work already done.[80]

---

78 As in *Hussey v Palmer* [1972] 3 All ER 744 or *Yaxley v Gotts* [2000] 1 All ER 711.

79 In force in all jurisdictions concerned.

80 Eg, *Arterial Drainage Co v Rathangan Drainage Board* (1880) 6 LR Ir 513; *Lodder v Slowey* [1904] AC 442; *Lusty v Finsbury Securities Ltd* (1991) 58 Build LR 66.

What amounts to 'benefit' so as to trigger a claim?

6-27   In most cases of contractual restitution, the defendant will have tangibly received something from the claimant – a part delivery of goods, an unfinished building. This is clearly a benefit, and the question is essentially one of valuing it (of which more below). But not always. Assume you agree to write me a book, or build me a ship, or to sell me a picture, having first cleaned it. After you have done some or all of the work, but before delivery is due, I say I do not want it and will refuse delivery. You may have a claim for breach of contract; but do you have a claim in restitution for the writing or cleaning you have done?

This was essentially the issue that arose in the old case of *Planché v Colburn*.[81] An author's commission was wrongfully countermanded when he had written an appreciable amount (but not delivered the manuscript). The author sought to recover in *quantum meruit*; the publishers argued that the claim was misconceived, since – in modern terms – they had received no benefit. The plaintiff nevertheless succeeded.

6-28   The result in *Planché* is controversial, and it has indeed been criticised.[82] How can a half-written book which a publisher has never seen and now does not want amount to a benefit to anyone? Is not the restitution issue a red herring and the author's claim really one for his own time wasted, that is, for damages?

It is, nevertheless, submitted that *Planché* is quite defensible. The key to the problem lies in what we regard as amounting to a 'benefit'. It was suggested above[83] that the concept is apt to include not only a physical receipt of goods or services, but also anything done as a result of a request addressed to the person providing them. If so, there is no difficulty in saying that in that case, the author's work benefited the publisher. Indeed, reasoning of this sort seems to underlie the Irish decision in *Folens and Co v Minister of Education*,[84] where McWilliam J reached the same result on facts similar to *Planché*.[85] The defendants who had commissioned the work concerned (an Irish language children's encyclopedia) and then cancelled the project had to pay for the work done by the would-be publishers; and this was, it was said, because it had been done 'with the approval or at the direction of the Department'.[86] This, in other words, was sufficient to overcome any 'no benefit' argument.

There is also a further point. The reasoning suggested above avoids what would otherwise be a highly arbitrary distinction. Change the facts of *Planché* slightly, and assume that a manuscript is to be typed on the publisher's own

---

81   (1831) 8 Bing 14, followed in Australia in *Brenner v FAM* [1993] 2 VR 221.

82   Eg, Goff & Jones, pp 20–21; Burrows, pp 8–9.

83   Above, § 1-12 *et seq.*

84   [1984] 1 ILRM 265. Cf *Premier Dairies Ltd v Jameson* (1983) unreported, 1 March, HC (Ire).

85   The difference was that there was no concluded contract between the parties, which if anything makes *Folens* an even stronger authority.

86   See [1984] 1 ILRM 265, p 276.

word processor, so as to be immediately available to him. It would be peculiar, to say the least, that this should make all the difference to the author's claim to a *quantum meruit* if the publisher later reneges on the deal.

Is the benefit freely accepted?

6-29   Another possible difficulty with benefits rendered under contracts terminated through breach lies in the concept of acceptance. Can the defendant, who contracted for, and presumably wanted, performance in full, be said to have accepted anything short of that? In the case of contracts where the claimant's failure to render complete performance results from his own breach, this is a powerful point.[87] Here, however, it is less convincing. Just as it should not lie in a defendant's mouth to say he did not want what he asked for, so, also, he should not be allowed to plead that he did not want part performance when the only reason he did not receive full performance was his own breach of contract.

Effect of a losing bargain

6-30   I agree to build you a house on your land for £100,000. In fact, I have under-priced the job: the reasonable value of my work, if completed, would be £120,000. If you wrongfully throw me off the site when it is half built, should I recover £60,000, being half the value of my labour and materials,[88] or should my claim nevertheless be capped at £50,000, representing the due proportion of the contract price? There seems to be no clear authority in England or Ireland on this point:[89] therefore, it falls to be discussed as a matter of principle.

If one draws the parallel with money paid, logically, the answer to the question just posed must be that there can be no cap. If the payer of *money* is allowed to escape from a bad bargain by recovering his whole expenditure, so also should the person performing in kind be able to do so, by claiming the full value of what he has done.[90] Moreover, it is abundantly clear the case that an action in *quantum meruit* or *quantum valebat* is not an action on the contract:[91] if so, why should it be governed by its terms?

---

87   Below, § 6-33 *et seq.*

88   Assuming, for the sake of simplicity, that the benefit from half a house is half that from a complete one. In practice, some adjustment will invariably have to be made to reflect the fact that it is not.

89   In *Lodder v Slowey* (1900) 20 NZLR 321, a New Zealand court refused to cap the award; when the case went to the Privy Council, the point was not discussed (see [1904] AC 442).

90   Burrows, p 268; *contra*, Goff & Jones, p 530 *et seq*, who discuss the American authorities in some detail.

91   Hence, it has been held that where work is done on the footing of a contract that turns out to be ineffective, there is no cap on the award: see *Rover International Ltd v Cannon Film Sales Ltd (No 3)* [1989] 3 All ER 423, discussed below, § 7-7. (Note, however, that Kerr LJ, p 436, emphasised that the case involved a void contract).

6-31 In restitution, as elsewhere, however, there must be limits to logic where it leads to absurd or counter-intuitive results. And to allow a part-performing contractor to recover an uncapped award will, on occasion, allow a contractor who performs only in part to recover more than he would have got if he had performed in full[92] – a result which is, to say the least, odd.

There is also an argument of principle against disregarding the contract price. Where a person contracts to receive goods or services for a given amount, this shows the value he placed on them. If it is sought to make him pay more than this sum, he ought to be entitled to invoke subjective devaluation against any such claim. The fact he may have broken the contract concerned, and indeed, that that contract may have been rescinded, should not (it is submitted) alter this state of affairs. The fact that technically a contract is at an end should not deprive a defendant of the right to rely on its terms to show the value he placed on what he got under it.

For these reasons, and subject to the problem of 'front loading', dealt with below, it is suggested that the contract price (or rate) should indeed cap the claimant's recovery. It is notable that in one case, namely, where the seller of goods part delivers, this solution is provided by statute.[93]

6-32 If it is permissible to limit the claimant's recovery in such cases, there remains the practical problem of 'front loading'. With fixed costs in account, a normal builder will charge a good deal more proportionately for half a house than for a whole one: should this be reflected in any restitutionary award, by awarding him more than 50% of the total price? There seems no reason why it should not: the customer, although the fixed costs thrown away did not enure directly to his benefit, ought to have known that they would have formed a larger element in half a house than a whole one, and that the price would have been accordingly higher.

(3) Claimant in breach

The general rule

6-33 The authorities are clear on this point. As a general rule, a claimant who is himself in breach cannot have restitution for his own limited performance if the reason why the contract was not performed in full was his own breach of it. A builder who walks off the site before he has finished, as in the leading authorities of *Sumpter v Hedges*[94] and *Callan v Marum*,[95] or a carrier who delivers

---

92 As happened in the well known American case of *Boomer v Muir*, 24 P 2d 570 (1933).

93 See the Sale of Goods Act 1979, s 30(1) (England) and the Sale of Goods Act 1893 (Ireland), giving a part deliverer of goods the right to be paid for them at the contract rate.

94 [1898] 1 QB 673.

95 (1871) 5 IR CL 315. See, too, *Coughlan v Moloney* (1905) 39 ILTR 153, and *Creagh v Sheedy* [1955–1956] Ir JR 85 (no remedy for labourer engaged for fixed period of 12 months who left during that period).

short of the delivery point,[96] forfeits his right not only to the contract price, but to any recovery at all. In this, he is treated remarkably worse than a contractor who performs fully but badly[97] (though it should be remembered that the line between the two is not entirely clear, and a contractor who does a job with very drastic defects may be regarded for these purposes as having failed to render complete performance at all).[98]

The only exceptions are where the contract is not regarded as entire, in that it expressly or impliedly provides for *pro rata* payments, and where (for instance, in the case of contracts of employment) the Apportionment Act 1870[99] applies so as to deem periodical payments to accrue due from day to day.[100]

6-34   There is no doubt that this is a drastic rule. The penalty on the contract-breaker is matched only by the windfall for the victim. The contrast between the incomplete performer and the complete, but defective performer is stark, as is the contrast with the position of the contract-breaker whose benefit took the form of a money payment – who, as we have seen, can recover his payment as on a total failure of consideration. The existing principle has, furthermore, been said to be inconsistent with *dicta* in the House of Lords in *Hain SS Co v Tate and Lyle Ltd*.[101] As a result, it has been castigated by Goff & Jones[102] and Burrows[103] as unfair, and recommended for reversal by the English Law Commission.[104]

6-35   This is powerful criticism. It is nevertheless submitted that the 'no recovery' rule is entirely correct, both on principle and as a matter of policy. The policy point is straightforward: it strongly encourages people to keep their contracts, and it must be remembered that in most cases of incomplete performance, the contractor concerned can assure himself of payment simply by completing the job.

---

96 *Metcalfe v Britannia Ironworks Co* (1877) 2 QBD 423. In practice, contemporary contracts for the carriage of goods by sea invariably oust this rule.

97 *Dakin v Oxley* (1864) 15 CBNS 646 (carrier delivering goods damaged). Cf *Hoenig v Isaacs* [1952] 2 All ER 176 (decorating work done for £750 which cost the client a mere £55 to bring up to standard).

98 Eg, *Kincora Builders Ltd v Cronlin* (1973) unreported, 5 March, HC (Ire), and *Bolton v Mahadeva* [1972] 1 WLR 1009. Cf *Hoenig v Isaacs* [1952] 2 All ER 176.

99 In force in all relevant jurisdictions.

100 One hopes *dicta* in *Moriarty v Regent's Garage Co* [1921] 1 KB 423, p 435, to the effect that an employee lawfully dismissed for misconduct cannot claim back pay, will be disregarded. Cf *Treacy v Corcoran* (1874) IR 8 CL 40, where an employee who resigned during what was otherwise a fixed period of employment successfully invoked the 1870 Act.

101 [1936] 2 All ER 597, p 612, where Lord Wright suggested that a sea carrier in repudiatory breach because of a deviation could claim a *quantum meruit* for freight. See, too, Lord Atkin, p 603 and Lord Maugham, p 616. But this remark was *obiter*, and it is arguable that the deviation cases are *sui generis* anyway.

102 Goff & Jones, p 546 *et seq*.

103 Burrows, p 276 *et seq*. Birks is more lukewarm: *Essays*, p 139 *et seq*.

104 See Law Commission Report No 121.

The principled justification for denying recovery to a claimant in breach lies in the concept of lack of free acceptance, and the presumption against forced exchange.[105] The point is that a person buying goods or services expects full performance. He probably does not want, and certainly never agreed to receive, anything short of that. Unless he has at some later time freely elected to accept the part performance in the knowledge that no more will be forthcoming, it is therefore wrong to make him pay for it, however harsh this may seem vis à vis the seller.[106] This also justifies the distinction between this case and that of the contract-breaker; for whereas it is true that the latter did not contract to pay for part performance, it does not lie in his mouth to oppose this argument to the claimant when it was his own wrong that prevented him receiving performance in full.

This argument could, it is admitted, be queried on the basis that part performance by a contract-breaker has been accepted, albeit implicitly. Burrows,[107] for instance, contends that by contracting to receive the whole performance, the recipient consented in advance to receiving every part of it. But this supposed consent, with respect, is a fiction. The defendant never in fact agreed to accept anything other than full performance. Had he been asked whether he was interested in part performance, he would almost certainly have said he was not: and the idea that the whole includes the part would not impress him at all.

Non-contractual acceptance

6-36 There is one important qualification to the reasoning above. It is always open to a contractor to change his mind about what he will accept: and if, knowing that part performance is all that he will get, he chooses to accept it, the objection to making him pay for it falls away. One example of this occurs in sale of goods law: the denial of recovery to a part performer in breach is modified in sales of goods where the buyer positively accepts the short delivery.[108] Here, he has the ability to reject what is offered and return it if he wants to; if he chooses not to, then this undermines any potential objection based on forced exchange. And, similar reasoning applies elsewhere. In the labour law context, for instance, it was said in *Miles v Wakefield MBC*[109] that where workers in breach of contract withheld part of their labour in the course of industrial action, and this reduced

---

105 Above, § 1-30 *et seq.*

106 Cf Garner (1990) 10 OJLS 42, p 54. This also explains cases such as *Hopper v Burness* (1876) 1 CPD 137, applying the rule even where, in the event, the recipient is better off as he is than he would have been had he received full performance.

107 Burrows, p 277.

108 Sale of Goods Act 1979, s 30(1) (England) and the Sale of Goods Act 1893 (Ireland) obliges the buyer who accepts part delivery to pay pro rata, and draws no distinction between the claimant who is, and who is not, in breach. Cf *Behrend v Produce Brokers* [1920] 3 KB 530.

109 [1987] AC 539 (the actual case turned on another point). Cf *Wiluszynski v Tower Hamlets London BC* [1989] ICR 493.

labour was accepted by the employers, a *quantum meruit* would lie in respect of it. Nevertheless, where services are involved, it is likely in practice to be very difficult to show a genuine acceptance on the part of the other party.[110] One thing is clear: the mere fact that he has after the event taken advantage of what was done, however profitably, will not do. Thus, in *Hopper v Burness,*[111] a sea carrier who delivered goods short of destination was held entitled to no payment, even though the goods owner had profitably made the best of a bad job by selling them where they were for more than he could have got had they been carried to their proper destination.

Miles v Wakefield MBC,[112] discussed above, is instructive in this connection for another reason. Lord Templeman there seemingly accepted that the workers would have had a right to claim a *quantum meruit* whether or not their contracts of employment were still on foot (there was no indication that the employers had dismissed them). It is suggested that this must be right, despite the argument of Burrows[113] to the contrary. Not only does it avoid the startling result that an employer, by refusing to dismiss workers engaging in industrial action, can escape paying them for the limited services they do provide and which he accepts: more importantly, it is a little difficult to see why the subsistence of a contract of employment between the parties should affect the employer's liability to pay for something independently accepted.

(4) Neither party in breach

Non-frustration cases

6-37   Leaving aside the special case of frustration of contract (dealt with below), what happens where the contract itself contains provisions allowing either party lawfully to put an end to it other than as a result of breach by the other? Will a party who has partly performed have a claim if the contract is thus terminated? On principle, it is suggested that he should. If it was the buyer of goods or services who terminated the contract, he by doing so deliberately chose to be satisfied with only part of what he ordered and cannot complain at being asked to pay. And even if it was the seller, the buyer by entering into a contract which allowed the seller to do so ought to be regarded as taking the risk of having to pay something for what he had got.[114] It must be admitted, however, that there is a decision of Gannon J in the High Court in Ireland that goes against this. In *Travers Construction Ltd v Lismore Homes Ltd,*[115] a building contract was

---

110 See, once again, *Miles's* case itself, where no such acceptance was shown.

111 (1876) 1 CPD 137. The earlier decision in *Christy v Row* (1808) 1 Taunt 299 seems difficult to reconcile with this.

112 [1987] AC 539. Cf *Wiluszynski v Tower Hamlets BC* [1989] ICR 493.

113 Burrows, p 280.

114 Note that the provisions of the Apportionment Act 1870, s 2, may apply in a suitable case. Thus, in *Treacy v Corcoran* (1874) IR 8 CL 40 an employee successfully invoked them to claim his salary pro rata when he resigned during his period of employment.

115 (1990) unreported, 9 March.

terminated by mutual consent before performance was complete. The builder was denied restitution for work done, apparently on the ground that the parties having contracted with one another, they should be limited to the remedies provided by the contract. It can only be said that this seems an excessively harsh decision, which ought not to be followed in England and should be reconsidered in Ireland.

Frustration cases[116]

6-38   Restitution in respect of contracts later frustrated is governed at common law by principles analogous to those outlined above in relation to other contracts, though for obvious reasons, the issue of breach by either party does not arise. However, in England, the Law Reform (Frustrated Contracts) Act 1943[117] has modified these rules and set up a largely self-contained code. Since there is no equivalent legislation in Ireland, the result is that the Irish and English positions differ considerably on this subject: the former being based on the common law, the latter to a large extent on statute.

6-39   *Money paid: the Irish position at common law.* As with breach of contract, money paid under a contract later frustrated is recoverable if there has been a total failure of consideration,[118] but not otherwise. Thus, in *Whincup v Hughes*,[119] a premium paid to apprentice the plaintiff's son to a watchmaker for six years was held entirely forfeit even though the watchmaker died a year later. Again, take the sort of contract exemplified in *Hyundai Heavy Industries Co Ltd v Papadopoulos*,[120] where a ship is to be paid for by instalments during construction. If delivery is frustrated after construction begins, presumably in Ireland repayment of instalments paid will be denied on the basis that the buyer has received at least something of what he bargained for.[121] (No doubt, however, the exceptions to the requirement of total failure, such as prepayments to a seller who short delivers,[122] apply here also.)

6-40   Where there has been total failure, the traditional view is that money paid is recoverable as of right, without question or deduction. If true, this may seriously prejudice the payee who has spent money – conceivably irrevocably – on preparations for performance. For example, in the English case of *Fibrosa Spolka Akcyjna v Fairbairn Lawson Combe Barbour Ltd*,[123] decided at common law,

---

116 See McKendrick in Burrows (ed), *Essays on the Law of Restitution*, Chapter 6.

117 In NI, the relevant statute is the Frustrated Contracts (NI) Act 1947, exactly mirroring the Act of 1943.

118 *Fibrosa Spolka Akcyjna v Fairbairn Lawson Combe Barbour Ltd* [1943] AC 32.

119 (1871) LR 6 CP 78.

120 [1980] 2 All ER 29.

121 At least so long as courts in Ireland continue to adhere to the 'total failure' requirement.

122 See *Behrend v Produce Brokers Ltd* [1920] 3 KB 530; above, § 6-16.

123 [1943] AC 32.

machine tool manufacturers who were prevented at the last minute from delivering them to buyers by the outbreak of war had to return the price in full, with no credit for any manufacturing expenses.[124]

It is, however, doubtful whether this absolute right to recovery at common law remains today. Assuming acceptance by Irish courts of the general defence of change of position adumbrated in *Lipkin Gorman v Karpnale Ltd*,[125] there seems no reason why at common law such expenses should not be deductible from any repayment, in so far as they would otherwise be irrecoverable. The degree of such deductibility will no doubt depend on the circumstances. For instance, if a manufacturer of machine tools is prevented from delivering them to one buyer, but can readily sell them to another for the same price, it is unlikely he will be able to show a sufficient change of position to justify any allowance.[126] Furthermore, any right of deduction will itself depend on the general law of change of position. If, for example, the narrow view were accepted in Ireland that pre-receipt expense can never give a defence of change of position,[127] this would seem to preclude any reliance on contractual expenses incurred before the prepayment.[128]

6-41   *Benefits in kind: the Irish position at common law.* The question here is effectively the same as with contracts lawfully terminated by act of parties. Since we suggested there that recovery ought to be allowed,[129] logically, frustration cases should be treated in the same way.

Authority, however, goes the other way. *Prima facie*, a contractor prevented by a frustrating event from rendering full performance recovers nothing at all. Thus, in *Appleby v Myers*,[130] a factory burnt down while being fitted out by the plaintiffs under a contract with the owners. The plaintiffs, it was held, were entitled to recover nothing for their pre-destruction services. Moreover, it has been held that the same applies where the contract expressly provides for termination if a frustrating event occurs. Hence, shipowners prevented from completing a voyage by an excepted peril such as government action have been denied any right to claim *pro rata* freight.[131] Unless and until altered by the Supreme Court, this no doubt remains the position in Ireland.

---

124 The potential unfairness was recognised in that case by all five Law Lords: see [1943] AC 32, pp 49, 54–55, 72, 76, 78.

125 [1991] 2 AC 548.

126 Cf the position in England under the Law Reform (Frustrated Contracts) Act 1943: see below.

127 See *South Tyneside Metropolitan BC v Svenska International plc* [1995] 1 All ER 545, discussed below, § 13-16.

128 Cf the position under the English Law Reform (Frustrated Contracts) Act 1943, ss 1(2) and 1(3), where there is no such bar.

129 See above, § 6-37.

130 (1867) LR 3 CP 651. See, too, *Cutter v Powell* (1795) 6 TR 320.

131 Eg, *Petrinovic v Mission Française* (1942) 71 Lloyd's List LR 208; *St Enoch Co v Phosphate Co* [1916] 2 KB 624.

It is, however, no doubt subject to the same exceptions as the rule denying recovery to a part-performing contract-breaker. Thus, an employee will have the right to salary *pro rata* up to a frustrating event under the Apportionment Act 1870,[132] and a buyer accepting short delivery must pay for what he gets.[133] And, of course, where services are freely accepted after a frustrating event, there is no reason why a *quantum meruit* should not lie in a suitable case. Thus in *The Massalia*,[134] a contract to ship goods from India to Italy was assumed to have been frustrated by the closure of the Suez Canal.[135] But the cargo-owners, having acquiesced in the carriers' transport of their goods by another route, were nevertheless held liable to pay a reasonable rate.

6-42   *Frustration in England: the Law Reform (Frustrated Contracts) Act 1943.* We now turn to the position in England, as governed by the Law Reform (Frustrated Contracts) Act 1943.

6-43   *England: money paid: statute.* Under s 1(2) of the 1943 Act:

> All sums paid or payable to any party in pursuance of the contract before [the time of discharge by frustration] shall, in the case of sums so paid, be recoverable from him as money received by him to the use of the party by whom the sums were paid, and, in the case of sums so payable, cease to be so payable: provided that, if the party to whom the sums were paid or payable incurred expenses before the time of discharge in, or for the purpose of the contract, the court may, if it considers it just to do so, having regard to all the circumstances of the case, allow him to retain or, as the case may be, recover the whole or any part of the sums so paid or payable, not being an amount in excess of the expenses so incurred.

Hence, all money paid pursuant to a contract subsequently frustrated[136] is recoverable, whether or not the consideration has totally failed (thus extending the common law rule laid down in the *Fibrosa* case,[137] which was limited to cases of total failure). There is one qualification. Anticipating, to some extent, what has been suggested may be the present position at common law following the decision in *Lipkin Gorman v Karpnale*,[138] the payee has a defence of change of position, in that in so far as he has incurred expenses in performing the contract, he may, if the tribunal thinks fit, be allowed to set these off against any repayment (see below).

---

132 Which was indeed passed partly to protect such people and to reverse the contrary decision in *Cutter v Powell* (1795) 6 TR 320.

133 Sale of Goods Act 1893, s 30(1).

134 [1961] 2 QB 278.

135 Wrongly so, in the light of subsequent authority. But this does not affect the point in the text.

136 If paid subsequently by a party who did not know of the frustrating event, it could not be recovered under s 1(2), but could doubtless be recouped as money paid by mistake.

137 *Fibrosa Spolka Akcyjna v Fairbairn Lawson Combe Burbour Ltd* [1943] AC 32.

138 [1991] 2 AC 548.

It should be noted that statutory claims under s 1(2) are limited to money paid to the other party to the contract. Money paid to third parties under the contract (for example, where A Ltd agrees to build a factory, but the client agrees for accounting reasons to pay the price to an associated company of A Ltd) is regarded as a 'valuable benefit' in kind and dealt with under s 1(3), below.

6-44   *England: other benefits: statute.* Section 1(3) provides as follows:

> Where any party to the contract has, by reason of anything done by any other party thereto in, or for the purpose of, the performance of the contract, obtained a valuable benefit ... before the time of discharge, there shall be recoverable from him by the other party such sum (if any), not exceeding the value of the said benefit to the party obtaining it, as the court considers just, having regard to all the circumstances of the case and, in particular –

> (a) the amount of any expenses incurred before the time of discharge by the benefited party in, or for the purpose of, the performance of the contract, including any sums paid or payable by him to any other party in pursuance of the contract and retained or recoverable by that party under [s 1(2)], and

> (b) the effect, in relation to the said benefit, of the circumstances giving rise to the frustration of the contract.

The main effect of this sub-section is to get rid of the general common law prohibition on recovery for part performance, and provide a generalised right to sue in respect of 'valuable benefits' conferred by one party on the other. Having introduced this right, the provision qualifies it once again with a limited change of position defence, allowing the recipient to deduct expenses incurred in or about the contract.

6-45   A number of particular issues arise.

First, what counts as a 'valuable benefit'? In the general law of restitution, it has been suggested that any provision of goods and services amounts to a benefit, whether or not the recipient ends with any 'end product' to show for it.[139] Furthermore, since s 1(3) clearly envisages the 'valuable benefit' as a ceiling, with the 'just sum' as often as not a good deal below it, a wide interpretation of 'benefit' seems appropriate, with questions of how much end product remains going to the issue of what sum, if any, it is just to make the recipient pay.

Nevertheless, Goff J, in his judgment in *BP (Exploration) Ltd v Hunt*[140] (which was later approved by the House of Lords)[141] felt constrained to construe the concept of 'benefit' itself more narrowly than this. The issue concerned how much BP should recover for prospecting services rendered in connection with a

---

139 See above, § 1-12 *et seq.*
140 [1982] 1 All ER 925.
141 See [1982] 1 All ER 986.

Libyan oil concession owned by Mr Hunt, which was nationalised shortly after becoming productive and well before it had repaid its costs. BP argued that the value of their services amounted in itself to a benefit: Mr Hunt, that the only benefit was the oil he had actually got out of it. Robert Goff J held for Mr Hunt. As a general rule, he said, the scheme of s 1(3) of the 1943 Act was to look merely to what end product remained.[142] He did, however, accept that where services in their nature produced no such end product, then they ought to be valued as such. Thus, a contract to design and build a factory, which is frustrated during the design stage, will give rise to no recovery. By contrast, if I agree to provide security guards for your factory for a year and it burns down after two months, I confer a benefit on you of two months' security service. It must be said that this is a somewhat unfortunate distinction to have to draw, particularly as it does not appear elsewhere in the law of restitution.

6-46   Secondly, assuming there is a benefit, it is valued after, not before, the frustrating event. This was held in the *BP* case to result from the wording of s 1(3)(b) of the 1943 Act, requiring the court to take into account 'the effect, in relation to the said benefit, of the circumstances giving rise to the frustration of the contract'. That provision, Goff J held, went to the actual valuation of the benefit, and not simply to the determination of the just sum to be awarded in respect of it. This obviously matters: thus, in *BP (Exploration) Ltd v Hunt*, BP's argument that the increased value of the concession due to their exertions ought to be in account was rejected. Given the frustrating event, this was something which (except to the extent of the miserly compensation paid by the Libyan Government) the defendant concessionaire no longer had. More generally, it means that where a frustrating event destroys the object of the contract – as where a building being constructed burns down – there will normally be no benefit to value in the first place.[143]

J's conclusion on this latter point has been attacked, on the basis that s 1(3)(b) ought to go not to the valuation of the benefit, but to the computation of the 'just sum',[144] thus giving greater discretion to the court to make an award against a recipient even where nothing remains of what he got. Although the language of the section might seem to sit more easily with such an interpretation (particularly the reference to benefits obtained *before* the time of discharge), it is nevertheless suggested that Goff J is right. As he pointed out in the *BP* case, the provision is best viewed as a statutory form of 'change of position' defence.[145] if so, however unfortunate this may be to plaintiffs, it seems right that it should be available as of right to the defendant rather than merely as a matter of statutory discretion in the court.

---

142 Cf the common law rule in *Planché v Colburn* (1831) 8 Bing 14, above.

143 As, apparently, at common law: cf *Appleby v Myers* (1867) LR 2 CP 651.

144 Treitel, *Law of Contract*, 10th edn, p 851 *et seq*; Burrows, p 292.

145 [1982] 1 All ER 925, p 938. Strictly, his Lordship was referring to the proviso to s 1(2): but his remarks must apply, *mutatis mutandis*, to s 1(3).

Thirdly, the 'just sum' is largely to be computed as in the ordinary law of restitution: notably, in the case of services, it is (subject to the 'valuable benefit' ceiling) likely to be the value of the service concerned.[146]

Fourthly, as in the case of money paid, it may be possible for the recipient of the benefit to set off expenses incurred against any award made against him: see below.

6-47 *England: expenses: statute.* The law could have taken the view that, since a frustrated contract is a joint enterprise neutralised through no one's fault, losses to either party should be split equitably. For better or worse, it has not done so;[147] what it has done is take the more limited step of giving the court a discretion (if it considers it just to do so) to allow a set off of expenses against a claim for money paid[148] or benefits conferred.[149]

Despite the use in the statute of the language of discretion, it has been said that this is, in effect, a statutory defence of change of position:[150] a factor, it is suggested, which ought to guide any decision on how the discretion ought to be exercised to allow expenses. Suppose my contract to supply you with machinery is frustrated by illegality after you have paid me and I have incurred expense in manufacturing components. How much I can retain for expenses should depend on whether I can sell them elsewhere: to the extent that I can turn them into money, I have not really changed my position and should receive no credit.[151]

Note, further that, although based on the idea of change of position, the statutory set off for expenses may well be both narrower and wider than change of position generally in restitution. It is, for instance, restricted to expenses 'in, or for the purpose of, the performance of the contract'. Other expenditure, for instance, prepayments made to a property developer which are later invested by it in other projects which yield no return, is not covered, however much it may represent a change of position. On the other hand, as mentioned above,[152] there is no restriction in s 1(2) and 1(3) to expenses incurred after receipt of the money concerned, whereas under the general law, there may well be.[153]

---

146 *BP (Exploration) Ltd v Hunt* [1982] 1 All ER 925, p 942.

147 For better, according to Stewart and Carter [1992] CLJ 66. Cf the Frustrated Contracts Act 1974 of British Columbia, s 5(3).

148 Including money that ought to have been paid before the frustrating event but was not: s 1(2). This is outside the law of restitution, but the thinking is obvious: a party liable to make payment, but who has failed to do so, should not be allowed to take advantage of his own wrong.

149 Thus leaving unprotected a party who spends money on a contract which is frustrated before his co-contractor has provided anything in return.

150 *BP (Exploration) Ltd v Hunt* [1982] 1 All ER 925, p 938.

151 But see *Gamerco v ICM/Fair Warning Ltd* [1995] 1 WLR 1226, where Garland J exercised his discretion under s 1(2) of the Act by declining to make any deduction even for entirely wasted expenditure, apparently on the basis that the plaintiff stood to suffer more grievous loss than the defendant. With respect, this decision seems open to some question on the point of principle.

152 See above, § 6-40.

153 Burrows, p 285.

CHAPTER 7

FAILURE OF ASSUMPTIONS (2)

I VITIATED CONTRACTS IN GENERAL

7-1   It would have been logical enough for the law to provide that, once a contract had been successfully impugned or shown to be ineffective (for example, for mistake, or duress, or illegality), its effects fell to be undone and cross-restitution for benefits conferred was therefore available to both parties as a matter of course.[1] But, it has not done this,[2] instead leaving the subject of extra-contractual restitution to be dealt with piecemeal under the existing heads of recovery.

As was suggested in the previous chapter in the case of valid agreements, it is submitted that the basis of recovery for benefits rendered under vitiated contracts, where it is allowed, is failure of assumptions. Just as with claims arising from performance of valid contracts, the claimant's complaint is that the assumption on the basis of which he made his payment has not been satisfied.

As with recovery for mistake, the form taken by any restitutionary remedy arising out of a vitiated contract will vary. In particular, the effect of setting aside a contract for mistake or undue influence may well be *ipso facto* to revest property transferred in the transferor, whether at law or in equity. Where this happens, it is the law of property, rather than doctrines peculiar to restitution, that will govern the reversal of the defendant's unjust enrichment.

(a) Vitiated contracts and failure of consideration

(1) Background

7-2   In the case of valid contracts, we mentioned in the previous chapter that failure of assumptions was traditionally referred to as 'failure of consideration'; and that, for these purposes, the 'consideration' which had to fail meant the contractual return which the claimant expected to get. In most cases, this referred to the actual return (that is, goods or services) rather than the promise to provide it: but where the essence of the transaction was the purchase of the promise itself, the analysis might be different.

---

1   As effectively exists in the case of frustration (see above, Chapter 6).

2   'That law [of restitution] might have developed so as to recognise a *condictio indebiti* – an action for the recovery of money on the ground that it was not due. But it has not.' *Per* Lord Goff in *Woolwich Equitable Building Society v IRC (No 2)* [1993] AC 70, p 172.

At one time, there was a tendency to apply this analysis to vitiated contracts, and to apply to them the same rules as to other contracts. Thus, in *Valentini v Canali*,[3] a buyer of furniture was held unable to recover his money once he had had the use of the furniture, despite the fact that he was a minor and the contract was void. The Irish High Court took the same attitude.[4] Again, Swift J said bluntly, in another English minors' case, that 'money paid under a void contract cannot be recovered unless there is a total failure of consideration'.[5] *Ultra vires* contracts were similarly treated: thus, a subscriber for shares which had in fact been issued *ultra vires* failed to get his money back from the company on the basis that he had got (and indeed sold on) exactly what he paid for.[6]

Today, however, it seems clear that the recovery of benefits rendered under void and voidable contracts is less straightforward.

(2) Voidable contracts: failure of consideration and counter-restitution

7-3   Where a contract is voidable (that is, effective unless and until avoided), the matter of failure of consideration and counter-restitution is complicated by a further principle. Where benefits are rendered pursuant to a contractual obligation, there is no doubt that restitution is unavailable if and so long as that obligation is still on foot. This is because, until it is got rid of, there is nothing unjust in the defendant retaining benefits received under it.[7] This point matters, for two reasons. One is that factors (such as mistake) that would give rise to restitution in respect of a non-contractual transfer may well not suffice to attack a contract: hence the presence of a contract may strengthen the defendant's position very considerably.[8] But there is a second, and much more important one.

7-4   The second reason is this. Where voidable contracts are concerned, the need of the claimant to make counter-restitution tends to be applied at the contractual stage, and to be regarded as part of the law of contract rather than restitution. A person cannot set aside a contract – and hence any restitutionary claim will fall

---

3   (1889) 24 QBD 166. See, too, *Steinberg v Scala (Leeds) Ltd* [1923] 2 KB 452.

4   *Stapleton v Prudential Assurance Ltd* (1928) 62 ILTR 56.

5   *Pearce v Brain* [1929] 2 KB 310, p 314 (similarly refusing relief to an infant who had exchanged goods).

6   *Linz v Electric Wire Co of Palestine Ltd* [1948] AC 371.

7   See above, § 1-43.

8   See, eg, *Bell v Lever Bros Ltd* [1932] AC 161. Employers paid employees large golden handshakes, believing (falsely) that the latter had not misbehaved while in office. Had the payments been non-contractual, there is little doubt that they would have been recoverable as of course. They were, nevertheless, held irrevocable, since they had been made under a contract, and the mistake was not sufficient to avoid that contract.

at the first fence – unless he is able and willing to make *restitutio in integrum*.[9] Moreover, in contrast to the situation with void contracts, where it seems there is no objection to benefits in kind being balanced by money payments from the recipient,[10] where it is sought to get rid of a voidable contract, the law *prima facie* insists on restitution in specie rather than in money. Thus, a buyer who has resold cannot set aside his contract for mistake or misrepresentation: provision of the monetary equivalent of what he received will not do, even where the other party is guilty of fraud,[11] and even where the subject matter is an item readily obtainable in the market, such as shares.[12] The same goes, too, for a buyer who has changed the nature of what he bought, however willing to make up the depreciation in money.[13]

On the other hand, the insistence of restitution in specie is only a *prima facie* rule. It is increasingly being relaxed, and in any case is subject to exceptions.

7-5   One such exception is best explained as arising from a rough and ready appreciation of who ought to bear certain risks. This is the rule that a person who induces a contract by fraud or misrepresentation cannot complain if what he gets back is depreciated or destroyed because of some feature he himself misrepresented. *Adam v Newbigging*[14] highlights the point. A retired army officer was duped into buying a business by misrepresentations as to its solvency. Finding out its true state, he sought to return it and get his money back, even though it had meanwhile become bankrupt. The court had no difficulty in allowing him to do so: even though the seller had made the representations entirely innocently, he and not the representee was the person who ought to bear the risk of subsequent deterioration in the business. Indeed, there is authority applying similar reasoning where depreciation or destruction results from entirely external factors: thus, in *Head v Tattersall*,[15] the buyer of a

---

9   There is one further complication. According to the law of contract in the Republic, a sale of land cannot (absent fraud) be set aside at all once it has been executed. This is because of the rule in *Seddon v North Eastern Salt Co* [1905] 1 Ch 326, which remains in force in all contracts save those for the sale of goods (in which it was abolished by the Sale of Goods and Supply of Services Act 1980, s 44(b)). In England and NI, no difficulty arises in this connection, since whatever vestiges of the rule remained were removed by the Misrepresentation Act 1967, s 1, and its NI equivalent.

10   *Rover International Ltd v Cannon Film Sales Ltd (No 3)* [1989] 3 All ER 423.

11   See *Smith New Court Securities Ltd v Scrimgeour Vickers (Asset Management) Ltd* [1994] 4 All ER 225, p 234 (the case went to the HL on another point: [1997] AC 254).

12   See *Smith New Court Securities Ltd v Scrimgeour Vickers (Asset Management) Ltd* [1994] 4 All ER 225.

13   See *Clarke v Dickson* (1858) 8 EB & E 148.

14   (1886) 34 Ch D 582; (1888) 13 App Cas 308. See, too, *Lagunas Nitrate Co v Lagunas Syndicate* [1899] 2 Ch 392.

15   (1871) LR 7 Ex 7. Strictly, the buyer here was cancelling the contract for breach of condition, not rescinding it for misrepresentation: but it is unlikely that this makes any difference.

misdescribed horse did not lose the right to reject it and reclaim the price when it fortuitously died in his hands.[16]

Similar thinking may well underlie the difficult case of *Mackenzie v Royal Bank of Canada*,[17] establishing that where a bank misleads a guarantor into providing security for a loan to its customer, the guarantor can recover that security even though neither he nor the principal debtor is in a position to restore the bank's position by returning the sums advanced.[18] As between the bank, which is guilty of misrepresentation, and the surety, who is not, the former should bear the risk that the transaction will be cancelled in circumstances where *restitutio in integrum* is impossible.[19]

7-6   The second exception arises from the rule applied in equity[20] that, provided the person seeking restitution can return substantially what he got, the non-returnability of a minor part will not defeat his claim. The difference may be made up in cash. So, a person duped into buying land can rescind provided he pays for his period of occupation of it:[21] in other kinds of contract, small incidental benefits can either be compensated for or even set off against one another.[22] The leading authority is *Erlanger v New Sombrero Phosphate Co*.[23] A company was set up by promoters, who then manipulated it into taking a doubtful guano mining business off their hands at a handsome profit to themselves. This was a flagrant breach of their fiduciary duty, and undoubtedly made the purchase voidable. Some time later, the company sued the promoters to recover its money. It succeeded, even though the mine was by then sadly depleted: the company merely had to return it and account in addition for profits made from working it in the interim.[24] And, in *O'Sullivan v Management*

---

16   Another such case is *Armstrong v Jackson* [1917] 2 KB 822. A broker who in breach of fiduciary duty surreptitiously unloaded shares of his own onto his client was forced to take them back and repay what he had got for them, despite an interim decline of over 90% in value.

17   [1934] AC 468. Treitel's explanation of this case as involving no benefit to the guarantor to be restored (*Law of Contract*, 10th edn, p 352) surely cannot be right: something done by A for B at C's request must be a benefit to C.

18   A rule assumed to apply in numerous subsequent cases, notably where the bank is guilty of undue influence: eg, *Lloyds Bank Ltd v Bundy* [1975] QB 326.

19   If the guarantor's agreement to give security were voidable for some other reason, such as shared mistake which was no one's responsibility, a court might well be a good deal less sympathetic to him. This could well arise in practice, eg, where a so called 'lease' of bogus goods was involved (cf *Associated Japanese Bank (International) Ltd v Crédit du Nord SA* [1988] 3 All ER 902).

20   It is arguable that the common law rule regarding rescission for fraud was much stricter: Treitel, *Law of Contract* (10th edn), p 342 *et seq*.

21   See *Hulton v Hulton* [1917] 1 KB 813, p 826. This situation cannot arise in Ireland except in the case of fraudulent misrepresentation: *Lecky v Walter* [1914] IR 378.

22   *Hulton v Hulton* [1917] 1 KB 813.

23   (1878) 3 App Cas 1218.

24   As Lord Blackburn put it, 'I think the practice has always been for a court of equity to give this relief [ie, rescission] whenever, by the exercise of its powers, it can do whatever is practically just, though it cannot restore the parties precisely to the state they were in before the contract': (1878) 3 App Cas 1218, p 1278.

Agency Ltd,[25] a similar approach was taken in an undue influence case. A singer agreed with music promoters to assign to them the copyright in his songs, the quid pro quo being regular cash payments and the promoters' services in developing his career. Having successfully attacked the agreement as vitiated by the promoters' undue influence, the singer was held able to rescind it and recover the vital copyrights. The promoters' argument that their management services could not be returned was met by ordering a payment from the musician in addition to any credit for cash received.

(3) Void contracts: counter-restitution and the place of failure of consideration

7-7 The early view, that void contracts deserved no special treatment and that the 'failure of consideration' requirement applied to them in the same way as valid ones, was finally abandoned in a series of cases in England dating from the 1980s. The first was *Rover International Ltd v Cannon Film Sales Ltd (No 3)*.[26] Rover agreed to pay Cannon for a number of films, to distribute them and to share any profits with Cannon. Rover paid Cannon various sums and received certain benefits in return. It then transpired that the whole contract had been void from the start because Rover had not been incorporated when it signed it. Rover sought its money back: Cannon riposted that there had been no total failure of consideration. Although Rover succeeded on other grounds,[27] Kerr LJ thought that there had been a total failure of consideration in any case. Rover had contracted for enforceable contractual rights against Cannon: they had not got them, and that was sufficient to allow recovery.[28]

If this was right, then radical conclusions followed. If failure to obtain valid contractual rights in return for a payment automatically amounted to 'failure of consideration', then effectively any sum paid under a void contract was recoverable, whatever return had actually been received.

7-8 Further suggestions that this might indeed be the case came from the Court of Appeal in *Westdeutsche Landesbank Girozentrale v Islington BC*.[29] A bank and a local authority concluded a 'swap' transaction, whereby the bank paid the authority £2.5 m there and then and thereafter, monthly payments were to be made by one or other party in an amount that varied according to fluctuations in market interest rates. The transaction was later found to be *ultra vires* the authority, and the bank (which was out of pocket at the time the authority ceased to honour the arrangement) sued to recover its net payments. It won, both at first instance and in the Court of Appeal.

---

25 [1985] QB 428.
26 [1989] 3 All ER 423.
27 Ie, that they had paid by mistake.
28 [1989] 3 All ER 423, p 433.
29 [1994] 4 All ER 890.

Unfortunately, it was not entirely clear whether *Westdeutsche* had actually followed the reasoning in *Rover*. Hobhouse J, with the apparent agreement of the Court of Appeal, said that where money was paid under a void contract, it was recoverable not for failure of consideration, but under the novel head of 'absence of consideration'. As Lord Goff pointed out,[30] when the case went to the House of Lords on another point,[31] this raised considerable difficulties.[32] In particular, it is difficult to reconcile Hobhouse J's position with the lack of a right of recovery in other contracts, such as those affected by statutory invalidity under the gaming legislation – or, indeed, with the irrevocability of gifts.[33] At least one other member of the House expressed views much more consistent with the 'failure of consideration' view.[34]

7-9 The matter now seems to have been settled beyond doubt in favour of the 'failure of consideration' view. In *Guinness Mahon and Co Ltd v Kensington BC*,[35] the facts were the same as in *Westdeutsche*, save that the 'swap' had run its course. The decision of the Court of Appeal, that this factor made no difference to the bank's right of recovery, was hardly surprising. It was clearly somewhat odd[36] if a potential right to recover several hundred thousand pounds on the day before the final payment was simply extinguished as soon as the final payment was made and the books were closed. But both Morritt and Walker LJJ accepted that in the case of void contracts, if not elsewhere,[37] 'failure of consideration' embraced failure to obtain a valid counter-promise, rather than non-receipt of actual counter-performance.[38] Morritt LJ explicitly expressed agreement with the proposition that 'in the case of a contract void from the start, there must for that reason have been a total failure of consideration'.[39]

---

30 See [1996] AC 669, pp 682–83.

31 Namely, whether the claimants had a right to compound interest by virtue of having a proprietary equitable claim or otherwise.

32 It is noteworthy that the reasoning of Hobhouse J has been comprehensively, and convincingly, attacked by Swadling in [1994] RLR 73. Much of Swadling's argument is gratefully adopted here.

33 As Hobhouse J himself recognised: [1994] 4 All ER 890, p 896. He was driven to regard gifts as an anomalous exception.

34 'The essence of the swap agreement is that ... the consideration for one party making a payment is *an obligation on the other party to make counter-payments over the whole term of the agreement*' (Lord Browne-Wilkinson [1996] AC 669, p 710: emphasis supplied).

35 [1999] QB 215.

36 But see Birks (1993) 23 UWALR 195.

37 Morritt LJ was at pains to dispel the idea that the rule must necessarily be the same in the case of void contracts and other contracts: see pp 226–27.

38 *Ibid*, p 227.

39 *Ibid*.

(b) Void contracts: claims for benefits in kind

(1) Generally

7-10   The question of recovery in respect of benefits in kind is unlikely to arise in the restitutionary context where voidable contracts are involved, since (as we pointed out above) such issues as the return of benefits received are generally dealt with at the contractual stage, in deciding whether or not to allow rescission, and if so whether to impose terms.[40] But, it may well arise in the case of void contracts; and here there seems no doubt about the availability of a claim in *quantum meruit* and *quantum valebat* in suitable situations, provided that it is clear that the services were not meant to be rendered gratuitously vis à vis the defendant.[41] Indeed, in the seminal case of *Rover International Ltd v Cannon Film Sales Ltd (No 3)*,[42] above, it was accepted that in so far as Rover had rendered services to Cannon under the putative contract, they were entitled to be remunerated for them.

(2) The effect of a losing bargain

7-11   With some trepidation, we suggested above[43] that there should be a 'contract price cap' in the case of valid contracts terminated by breach. To allow the victim of a breach of contract to claim more by way of *quantum meruit* (or *valebat*) than he would have got had he claimed under the contract itself was distinctly curious, and would effectively subvert the contractual terms agreed between the parties.

With void contracts, the point is less easy. *Ex hypothesi*, a party to a void contract cannot say that he contracted to pay a limited sum and no more: on the contrary; he never entered into any contract at all. And, indeed, the English Court of Appeal has now decisively accepted that this point precludes any 'contract price cap'. In *Rover International Ltd v Cannon Film Sales Ltd (No 3)*,[44] referred to above, film distributors took certain films from C pursuant to a supposed contract (which was, in the event, entirely ineffective) whereby they would distribute them under a profit-sharing arrangement. After a few films had been distributed, the defect in the contract was discovered, and it was accepted that Rover had a claim for what they had done. It was held that, in deciding how much they were entitled to, no limit should be set by reference to

---

40   For a case where de facto restitutionary recovery for such benefits was granted as part of the rescission process, see, eg, *O'Sullivan v Management Agency and Music Ltd* [1985] QB 428.

41   For a case where they were so intended, see *Bridgewater v Griffiths* [2000] 1 WLR 524 (where legal aid certificate void, no personal liability in would-be assisted person to pay).

42   [1989] 3 All ER 423.

43   See above.

44   [1989] 3 All ER 423.

the payment terms of the putative contract. As Kerr LJ put it, if it were otherwise, the court would, in deciding questions of restitutionary *quantum*:

> ... always be called on to analyse or attempt to forecast the relative position of the parties under a contract which is *ex hypothesi* non-existent. This is not an attractive proposition, and I can see no justification for it in principle or on any authority.[45]

The Irish High Court has since suggested that it is likely to follow suit. In *Callinan v VHI Board*,[46] a private hospital, confidently expecting the renewal of a contract with the Board for treatment of patients covered by the VHI scheme, continued to treat them after existing arrangements had expired. In the event, no contract was concluded; in an action by the hospital for a *quantum meruit*, Keane J declined to impose a rigid 'contract ceiling' in respect of its claim.

On the other hand, as Burrows correctly points out,[47] there is a strong argument for allowing the putative contract price to be a relevant factor even if not a decisive one in such cases.[48] In particular, it may well establish a clear valuation put by the defendant on the benefit received, and hence potentially enables him to invoke 'subjective devaluation' in answer to the claimant's claim.

II CONTRACTS AFFECTED BY MISTAKE

(a) Generally

7-12   There is no unified doctrine of error in the Anglo-Irish law of contract. Different mistakes have different effects, and this is reflected in restitution law. Some mistakes are regarded as rendering a contract void – that is, as preventing the would-be contractors from reaching any valid agreement at all. Others merely make it voidable, in which case there is a contract, *prima facie* effective, but one or other party has the right to set it aside on account of some error on his part. In practice, most mistakes fall into the latter category. The former class is now of little practical significance in cases either of misrepresentation,[49] or where both parties share the same mistake.[50] It is, however, still potentially important where (owing, for instance, to the actions of a dishonest intermediary) the parties are at

---

45 [1989] 3 All ER 423, p 436.
46 [1994] 3 CMLR 796.
47 Burrows, p 268 *et seq*.
48 As it was in the 'use and occupation' case of *Lewisham BC v Masters* (1999) unreported, CA, 25 November (occupation of land in anticipation of lease never in fact granted: putative rent under lease relevant in valuing that use and occupation).
49 Since *Lewis v Averay* [1972] 1 QB 198.
50 Since *Bell v Lever Bros Ltd* [1932] AC 161. But see *Associated Japanese Bank (International) Ltd v Crédit du Nord* [1988] 3 All ER 902.

cross purposes either as to the subject matter of the contract[51] or as to the terms on which they have agreed.[52]

(b) Contracts void for mistake

(1) Money paid

7-13   The decision in *Guinness Mahon and Co Ltd v Kensington BC*,[53] above, confirmed that where money is paid under a void contract, it can on principle be recovered on the grounds of failure of consideration, and, further, that this remains the case even though it has been partly or completely performed on the other side. There is little doubt that this reasoning must apply to money paid pursuant to a contract void for mistake. Authority is hardly plentiful: but an early case is *Strickland v Turner*,[54] where the buyer of an annuity got his money back when it transpired that the annuity had in fact expired prior to the sale. The contract was void: he got nothing for his money, and the consideration had totally failed. A more topical example might be where a bank guaranteed the liabilities of a buyer of non-existent goods, as in *Associated Japanese Bank (International) Ltd v Crédit du Nord SA*,[55] and paid sums under the guarantee before discovering the truth. Such sums would, it is suggested, be recoverable on the basis of failure of consideration.

In fact, however, this is likely to be of little importance practically. Unless the payer knows at the time of payment that the contract is void (which is unlikely), his payment will, in any case, be recoverable on the basis of mistake, without the need to invoke failure of consideration.[56]

(2) Benefits in kind

7-14   If money paid under a contract void for mistake can be recovered on the basis of failure of assumptions, similar reasoning must apply to benefits in kind. So much has, indeed, been held to be the case with contracts void for incapacity,[57]

---

51   As in, eg, *Raffles v Wichelhaus* (1864) 2 H & C 906.

52   As in, eg, *Armagas Ltd v Mundogas SA* [1986] AC 717 (where, however, no restitutionary point arose). Cf the Massachusetts decision in *Vickery v Ritchie* 88 NE 835 (1909).

53   [1999] QB 215.

54   (1852) 7 Ex 208.

55   [1988] 3 All ER 902. The contract there was held void by the Court of Appeal.

56   Compare *Rover International Ltd v Cannon Film Sales Ltd (No 3)* [1989] 3 All ER 423 and *Kleinwort Benson Ltd v Lincoln CC* [1999] 1 AC 221. Both were cases of payment made under contracts which were (unknown to the payers) void for incapacity: in both it was accepted that the claimant could sue either on the basis of mistake or of failure of consideration.

57   *Rover International Ltd v Cannon Film Sales Ltd (No 3)* [1989] 3 All ER 423.

and there is no reason to treat contracts affected by mistake any differently. The Irish decision in *Fanning v Wicklow CC*[58] provides an example. A contractor did work for a local authority under a contract ineffective for lack of correspondence between offer and acceptance: although the court had to hold that no contractual action lay, the contractor recovered the reasonable value of what he had done in *quantum meruit*. Again, suppose a solicitor prepares documentation for the sale of a ship at the urgent request of the owner: it then appears that the ship had sunk shortly before the solicitor was instructed. Assuming the contract is void, it is submitted that the solicitor will recover a *quantum meruit*.

In the case of property transferred under a void contract, no doubt *quantum valebat* will equally lie,[59] assuming the property has been accepted by the defendant and subject, of course, to any defences, such as subjective devaluation.[60]

On the other hand, where chattels are involved, there may also be a *de facto* right of recovery based on property. The law conditions the validity of any transfer of title on that of the underlying contract: no contract, no title. *Cundy v Lindsay*[61] illustrates the point. A, a fraudster masquerading as B, induced C to send him goods on credit: when he got them, he sold them on to D and disappeared. C was held able to recover the goods by an action in conversion, not only against A,[62] but against anyone else into whose hands they might have come, including D. However pragmatic, this is hardly satisfactory: the effect on third parties is unfortunate, as is the lack of any of the defences, such as change of position, normally available against a restitution claimant.

(c) Contracts voidable for mistake

(1) Money paid

7-15   Where money is paid under a contract merely voidable for mistake, the position is slightly different, since there can (as mentioned above)[63] be no restitutionary recovery at all unless and until the contract is avoided. Once it has been avoided, however, it is suggested that money paid will be recoverable in the same way as

---

58 (1984) unreported, 30 April.

59 Arguably, the transferor may also have the benefit of a trust. If shares are transferred under a void contract, the transfer is probably voidable: once avoided, presumably the transferee will hold them on trust for the transferor. Cf *Re French's Wine Bar Ltd* [1987] BCLC 499.

60 Above, § 1-33.

61 (1878) 3 App Cas 459.

62 Note, however, that if A is innocent (eg, if both A and C have been duped by a third party B) and A has disposed of the chattels without negligence, he escapes liability in conversion: *Elvin Powell v Plummer Roddis* (1933) 50 TLR 158. But this is due to the vagaries of the law of conversion rather than to any deep-seated restitutionary principle.

63 § 7-3.

with void contracts. On the other hand, issues of counter-restitution are less likely to arise for the reason referred to above, § 7-12: namely that such questions are normally dealt with at the contractual stage by putting the person seeking restitution on terms as to return of any benefits which he himself may have got.[64]

(2) Benefits in kind

7-16　There seems no decided case dealing with services rendered under a contract voidable for mistake.[65] It is submitted, however, that there is no reason to draw any distinction here between a void contract and a voidable contract which has been avoided. If so, *quantum meruit* is presumably available on principle.

As for property transferred under contracts voidable for mistake (or, more commonly in practice, misrepresentation), presumably once the contract has been avoided, the position is the same as with void contracts: that is, an action should lie for *quantum valebat*. With chattels, there is a similar complication: the title gained by the transferee stands or falls with the validity of the contract itself, so once the contract is avoided, ownership automatically revests in the transferor. But, since a contract may not be avoided so as to prejudice the interests of an innocent transferee for value, it follows that in practice, this rule only affects the actual parties to the contract.

III CONTRACTS AFFECTED BY DURESS AND UNDUE INFLUENCE

The definition of these concepts has already been dealt with in Chapter 4. Suffice it to say here that the forms of pressure that will suffice to allow restitutionary recovery in the absence of contract are the same as those which will allow a contract induced thereby to be attacked.

Undue influence and duress will, it seems, normally have the effect of rendering a contract voidable and not void. This is clearly so with undue influence,[66] and also with economic duress (for example, where I coerce you into contracting with me by threatening a breach of contract or a tort).[67] Matters

---

64　As arguably happened in the Irish case of *Cooper v Phibbs* (1867) LR 2 HL 149. The lessee of fishing rights who turned out to be the real owner of them recovered payments made under the lease, but only subject to giving credit for improvements wrought by the *soi-disant* lessor.

65　Though cf cases such as *Cooper v Phibbs* (1867) LR 2 HL 149, above, where recovery for such services was given negatively, ie, by imposition of terms on the party seeking rescission.

66　Hence the availability of bars to relief such as the rights of a *bona fide* purchaser.

67　See *dicta* in *Pao On v Lau Yiu Long* [1980] AC 614, pp 635–36 (Lord Scarman); and *The Atlantic Baron* [1979] QB 705 (Mocatta J). Both cases are discussed above, in Chapter 4.

are slightly less clear in the case of threats of physical violence, but it is suggested that the better position is that the resulting contract is void.[68] It would seem to follow from this that, physical violence aside, the rules of restitutionary recovery which apply where a contract has been successfully impugned for duress are likely to be the same as those obtaining in the case of contracts voidable for misrepresentation.

7-17   As for setting aside the contract, it is suggested that on principle, there is no reason not to require, as in other voidable contracts, *restitutio in integrum*.[69] If A Ltd forces B Ltd to buy securities by threatening a breach of contract or other form of economic duress, B should clearly have to give up the securities as a condition of recovering its money: and, if it has sold them, it is not easy to see why it should be in a better position than if it had been defrauded into buying them. On the other hand, any requirement of *restitutio* would have to be applied sensitively. In so far as, say, a person were forced to accept and pay for services under duress, it would be monstrous if he came under an obligation to pay a reasonable price for them as a condition of getting his money back: he should have, and surely will be given, the ability to plead that benefits which have not been freely accepted should not figure in any computation of counter-restitution.[70]

IV CONTRACTS AFFECTED BY MINORITY

(a) Contractual capacity: the general law

7-18   Contracts entered into by a minor, while generally accepted to be enforceable by him,[71] can only be enforced against him to a limited extent. The majority of contracts (which we will call Category 1) are entirely unenforceable against him, in England because of the common law, and in Ireland under s 1 of the Infants'

---

68 In *Barton v Armstrong* [1976] AC 104, p 121, where a contract was procured by threats of physical violence, it was said that the contract was 'void' as against Armstrong (the victim), but no opinion was expressed as to its effect on the rights of third parties. It is suggested, however, that a transfer in such circumstances should be void for all purposes. If the transfer is documentary, eg, by deed, presumably the victim could establish voidness by pleading *non est factum*.

69 Subject to the criticisms above, § 7-7.

70 No doubt this is why Burrows, p 168, doubts whether the requirement applies at all to duress cases.

71 Eg, *Bruce v Warwick* (1815) 6 Taunt 118, and (possibly) *Harnedy v National Greyhound Racing Co* [1944] IR 160. And there never seems to have been any difficulty about a minor suing the seller of defective goods for injuries suffered: see, eg, *Godley v Perry* [1960] 1 WLR 9.

Relief Act 1874.[72] However, in England and Northern Ireland (but not the Republic),[73] it is open to the minor to ratify the contract on coming of age.[74]

A small, separate class of contracts (Category 2), notably those concerning leases and shareholdings, are valid unless and until disaffirmed. By contrast, some contracts, such as those for necessaries or beneficial contracts of service, are binding on all parties in the normal way (Category 3).

However, these rules only apply to actions to enforce the contract. How far it is open to either party to take the alternative course of seeking restitution for benefits conferred is the question we must turn to.

(b) Claims by minors: money paid

7-19 If we limit the effectiveness of minors' contracts in order to protect minors from their own improvidence, the obvious approach would be straightforward. The minor would be able simply to recover back anything he had paid, subject where necessary to providing counter-restitution, in cash or in kind as appropriate (and also subject to any other defences, such as change of position). Oddly enough, however, the law accepted such a common sense solution. Instead, it treats minors' contracts surprisingly like any other contract. In particular, it seems that in both Category 1 and Category 2 contracts, there can be no recovery at all, save where either the minor has got nothing in exchange or, if he has, he can return it so as to restore the status quo ante. *Steinberg v Scala (Leeds) Ltd*,[75] a Category 2 case, demonstrates the point. A minor who bought shares, but later repudiated the transaction, failed to recover back the price: she had had the benefit of the shares, together with the right to receive dividends (although, in the event, there had been none), and this meant that there had been no total failure. Similarly, in *Valentini v Canali*[76] a minor who bought and used furniture was held unable to give it back and recover a down payment, on the basis that he had taken a benefit under the contract. The only indulgence shown to the minor is that apparently, he may recover a deposit paid, even though it was intended to be security for his own performance and even though it was he who repudiated the contract.[77]

---

72 Which provides as follows: 'All contracts, whether by specialty or simple contract, henceforth entered into by infants for the repayment of money lent or to be lent, or for goods supplied or to be supplied (other than contracts for necessaries), and all accounts stated with infants, shall be absolutely void ...' The Act was repealed for England by the Minors' Contracts Act 1987 and in NI by equivalent legislation.

73 Because of the Infants' Relief Act 1874, s 2 (since repealed in England and NI).

74 *Williams v Moor* (1843) 11 M & W 256.

75 [1923] 2 Ch 452.

76 (1889) 24 QBD 166 (a Category 1 case). See too *Pearce v Brain* [1929] 2 KB 310, where, however, the contract was one of exchange and not a sale.

77 *Corpe v Overton* (1833) 10 Bing 252. This is not so in the case of other unenforceable contracts: *Thomas v Brown* (1876) 1 QBD 714 (deposit under contract unenforceable under Statute of Frauds).

On the other hand, this rule does seem tough on the minor. Even if restitution is not available simply on the ground of minority, there is much to be said for a rule that a minor who has received something in return should be entitled to restitution if he can return it. In other words, restitution should be denied only if the minor cannot in substance give back what he has got. It is worth noting that in most of the cases in which restitution has been denied to the minor on the basis that there has been no failure of consideration, there was, in fact, just such an inability: if so, the solution just suggested still seems open to a suitably creative court.

(c) Claims by minors: property and services

7-20 Where a minor transfers property under a contract which is not binding on him, there seems little doubt that title passes. Thus, in *Chaplin v Leslie Frewin (Publishers) Ltd*,[78] where a minor assigned to a publisher the copyright in a book, the publisher was held to have title to the copyright concerned. What is less clear is whether the minor has any restitutionary claim for the return of that property once he has received the bargained-for exchange. In *Pearce v Brain*,[79] Swift J seems to have thought that he had. A youth exchanged his motorcycle for a car. When the axle of the car broke, he sought to undo the transaction and recover the motorcycle. His action failed, but only on the basis that he could not show a total failure of consideration since he had had the use of the car for some little time. Had he offered to return the car immediately, it seems to have been accepted by Swift J that his claim would have succeeded.[80] On the other hand, in *Chaplin v Leslie Frewin (Publishers) Ltd*,[81] a majority of the Court of Appeal clearly thought differently. The minor who had transferred the copyright later regretted the transaction, but two judges clearly thought that the transfer remained irrevocable even if the contract was not binding on him and even if he gave credit for moneys received in exchange.[82] It is respectfully suggested that the view of Swift J in *Pearce v Brain* is to be preferred. It would be distinctly odd if property could be recovered if transferred under a contract voidable for mistake, or, for that matter, a contract ineffective because of the *ultra vires* doctrine, but not if transferred by a minor in circumstances where the law deems him in need of protection.

---

78 [1966] Ch 71.

79 [1929] 2 KB 310.

80 Although Swift J thought he could claim the car *in specie*, this view seems untenable in view of *Chaplin v Leslie Frewin Ltd* [1966] Ch 71.

81 [1966] Ch 71.

82 In fact, the contract was held to be for the minor's benefit, so the point did not arise.

(d) Claims against the minor

7-21   Although the ineffectiveness of minors' contracts does not, as such, bar restitutionary recovery, the policy behind it does demand the limitation of such actions against them where it might approximate to the enforcement of the contract itself. The position here is different in the two jurisdictions, the English and Northern Irish rules being largely altered by the Minors' Contracts Act 1987 and equivalent legislation.

Under the common law, which is in effect in the Republic, restitution is severely restricted. In particular, it was held in *Cowern v Nield*[83] that a minor who agreed to sell goods, but failed to deliver them, could not be sued for return of the price as money paid for a consideration that had totally failed. In the later case of *Leslie (R) Ltd v Shiell*,[84] a similar result followed, denying any restitutionary remedy to a lender of money against a minor who had lied about his age. The only exceptions were that if the minor was guilty of fraud and still had the money or property concerned, equity could order him to return it;[85] and that, where he obtained property by fraud which he then sold, he could similarly be made liable for the sale proceeds by way of restitution for the wrong of deceit.[86] Similarly, it would seem that a person supplying goods and services to a minor under a contract later rescinded for breach by the latter would not be entitled to restitutionary recovery, since it would offend against the policy of denying effect to minors' contractual obligations to make them pay even a reasonable price for what was supplied.[87]

7-22   These results are hard to rationalise or justify. In so far as both of them were expressed to result from the 'implied contract' theory of money had and received, their doctrinal basis is, to say the least, shaky. Moreover, although *Leslie v Shiell*[88] could be defended[89] on the basis that to allow recovery there is, in effect, enforcing the contract of loan,[90] the result in *Cowern v Nield*[91] cannot be upheld even on that basis: making someone repay money he has received without providing the promised return is simply not the same as making him liable in damages for not providing that return. Furthermore, even in cases such

---

83   [1912] 2 KB 419.

84   [1914] 3 KB 607.

85   See *R Leslie Ltd v Shiell* [1914] 3 KB 607, p 619 (Lord Sumner). The Divisional Court also accepted that this was the case in *Cowern v Nield* [1912] 2 KB 419.

86   *Stocks v Wilson* [1913] 2 KB 235.

87   Cf *ibid*, pp 242–43.

88   [1914] 3 KB 607.

89   As it is by Goff & Jones: see p 649 *et seq*.

90   True, Burrows argues (Burrows, p 452) that there are differences, particularly in that interest would not be recoverable as of right in a restitutionary action. But, with respect, this is a very narrow distinction, and arguably not enough to justify distinguishing between contractual and restitutionary recovery.

91   [1912] 2 KB 419.

as *Leslie v Shiell*[92] it is not clear that the policy of protecting minors from their own improvidence necessarily requires denial of any extra-contractual remedy; for instance, if the minor still has the money or has used it for expenditure which he would have made anyway. For these reasons, it was clearly right for the Irish Law Reform Commission to propose that the court should have at least some discretionary power to allow a restitutionary remedy against the minor in such circumstances,[93] though the breadth of the discretion suggested opens their proposal to the charge of unnecessary uncertainty.[94]

7-23   In England, s 3 of the Minors' Contracts Act 1987 has considerably altered the situation. It has partly ameliorated the claimant's position by allowing the court in its discretion to order the minor to restore property obtained under the contract or other property representing it, but only provided that (in either case) he still has it. For these purposes, it seems that 'property' includes money.[95] Although this has been criticised as not going far enough and as embodying an unwarrantable confusion of personal and proprietary restitution,[96] it is arguably a fair compromise. In effect, it gives the minor a kind of extended change of position defence; the fact that it apparently applies even where he knew of the potential claim against him can no doubt be justified on the basis that the minor should be protected against his own improvidence and should not be actually impoverished as a result of it.

V CONTRACTS AFFECTED BY ILLEGALITY[97]

(a) In general

7-24   As a general rule, the fact that a contract is illegal is merely a reason for not enforcing it. It is not an 'unjust factor' within the law of restitution, or a ground for making either party restore benefits gained under it. There is, therefore, no doubt that an executed illegal contract cannot be undone by either party simply on the ground that it should never have been entered into in the first place:[98]

---

92 [1914] 3 KB 607.

93 Report on *Minors' Contracts*, 1985 LRC No 15, Recommendation 3.

94 The considerations proposed included, besides the amount of the benefit retained by the minor, his financial position, the reasonableness of the parties' conduct and 'all other circumstances that appear to the court to be relevant': Recommendations, § 3.

95 Treitel, *Law of Contract*, 10th edn, p 512. The English Law Commission, on whose report the 1987 Act was based, certainly envisaged this: see Law Commission No 134, 4.21.

96 See Burrows, p 453.

97 In England, see Law Commission Consultation Paper No 154 (1999).

98 If authority is needed, *Shaw v Shaw* [1965] 1 All ER 638 is a straightforward instance (no recovery of money paid contrary to exchange control on that ground alone).

witness *Lowry v Bourdieu*,[99] where the plaintiff took out an illegal marine insurance policy on a ship which, in the event, arrived safely at its destination. Later, he sought to recover back the premium, but in the absence of any independent ground of restitution, the court had no difficulty in dismissing his claim. To this extent, the suggestion in *Guinness Mahon and Co Ltd v Kensington BC*,[100] that wherever payments were made under a void contract, there was automatically a failure of consideration, clearly cannot apply.

Furthermore, it is now clear that even though illegal contracts are traditionally described as 'void', the transferee of property pursuant to such a contracts gets an indefeasible title to it notwithstanding. Thus, in *Singh v Ali*,[101] a person who sold and delivered a lorry under an illegal contract was held liable in conversion when, not having been paid for it, he chose to exercise self-help by repossessing it.

Nevertheless, the illegality of a contract is relevant to restitutionary liability in two ways. First, it may act as a bar to restitution that would otherwise be available in connection with the contract: to that extent, people enter into illegal arrangements at their own risk. This matter is covered in Chapter 13. Secondly, in one case, illegality may actually create a right to restitution: namely, where a contract is made illegal in order to protect one party to it. This idea, which can be referred to as 'protective illegality', is dealt with in this chapter.

(b) Illegality as an unjust factor: protective illegality

7-25   Where the sole purpose of regarding a contract as illegal or contrary to public policy is to protect a vulnerable party from exploitation, then exceptionally, that party may be able to use this as a means to invalidate the contract and recover benefits rendered pursuant to it. The principle is normally applied in cases of statutory illegality, on the basis of Lord Mansfield's *dictum* in *Browning v Morris*:[102]

> Where contracts or transactions are prohibited by positive statutes, for the purpose of protecting one set of men from another set of men ... there the parties are not *in pari delicto*; and in furtherance of these statutes, the person injured, after the transaction is finished and completed, may bring his action and defeat the contract.

---

99 (1780) 2 Doug 468. See, too, *Sumner v Sumner* (1935) 69 ILTR 101 (no cancellation of settlement under contract illegally contemplating divorce, contrary to the Constitution), and *Shaw v Shaw* [1965] 1 All ER 638.

100 [1999] QB 215, p 226.

101 *Singh v Ali* [1960] AC 167. See, too, *Hortensius v Bishops* [1989] ILRM 294 and *Chief Constable of West Midlands v White* (1992) *The Times*, 25 March.

102 (1778) 2 Cowper 790, p 792.

Thus, in a series of cases under former moneylending legislation, it was held that securities given for repayment of loans which illegally failed to observe the correct formalities could be recovered.[103] But, the principle is broad enough to cover cases of common law illegality as well, as shown by the old case of *Atkinson v Denby*.[104] A debtor in difficulties wished to compound with all his creditors, but one of them refused to agree to this arrangement unless paid in full without the knowledge of the others. Such a contract was unenforceable as against public policy; nevertheless, having paid the creditor concerned, the debtor was held entitled, on the basis of Lord Mansfield's view in *Browning v Morris*, to recover his money.

7-26   Another line of cases depending on the same principle, it is suggested, are the authorities allowing recovery of fees paid to marriage brokers by hopeful suitors, such contracts having long been regarded as contrary to public policy.[105] Yet another concerns the decisions such as *Kiriri Cotton v Dewani*,[106] which held recoverable premiums demanded by landlords contrary to statute.[107] Although in *Kiriri Cotton* mention was also made of the fact that the payment was made under a mistake,[108] this can hardly be crucial: a tenant from whom an illegal premium is extorted can hardly be in a worse position merely because he knows the demand is illegal.

One interesting feature of 'protective illegality' cases is that there appears to be no requirement of total failure even where it would normally apply to the claim in question. The authorities are clear, for instance, that marriage brokerage payments are recoverable even after the arranged marriage:[109] again, in *Atkinson v Denby*[110] (referred to above), recovery was given although the arrangement had been carried out. From this, however, another question naturally follows: must the claimant who has received a benefit under such an arrangement make counter-restitution as a condition of obtaining restitution? Barring one case,[111] since largely distinguished,[112] the consistent answer given in the cases has been

---

103 Notably *Lodge v National Union Investment Co* [1907] 1 Ch 300 and *Kasumu v Baba-Egbe* [1956] AC 539.

104 (1862) 7 H & N 934. This case is apparently regarded by Burrows as one of duress (see Burrows, p 468): *sed quaere*. The creditor committed no wrong against the debtor in making his demand.

105 They run from *Smith v Bruning* (1700) 2 Vern 392 to *Hermann v Charlesworth* [1905] 2 KB 123.

106 [1960] AC 192. See too *Gray v Southouse* [1949] 2 All ER 1019.

107 Today, statute normally gives an express right of recovery – eg, in England, the Rent Act 1977, s 57.

108 See [1960] AC 192, p 203 *et seq*.

109 Eg, *Smith v Bruning* (1700) 2 Vern 392, where the then substantial sum of £50 paid to a marriage broker was ordered to be repaid even though the plaintiff had indeed married the lady procured.

110 (1862) 7 H & N 934.

111 *Lodge v National Union Investment Co* [1907] 1 Ch 300.

112 Eg, *Kasumu v Baba-Egbe* [1956] AC 539.

no. Thus, in *Kasumu v Baba-Egbe*,[113] borrowers under a moneylending contract that was made illegal and void under a Nigerian ordinance successfully obtained cancellation of the security they had given without being put on terms as to the repayment of the actual amount lent. As the Privy Council pointed out in *Kasumu*, this is on the basis that if public policy demands that the defendant be disabled from suing on the contract, he should not be able to get the same result[114] by the back door in the shape of an order that he be allowed to set off against the plaintiff's claim any performance provided by him.

VI CONTRACTS AFFECTED BY *ULTRA VIRES*

7-27   At common law, *ultra vires* contracts entered into by companies and public bodies are void and unenforceable, both against[115] and (probably) by[116] the organisation concerned. As regards companies, both England and Ireland have modified this rule, but not entirely removed it. In England, s 35(1) of the Companies Act 1985 has abolished it as regards companies registered under the Companies Acts, save as to transactions with insiders such as directors,[117] but it continues to apply to companies not so registered, and to charitable companies.[118] The Irish reform has been more cautious: by s 8(1) of the Companies Act 1963,[119] a transaction is effective as regards anyone who does not actually know it is *ultra vires*, but the rule remains as against anyone who does. In both jurisdictions, the common law rule continues to apply with full force to contracts with public bodies such as local authorities.

(a) Restitutionary claims by the corporation[120]

7-28   As early as 1966, it was suggested that a corporation's inability to enforce an *ultra vires* contract might not preclude restitutionary liability for such benefits as

---

113 [1956] AC 539.

114 Or, more accurately, nearly the same result: even if the borrower did have to return the amount lent, he would still presumably not have to pay the agreed interest on it.

115 *Ashbury Carriage and Wagon Co v Riche* (1875) LR 7 HL 653.

116 See *Bell Houses Ltd v City Wall Properties Ltd* [1966] 1 QB 207. The point was left open when that case went to the Court of Appeal ([1966] 2 QB 656): but Hobhouse J in *Westdeutsche Landesbank Girozentrale v Islington BC* [1994] 4 All ER 890 (affirmed by the HL [1996] AC 669) clearly assumed its correctness.

117 Companies Act 1985, s 322A. (In NI, references should be read as to the Companies (NI) Order 1986 SI 1986/1032.)

118 Companies Act 1985, s 35(4).

119 See too European Communities (Companies) Regulations 1973 SI 1973/163.

120 'Corporation' is used in this part as an umbrella term to cover both companies and other bodies, such as local authorities.

were provided.[121] And the matter was put beyond doubt by one of the later 'swaps' cases, *South Tyneside BC v Svenska International*,[122] where a local authority successfully recovered net payments made to a bank under an *ultra vires* interest rate swap agreement. Similarly, there is no doubt that a company, say, which pays in advance for goods to be delivered under a contract *ultra vires* can itself recover its money if it does not get them.[123] It is not as if the policy behind the *ultra vires* rule, which is no doubt the protection of corporate and public funds, would be in any way infringed.[124]

Nor, it is suggested, should it make any difference that the contract has been completely carried out. There is *ex hypothesi* no binding agreement between the parties: provided that the claimant corporation is able to afford counter-restitution so as to cause a failure of consideration, there seems no reason why it should not recover. Furthermore, this would underpin the rationale behind the *ultra vires* rule, namely, to protect the funds of the body concerned from unlawful dissipation. In any case, the same result can be reached another way, namely, by regarding the fact that a payment is made *ultra vires* as itself creating an 'unjust factor' allowing restitution (subject to a defence, where appropriate, of change of position).[125]

(b) Claims against the corporation

7-29 Since *Westdeutsche Landesbank Girozentrale v Islington BC*,[126] there has been no doubt that money paid to a corporation under an *ultra vires* contract is recoverable. Although, in that case, Hobhouse J put the grounds of recovery down to 'absence of consideration', it has been suggested above[127] that because of the ability of the corporation to recover what it has paid, recovery is better based on the orthodox basis of failure of consideration.[128] And, subject to what is said below, presumably the same applies to benefits in kind.

---

121 *Bell Houses Ltd v City Wall Properties Ltd* [1966] 1 QB 207, p 226 (Mocatta J).

122 [1995] 1 All ER 545. See too *Re Frederick Inns Ltd* [1981] ILRM 582 (recovery *in personam* of *ultra vires* payment by a company of debts owed by other companies in same group).

123 Indeed, it seems from the 'swaps' cases that, provided it can produce counter-restitution by tendering the goods back, it can recover its money even if it does get them: see the next paragraph.

124 See Arrowsmith (1989) 9 LS 307, p 309.

125 See Chapter 13.

126 [1994] 4 All ER 890 (upheld in the HL [1996] AC 669).

127 See § 6-12 *et seq.*

128 Cf the reasoning in *Hicks v Hicks* (1802) 3 East 16, where it was held that where the grantee of a void annuity chose to take the point, he could recover his money on giving credit for what he had himself received. It is suggested that this is another case where the availability of cross-restitution causes a total failure of consideration.

Until the House of Lords' decision in *Westdeutsche Landesbank*,[129] it was thought that one type of contract might – at least in England – be treated differently: namely, a contract to lend money to an *ultra vires* borrower. This was the result of the notorious decision in *Sinclair v Brougham*,[130] where depositors with the Birkbeck Bank belatedly discovered that it had been carrying on business *ultra vires* and hence that they could not sue it on its promise to repay their money. Their claim to restitution *in personam* was also denied, on the basis that to allow it would, to some extent, be tantamount to enforcing a contract otherwise ineffective. But, it is submitted that this decision is now thoroughly discredited. The Irish courts understandably disowned it in *Re PMPA Garage (Longmile) Ltd*,[131] where it was said that as regards Irish law, there would no longer be any bar to restitution in such a case. And in the *Westdeutsche* case,[132] the denial of a personal claim in Sinclair was said by two members of the House of Lords[133] to have been wrong, while a third Law Lord expressed grave reservations as to its correctness.[134] In these circumstances, it is suggested that the earlier case is extremely unlikely to be followed and need not worry restitution lawyers overmuch in the future.

7-30   Two further points need to be noted. First, should it make any difference to a claim against the corporation that the contract is fully executed? In *Kleinwort Benson v Sandwell BC*,[135] a 'swaps' case decided at the same time as Westdeutsche, the facts were the same save that the 'swap' had run its course, leaving the plaintiff bank the net payer. Having decided *Westdeutsche* on the basis of 'absence of consideration', it is not surprising that Hobhouse J and the Court of Appeal held that the bank could recover. This conclusion has been questioned by Swadling,[136] on the basis that the bank got all it paid for and hence should not be in a position to complain; nevertheless, it is respectfully submitted that the result is correct. The bank paid on the assumption not only that it would get paid by Sandwell, but that it would get an indefeasible title to keep the payment. This it did not get (assuming there would have been no bar to the authority recovering its money if it wished); if so, there is no reason why it should not be able to show failure of consideration in the ordinary way.

Secondly, should it be relevant that the claimant has already recovered its money elsewhere, as (for instance) where a public authority has made good a shortfall by increasing taxation, or where a bank entering into an ineffective 'swap' transaction has successfully hedged its position with a third party? The

129 [1996] AC 669.
130 [1914] AC 398.
131 [1992] 1 IR 332.
132 [1996] AC 669.
133 Ie, Lords Browne-Wilkinson and Slynn.
134 Lord Goff.
135 [1994] 4 All ER 890.
136 See [1994] RLR 73, p 80.

English Court of Appeal has answered this question in the negative;[137] and, it is respectfully submitted, rightly so. The position as between the claimant and a third party ought to be regarded as *res inter alios acta;* the claimant may itself be under a restitutionary liability to the third party (depending on any agreement entered into between them), and, in any case, it is hard to see why the defendant's enrichment is any less unjustified merely because the claimant may have indemnified itself elsewhere.

VII CONTRACTS AFFECTED BY LACK OF FORMALITY

7-31   This topic is less important than it was, but still may raise difficulties. In both England and Ireland, contracts for the sale of land are subject to strict formal requirements: in England, by s 2 of the Law of Property (Miscellaneous Provisions) Act 1989, requiring such contracts to be entirely reduced to writing, signed by both parties, and in Northern Ireland and the Republic by the Statute of Frauds (Ireland) 1695, s 2 of which requires a note or memorandum evidencing the contract and signed by the person against whom it is sought to enforce it. In addition to this, the law of the Republic requires a note or memorandum of contracts for the sale of goods for more than £10,[138] and for contracts not to be performed within one year.[139] Furthermore, there are a number of other miscellaneous statutes requiring writing or other forms, for instance, in the case of consumer credit contracts[140] or contracts for estate agency work.[141]

7-32   On principle, the fact that a contract is unenforceable ought not to be a reason as such to deny restitutionary recovery on ordinary failure of consideration principles. The mere fact that a defendant cannot be forced to perform his contract or to pay damages in lieu does not make his enrichment any less unjust if, having accepted some payment or other benefit under it, he fails to provide the *quid pro quo.* There is, for instance, no doubt that deposits under oral contracts for the sale of land are recoverable if the vendor fails to convey:[142] and, in the important case of *Deglman v Guaranty Trust,*[143] the Supreme Court of Canada held that where a plaintiff rendered housekeeping services to the defendant pursuant to an unenforceable oral agreement to devise his house to her on his death, the fact that she could not obtain the house did not prevent her

---

137 See *Kleinwort Benson Ltd v Birmingham CC* [1997] QB 380.
138 Sale of Goods Act 1893, s 4.
139 Statute of Frauds (Ireland) 1695, s 2.
140 Eg, Consumer Credit Act 1974, ss 60, 61 (England).
141 Eg, Estate Agents Act 1979, s 18 (England).
142 In *Gosbell v Archer* (1835) 2 Ad & El 500, as much was admitted.
143 [1954] 3 DLR 75.

recovering the reasonable value of her services. As Rand J put it: 'The [Statute of Frauds] in such a case does not touch the principle of restitution against what would otherwise be an unjust enrichment of the defendant at the expense of the plaintiff.'[144]

7-33 Similarly, too, with other performance in kind, for instance where (in Ireland) services are rendered under a contract not to be performed for a year. The person rendering the services, while unable to sue for the contracted remuneration, is entitled to reasonable payment for what he has done.[145] The Australian decision in *Pavey and Matthews Pty Ltd v Paul*[146] is a more recent illustration of the same thinking. Building work was carried out under a contract which, because of a local statute, was unenforceable because it was not in writing. In a very careful and closely reasoned judgment, the High Court of Australia held that the unenforceability of the contract was of itself no bar to the builder recovering a reasonable sum for what he had done.

On the other hand, a proper interpretation of the statute invalidating the contract for lack of form is vital. If, for instance (as with the (English) Consumer Credit Act),[147] it provides specifically for enforcement of the defective contract with the leave of the court, this may well indicate that the statutory remedy is exhaustive and that any restitutionary remedies outside it ought to be barred.[148] Again, in *Pavey and Matthews v Paul*,[149] referred to above, it is instructive that much of the discussion centred round whether the intent of the statute there in issue would be frustrated by an action in restitution: only after a determination that it would not was the action allowed.

VIII NON-CONTRACTUAL CASES

7-34 As mentioned above,[150] there is no necessary connection between failure of consideration and contract: the concept applies equally to benefits rendered in anticipation of a contract that never materialises, and indeed, where no contract is ever concluded[151] or even contemplated. A clear example of a 'no-contract' case would arise were A to pay B under an agreement binding in honour only for goods which B failed to deliver, or give him £50,000 towards the purchase of a house which, in the event, he did not buy. In either case, it is suggested that A would be able to recover the price of the goods or £50,000 as the case may be.

---

144 [1954] 3 DLR 75, p 78.
145 Eg, *Mavor v Pyne* (1825) 3 Bing 285; *Savage v Canning* (1867) IR 1 CL 434.
146 (1986) 162 CLR 221.
147 Section 127. See too Estate Agents Act 1979, s 18.
148 Cf *Dimond v Lovell* [2000] 2 All ER 897; below, § 13-32.
149 (1986) 162 CLR 221.
150 See above, § 6-5.
151 *Chillingworth v Esche* [1924] 1 Ch 97.

7-35   In fact, most real-life examples concern land, where (perhaps oddly) a proprietary remedy may be available. Cases such as *Hussey v Palmer*[152] illustrate the point. A paid for improvements to B's premises in the (arguably non-contractual) expectation of being able to live there for life. When the relationship later broke down, she successfully obtained a declaration that the house was subject to a trust in her favour for an amount proportional to her expenditure. But, even here, restitution is in practice not very important. The grant of relief to someone acting, or incurring expenditure, on property in the expectation of some future benefit is a creature of equity based on constructive trust: and while this remedy may, as in *Hussey v Palmer*, be based on unjust enrichment, it may equally go further and give the claimant what he hoped to get,[153] thus in effect giving a contractual right where otherwise there would be none.[154] Important as this is, it is not part of the subject of this book.

7-36   Much more significant is the subject of work done, or goods supplied, in the confident expectation that there will be a contract between the parties and that remuneration will be available under the terms of the contract. For example, while landlord and tenant are negotiating the terms of a new lease, the tenant asks the landlord to carry out certain alterations or improvements. Or, during negotiations for what promises to be a complex, but urgent construction project, a building contractor is requested to start certain work – or a supplier to supply materials – before the contract is concluded. If, in the event, the parties do not agree, is restitution available?

7-37   Logically, the answer to this question must be yes – at least *prima facie*. There can be no doubt as to enrichment, there having been a request for the goods or services concerned; nor, for the same reason, can the recipient say he did not want them. And, *ex hypothesi*, there has been a failure of consideration: the recompense contemplated, namely part (or conceivably all) of the consideration to be provided by the other party under the contract, has not been and will not be provided. And so we have cases like *William Lacey (Hounslow) v Davis*.[155] Builders tendered in respect of reconstruction work on war-damaged premises. Having been assured their tender would be accepted, at the landowner's request they prepared detailed estimates with a view to extracting the maximum contribution from the Exchequer towards the cost; they also took out detailed bills of quantities in preparation for the work itself. At the last minute, however, the owner decided to cut his losses and sell rather than repair. Barry J had no

---

152 [1972] 3 All ER 744. Cf *Chalmers v Pardoe* [1963] 3 All ER 552.

153 'The equity having thus been raised ... it is for the courts of equity to decide in what way that equity should be satisfied' (*per* Lord Denning MR in *Greasley v Cooke* [1980] 3 All ER 710, p 713). The plaintiff there got her full expectation, not just her expenditure. See, too, *Re Basham* [1987] 1 All ER 405, and cf *Inwards v Baker* [1965] 2 QB 29.

154 See Birks, p 290 *et seq*.

155 [1957] 2 All ER 712. See, too, *Peter Lind Ltd v Mersey Docks and Harbour Board* [1972] 2 Lloyd's Rep 234; and *Fanning v Wicklow CC* (1984) unreported, 30 April, HC (a decision very similar to the *William Lacey* case).

difficulty in allowing the builders a *quantum meruit* claim; the fact that they expected to recoup themselves out of the profits of the contract, but now would not, was ample ground for making the owner pay a reasonable sum for what they did. Similar is *British Steel Corp v Cleveland Bridge and Engineering Co*,[156] where building contractors in a hurry to start a project in the Gulf ordered steel to be supplied immediately, in the firm belief that a contract would eventuate between them and the steel suppliers. When it did not because the parties could not agree on price, the suppliers recovered a reasonable sum in *quantum meruit*.

7-38   When, then, should recovery not be granted? The only possible answer, it is suggested, is based on risk: we should deny a remedy if, and only if, the party providing the benefit should in the circumstances be regarded as having taken the risk of not being paid. But how do we know?

On one view, it should depend on whose fault it was that negotiations broke down· if the claimant's, he should forfeit his claim. Birks provides some support for this view,[157] as does an Australian decision, *Sabemo v North Sydney Municipal Council*.[158] Contractors had been chosen to build a major municipal development; after they had at the authority's request done a good deal of preliminary work by way of planning and costing, the authority unilaterally cancelled the project. The contractors recovered reasonable remuneration for what they had done, Sheppard J stressing in particular[159] that the Council's withdrawal had been opportunistic and culpable, and not due to *bona fide* disagreement. But this is hardly satisfactory, since:

(a) it gives too little weight to negotiating parties' normal understanding that until agreement, they can withdraw for any reason they see fit;[160]

(b) distinguishing between culpable and non-culpable failure to contract is likely in practice to be very difficult; and

(c) elsewhere, for instance in the case of money paid for a consideration that totally fails, the fact that the claimant acted wrongfully is correctly regarded as irrelevant to his claim to restitution.

7-39   Much better, it is suggested, is to ask the following question: had the expected contract been concluded, would the work done have been regarded as performance of it or merely as preparation for performance? If the latter, *prima*

---

156 [1984] 1 All ER 504.

157 Birks, p 283 *et seq*.

158 [1977] 2 NSWLR 880. See, too, *dicta* of Somervell and Denning LJJ in *Brewer Street Investments v Barclays Woollen Co* [1954] 1 QB 428, pp 434, 436.

159 See [1977] 2 NSWLR 880, p 902.

160 As was accepted by Rattee J in *Regalian Properties v London Docklands Development Corp* [1995] 1 All ER 1005, p 1024. Cf *Walford v Miles* [1992] 2 AC 128, questioning the whole concept of an obligation to act reasonably or in good faith during contractual negotiations.

facie there should be no claim. It is something done as a necessary overhead, or indeed to persuade the other party to contract at all (for example, the house owner who at a prospective purchaser's suggestion repairs the roof); in the circumstances it would entirely defeat the parties' expectations to allow a charge to be made for without express provision.

It is suggested that most cases of work done by a person on his own property will fall into this category: see, for example, *Jennings v Woodman*,[161] where potential lessors who did work on their premises at the prospective lessees' insistence were held disentitled to recovery even though no lease in fact ensued.[162] Admittedly, a contrary result was reached in *Brewer Street Investments Ltd v Barclays Woollen Co Ltd*,[163] where lessors successfully recovered the cost of improvements: but, it is suggested that each case depends very much on its own facts, particularly since there the lessees had accepted in so many words that they would be responsible for the cost of any improvements. Certainly, Denning LJ's suggestion that the works were done for the lessees' benefit[164] is difficult to accept: it is odd, to say the least, to argue that a person who improves his own property with a view to persuading someone else to buy or lease it acts for anyone's benefit other than his own.

7-40   Cases where claims for work, done by the claimant not on his own property, have been defeated on the basis of risk are less common, but they do occur. One such, it is submitted, is *Regalian Properties Ltd v London Docklands Development Corp*.[165] Developers provisionally agreed to build a number of houses in the London Docklands on land owned and marked down for comprehensive redevelopment by the LDDC. Under the proposed scheme, the LDDC would sell the houses to the developers, they would resell them to purchasers, and the profit would be split. The plans submitted by the developers were drastically, and expensively, modified at the corporation's insistence; but then, land values increased ruinously, and the deal was abandoned. The developers failed in a claim against the authority for £3 m, representing their extra planning work and professional fees incurred, Rattee J stressing that this was merely preparatory work[166] and distinguishing cases like *Cleveland Bridge* on that basis.

7-41   One further point should be noted in connection with benefits provided under anticipated contracts (though theoretically it may arise in connection with any non-contractual claim for goods supplied or services rendered). What if what the

---

161 [1952] 2 TLR 309.

162 Birks, p 284, observes that it was pretty clearly the lessors' fault that the lease went off (they had failed to notice a vital covenant as to user). But, for the reason suggested above, it is suggested that this ought to be regarded as being of little, if any, relevance.

163 [1954] 1 QB 428.

164 *Ibid*, p 437.

165 [1995] 1 All ER 1005.

166 Cf *Marston Construction Ltd v Kigass Ltd* (1989) 15 Const LR 116, where such a claim had apparently been accepted, but which was doubted by Rattee J in *Regalian*.

claimant provides is somehow defective, so as to cause the defendant to incur loss or expenditure? *Ex hypothesi*, there can be no claim for breach of contract, but is there any other basis for allowing him to set off that loss or expenditure against the claimant's claim? Goff J, in the *Cleveland Bridge* case,[167] clearly thought not: even though the defendants there claimed that because the steel fabrications had been delivered defective and out of sequence they had suffered loss exceeding the claim against them, they were held liable to pay without deduction. But this may not necessarily be so. In *Crown House Ltd v Amec plc*,[168] a case involving building work done before contracts were finalised, Slade LJ thought, *obiter*, that there might be room for a deduction on the basis that the value of the work *to this defendant* might be regarded as diminished by loss he suffered as a result of defects in it. The result certainly seems fair, though perhaps a better way of explaining it is on the basis of reasoning analogous to the 'extended' change of position defence: that is, that where as a result of receipt of the benefit the defendant suffers unrecoupable loss, then whether or not that loss results from the defendant's positive act in relying on the benefit he ought to have a defence *pro tanto*.

---

167 [1984] 1 All ER 504.
168 (1989) 48 Build LR 37, p 54.

CHAPTER 8

RECOUPMENT AND CONTRIBUTION

I GENERALLY

8-1 The right to recoupment or contribution arises in order to deal with the situation where a claimant, C, is constrained to discharge an obligation to a third party, T, that for some reason ought more appropriately to have been borne by the defendant, D, alone (recoupment), or by C and D together (contribution). Typical examples of the right to recoupment are the surety's claim to indemnity from the principal debtor on discharging the latter's obligation, and the right to repayment of a person who has to pay someone else's debt in order to free his own property from some charge or lien affecting it. Rights to contribution are epitomised by the claims inter se of co-debtors and of wrongdoers, such as joint tortfeasors or trustees collectively answerable for a breach of trust. The 'unjust factor' behind both is similar to that involved in duress: C has been forced against his will to confer a benefit on D. Nevertheless, the liability is clearly different from duress, in that the claimant has been forced to benefit the defendant not by unlawful means, but instead by lawful means employed by a third party.

8-2 The right to recoupment and contribution is, it seems fairly clear, a restitutionary right independent of the underlying obligation.[1] If so, it should be no defence that at the time it is sought, the creditor's claim against the person from whom relief is sought would be statute barred, provided that it would not have been so barred when the claimant was sued or paid it.[2] This is specifically provided by statute in respect of concurrent wrongdoers in both Ireland[3] and England;[4] but, independent of statute, the same reasoning has been applied to other defences which become available to the would-be contributor as a result of subsequent events. One example of such is a compromise by him of the claimant's demand.[5] Another is provided by the Privy Council's decision in *Legal and General*

---

1 Explicitly so in Ireland in the case of concurrent wrongdoers: see Civil Liability Act 1961, s 30.

2 A case specifically provided for in certain cases: see the Civil Liability Act 1961, ss 23(4), 31 (Ireland), and the Civil Liability (Contribution) Act 1978, s 1(2) (England).

3 Civil Liability Act 1961, s 23(4).

4 Civil Liability (Contribution) Act 1978, s 1(2) and (3).

5 See *Logan v Uttlesford DC* (1986) 136 NLJ 541 and *Jameson v Central Electricity Generating Board* [1998] QB 323 (reversed in the HL on other grounds [2000] 1 AC 455) (both concerning statutory contribution under the English Civil Liability (Contribution) Act 1978).

Assurance Soc Ltd v Drake Insurance Co Ltd.[6] Two underwriters insured the same risk. One paid the claim in full; he recovered contribution from the other, despite the defence raised by the latter that the assured had lost his right to claim against it by failing to give timely notice of the loss.

8-3   More generally, in order to claim recoupment or contribution, the claimant must show three things:

(a) that he discharged an obligation of the defendant;

(b) that he was compellable to do so,[7] either by action or by seizure of his property; and

(c) that, as between himself and the defendant, it was an obligation which the latter was primarily liable to discharge in whole or in part.

(a) Discharge of obligation

8-4   Recoupment is unavailable unless a liability of the defendant is in fact discharged:[8] it is not enough to show merely that the claimant has been forced to make a payment, and that that payment benefits the defendant in some other way.[9] Thus, where a customer successfully sued his bank for negligence in failing to collect a number of cheques paid in by a debtor who subsequently went bankrupt, the bank was denied any remedy against the bankrupt's estate which had been *de facto* relieved.[10] Again, it has been held in England[11] that an employer cannot recover sick pay he has had to pay his employee from the tortfeasor responsible for injuring him in the first place: to the extent that his employer continues to pay him, the employee has suffered no loss for which he can sue, and hence no liability of the wrongdoer has been discharged by the payment. And, *a fortiori*, where a claimant, C, has indemnified X against a

---

6   [1992] QB 887.

7   *Stott v West Yorkshire Road Car Co Ltd* [1971] 2 QB 651 (contribution between tortfeasors: plaintiff failed because he could not show he was legally compellable to pay at all). But note that there is now a statutory exception in the case of concurrent wrongdoers who settle with a claimant even though not in fact liable: see the Civil Liability (Contribution) Act 1978, s 1(4) (England), and the Civil Liability Act 1961, s 29(1) (Ireland).

8   Cf *Re TH Knitwear (Wholesale) Ltd* [1987] 1 WLR 371 (Customs repay VAT wrongly paid by customer of company in liquidation: no claim against company since customer retained claim against company, even though it would have to account for proceeds to Customs).

9   Cf, however, the statutory right of the Crown in England to recover social security payments from tortfeasors, which operates independently of whether the injured person's claim against the tortfeasor has been *pro tanto* discharged: Social Security (Recovery of Benefits) Act 1997.

10   *Re Towey, A Bankrupt* (1994) unreported, 24 March, Irish HC (Carney J)).

11   See *Metropolitan Police Receiver v Croydon Corp* [1957] 1 All ER 78. A similar result was reached by the Supreme Court in *AG v Ryan's Car Hire Ltd* [1965] IR 642, but discussion there centred on the non-availability of the tortious *actio per quod servitium amisit*, rather than on the possibility of a restitutionary claim. See too *Hogan v Steele & Co Ltd* [2000] 1 ESC 26.

liability to Y, he cannot claim contribution from D on the basis that D would also have been liable to Y.[12]

This requirement of an obligation discharged, rather than simply an abstract benefit conferred, is a little difficult to rationalise; but, it is perhaps best regarded as resulting from 'incidental benefit' thinking: the person who is forced to do good to someone else other than by direct discharge of his obligation is regarded in the same light as the person who happens to benefit another as a result, say, of saving his own property.[13]

Discharge: the problem of unrequested payment of another's obligation

8-5 Moreover, the requirement of an obligation discharged must be read in the light of a further rule, namely that where a third party voluntarily purports to pay a debt for the debtor, such payment will not necessarily have the effect of extinguishing the obligation concerned.[14] Thus, with unrequested payment of another's debt, it seems from the authorities[15] that such a payment will only discharge the debt in two cases. One is where payment is made by the claimant on account of the debt and that payment is later ratified by the debtor.[16] The other is where the creditor could have sued the claimant for it or otherwise enforced its payment against him (for instance, by seizing his goods): although there is no direct authority here, a number of cases, including *Owen v Tate*,[17] clearly proceed on the assumption that if paid, the obligation is indeed extinguished. Apart from *Owen v Tate*, which is discussed below, one such is *Midland Great Western Rly Co v Benson*[18] in 1878. A seller of butter, having received an advance payment of £40 towards the price, despatched the butter by train to the buyer, to whom property passed. He then wrongfully persuaded the railway to stop it in transit. Under threat of legal action by the buyer, the railway paid him £40, which sum they then successfully recovered from the seller on the basis that their payment had gone to discharge the latter's own liability to the buyer.

8-6 On the authorities, it is similarly difficult for a liability for wrongdoing to be extinguished. Payments received by the victim of a breach of contract or a tort, even if intended to recoup his losses in fact, do not go to reduce or discharge the

---

12 *Birse Construction Ltd v Haiste* [1996] 2 All ER 1.

13 See above, § 1-42.

14 Most recently, see the subrogation case of *Crantrave Ltd v Lloyds Bank plc* [2000] 4 All ER 273.

15 They are usefully summarised in Burrows, p 222 *et seq*, and in Beatson, *The Use and Abuse of Unjust Enrichment*, Chapter 7.

16 This results from a combination of *Belshaw v Bush* (1851) 11 CB 191 and *Walter v James* (1871) LR 6 Ex 124. For a review of the authorities generally, see Beatson in *The Use and Abuse of Unjust Enrichment*, Chapter 7.

17 [1976] QB 402, discussed below, § 8-8.

18 (1878) 2 LR (Ir) 548.

victim of the wrong unless paid on his account. Thus, in *The Esso Bernicia*,[19] a tanker ran ashore on the Scottish coast while under tow, allegedly because the tug had been improperly constructed. A good deal of oil escaped. The tanker owners indemnified local crofters for the consequences of the resulting pollution under a voluntary environmental protection scheme known as TOVALOP. They then sought recoupment from the builders of the tug, arguing that they could equally have been sued by the crofters. The claim failed: assuming the builders would have been liable in tort to the crofters, this liability had not been discharged.

It seems, however, that where A is actually held liable by a court for a liability properly payable by B, then his payment of it will discharge B. This is the result of *East Cork Foods Ltd v O'Dwyer Steel Ltd*.[20] X, injured in an accident, sued E and O. At first instance, they were held equally liable and E paid his share, but on appeal O was held to be solely responsible. E successfully brought an action against O to recover the amount of his payment on the basis that he had been forced to discharge O's liability to X. This is a clearly sensible result, but only defensible on the assumption that O's liability was in fact discharged.

(b) Compellability

8-7   As a general rule, it is not enough that the claimant has paid off some obligation of the defendant. He must show that he was legally compelled, or compellable,[21] to do so.[22] Subject to one statutory exception in the case of contribution between wrongdoers (applicable in both England and Ireland),[23] a person who pays when he is not liable to do so, even by way of *bona fide* compromise[24] or otherwise for good reason, has no right of recourse.[25] However, where a payment is voluntary only because some procedural precondition of liability has not been satisfied (such as a demand in writing from

---

19 [1989] AC 643 (a Scots case, but the principles were said to be the same as in England). See, too, *Jones v Stroud DC* [1988] 1 All ER 5.

20 [1978] IR 103.

21 A term which includes liability established in a foreign court: *Liberian Insurance Agency Inc v Mosse* [1977] 2 Lloyd's Rep 560.

22 See, eg, *Legal and General Assurance Soc Ltd v Drake Insurance Co Ltd* [1992] QB 877 (contribution between insurers: to the extent that insurer who pays out was not in fact liable, no contribution).

23 See the Civil Liability (Contribution) Act 1978, s 1(4) (England), and the Civil Liability Act 1961, s 29(1) (Ireland).

24 It never seems to have been argued that the payer should have a right to recover in such circumstances on the basis that by paying off the defendant's obligation he has benefited him as a result of a mistake.

25 *Legal & General Assurance Soc Ltd v Drake Insurance Co Ltd* [1992] QB 877; *Bovis Construction Ltd v Commercial Union Assurance Co plc* [2001] Lloyd's Rep IR 321.

the creditor) and would otherwise have been due, then that payment is regarded as being compelled.[26]

One might be forgiven for thinking that this was merely an aspect of the rule that voluntary payment of another's obligation does not discharge it. If the payment was not compelled, then the obligation would not be discharged: and if that is so, then there is no enrichment at all, let alone any unjust enrichment. But this is to oversimplify matters. Even where the payment is in form compulsory, and hence there is a discharge, it is submitted that there still may be cases where the person who made it is nonetheless disentitled to recoupment on the ground that he was not in substance compelled to pay. Take the case where D owes T £100. If C pays the £100 to T, D's debt remains undischarged. But what if D contracts with T to pay the debt and then actually pays it five minutes later? The debt may now be discharged by the payment, but C has still in substance acted voluntarily. It would be absurd if his position as against D were radically different according to whether he paid the debt immediately, or went through the form of voluntarily assuming an obligation to pay it first.[27]

8-8   It is this principle which, it is suggested, underlies the difficult decision in *Owen v Tate*.[28] The defendants owed money to a bank, secured as to £350 on property belonging to L. The plaintiff, acting out of kindness to L, agreed with the bank to guarantee the £350 debt and then subsequently paid it off. L's property thereby became unencumbered. The plaintiff's action for recoupment against the defendants, that is, the debtors, nevertheless failed. As against them, he was held to have acted entirely voluntarily[29] and, indeed, officiously.

Admittedly, this decision has been criticised. Burrows[30] argues that even if compulsion is negatived as an unjust factor, the claimant ought to have been able to plead failure of consideration instead – namely, that he expected by paying the debt to get reimbursement from the defendants, but did not. But this surely cannot be right. There was no agreement or common assumption between the parties as to the return to be got by the claimant in exchange for his payment: all there was was a mere unilateral expectation on his part, which is

---

26   *Stimpson v Smith* [1999] 2 All ER 833.

27   Cf *Beresford v Kennedy* (1887) 21 Ir LTR 17, denying restitution to one who was compelled to pay a debt, but only because of his own wrongful act. *Contra*, however, Burrows, p 215 *et seq*.

28   [1976] QB 402.

29   Goff & Jones argue (Goff & Jones, pp 128–29) that the plaintiff, however voluntarily he may have acted vis à vis the debtor, did not so act as against the bank. But, with respect, this seems an over-narrow distinction.

30   See Burrows, p 215. Burrows also contends (*ibid*) that subrogation ought to have been granted in *Owen* under the Mercantile Law Amendment Act 1856, s 5, to the security held by the bank (a point not, in fact, argued). But this is also difficult. Presumably that section is only intended to apply where restitution would otherwise be available, and not (for instance) where a debt is guaranteed purely as a gift to the debtor: if so, then assuming the claimant's non-statutory claim was barred, the same must go for the statutory one.

something quite different, and (it is suggested) cannot be sufficient of itself to ground recovery.

8-9   Assuming *Owen v Tate* to be correct, when will an obligation to pay be regarded as having been assumed voluntarily in this sense? The mere fact that it was done without a prior request of the debtor is not of itself enough, as shown by *The Zuhal K*.[31] Shipowners faced with a claim for cargo damage sought a guarantee from their P & I club to free the vessel from arrest. The club (which was in financial difficulty) at the cargo-owners' insistence obtained a further guarantee from an insurance company. Having paid off the cargo-owners, the company successfully claimed from the shipowners, despite the latter's argument that vis à vis themselves, the company had acted voluntarily. Again, in *Belger v Belger*[32] a house was charged with monthly repayments due on a loan to a husband and wife jointly. As between these two, the husband was primarily liable to make the payments. The parties were subsequently divorced, whereupon the wife sold the house; as a result of this, the loan had to be paid off immediately out of the proceeds. It was held that, even though she had not literally been compelled to sell the house,[33] in substance this was a case of compulsory payment. Hence, she had an immediate right of indemnity against her ex-husband, despite the latter's plea that she had voluntarily exposed herself to an immediate and not a deferred liability.

In the light of cases of this sort, the best formulation is, it is submitted, that a claimant will be allowed to recover provided he undertakes liability for the defendant's debt for good business reasons,[34] such as protecting his own property rights,[35] or for other considerations not amounting simply to a desire to discharge the defendant; and that this will apply even if he does not act at the defendant's actual request.[36] On the other hand, someone who has no such reason, or *a fortiori* someone who was only compelled to pay the defendant's debt because of his own wrongful act,[37] will not be so successful.

---

31   [1987] 1 Lloyd's Rep 151.

32   (1989) unreported, 17 July, CA.

33   In that she could have retained it, provided the payments were kept up.

34   A possible further instance of this thinking is where a person (known as an accommodation party – Bills of Exchange Act 1882, s 28) puts his name to a bill of exchange to guarantee the credit of someone already a party to it. He is treated as a surety to that person; his payment of the bill discharges it; and he has all the rights otherwise inhering in a guarantor. See *Oriental Finance Corp v Overend Gurney and Co* (1874) LR 7 HL 348; *Chalmers and Guest on Bills of Exchange*, 15th edn, p 801 et seq.

35   See, eg, *Kleinwort Benson Ltd v Vaughan* (1995) unreported, 13 December, CA (discharge of mortgagee by holder of equitable charge over house, where chargee's interest arose from owner's use of moneys stolen from chargee in its purchase).

36   See *Owen v Tate* [1976] QB 402, where Scarman LJ, pp 409–10 opined that recoupment was available to those who paid in circumstances of reasonableness or necessity.

37   Eg, the person who leaves his cattle unlawfully on someone else's land, whereupon they are distrained for rates owing by the latter: cf *Beresford v Kennedy* (1887) 21 Ir LTR 17. And cf *Gormley v Johnston* (1895) 29 Ir LTR 69.

8-10   It should be noted, however, that 'compellability' does not necessarily mean 'liability to be sued'. The principle of recoupment applies equally to anyone otherwise forced by operation of law to discharge another's obligation. Thus, in *Exall v Partridge*,[38] the plaintiff left a vehicle on premises leased to the defendant, whereupon the landlord lawfully distrained on it for rent owing. Having paid off the landlord, the plaintiff successfully recovered his outlay from the defendant. Again, if my property is wrongfully, but effectively, charged for someone else's debt, I have a right to recoupment from the debtor or any surety of his,[39] together with a right to invoke the rules of marshalling to obtain the benefit of any other security pledged for the same debt.[40] A similar rule applies to liens: if (for example) I buy property over which, unknown to me, some third party has a charge and, in order to avoid their seizure, I have to pay it off.[41] There are numerous other miscellaneous instances.[42]

(c) An obligation lying primarily on the defendant

8-11   The right to recoupment, for obvious reasons, can only work one way round: the defendant must be shown to have been primarily liable as against the claimant. This explains why a surety, while he can claim against the debtor, cannot claim against a sub-surety;[43] and a surety who guarantees a debt as a gift to the principal debtor cannot claim reimbursement at all.[44] Normally, it will be clear from the circumstances who is primarily liable as between the parties; furthermore, it goes without saying that there is no objection to the normal order of liability being reversed or varied by agreement *inter se*. Thus, in *Belger v Belger*,[45] the incidence of a joint debt undertaken by husband and wife was held to have been varied by a subsequent divorce settlement so as to make it primarily payable by the husband alone, and to give the wife a claim against him for the whole amount paid by her to discharge it.

---

38   8 TR 308. But not where the only reason the plaintiff's goods are seized is because he left them unlawfully on the defendant's land: see *Beresford v Kennedy* (1887) 21 Ir LTR 17. The element of compulsion is no doubt lacking here.

39   *Ex p Salting* (1883) 25 Ch D 148.

40   *Ex p Alston* (1868) LR 4 Ch App 168.

41   See, eg, *Ker v Ker* (1869) 4 Ir R Eq (buyer of part of land subject to charge affecting the whole has right of contribution); and cf the shipping cases of *Johnson v Royal Mail Steam Packet Co* (1867) LR 3 CP 38 and *The Orchis* (1890) 15 PD 38 (both concerned with mortgagees discharging maritime liens).

42   For a case concerning the discharge of a mortgage by the holder of an equitable charge, see *Kleinwort Benson Ltd v Vaughan* (1995) unreported, 13 December, CA.

43   *Craythorne v Swinburne* (1807) 14 Ves 160, below.

44   Cf *Anson v Anson* [1953] 1 QB 636 (had presumption of advancement applied between surety and principal, would have ousted indemnity).

45   (1989) unreported, 17 July, CA.

II PARTICULAR CASES OF RECOUPMENT

(a) Sureties

It is well established that a surety,[46] or anyone in an analogous position,[47] who is called on to pay the principal debt can recoup his payment from the debtor once he has paid the creditor.[48] A similar result follows where the surety compounds for the debt (though he can only recover up to the amount actually paid.[49] He can also claim to be subrogated to any security for the debt held by the creditor,[50] whether or not he knew about it,[51] and even though he himself took a lesser security from the principal.[52] Where he has undertaken joint liability with the debtor as against the creditor, s 5 of the Mercantile Law Amendment Act 1856[53] preserves his right to take over the securities, even though at common law they would be regarded as discharged by his payment.

A sub-surety has a similar restitutionary right against the surety, over and above any right he may have in contract,[54] and (it is submitted) against the principal debtor as well.[55]

For obvious reasons, however, this does not work the other way round. A surety can never sue a sub-surety, however much he may have saved him.[56] Traditionally, this is put on the ground that surety and sub-surety are not sureties 'in the same degree': the real reason is that, as between them, the sub-surety's liability is regarded as secondary to the surety's, and hence any enrichment on the part of the former is not unjustified.

---

46 Including a person who, while not legally liable for the principal debt, has charged his property to guarantee it. See, eg, *Smith v Wood* [1929] 1 Ch 14 and *Re Marley* [1976] 1 WLR 952.

47 Eg, the issuer of a professional indemnity bond (*Irish National Insurance Co v Scannell* [1959] Ir Jur Rep 41); the drawer of a bill of exchange vis à vis the acceptor (*Duncan Fox v North and South Wales Bank* (1879) 6 App Cas 1), or a transferor of shares later made liable as contributory (*Nevill's* case (1870) LR 6 Ch App 43).

48 Though not before: *Re Richardson* [1911] 2 KB 712.

49 *Smith v Compton* (1832) 3 B & Ad 407. Similarly, it seems, where property is transferred in settlement of the debt: cf *Fahey v Frawley* (1890) 26 LR Ir 78 and *Gore v Gore* [1901] 2 IR 269. Presumably, the justification is that the debtor might have compounded for the same amount and hence is enriched to that extent only by the surety's action.

50 *Morgan v Seymour* (1638) 1 Ch R 120; *Mayhew v Crickett* (1818) 2 Swan 185, p 191. Similarly with a surety for part of a debt, who can claim subrogation *pro rata*: *Re Butler's Wharf Ltd* [1995] 2 BCLC 43.

51 *Mayhew v Crickett* (1818) 2 Swan 185, above.

52 *Re Chipboard Products Ltd* [1994] 3 IR 164.

53 In force in both jurisdictions.

54 See *Re Denton* [1904] 2 Ch 178. The right, which is independent of contract, will matter where A and B are co-sureties and C, a sub-surety of A, seeks to recover from B.

55 So held in Canada: *Fox v Royal Bank of Canada* (1975) 59 DLR (3d) 258.

56 *Craythorne v Swinburne* (1807) 14 Ves 160.

(b) Leases

8-12 At common law, a lessee who assigns his lease remains liable under the contract of lease vis à vis the lessor to pay the rent for the rest of the term, notwithstanding that he has ceased to have any interest in the property.

In Ireland, this common law rule was supposedly abolished by Deasy's Act[57] in 1860. Nevertheless, it remains open to the lessor as a condition of granting a licence to assign to extract an express covenant to the same effect, and since this is common practice, the position in practice remains much the same.

In England, by contrast, reform has been more drastic. For all leases granted after 1 January 1996, the common law rule is abrogated by s 5 of the Landlord and Tenant (Covenants) Act 1995 and the landlord limited to extracting a covenant to pay the rent during the immediate assignee's own occupation, but no further. Nevertheless, the old rules continue – significantly – to govern pre-1996 leases. For this reason, the position of the tenant forced to pay rent for a period during which he has been out of possession is, and will remain, worth discussing in the English context too.

8-13 The significance of all this to restitution lawyers is that a tenant called on to pay rent in respect of a period after he has assigned the lease can, under the rule in *Moule v Garrett*,[58] exercise in turn a restitutionary right of recovery against the present tenant.[59] In addition, it has been held that he can recover on similar principles from a surety for the defaulting tenant.[60] Furthermore, if the landlord holds any security for the rent, it is suggested that the assignor can claim to be subrogated to it.[61] Indeed, there is no need for the lessee-claimant to be liable to be sued for the rent: it is enough if he is liable to distress in respect of it.[62] On principle, it is suggested that a sub-lessee ought to have a similar right against

---

57 Ie, the Landlord and Tenant Law (Amendment) Act 1860, s 16. This Act also applies in Northern Ireland.

58 (1872) LR 7 Ex 101. As against the immediate assignee, the assignor has a parallel right in contract, since any assignment of a lease contains an implied promise by the assignee to indemnify the assignor. But this will obviously not work as against a subsequent assignee, who will not be in privity of contact with the assignor.

59 And so too, it seems, with an intermediate assignee who has covenanted with the landlord to pay rent for the remainder of the term. This was assumed to be the case in *Electricity Supply Nominees Ltd v Thorn EMI plc* (1991) 63 P & CR 143.

60 See *Becton Dickinson (UK) Ltd v Zwebner* [1989] QB 208. It has been said in England that the original tenant cannot claim to be subrogated to the surety's right of recoupment against the defaulting tenant or anyone else (see *RPH Ltd v Mirror Group Ltd* (1993) 65 P & CR 252). But it is difficult to see why not.

61 Cf *Harberton (Lord) v Bennett* (1829) Beatty 386.

62 *Whitham v Bullock* [1939] 2 KB 81 (lessee divided land and assigned part to A, part to B: A held able to recover from B when landlord lawfully distrained on A for B's rent, whether or not A could in strict law be sued for it).

the headlessor if forced (for example, by distress) to pay the headrent,[63] though such claims are likely to be rare in practice.[64]

However, the doctrine is limited in two ways. First, a headlessee cannot claim against an assignee's sub-tenant even if he has been forced to pay the rent under the headlease and hence saved the sub-lessee from a *de facto* liability.[65] Although it may seem odd to deny an ex-lessee out of possession recompense from a sub-lessee in it, this is an aspect of the rule limiting recoupment to payment off of obligations owing by the defendant: the sub-lessee, while the landlord may have means (for example, distress) to make him pay the rent, could not have been actually sued for it. And secondly, for similar reasons, it has been held that one of several sub-lessees cannot recover from the others if he pays the whole of the headrent, for instance, under the threat of distress.[66]

(c) Co-owners

8-14 There is an old line of authority that where land was subject to a mortgage or charge, anyone interested in the equity of redemption could effectively discharge the incumbrance,[67] and that having done so he would *prima facie* be subrogated to the rights of the incumbrancer.[68] This right applied to second mortgagees,[69] part owners,[70] tenants for life[71] and remaindermen[72] (though it could not be used by a mortgagor who granted a second mortgage to elevate himself above the second mortgagee, since a mortgagor cannot set up against his

---

63   See *Eaton v Donegal Tweed Co Ltd* (1934) LJCCR 81. In Ireland, such payments may give rise to a charge over the property in addition to any personal claim, under the doctrine of 'salvage': see *Locke v Evans* (1823) 11 Ir Eq R 52n, and below, § 9-16.

64   Doubtless because most sub-lessees will choose instead to apply for relief against forfeiture under the Law of Property Act 1925, s 146 (England) or the Conveyancing Act 1892, ss 4, 5 (Ireland). But even here, the question might be important, eg, if the headrent was larger than the sub-rent, or if the sub-lease was of only part of the land subject to the headrent.

65   *Ahearne v McSwiney* (1858) IR 8 CL 568; *Ryan v Byrne* (1880) 17 ILTR 102; *Johnson v Wild* (1890) 44 Ch D 146; *Bonner v Tottenham Building Society* [1899] 1 QB 161. But cf *Electricity Supply Nominees Ltd v Thorn EMI plc* (1991) 63 P & CR 143 (right against own sub-tenant where headlease no longer extant).

66   *Hunter v Hunt* (1845) 1 CB 300 (contra, *Webber v Smith* (1689) 2 Vern 103). But in Ireland, this can be regarded as a 'salvage' payment giving rise to a lien, though not a positive claim: *Allison v Jenkins* [1904] 1 IR 341.

67   Thus providing an exception to the normal rule that a stranger cannot effectively discharge another's debt: above, § 8-5.

68   For an explanation see *Morley v Morley* (1855) de Gex, M & G 610, pp 619–20. The matter is dealt with exhaustively by Sutton in Burrows (ed), *Essays on Restitution*, Chapter 4. More recently, cf *Re Hunter* (1998) unreported, 3 March, Ch D, NI) (joint tenant paying off mortgage debt entitled to subrogation to mortgage protection policy).

69   Cf *Re Power's Policies* [1899] 1 IR 6.

70   *Ker v Ker* (1869) 4 Ir R Eq 15; *Re Pride* [1891] 2 Ch 135; *Re Hunter* (1998) unreported, 3 March, Ch D, NI.

71   *Ravald v Russell* (1830) You 9.

72   *Re Chesters* [1935] 1 Ch 77.

own mortgagee an incumbrance he himself created).[73] The only reasonable explanation for this principle, it is suggested, is on the basis of practical compulsion: like the plaintiff in *Exall v Partridge*,[74] a person who has to pay off someone else's debt in order to get back his own property does so in essence, if not in strict law, under compulsion.

Attempts to extend this reasoning to cases of other co-owners in other contexts have largely been unsuccessful, at least in England. In *Re Leslie*,[75] a husband paid premiums on a life policy then owned by his wife but in circumstances where, had she died before him, he would have become beneficially entitled to it. In the event, he predeceased her; nevertheless, his executors were refused a claim over the policy proceeds for the sums paid. This was on the ground that as regards payments by one part owner, 'except by contract, such payments give no title to the party making them against the other part owner or part owners of the policy':[76] the only effective exception being where a mortgagee paid to preserve his own security. And similar reasoning was later applied in *Falcke v Scottish Imperial Insurance Co*[77] (although the claimant there was a mortgagor seeking to rely on his payment of premiums to defeat his own mortgagee, which even on the basis of the land law cases should not have been allowed).

8-15   Irish law, by contrast, may be more generous to those discharging incumbrances to save their own interests. Under the doctrine of 'salvage',[78] any payment made to discharge burdens on property gives rise to a lien over it, provided:

- it has the effect of saving the property for all interested in it;
- it is made by someone with a charge over or interest in that property; and
- it is made in the payer's own interest and not pursuant to some duty.[79]

This rule, which has (rightly) been said to be justified on the basis of practical compulsion,[80] is thus apt to cover cases such as the sub-lessee who pays the headrent to protect his own interests[81] and the second mortgagee paying off a prior incumbrance.[82]

---

73   See *Otter v Lord Vaux* (1856) 6 de Gex, M & G 637, p 643.

74   (1799) 8 TR 308.

75   (1883) 23 Ch D 552.

76   *Ibid*, p 563. Sutton, in Burrows (ed), *Essays on Restitution*, Chapter 4, points out that this is inconsistent with earlier authority, notably *Burridge v Row* (1842) 1 Y & CCC 143.

77   (1886) 34 Ch D 234.

78   Sometimes known as 'graft': *Re Power's Policies* [1899] 1 IR 12, p 23.

79   See *Re Power's Policies* [1899] 1 IR 12, p 27 (Holmes LJ).

80   'I have always understood that the reason of the priority which Courts of Equity give to the salvage creditor is this, that the payment is in a manner compulsory and that, in the common danger, it is for the benefit of all to encourage an advance of money, without which the mortgagor himself and every one of his creditors must suffer a serious loss.' See *Fetherstone v Mitchell* (1848) 11 Ir Eq R 35, p 42 (Brooke MC).

81   See *Locke v Evans* (1823) (1848) 11 Ir R Eq 52n.

82   See, eg, *Kelly v Staunton* (1826) 1 Hogan 393, and *Re Power's Policies* [1899] 1 IR 6. And cf *Ker v Ker* (1869) 4 Ir R Eq 15 (buyer of portion of charged land given relief).

These last two categories of claimant are admittedly protected even on the less generous principles applied in England. Nevertheless, a 'salvage' claim remains more advantageous to them, for two reasons. First, it gives rise to a proprietary remedy in the form of a lien, rather than a mere personal liability.[83] And secondly, there are some cases where a 'salvage' claim will lie even though a claim under the general law will not. Thus, in *Allison v Jenkins*[84] one of two sub-tenants who paid rent owing under the headlease was able to claim contribution from the other; and in *Fetherstone v Mitchell*[85] a judgment creditor was allowed to take advantage of the rule when, to preserve his interests, he paid off moneys owing to the landlord of property available to satisfy his debt.

(d) Other rights of recourse

8-16   On similar principles to those applicable to sureties and lessees, anyone who has become legally liable to pay a debt primarily owed by someone else can *prima facie* recover from the main debtor once he has paid it, and claim the benefit of any security held by the creditor.[86] This category also includes those, such as bonded warehouse owners, who are statutorily liable to pay excise duty on goods not owned by them, but removed unlawfully from their premises (as happened in the case of *Brook's Wharf and Bull Wharf Ltd v Goodman Bros*);[87] sellers of partly paid shares;[88] and indorsers[89] and other transferors[90] of bills of exchange. The categories are presumably not closed;[91] however, any extension must be pragmatic, and must presumably not subvert other areas of the law. Property insurers, for instance, cannot as a matter of tort recover against those responsible for damaging property except by relying on subrogation or assignment;[92] nor can underwriters of personal injury insurance claim from tortfeasors.[93] It is unlikely that the courts will allow these rules to be upset by the use of unjustified enrichment.[94]

---

83   This was established relatively early: see *Hill v Browne* (1843) 6 Ir Eq R 406.

84   [1904] 1 IR 341.

85   (1848) 11 Ir Eq R 35.

86   *Duncan, Fox v North and South Wales Banking Co* (1880) 6 App Cas 1.

87   [1937] 1 KB 534. Cf *The Pindaros* [1983] 2 Lloyd's Rep 635.

88   Eg, *Nevill's* case (1870) LR 6 Ch App 43.

89   *Sleigh v Sleigh* (1850) 5 Ex 514: see, now, Bills of Exchange Act 1882, s 55(2).

90   *Ex p Bishop* (1880) 15 Ch D 400.

91   Cf *East Cork Foods Ltd v O'Dwyer Steel Ltd* [1978] IR 103.

92   *Simpson v Thomson* (1877) 3 App Cas 279.

93   Note that *Metropolitan Police Receiver v Croydon Corp* [1957] 2 QB 154 will not help the tortfeasor here, since insurance payments are not deducted from damage awards.

94   Cf *The Esso Bernicia* [1989] 1 AC 643.

III THE RIGHT TO CONTRIBUTION

8-17   Contribution is, in essence, a sub-species of recoupment. In recoupment, my claim is that I have involuntarily discharged an obligation that should have been wholly borne by you, rather than me. In contribution, it is that both of us were (as between ourselves) equally liable to bear it, but that I have paid more than my fair share.

Contribution claimants mainly (though not exclusively) fall into four categories: (a) concurrent debtors; (b) co-sureties; (c) insurers; and (d) those concurrently liable for the same damage at common law (that is, concurrent tortfeasors and contract-breakers), and trustees jointly liable for the same breach of trust. However, since the latter two are now covered by statute, they will be dealt with together.

(a) Concurrent debtors

8-18   Where two or more people are concurrently liable for the same debt, any debtor who pays more than his fair share has a right to contribution against the others. This rule applies not only to concurrent debtors as such, but also to those in analogous positions, such as partners in respect of partnership debts.[95] It has been held that a similar right accrues to a surety for a co-debtor, so as to allow him to claim contribution from the other debtor.[96] It is, of course, open to co-debtors to agree among themselves the proportions in which they are to bear the ultimate responsibility:[97] if they do not, the solvent debtors[98] each pay equally.

(b) Co-sureties

8-19   A similar principle applies to co-sureties.[99] One surety having paid can recover a proportion against the others,[100] provided of course that he had himself

---

95 See, eg, *Re Royal Bank of Australia* (1856) DM & G 572.

96 See *Guinness v CMD Ltd* (1995) 45 Con LR 48. *Quaere* whether he would have a similar right against a surety for the other debtor.

97 Eg, so as to give one a right to full indemnity, as in *Belger v Belger* (1989) unreported, 17 July, CA.

98 It is clear in the case of co-sureties that the liabilities of insolvent sureties are disregarded for these purposes, at least in equity (see *Re Arcedeckne* (1883) 24 Ch D 709). It is suggested that concurrent debtors should be in no different position.

99 Eg, *Gore v Gore* [1901] 2 IR 269.

100 Including those whose property is charged, but who are not personally liable: *Smith v Wood* [1929] 1 Ch 14.

become liable to pay the principal debt,[101] and whether or not he knew of the existence of the others when guaranteeing the debt.[102] *Prima facie*, individual sureties, like concurrent debtors, pay equally in the absence of agreement between them.[103] But this is displaced where the liability of one or more sureties is limited, and the maximum sums concerned are different. Here, it seems, liability is apportioned proportionately to the respective maximum limits[104] (save that, if any surety's liability is unlimited, his maximum is reckoned as the amount of the debt).[105]

(c) Concurrent insurers

8-20   Where the same loss is insured by more than one insurer, an insurer who pays the whole loss can recover against any other insurer liable[106] in respect of it. Here, however, an awkward limitation applies: the insurers must have insured not only the same loss, but the same risk. Thus in *North British and Mercantile Insurance Co v London, Liverpool and Globe Insurance Co*[107] it was held that where bailees and bailors both insured goods, the bailees' insurer could not claim contribution from the bailors' underwriter; the insurances may have been on the same goods, but they were not on the same interests in those goods.[108]

There is similarly difficulty where the insurer who pays has a clause in the policy limiting his liability to a rateable proportion in the case of double insurance. Having paid the whole claim, can he then claim contribution against

---

101 On what this entails, see *Hay v Carter* [1935] Ch 397. The fact that the surety could not technically have been sued because of the non-fulfilment of some procedural precondition, such as a demand in writing, will not render his payment voluntary: *Stimpson v Smith* [1999] 2 All ER 833.

102 Eg, *Re Ennis* [1893] 3 Ch 238.

103 *Ward v National Bank of New Zealand* (1883) 8 App Cas 755, p 765.

104 *Ellesmere Brewery Co v Cooper* [1896] 1 QB 75.

105 See *Naumann v Northcote* (1978) unreported, 7 February, CA.

106 Including an insurer who was liable, but has ceased to be because of failure to give due notice of a claim: *Legal and General Assurance Soc Ltd v Drake Assurance Co Ltd* [1992] QB 877.

107 (1876) 5 Ch D 569. The principle in this case was applied with unusual ferocity by the Supreme Court of Ireland in *Zurich Insurance Co v Shield Insurance Co* (1987) unreported, 18 December. D, an employee of Q, injured S, another employee, by negligent driving. Q's motor insurers paid in full, but were denied contribution against Q's employer's liability underwriters on the basis that their own policy covered D personally, whereas the defendants' did not, and hence the risks were different.

108 There is a plausible argument that the principle has actually been repealed in England by the Civil Liability (Contribution) Act 1978, s 1 of which enacts a general right to contribution as between those liable in respect of the same damage, whether in contract, tort or otherwise. Bailees' and bailors' insurers seem to come within this criterion, especially since it now seems that the liability of an insurer to pay out on a loss is a liability for damage and not a simple debt (see Hirst J's decision in *The Italia Express* [1992] 2 Lloyd's Rep 281). However, there is first instance authority that the 1978 Act does not apply to contribution between insurers: *Bovis Construction Ltd v Commercial Union Assurance Co plc* [2001] Lloyd's Rep IR 321 (*sed quaere*).

the other insurer? The answer logically has to be 'No', since the excess over and above his own rateable proportion is regarded as a voluntary payment and hence irrecoverable, whether or not at the time he knew of the existence of the other insurer.[109]

The distribution of the loss in the case of differing limits on liability is also a matter of controversy. As between liability insurers, it is on the basis of the amount each insurer would have had to pay under the claim had he been solely liable;[110] with property insurers, it is probably the same as in the case of sureties (that is, the proportion between the maximum liabilities under the policies).[111]

(d) Concurrent wrongdoers and trustees

8-21　At common law, there was no provision for contribution between tortfeasors[112] or contract-breakers, even though they might both be liable for the same loss. Equity, however, always allowed it between co-trustees in breach of trust.[113] Today, the basis for contribution between wrongdoers is entirely statutory. Section 1 of the English Civil Liability (Contribution) Act 1978, and Chapter 2 of the Irish Civil Liability Act 1961, now provide for a general right of contribution between anyone liable[114] for the same damage,[115] as is normally the case with concurrent tortfeasors[116] and trustees committing a breach of trust. Moreover,

---

109 *Legal and General Assurance Soc Ltd v Drake Insurance Co Ltd* [1992] QB 877. An argument that this rule had been reversed in England by the Civil Liability (Contribution) Act 1978 (see, generally, above, fn 108) was rejected by Steel J in *Bovis Construction Ltd v Commercial Union Assurance Co plc* [2001] Lloyd's Rep IR 321.

110 *Commercial Union Assurance Co Ltd v Hayden* [1977] QB 804.

111 Assumed, but not decided, in *Commercial Union Assurance Co Ltd v Hayden* [1977] QB 804.

112 Apparently on the basis that *ex turpi causa non oritur actio*: eg, *Merryweather v Nixan* (1799) 8 TR 186.

113 Eg, *Bahin v Hughes* (1886) 31 Ch D 390. But only equal contribution could be awarded, whatever the relative degrees of fault: ibid.

114 In England, 'liable' means 'able to be sued': *Wimpey v BOAC* [1955] AC 169. Ireland, oddly, allows contribution claims against those who would be liable, but are protected by some immunity (eg, trade unions against whom action is barred by the Industrial Relations Act 1990): see the definition of 'liable' in s 2 of the 1961 Act. This is peculiar: if I could not be sued for a given sum, how can I be enriched if you pay it for me? Where the would-be contributor has been unsuccessfully sued by the claimant, the contribution action is barred in England (1978 Act, s 1(5)) but not in Ireland (1961 Act, s 29(8)).

115 For what counts as the 'same damage', see *Birse Construction Ltd v Haiste Ltd* [1996] 2 All ER 1 and *Eastgate v Lindsey Morden Group plc* [2001] PNLR 953.

116 Subject to one exception. In maritime collisions, there is no joint and several liability for property damage, each vessel only being liable according to her own share of blame (see Merchant Shipping Act 1995, s 187 in England, and in Ireland, the Civil Liability Act 1961, s 46). It follows that no question of contribution *inter se* arises, as indeed s 46(2) of the 1961 legislation makes explicit.

they do so whether the liability arises in contract, tort or equity,[117] thus allowing claims between different sorts of wrongdoer. Thus, for instance, where a buyer of defective goods sues the seller for damages under the Sale of Goods Act, there is no reason why the seller should not be able to claim contribution from the manufacturer in so far as the latter would himself have been liable in tort to the buyer.

The measure of contribution is fixed at whatever sum the court considers just and equitable;[118] but this sum must be fixed as between those parties before the court, with no account being taken of anyone else's possible liability[119] (though there is nothing to bar a subsequent claim against a third party by someone who as a result has paid more than his fair share).[120]

A limited exception is introduced by statute in both jurisdictions to the normal rule in contribution and recoupment cases, that reimbursement is only available to a claimant who was *compellable* to discharge the liability concerned. In England, s 1(4) of the 1978 Act provides that a defendant who has *bona fide* settled a claim against him can claim contribution whether or not he was in fact liable to pay,[121] though (oddly) not if the facts alleged against him gave no cause of action as a matter of law. Ireland has a similar provision in s 29(1) of the Civil Liability Act 1961,[122] but shorn of this rather bizarre limitation.

(e) Other cases of contribution

8-22 The four categories above are not exhaustive, but reflect a more general rule that where several people are commonly subject to some obligation, any one of them who bears more than his fair share of it is entitled to reimbursement from the others.[123] Other examples include (for example) partners,[124] company directors

---

117 England: 1978 Act, s 2(1). Ireland: see the 1961 Act, s 2, defining 'wrong' as including tort, breach of contract or breach of trust. The English statute has been interpreted, surprisingly expansively, as allowing contribution against a person liable to repay money received as a result of a mistake of fact (*Friends' Provident Life Office v Hillier Parker* [1997] QB 805); but this would not apply in Ireland, where contribution is limited specifically to 'wrongdoers'.

118 England: 1978 Act, s 2. Ireland: 1961 Act, s 21(2). On apportionment see, eg, *Randolph v Tuck* [1962] 1 QB 175, and *Patterson v Murphy* [1978] ILRM 85.

119 In Ireland, this is statutory: 1961 Act, s 25. For the English position see *Mayfield v Llewellyn* [1961] 1 WLR 119. This is admittedly a rough and ready way of dealing with the question of enrichment: but it is probably justified on practical grounds.

120 Specifically made clear in Ireland: 1961 Act, s 25.

121 The previous rule was different: *Stott v West Yorkshire Road Car Co Ltd* [1971] 2 QB 651.

122 See, too, s 22.

123 For an example of such reasoning, cf Derham (1991) 107 LQR 126 (discussing the case of two assignees of different debts who are both vulnerable to a single set-off available to the debtor against the assignor).

124 Eg, *Re Royal Bank of Australia* (1856) 6 D M & G 572.

jointly liable for misfeasance[125] and buyers of part of land subject to a charge affecting the whole.[126]

IV POSSIBLE EXTENSIONS OF RECOUPMENT AND CONTRIBUTION

8-23   Recoupment and contribution proper concern forced discharge of obligations. What they have in common is a debt or other obligation affecting the defendant, which: (a) the claimant has been compelled to discharge; and which (b) as between claimant and defendant, ought wholly or partly to have been discharged by the latter.[127] Logically, however, it can be argued that there is no need to limit it to these instances: the principle behind it should be extended to any case where A has been effectively forced to confer any benefit whatever on B.

In at least one case this logic, or something like it, is applied: this is the doctrine of general average (dealt with below). It is an open question whether similar thinking can be applied by analogy to cover other benefits, in particular in the case of emergency action taken for the defendant's benefit which incidentally affects others' interests. Suppose, for instance, that, in the course of putting out a fire in my house, firemen enter on your land and do substantial damage to it. You clearly cannot sue the fire authority, since they had a right to act as they did;[128] on the other hand, you have been forced to suffer considerable prejudice for my benefit, and there is much to be said for allowing you a measure of restitutionary recovery in respect of this. Again, imagine two ships owned by A and B moored together in an exposed position. A storm blows up; fearing for their safety, the crew of A's ship cast off the mooring lines and stand out to sea; B's ship thereupon goes adrift and is damaged. The emergency precludes any liability of A to B in tort;[129] on the other hand, it seems hard that B should bear the entire loss of saving A's property. At this stage it must remain an open question whether the law of restitution may come to the rescue.[130]

---

125 Eg, *Ramskill v Edwards* (1885) 31 Ch D 100.

126 Eg, *Ker v Ker* (1869) 4 Ir R Eq 15.

127 Or, put another way, that the defendant's enrichment is unjustified. This also explains why the surety cannot claim against the sub-surety: there is nothing unjust about the latter taking the benefit of the former's payment.

128 The fire services understandably have extensive powers of entry on, and interference with, property in the course of their operations: eg, Fire Services Act 1947, s 30 (England).

129 See, eg, *The Highland Loch* [1912] AC 312.

130 Cf the Minnesota decision in *Vincent v Erie Transport* 124 NW 221 (1910). True, in the cases discussed above it has always been assumed to be necessary that the claimant has discharged a legally enforceable liability. But it is suggested that there is no logical reason why this should be a general requirement.

V A SPECIAL CASE – GENERAL AVERAGE

8-24   Suppose a cargo-carrying vessel gets into difficulties. In order to complete the voyage, extraordinary expenses are incurred for (for example) towage or repairs; or – more drastically – some of the cargo has to be jettisoned or discharged. In such a case the shipowner or cargo-owner, as the case may be, has a claim against the other participants in the adventure for rateable contribution to the loss according to the benefit received by the latter. Although as between ship and cargo this is largely regulated by contract,[131] the right is a general one and equally applies as between cargo-owners who are not in privity of contract. The expenses must be extraordinary[132] and reasonable, and incurred in order to avert an actual danger[133] to the whole adventure; rather oddly, they must also be forced on the participants by force of circumstances, and not by (for example) government action.[134] Reflecting the principle that restitutionary rights are subject to any contrary agreement between the parties, no claim lies by the shipowner in respect of loss or expenditure arising from a cause for which he is responsible under the contract of carriage.[135]

---

131 Virtually all contracts for carriage of goods by sea provide for adjustment of general average according to extra-statutory provisions known as the York-Antwerp Rules.

132 Eg, *Société Nouvelle d'Armement v Spillers and Bakers Ltd* [1917] 1 KB 865.

133 *Watson and Son Ltd v Fireman's Fund Insurance Co of San Francisco* [1922] 2 KB 355.

134 *Athel Line Ltd v Liverpool and London War Risks Association Ltd* [1944] KB 87.

135 *Strang Steel and Co v Scott and Co* (1889) 14 App Cas 601. See, in particular, the Hague Rules, r 4(2), enacted in England by the Carriage of Goods by Sea Act 1971, and in Ireland by the Merchant Shipping Act 1947.

CHAPTER 9

NECESSITY

9-1   While away on holiday, you are taken ill and cannot get back for some weeks. As your neighbour, I make the necessary arrangements and incur expenses to keep up your mortgage and insurance payments, repair burst pipes in your house, and so on. Or again: you lose your dog, whereupon I find it and feed it until reclaimed. Do I have a claim to reimbursement? Cases of this sort form the subject of this chapter. The main part deals with claims for necessitous intervention in general: the second with the specialised area of maritime salvage, which (as will be seen) is something of a law unto itself, and arguably not best regarded as a part of the law of restitution at all.

1 NECESSITOUS INTERVENTION:
THE GENERAL RULE OF NON-RECOVERY

9-2   Despite an instinctive feeling of sympathy for him, the immediate reaction of English law to the necessitous intervener is to deny him recovery. However clearly beneficial his intervention was to the recipient, there are many cases in which it has been reiterated that necessitous payment, or the rendering of other services beneficial to the interests of the defendant in an emergency, do not without more give rise to a claim for payment[1] or any other relief.[2]

It is true that in a number of cases, necessitous interveners have been granted a measure of relief. The best known example is the maritime salvor: but he is not the only one. Others (dealt with in greater detail below) include agents of necessity, bailees put in a quandary as to what to do with goods in their charge, and those intervening to discharge duties, such as the burial of the dead, which by law ought to be shouldered by someone else. But, as yet, little evidence is available of any judicial attempt to regard these as anything other than a series of discrete exceptions.

---

1   See, eg, *The Tojo Maru* [1972] AC 242, p 268: 'On land a person who interferes to save property is not in law entitled to any reward' (Lord Reid). See, too, *Sorrell v Paget* [1950] 1 KB 252, p 260 (Bucknill LJ).

2   Eg, a lien: see *Nicholson v Chapman* (1793) 2 H Bl 254 (feeding a lost animal); *Re Leslie* (1883) 23 Ch D 552; *Falcke v Scottish Imperial Insurance Co* (1886) 34 Ch D 234 (payment of premiums to keep up insurance policy); *O'Callaghan v Ballincollig Holdings Ltd* (1993) unreported, 31 March (Ireland) (Blayney J).

In particular, the opportunity to generalise and create a new head of restitutionary recovery was pointedly not taken in *The Winson*.[3] Salvors rescued a cargo of wheat and, having done so, paid to warehouse it on shore. Some time later, the owners took charge of it, but refused to pay the accrued storage charges. Lloyd J at first instance held for the salvors, arguing *inter alia* that even if the salvage contract had been at an end, the owners were bound to pay on the basis of necessity.[4] The House of Lords, however, while upholding his decision, did so on the much narrower ground that it was the salvors' status as bailees which provided them with a right of recovery.[5]

II NECESSITOUS INTERVENTION: THE EXCEPTIONS TO NON-RECOVERY

9-3 We now turn to the various exceptions to the general rule of non-recovery. As might be expected, there is no general explanation that can justify them all. Nevertheless, most fall into two groups. First, there are the cases where the terms of some pre-existing relationship between the parties can be invoked so as to give rise to an obligation to pay for necessitous intervention.[6] Secondly, in a number of other instances, recovery is allowed (it is suggested) largely on the basis of public policy, as with emergency medical attention or actions to save animals, or where some public duty of A's is in fact carried out by B in circumstances of urgency.

It should be noted that another possible exception, maritime salvage, is dealt with elsewhere in this chapter.

(a) Agency of necessity[7]

9-4 Suppose an agent is in possession of his principal's goods or otherwise conducting the principal's affairs and an emergency arises requiring immediate action. Suppose, further, that it is impracticable to make contact with the

---

3 [1982] AC 939.

4 See [1979] 2 All ER 35, p 44.

5 It might be thought that *The Goring* [1988] AC 431, where the House of Lords declined to extend the principle of maritime salvage to inland waters, was a similar case. In fact, however, they had little choice in the matter, since the proceedings were in Admiralty, and this jurisdiction was held to be limited to salvage cases proper.

6 '[I]n English law a mere stranger cannot compel an owner of goods to pay for a benefit bestowed upon him against his will; but this latter principle does not apply where there is a pre-existing legal relationship between the owner of the goods and the bestower of the benefit, such as that of bailor and bailee ...': Lord Diplock in *The Winson* [1982] AC 939, p 961.

7 Bowstead, *Agency*, 16th edn, Chapter 4.

principal. A number of cases[8] decide that the agent is entitled not only to do whatever is necessary without incurring liability to the principal,[9] but to go further and charge the latter for what he does. Thus, in *The Argos*[10] and *Tetley v British Trade Corp*,[11] carriers who took steps to deal with goods in an emergency and in the absence of any possibility of contact with cargo-owners were held entitled to reimbursement. And again, at least partly on the basis of the agency of necessity cases, it was decided in *Great Northern Rly Co v Swaffield*[12] that a carrier who conveyed a horse only to find nobody available to collect the beast on arrival was entitled to charge the consignor for expenses incurred in feeding and stabling it.

9-5   The doctrinal basis for agency of necessity is, it would seem, the idea that the relation between principal and agent is deemed to include an implied obligation[13] to this effect which comes into operation in the event of some unforeseen catastrophe.[14] More recently, however, the English Court of Appeal has suggested that the doctrine may extend further and embrace a claimant with no previous relation with the defendant, such as a garage engaged by the police to fish a car out of a pond where it has been abandoned by joyriders.[15] If this development is taken further, the doctrine of agency of necessity could well expand into something like a general right of recovery for necessitous intervention.

In practice, however, it should be noted that the doctrine of agency of necessity is more often invoked than applied. Many of the cases date from before the time of widespread instantaneous communication; today, it is likely to be rare in practice for an agent to be able to show that it was impossible to obtain proper instructions.[16] Furthermore, it goes without saying that the rule can be excluded by contrary agreement between principal and agent.

---

8 Eg, *Notara v Henderson* (1872) LR 7 QB 225; *The Argos* (1873) LR 5 PC 134. See, generally, Bowstead, *Agency*, 15th edn, p 84 *et seq*.

9 Eg, for breach of contract or conversion; see, eg, *Sims v Midland Rly Co* [1913] 1 KB 103, or *Prager v Blatspiel Stamp & Heacock Ltd* [1924] 1 KB 566 (where the defence failed on the facts). And cf *Flannery v Dean* [1995] 2 ILRM 393. The agent may also be able to bind the principal vis à vis third parties, eg, where a ship engages salvors on behalf of cargo; cf *The Choko Star* [1990] 1 Lloyd's Rep 506. (Note that the latter point is now governed by statute in England: see Merchant Shipping Act 1995, Sched 11, Part I, s 6.2.)

10 (1873) LR 5 PC 134.

11 (1922) 10 Lloyd's List LR 678.

12 (1874) LR 9 Ex 132. Cf *Flannery v Dean* [1995] 2 ILRM 393.

13 If the agency is contractual, this will be an implied term: but there seems no reason not to apply the doctrine to a gratuitous agent who does not act under a contract.

14 Cf *Gt Northern Rly Co v Swaffield*, above, fn 12, where Kelly CB, p 136, referred to an implied contract to pay the railway company for looking after the horse.

15 *Surrey Breakdown Ltd v Knight* [1999] RTR 84 (England). The claim based on agency of necessity failed on the facts because it would have been perfectly possible to contact the owner.

16 As happened in *Surrey Breakdown Ltd v Knight* [1999] RTR 84.

(b) Bailment

9-6 By an analogous principle, it was held in *The Winson*[17] that a bailee of goods, in so far as he was under a duty to take steps to look after them,[18] may at least in a commercial bailment[19] be able to charge the bailor his reasonable costs of doing so. Hence, salvors who took steps to preserve wheat after they had finished salving it from a stranded vessel (having received no instructions from its owners as to what to do with it) successfully recovered from those owners their costs incurred in doing so.

This right of the bailee is distinct from agency of necessity, in that it applies in circumstances when the latter would not.[20] However, it is submitted that it is likely in practice to be limited to emergency, rather than foreseen, preservative measures. If you employ me to look after your horse while you are away, no doubt I can charge you for emergency veterinary treatment if it becomes ill: on the other hand, it seems unlikely that, without specific agreement, you would become legally liable to pay me the cost of merely feeding it.

(c) Trustees' rights

9-7 A trustee has no implied right to payment for acting as such. If the trust instrument provides for remuneration, he is normally limited to that stipulated; if it does not, he must act for nothing. Nevertheless, he has two *de facto* ways of claiming for emergency measures connected with the trust estate.

First, his well established right to reimbursement of reasonable outgoings incurred in and about the administration of the trust[21] for the benefit of the beneficiaries would clearly extend to emergency expenditure such as (for instance) arranging for the preservation of a trust building damaged in a storm, or paying premiums to keep afoot a life policy vested in them on behalf of a beneficiary.[22] Such a right is normally limited to a claim to be reimbursed out of the property forming the trust estate, thus effectively amounting to an equitable

---

17 [1982] AC 939. See, too, *Great Northern Rly Co v Swaffield* (1874) LR 9 Ex 132, above (though the basis of this decision is unclear. It may have been a case of agency of necessity, above; or possibly a 'public policy' case: see below).

18 But, it seems, no further: [1982] AC 939, p 960 (Lord Diplock). So the gratuitous lender of a car will not, it would seem, be liable to meet emergency repair bills.

19 Lord Simon in *The Winson* [1982] AC 939, p 964 doubted whether any such principle applied to bailees generally.

20 Agency of necessity was specifically negatived in *The Winson*, since it was not impossible to get into contact with the principal in that case.

21 In England, indeed, this is provided for by statute: Trustee Act 1925, s 30(2). See, generally, Snell's *Equity*, 30th edn, § 11-95.

22 As in *Re Smith's Estate* [1937] Ch 636.

lien over it. However, where the trust is a bare one and all beneficiaries are *sui juris*, they may be personally liable as well.[23]

9-8 However, the trustee's right is essentially to an indemnity for expenditure, not to payment for work carried out personally. As mentioned above, in the absence of specific provision a trustee is *prima facie* expected to act for nothing. Nevertheless, the court has inherent jurisdiction[24] to allow or increase remuneration, a power that will be exercised in respect of extra work not contemplated when the trust was set up.[25] In a suitable case, there seems no reason why this should not be invoked to allow a trustee to claim for emergency services rendered personally.[26] This could arise, for example, were a professionally qualified trustee to intervene to prevent disastrous mismanagement in a company in which the trust had a sizeable shareholding.[27]

(d) Liquidators and receivers

9-9 Company liquidators are not strictly trustees, and do not have title to the assets under their tutelage;[28] nevertheless, they have control over, and a duty to realise, things to which others have an equitable claim. As against assets to which the company has beneficial title they have (at least in England) a statutory lien for their charges in realising them,[29] but this does not extend to property held by the company on trust. Nevertheless, Edward Nugee QC decided in *Re Berkeley Applegate (Investment Consultants) Ltd*[30] that here, they had an equitable claim to satisfy themselves out of that property, on the basis that their efforts were necessary to its recovery.[31]

---

23 See, eg, *Hardoon v Belilios* [1901] AC 118; *Buchan v Ayre* [1915] 2 Ch 474; Snell's *Equity*, 30th edn, § 11-96.

24 And, in England, a statutory power as well: Trustee Act 1925, s 57.

25 Eg, *Re Duke of Norfolk's Settlement Trusts* [1982] Ch 61, and cases there cited.

26 And cf *Re Berkeley Applegate (Investment Consultants) Ltd* [1989] Ch 32 (liquidator of company holding assets on trust, though not a trustee as such, has similar right of reimbursement against trust assets).

27 Cf *Re Keeler's Settlement Trusts* [1981] 1 All ER 889 and *Re Duke of Norfolk's Settlement Trusts* [1982] Ch 61, where remuneration was granted to trustees for work done over and above the call of duty in such a case, even though strictly, these were not situations of necessity.

28 In this, they differ from trustees in bankruptcy, who actually take title to the bankrupt's estate.

29 Insolvency Act 1986, s 234(4).

30 [1989] Ch 32 (see, too [1989] BCC 803). And see *Re Eastern Capital Futures Ltd* [1989] BCLC 371.

31 See, too, *Re Oriental Hotels Co Ltd* [1908] 1 IR 473.

(e) Medical attention

9-10   In England, the problem of whether a patient should have to pay for emergency medical attention has never had to be faced: but if such a claim were brought, it would probably fail. Restitution law has to take account of surrounding social circumstances and, in a country where medical attention is free for the asking even in the absence of an emergency, it would be odd if the mere fact of an emergency made all the difference. Put more formally, it would normally be inferred that such services were rendered with donative intent, hence ousting any restitutionary claim. Nor does there seem to be any direct authority in Ireland on the point.[32] On the other hand, the problem has arisen elsewhere. In the US, recovery in such circumstances is common, at least provided there is no evidence that the doctor intended to act gratuitously,[33] and in Canada, the leading case allowed recovery to a doctor who attempted (unsuccessfully, as it turned out) to revive a suicide victim,[34] on the basis of the decisions about the supply of necessaries to incompetents (see below).

(f) Supply of necessaries to incompetents

9-11   This is not a problem that often arises. Nevertheless, it has spawned some interesting case law, and is worth a brief look for that reason.

A mentally disordered person is liable on a contract except in so far as he is unable to understand the nature of the transaction,[35] and at least in English law he is liable even then if the other party does not know of his disability.[36] Nevertheless, if he is obviously incapable of any rational action at all, there is clear authority that he is liable for necessaries supplied.[37] This may well also explain the Irish decision in *Re Pike*,[38] referred to below. The Dublin police found an elderly woman incapacitated in her house and removed her to hospital. The police authority was held entitled to a lien for its subsequent costs incurred in looking after her house for some days until her relatives could be contacted.[39]

---

32 But cf *Callinan v VHI Board* [1994] 3 CMLR 796.

33 See Palmer, G, *Law of Restitution*, § 10.4, for the authorities.

34 *Matheson v Smiley* [1932] 2 DLR 787.

35 Cf *Re K* [1988] 1 All ER 358 (power of attorney).

36 *Hart v O'Connor* [1985] AC 1000. The position in Ireland is less certain: see *Hassard v Smith* (1872) IR 6 Eq 429 and Clark, *Contract Law in Ireland*, 3rd edn, p 374 *et seq*.

37 Eg, *West Ham Union v Pearson* (1890) 62 LT 638; cf *Pontypridd Union v Drew* [1927] 1 KB 214. But not where the person supplying the necessaries evinced a donative intent: *Re Rhodes* (1890) 44 Ch D 94.

38 (1889) 23 LR Ir 9.

39 It might be argued that this decision is a reflection of the specifically Irish doctrine of 'salvage', referred to below, § 9-16. But this is difficult, since traditionally one of the requirements of a successful claim is that the claimant had an interest in some property saved (see *Re Power's Policies* [1899] 1 IR 6, p 12).

Indeed, this liability is now statutory in one case. Under the Sale of Goods Act,[40] an incompetent is liable to pay a reasonable price for necessary goods sold and delivered to him.

9-12   As regards minors, the law of contract once again normally provides a remedy: a minor is capable of agreeing to pay a reasonable sum[41] for necessaries supplied,[42] and emergency services will nearly always be necessaries. Presumably as regards very young children, a similar rule applies as with entirely irrational persons of unsound mind.

(g) Caring for animals

9-13   You omit to feed your dog or allow it to stray. If I give it something to prevent it starving, can I claim for my time or expense? Older authority suggests the answer no; I have neither a claim against you, nor even a lien over the beast.[43] But since *Great Northern Rly Co v Swaffield*,[44] the matter has been less certain. The plaintiffs were carriers who had conveyed a horse from London to a country station. Finding no one on hand to collect it, they paid to stable it locally. However, the owner refused to sanction or approve this arrangement. In the course of the stand-off that resulted, a bill for £17 was run up. The plaintiffs successfully sued the owner for that £17, one ground of decision being the agency of necessity cases referred to above.

It must be said, however, that although this case can be cited as an instance of restitution for necessitous benefits conferred,[45] it is hardly strong authority. There was a contract of carriage between plaintiff and defendant, and the judgments can be read as based on a sort of extended contractual liability. It is by no means clear that the result would have been the same had the defendant been a consignee not otherwise in any contractual relation with the carriers. Furthermore, there is the difficulty that before most of the bill was run up, the defendant had said that he wished to have nothing more to do with the plaintiffs' stabling arrangements, which would normally bar a restitutionary claim.

---

40   See (Ireland) Sale of Goods Act 1893, s 2; (England) Sale of Goods Act 1979, s 3(2).
41   See *Pontypridd Union v Drew* [1927] 1 KB 214, p 220.
42   Eg, *Nash v Inman* [1908] 2 KB 1; *Dickson v Buller* (1859) 9 Ir CLR (Appendix).
43   See *Binstead v Buck* (1777) 2 W Bl 1117; *Nicholson v Chapman* (1793) 2 H Bl 254.
44   (1874) LR 9 Ex 132.
45   As in Burrows, p 233, or Birks, p 200.

(h) Performance of public duties

9-14   It is clear law that if I am legally compelled to perform your public duty, I will in certain cases have a claim against you. A straightforward instance is the English decision in *Gebhardt v Saunders*.[46] A lessee was forced by law to take steps to abate a statutory nuisance that was in fact the landlord's primary responsibility. Having done so, he recovered from the landlord.

But, can there also be recovery where my performance of your public duty was not forced, but was carried out reasonably and in a situation of urgent necessity? In certain cases, this step has been taken. Thus, where those responsible for the burial of a dead body have failed to carry out their responsibility, other persons who have shouldered the responsibility have been given a right of recovery against them, on the basis that the persons responsible have thereby been saved the expense.[47] And in Canada, a doctor who provided emergency assistance to a pauper, where this was in fact a statutory duty laid on the municipality, successfully recovered his fee from it.[48] This right, in so far as it applies, should presumably be limited to cases where the intervention was not intended to be gratuitous, and where the intervening party had some reasonable excuse – such as a close relationship with the deceased – for interfering.

9-15   It would have been perfectly possible for the law to generalise from the 'public duty' cases and create a sort of restitutionary *actio popularis* whenever my performance of your duty, albeit not forced, was carried out reasonably and necessarily. But so far, there is little sign of any such development. Thus, in *Macclesfield Corp v Great Central Rly Co*,[49] a railway company responsible for maintaining a stretch of highway allowed it to get dangerously potholed. The local authority, having notified them of their duty to repair it, but to no effect, did the job itself. In the absence of proof that the authority was bound in law to do as it had done, its action for the costs incurred failed.

It is also worth mentioning in this connection, however, that numerous statutory provisions give equivalent rights of recovery to public authorities, with the result that the courts have had limited opportunities to develop common law doctrine in this field. Thus, authorities who carry out works, normally connected with health or safety, are often specifically empowered to recover the cost from the owner or occupier concerned who ought to have had them done in the first place.[50] And, to put the burial cases in context, a similar provision applies to a

---

46   [1892] 2 QB 452.

47   Eg, *Jenkins v Tucker* (1788) 1 H Bl 90; *Tugwell v Heyman* (1812) 3 Camp 298.

48   See *Hastings v Seaman's Village* [1946] 4 DLR 695. And cf *Callinan v VHI* [1994] 3 CMLR 796.

49   [1911] 2 KB 528. As Burrows points out, p 240, however, this case is not conclusive authority, since the point of necessity was not as such argued.

50   See, for a random English example, the Highways Act 1980, s 165(3) (removal of dangers to highway users by highway authority).

local authority exercising its statutory function of disposing of corpses that would otherwise go unburied.

(i) Ireland: the doctrine of 'salvage'

9-16   As was seen in Chapter 8,[51] the doctrine of 'salvage' recognised in the Republic may provide a remedy where a person with an interest in property incurs necessary expense for its preservation, to the advantage of others interested in it. Although most of the cases involve at least practical compulsion, 'salvage' principles have been successfully invoked by volunteers as well. A neat example is *Rathdonnell (Lord) v Colvin*.[52] The tenant for life of an oversized mansion volunteered to carry out necessary rationalisation works. He was given leave to do so by the court, and the expenses of so doing were declared then and there to qualify as a 'salvage' payment, so as to give him a charge over the interests of the remaindermen concerned.

(j) Other cases

9-17   A few cases do not fall under any of the above heads.

One such is the briefly reported Irish decision in *Re Pike*,[53] referred to above, where the Dublin police, having found a woman at home in no fit state to look after herself, took her to hospital and then kept a round-the-clock watch on the premises for three days until her relatives arrived. Shortly thereafter, she died. The police authority were held entitled to a lien on the house, which formed part of her estate, for some £18, being their reasonable charge for three days' use of a policeman's time. The ground of the decision is not clear, but arguably, this was a case of pure necessity.

Secondly, there is the case of the acceptor for honour of a bill of exchange.[54] Under s 65 of the Bills of Exchange Act 1882,[55] where a bill has been dishonoured, it is open to any person to accept liability on it 'for the honour' of the drawer or acceptor. Having done so and paid it, that person is by s 68(5) subrogated to any rights of the holder. It must be admitted, however, that this is hardly a strong example. To begin with, while it is true that the acceptor for honour need not act at the request of the acceptor, he often will: and if he does, no question of liability for necessitous intervention pure and simple arises. More importantly, it is not only those who become parties to a bill in the case of necessity who gain the right to sue the acceptor: any indorser has a similar right,

---

51 See § 8-15, above.
52 [1952] IR 297.
53 (1889) 23 LR Ir 9.
54 *Chalmers and Guest on Bills of Exchange*, 16th edn, § 1697 *et seq.*
55 Which remains in force in all relevant jurisdictions.

and indeed (it seems) anyone else who signs the bill other than as an indorser.[56] It may well be that bills of exchange fall to be regarded as *sui generis* in this connection; when accepting a bill, one should know that others are likely to put their names to it and gain potential rights under it.

III A GENERAL PRINCIPLE?

9-18   In the light of the above cases, the question as regards the future development of restitution law comes to this. Should they continue to be regarded as exceptional cases, or has the time come to generalise and recognise 'necessity' in its own right as an 'unjust factor'?

Hitherto, the traditional approach has been to say no, on the basis adumbrated by Bowen LJ in *Falcke v Scottish Imperial Insurance Co*. Liabilities, he said, 'are not to be forced on people behind their backs any more than you can confer a benefit upon a man against his will'.[57] But this, of itself, will hardly do. One may understandably feel unwilling to reward the officious bystander who insists on rendering services to someone who, for all he knows, may not want them at all. But there is a world of difference between him and someone who, for good reason, confers a benefit which it is almost certain the recipient: (a) would have wanted; and (b) would have obtained, and doubtless paid for, had he had the chance.

9-19   On the other hand, the present approach, which generally denies even the latter a remedy, may well be justified for another reason. In most other cases of restitution, the claimant has been able to show something more than mere benefit to the defendant, however incontrovertible. In particular, he can normally demonstrate either or both of: (a) a lack of voluntariness on his part (for example, mistake, duress) in rendering the benefit; and (b) acceptance by the defendant – or at the very least, a rejected opportunity to decline it. The difficulty with necessitous intervention, by contrast, is that neither of these is present. I do not have to help you in an emergency, and I know this: if I choose to do so, you have no choice whether to benefit from what I have done.[58] It follows that, in order to give a remedy here, we must find some reason to relax either the need for involuntariness, or the requirement of free acceptance.

---

56   Such a person becomes liable as if he were a true indorser to a holder in due course: Bills of Exchange Act, s 56. And it seems that, on principle, he has the rights of one too, including the right to sue the acceptor (*Chalmers and Guest on Bills of Exchange*, 15th edn, § 1426).

57   See (1886) 34 Ch D 234, p 248.

58   Cf *O'Callaghan v Ballincollig Holdings Ltd* (1993) unreported, 31 March, HC (Ireland) (Blayney J) (tenant repairing leased premises: landlord had no right to prevent repairs: no claim in unjust enrichment). Of course, in some cases of emergency intervention you do have an effective choice, for instance where I pay your debts in your name and you then ratify my acts: but then you can be held liable on free acceptance principles anyway.

The first possibility effectively involves replacing 'involuntary' with the wider 'non-officious': meritorious claimants such as the necessitous intervener being able, of course, to satisfy the latter, but not the former criterion. This obviously raises difficult issues of the place of officiousness in restitution law (in particular, should it merely be a bar to recovery that would otherwise be available, or should the lack of it in some cases be an independent ground for relief?).[59] Suffice it to say here that, in the author's view, no sufficient justification has ever been shown. On the contrary: rewarding the necessitous intervener merely because he is non-officious overly undermines the principle that altruism should be its own reward. Voluntary transfers of wealth, however unmeritorious the recipient, should generally be allowed to lie where they fall: there is no reason to give the morally deserving claimant anything more than a moral claim to be paid.

9-20 Alternatively, one can attack the problem from the 'free acceptance' angle, arguing that just as the person who receives a benefit willy-nilly from someone not acting voluntarily may be forced to pay for it if it was in fact 'incontrovertible', a similar rule should apply in the case of necessitous intervention. But this, it is submitted, is open to two objections. One arises from the argument above, § 1-31, that the whole idea of 'incontrovertible benefit' ought to be regarded as questionable on the ground that it seriously underplays the value of freedom of property and the principle against forced exchange. But even accepting, for the sake of argument, that there should be some role for 'incontrovertible benefit' in the law of restitution, it is by no means clear that it ought to apply here. In cases such as mistake or compulsion, where the benefit is one the defendant never consented to receive, nor the claimant to give, the equities are, so to speak, equal: injustice must be done to one or other, and a balancing claim may well be justified. But this cannot be so if the claimant acted voluntarily; however meritorious he was, and indeed, even if he had a moral duty to do as he did, the fact remains that he did so out of choice, and this, it is respectfully submitted, is a powerful reason not to upset the status quo.

IV MARITIME SALVAGE: A FURTHER ISSUE[60]

(a) In general

9-21 We have deliberately left until last the discussion of the principles of maritime salvage. There is no doubt that this does give a claim of sorts to the necessitous intervener, and a right that is independent of any pre-existing relationship or

---

59 See above, § 1-45.
60 Kennedy on *Civil Salvage*, 5th edn. In the Republic, salvage law is largely codified: Merchant Shipping (Salvage and Wreck) Act 1993, Part III.

other ground for intervention. In contrast to the position on land, the right of the maritime[61] salvor to remuneration is well established, both at common law and now by statute.[62] Moreover, he obtains both a personal liability and a proprietary claim in the shape of a maritime lien over the vessel salved.

9-22   The right to salvage remuneration arises whenever a ship or cargo is, or reasonably seems to be, in danger,[63] and is voluntarily saved by the efforts of those who are not bound by the terms of their employment or otherwise to do so.

In practice, the great majority of contemporary salvage operations are carried out contractually, in particular under standard forms of contract such as Lloyd's Open Form, under which services are requested before the event[64] on the terms laid out in it, with remuneration and any other disputes to be settled by arbitration afterwards. Hence, most salvage disputes today are (at least in form) contractual rather than restitutionary.[65]

Nevertheless, the general extra-contractual rules remain important, since: (a) the principles applicable under Lloyd's Open Form are often similar to those that would apply even in the absence of contract; and (b) some salvage work is still effected subject to them.

9-23   The requirement of 'voluntariness' means that normally, the crew of a ship cannot claim salvage from the owners for saving it,[66] though they can once the vessel has been abandoned[67] if they then voluntarily return to her. On the other hand, it seems clear that the mere fact that it may be a criminal offence for the owner or master of a ship to fail to go to the assistance of another vessel in distress[68] will not affect the right to salvage.

---

61 'Maritime' in this context was interpreted at common law as limited to tidal waters: *The Goring* [1988] 1 All ER 641 (non-tidal waters of the Thames not maritime). Under the Merchant Shipping Act 1995, Sched 11, by contrast, it includes all waters other than 'inland' waters of the UK – see Sched 11, Part II, s 2(1).

62 Ie (Ireland), Merchant Shipping (Salvage and Wreck) Act 1993, Pt III; (England), Merchant Shipping Act 1995, Sched 11 (enacting the provisions of the 1989 Salvage Convention).

63 Eg, *The Troilus* [1951] AC 820 (at common law): see now Merchant Shipping Act 1995, Sched 11, Pt I, s 1(a).

64 Though it is entirely possible, and not uncommon in practice, for Lloyd's Open Form to be agreed *ex post facto* after the salvage has commenced.

65 Thus the (English) Merchant Shipping Act 1995, Sched 11, specifically provides in s 6(1) that it is subject to nay contract between the parties.

66 Eg, *The Portreath* [1923] P 155. In the Republic, this rule is enshrined in statute: Merchant Shipping (Salvage and Wreck) Act 1993, s 30, providing that employees cannot claim salvage except in so far as their services went beyond what was reasonably required under their contract of service.

67 See, eg, *The Albionic* [1942] P 81 (in fact, the ship was held not to have been abandoned, so the claim failed).

68 England: Merchant Shipping Act 1995, ss 92, 93. Ireland: Merchant Shipping (Salvage and Wreck) Act 1993, s 23.

9-24   Entitlement to salvage relates to property that the salvor has saved, or at least contributed to the rescue of.[69] The burden of a salvage award falls on all those who have any interest in the property saved. Moreover, 'property', it should be noted, is widely construed in the salvage context. Where ship and cargo are salved, for instance, then the salvor has a claim not only against the physical corpus of both, but also against the shipowner's claim for freight relating to that cargo: again, where a passenger ship is salved, the salvor has a claim against any unpaid passage moneys. In neither case would the moneys have been earned but for the salvor's efforts.

On the other hand, it is a vital principle of salvage that the value of property saved marks the limit of any entitlement of the salvor. If he saves nothing, his award is nil, however meritorious he may have been. 'No cure, no pay' is a fundamental principle of the law of salvage.[70] Again, if what he successfully saves is of small or trifling value, so also will be his recovery.

Salvage of life alone is on a different footing. In England it does not, as such, carry the right to any reward. (It is not, however, irrelevant. If property and life are saved at the same time, the amount of any award against the property may be increased: and there is a statutory jurisdiction[71] to reward life salvors out of public funds in cases of 'pure' life salvage). In the Republic, a life salvor has a statutory right to remuneration out of the proceeds of any property saved.[72]

9-25   Technically, a shipowner who refuses salvage services can be made to pay for them notwithstanding, at least if he acts unreasonably.[73] On the other hand, salvage services in practice are nearly always rendered by agreement between the parties, except occasionally in the case of abandoned cargo.

The amount of any salvage award is settled, in the case of Lloyd's Open Form and similar standard form agreements by arbitration, and in the absence of any contractual means by the court. There is no fixed formula, except that the award cannot be for more than the value of the property saved: matters in account include the value of property saved, whether the salvor was a professional salvor with vessels constantly on standby (if he was, he gets more); the amount of effort and danger to the salvor and to the salved vessel; the competence and speed of the salvage services; the availability of other salvage services, and so on.[74]

---

69 Eg, *The Camellia* (1884) 9 PD 27.

70 Specifically provided for in England in the Merchant Shipping Act 1995, Sched 11, Pt I, s 12(1), and in the Republic by the Merchant Shipping (Salvage and Wreck) Act 1993, s 25.

71 Merchant Shipping Act 1995, Sched 11, Pt II, s 5.

72 Merchant Shipping (Salvage and Wreck) Act 1993, s 29.

73 Eg, *The Kangaroo* [1918] P 327 (at common law). The same applies under statute. In England, the Merchant Shipping Act 1995, Sched 11, s 19, denies salvage to a person who acts against the wishes of the salvee, but only in so far as the latter acts reasonably. The equivalent Irish provision is the Merchant Shipping (Salvage and Wreck) Act 1993, s 32.

74 See, eg, Kennedy on *Civil Salvage* (5th edn, 1985), Ch 12, for the common law position. The same applies under the (English) Merchant Shipping Act 1995 (Sched 11, Pt I, s 13), and in the Republic (Merchant Shipping (Salvage and Wreck) Act 1993, s 26).

(b) The place of salvage in restitution law

9-26   Despite its traditional treatment in books on restitution, there is room for some doubt as to the precise relation between salvage and the rest of the law of restitution. True, salvage is about benefit to property owners, in that salvage awards depend on some benefit having been rendered, and are to some extent governed by the amount of any such benefit. It is also the case that the distinction drawn in English law between land and sea salvage can, to some extent, be justified in terms of general restitutionary principles. It is also true that the public policy arguments in favour of recovery for the necessitous intervener, such as may have applied in cases such as *Great Northern Rly Co v Swaffield*,[75] are extremely strong in the case of maritime salvage. Not only is there likely to be a lack of alternative sources of assistance for a vessel in distress to call on, but life as well as property is more likely to be in serious danger: furthermore, almost universal insurance including cover for salvage charges means that it is less likely that parties will be saddled with a liability they cannot reasonably bear.

On the other hand, it is perhaps more realistic to regard salvage as *sui generis* rather than to try to integrate it too closely into restitution law as a whole. The connection between awards and the value of property saved (and hence benefit to the recipient of the services) is by no means direct: the element of reward given to professional salvors for keeping vessels permanently on standby, which is a vital feature in the computation of salvage awards, can hardly be said to reflect the benefit to any particular vessel owner. Furthermore, as has already been mentioned, a great deal of salvage is effected under standard forms of contract which provide for the amount payable to be settled by arbitration. The liabilities incurred under such a contract can hardly be called restitutionary.

---

75   (1874) LR 9 Ex 132.

CHAPTER 10

BENEFITS CONFERRED THROUGH THIRD PARTIES: 'TRACING'

I GENERALLY

10-1 Most of this book deals with claims for reimbursement for benefits received at the hands of the claimant. I pay you money by mistake; I pay off a debt owed jointly by you and me; I do work for you assuming that there will be a contract between us but we fail to agree; and so on. In all these cases the person providing the benefit and the person as the person seeking restitution are one and the same.

In this chapter, by contrast, the defendant's enrichment comes through the intervention of a third party, X. This can happen in one of two ways. First, the third party may have transferred to the defendant an asset which is the proceeds of, or otherwise represents, some item of property wrongfully taken from the claimant. For example, my trustee helps himself to £10,000 of trust money, buys shares with it and then gives them to you. This involves the legal process commonly, but deceptively, known as 'tracing'. Alternatively, the claimant may complain that the defendant has received money or property which never belonged to the claimant, but for some reason ought to have gone to him rather than the defendant. For example, you assign to me a debt of £10,000 owed to you by X, but X then proceeds to pay you rather than me. For brevity, we will call the first of these situations 'tracing' and the second 'diversion' (since the essence of my claim in cases of this sort is that something which was, or ought to have been, on its way to me has been diverted, directly or indirectly, to you).

II 'TRACING'[1]

(a) In general

10-2 In the first case, that is, 'tracing', the unjust factor concerned is that *prima facie*, any enrichment obtained through property of which someone has been unjustifiably deprived calls for reversal.[2] Typically, we are talking about unravelling the consequences of fraud: the third party being the villain, the

---

1 Smith, *The Law of Tracing*.
2 See above, § 1-20.

claimant his victim and the defendant a person who receives or handles the fruits of peculation later on. But dishonesty is not *de rigueur*: trustees, executors and banks equally can and do make mistakes that divert to me assets that should have gone to you, and hence raise questions of how the resulting imbalance should be corrected.

Before we start, however, a terminological point. Taken at its widest, this chapter could swallow up the whole of the law of property. Suppose your car is stolen and I buy it; or suppose your trustee makes a present to me of shares belonging to the trust. If I still have the car (or the shares) you have a good claim against me to get them back. But it is not a *restitutionary* claim; it is simply to be given back what remained yours all along, whether at law or in equity.[3] We will, therefore, not be dealing with it here. Instead, we will concentrate on cases where what is received is not the claimant's property itself, but instead something else alleged to be representative of it: as where (for instance) I have sold the car or the shares before you approach me, and you then look to me to reimburse to you the amount I got for them.

10-3   The starting point in any tracing claim is a straightforward, if bald, proposition. Where a person in control of an asset of mine changes it into, or substitutes for it, some other asset, then subject to certain conditions I will have a claim to the substituted asset.[4] Typically, the person controlling the asset will be a trustee, agent or other fiduciary of mine: but the principle applies equally to a thief, or a mere bailee.

Two recent cases provide straightforward examples. In *Jones (FC) and Sons (Trustee) v Jones*,[5] a bankrupt without authority drew a cheque for some £11,000 in favour of his wife. She used the proceeds to speculate successfully and came to be owed about £50,000 by her commodity brokers. The bankrupt's trustee, who had owned all the bankrupt's property at the time the original cheque was drawn, successfully claimed the whole £50,000 from the wife. In the later *Foskett v McKeown*,[6] a fraudster obtained moneys to be laid out in the purchase of Portuguese real estate, but instead spent a good deal of them in paying the premiums on a policy for £1 m on his own life. After he died, the depositors who had held the beneficial interest in those moneys successfully claimed part ownership of the insurance proceeds in proportion to the trust moneys that had gone to pay the premiums.

10-4   In any claim to substituted assets, two questions come to the fore. One is the legal nature of the claimant's interest in, or claim to, the substitute. The other is

---

3   Cf the discussion above, § 1-50; Virgo, *Principles of the Law of Restitution*, p 592 *et seq*. Others have taken a different view: eg, Burrows, p 369.

4   The claimant 'will normally be able to maintain the same claim to the substituted asset as he could have maintained to the original asset': *Foskett v McKeown* [2001] 1 AC 102, p 128 (Lord Millett). See too *Barclays Bank plc v Buhr* [2001] EWCA 1223.

5   [1997] Ch 159.

6   [2001] 1 AC 102; Rotherham [2000] CLJ 440.

what counts as a substitute for the purpose of bringing that claim: how, in other words, we can or should identify Asset A (now in the defendant's hands) with Asset B (that was once in the claimant's) and say that the former represents, or can be 'traced' from, the latter.[7] It will be noticed that the second of these questions is ancillary to the first. Until we know what asset we wish to claim, and the nature of the interest we wish to claim in it, the question of 'tracing' is a mere theoretical exercise. As the leading commentator has put it,[8] tracing is of itself neither a right nor a remedy. It is a mere process of identification, a rule for creating a legal link between two or more assets, for the purpose of bringing some other substantive claim.[9]

Unfortunately, answering these two questions is remarkably awkward, not least because equity and the common law give different answers to each of them. As regards the first – the nature of the claim to substitute assets – this is not surprising, given the historical variance between legal and equitable rights and remedies. The failure of common law and equity to agree on the answer to the second – the process of deciding whether Asset A is indeed a substitute for Asset B – is remarkable and, by common consent, indefensible, given that the question is essentially an evidentiary one.[10] Nevertheless, pending resolution of the issue by either the House of Lords or the Supreme Court, the common law and equitable rules must continue to be dealt with separately.

(b) Tracing: the common law rules

Common law – the nature of the claimant's rights in substitute assets[11]

10-5   You take my horse and exchange it for a cow. What claim, if any, do I have at common law to the cow? Surprisingly, the matter is almost uncovered by direct authority. For a long time, *Taylor v Plumer*[12] was thought to have settled the matter. A stockbroker, W, embezzled P's money, and used it to buy bonds and bullion. He was stopped when about to sail for America and relieved of the bonds and gold by P's agents. An action by his trustee in bankruptcy against P failed, thus suggesting that P had some kind of legal title to the bonds. However,

---

7   Unless, of course, we say that the question whether the claimant should have rights against property in the defendant's hands should depend on factors other than whether that property is derived from an asset of the claimant. Cf Evans (1999) 115 LQR 469.

8   Smith, *The Law of Tracing*, Chapter 1. See, too, Birks (1997) 11 Trust Law Int 2; Millett (1998) 114 LQR 399, p 409.

9   A point now accepted on high authority: see Lord Millett's comments in *Foskett v McKeown* [2001] 1 AC 102, p 128. See, too, *Boscawen v Bajwa* [1995] 4 All ER 769, p 776.

10   *Jones (FC) and Sons (Trustee) v Jones* [1997] Ch 159, pp 169–70; *Foskett v McKeown* [2001] 1 AC 102, pp 113, 128–29; Goff & Jones, p 93; Virgo, *Principles of the Law of Restitution*, p 655; Smith, *The Law of Tracing*, Chapter 3; Birks in Cranston (ed), *Making Commercial Law*, Chapter 9.

11   Fox [1999] RLR 55.

12   (1815) 3 M & S 562. Cf *Golightly v Reynolds* (1772) Lofft 88.

it has now been convincingly shown that P's claim in this case was equitable and not legal,[13] and hence that it does not cover the question.

One thing is clear: in the scenario above, I do not actually own the cow. If I did, I could sue anyone who bought it from you, however innocently, for the strict liability tort of conversion. But *Commercial Banking Co of Sydney v Mann*[14] establishes that I cannot do this. Mann's partner stole cheques from the partnership and then changed them for banker's drafts which he cashed at the defendant bank. An action by the partners against the bank for conversion failed. Even if the drafts in the bank's hands derived from their property, this did not make them owners so as to allow them to bring conversion in respect of them. There is also another reason. Despite the fact that you have alienated my horse I still own it: to say I owned the cow too would potentially double my money.[15]

10-6   The true position, it is suggested, is that I do have a common law proprietary claim to the cow,[16] but a more limited one than outright ownership. While the animal is in your hands, I may elect[17] *as against you* to claim a right to immediate possession of it, with all the legal consequences that entails (including, it is submitted, a prior claim to the cow against your trustee in bankruptcy should you be insolvent). This proposition seems to follow by analogy from *Jones (FC) and Sons (Trustee) v Jones*.[18] A bankrupt, at a time when all his assets had vested in his trustee in bankruptcy, drew a cheque for nearly £12,000 in favour of his wife. The wife deposited it with futures brokers, traded successfully and ended with a credit balance of £50,000. The brokers were held, on entirely common law principles, to owe this sum to the trustee in bankruptcy. The wife's credit balance, a chose in action, was the proceeds of the bankrupt's moneys, to which he had no title. As against her, therefore, the trustee was to be treated as legal owner of the chose in action concerned. Similarly, it is submitted, in the example of the horse and the cow I may claim as against you the rights of an owner in respect of the cow.

But, as shown by *Commercial Banking Co of Sydney v Mann*,[19] this right is truncated. It will not subsist against anyone else through whose hands it passes,

---

13 W clearly being a fiduciary, and trustees in bankruptcy being bound to recognise equitable defences even in actions at law. See *Jones (FC) and Sons (Trustee) v Jones* [1997] Ch 159, p 169 (Millett LJ); Khurshid and Mathews (1975) 95 LQR 78; Smith [1995] LM and CLQ 240.

14 [1961] AC 1.

15 Birks, p 91 *et seq*.

16 As suggested by Fox LJ in *Agip (Africa) Ltd v Jackson* [1991] Ch 547, p 563 and by Lord Goff in *Lipkin Gorman v Karpnale Ltd* [1991] 2 AC 548, p 572 *et seq*. Although their Lordships' reliance in *Agip* on *Taylor v Plumer* has now been shown to have been misconceived (see above, fn 13), it is suggested that what they said remains good law on principle.

17 For a statement that what is involved here is an election, see *Foskett v McKeown* [2001] 1 AC 102, p 127 (Lord Millett).

18 [1997] Ch 159.

19 [1961] AC 1.

at least where he has acted in good faith.[20] As Lord Goff laconically put it in *Lipkin Gorman v Karpnale Ltd*, a common law claim to substitute assets 'cannot be relied on so as to render an innocent recipient a wrongdoer'.[21]

10-7   So far, we have been dealing with substitute assets other than money. As regards money, the general principle at common law can, it seems, be expressed thus. If a third party without lawful excuse causes a payment to be made to you which derives from money or assets belonging to me, I can *prima facie* sue you for money had and received. Assume my butler abstracts my cheque book, forges my signature on a cheque and gives it to you; you then cash it. Or my agent, whom I authorise to transfer funds on my behalf for my business, fraudulently transfers money to you in order to pay a debt of his in circumstances where you are not a *bona fide* purchaser. Again, imagine a bank computer error causes £1,000 to be debited to your account and credited to mine. In all three cases, you can sue me for the amount I received:[22] to that extent, I am unjustifiably enriched at your expense.

Take, for example, the old case of *Marsh v Keating*.[23] Brokers in good faith received the price of stock owned by the plaintiff which had been sold by someone else under a forged transfer. They were held liable to account to the owner for the price as money had and received to her use. A similar, more recent, decision is *Lipkin Gorman v Karpnale Ltd*.[24] A fraudulent solicitor filched funds from his firm and gambled them away at a Mayfair casino.[25] The casino was held liable to account to the firm for the moneys it had received (though subject to a defence of change of position to the extent that it had paid out any winnings to its customer).

For these purposes, it does not matter whether my property from which your gain was derived was in the form of money, or a bank balance, or some other thing: if X steals my car, sells it and immediately hands the price to you, you must still account to me.[26] Nor does it matter that you were not the direct recipient. In the example of the butler, it would make no difference if the cheque

---

20 Thus protecting, for example, the auctioneer who sells the cow on your behalf. Normally, such a person who deals with goods to which his client has no title is strictly liable to the true owner: *Willis and Son (A Firm) v British Car Auctions Ltd* [1978] 2 All ER 392.

21 See [1991] 2 AC 548, p 580.

22 Forgery: *Banque Belge pour l'Étranger v Hambrouck* [1921] 1 KB 321 (as interpreted in *Agip (Africa) v Jackson* [1991] Ch 547, p 564); cf *Jones (FC) and Sons (Trustee) v Jones* [1997] Ch 159, where it was accepted that the wife would equally have been amenable to an action in money had and received. Fraud: *Lipkin Gorman v Karpnale Ltd* [1991] 2 AC 548. For bank error, cf *Re PMPA Insurance Co Ltd* [1986] ILRM 524 (cheques and contra-entries mistakenly posted by bank to wrong account: restitution granted to rectify the position as between customers).

23 (1834) 1 Bing NC 198.

24 [1991] 2 AC 548.

25 The Playboy Club.

26 'But an action for money had and received is maintainable whenever the money of one man has, without consideration, got into the pocket of another': see *Hudson v Robinson* (1816) 4 M & S 475, p 478 (Lord Ellenborough).

had been made out to a friend of yours who had cashed it and immediately given you the proceeds.[27]

10-8   Claims for money had and received in respect of cash proceeds, like claims to chattels substituted, give way to the rights of a good faith purchaser. If the recipient, or any predecessor in title of his, has given value in exchange for moneys alleged to represent the claimant's assets, he is protected from liability.[28] Moreover, where it applies, this protection is complete, and does not simply extend to the extent of the value given, as would be in the case of change of position.

'Value', for these purposes, means consideration under a valid contract. A void transaction such as a gaming contract will not do.[29] Presumably, the same goes for a contract binding in honour only.[30] Nevertheless, such circumstances may give rise to a defence of change of position.[31]

10-9   At first sight, the head of money had and received just outlined looks like a simple property claim: the claimant pointing to a sum of money in the hands of the defendant and saying: 'That is mine, because it is derived from my property.' For this reason, and also because the claimant cannot even get his action off the ground unless he can show some original legal proprietary interest infringed, it is often referred to as 'common law tracing'.

But, this useful shorthand conceals one misconception. True, the action may depend on the claimant having been deprived of an item of property. Nevertheless, it lies not *in rem* but *in personam*, and for a money judgment only. Indeed, liability is based purely on receipt by the defendant, not (as would *ex hypothesi* be the case with a proprietary claim) retention of the moneys concerned at the time of the claim. Indeed, it lies (subject to the defence of change of position, below) even though there is nothing remaining in the defendant's hands representing what the claimant originally lost.[32]

From this, one important consequence follows. Suppose I cash a cheque in my favour drawn on your account but in fact forged by your butler: before I

---

27 *Banque Belge pour l'Étranger v Hambrouck* [1921] 1 KB 321 suggests this, in so far as it held Mlle Spanoghe liable to the plaintiffs. Mlle Spanoghe was an indirect, not a direct, recipient.

28 Eg, *Clarke v Shee* (1774) 1 Cowp 197, p 200; *Lipkin Gorman v Karpnale Ltd* [1992] 4 All ER 409, CA. In fact, the House of Lords held in the latter case that the defendant was not a *bona fide* purchaser at all (see [1991] 2 AC 548); but that does not affect the point in the text.

29 *Lipkin Gorman v Karpnale Ltd* [1991] 2 AC 548 (receipt in payment of gambling debts does not count as *bona fide* purchase). Presumably receipt under an illegal contract would have the same result.

30 *Quaere* how far this goes, however. If a convicted fraudster has paid his counsel with stolen money, must counsel (who does not act under a contract, and cannot sue for his fees) refund in full to the victim of the theft? Or would he have a defence of change of position?

31 *Lipkin Gorman v Karpnale Ltd* [1991] 2 AC 548.

32 'Since liability depends on receipt the fact that the defendant has not retained the asset is irrelevant': Fox LJ in *Agip (Africa) Ltd v Jackson* [1991] Ch 547, p 563.

have spent the cash, I go bankrupt. Your claim against me remains a personal one: therefore, you will have to take your place with my general creditors.[33] On the other hand, this seems to be limited to where the money was received before my bankruptcy; if I steal your car and sell it on credit, and after my insolvency my trustee in bankruptcy receives the price, you will have a direct claim against my trustee for the whole amount.[34]

Common law – identifying the proceeds

10-10 The full name of the action for money had and received is 'money had and received *to the use of the claimant*'; in other words, to establish the cause of action, I must show that your gain derives from something that was mine. Similarly, where I wish to lay claim to an asset in your hands I must show either that the asset is itself mine, or that it is derived from something that was.

This, in turn, breaks down into two separate requirements.

The first necessity is that the ultimate source of my gain must have been something you had title to at common law but have since been deprived of: this is, after all, a common law cause of action. So a car stolen from you will do, as will money filched from your bank account: on the other hand, an interest under a simple trust in your favour will not.

Secondly, and more importantly, before you can make a claim against me you must be able to identify the money received by me with that property: you must, that is, be able to link your loss to my gain, or your action cannot get off the ground. What sort of tie does this entail? On the authorities, it must be one satisfying three criteria:

(a) you must have been wrongfully deprived of your property;

(b) the money I received must have been derived from that property, directly or indirectly, by means of one or more sales or exchanges; and

(c) the process of exchange must not have involved mixing at any intermediate stage.

10-11 To demonstrate point (a), assume I pay X £100 cash as prepayment for goods, whereupon X gives the very same notes to you. X then fails to deliver the goods. I have a right against X, but not against you: I have not been wrongfully deprived of any proprietary interest with which the notes you received can be identified.[35]

---

33   See Goode (1976) 92 LQR 360, p 401.

34   See *Scott v Surman* (1742) Willes 400, p 403.

35   See *Box v Barclays Bank plc* (1998) *The Times*, 30 April. Cf *Eldan Services Ltd v Chandag Motors Ltd* [1990] 3 All ER 459. A person who pays for something in advance is not wrongfully deprived of his money even if he does not get what he paid for.

Points (b) and (c) are neatly illustrated by *Agip (Africa) Ltd v Jackson*.[36] As a result of the activities of a fraudster named Zdiri, Agip's bank in Tunisia debited Agip's account by $526,000 and instructed Lloyds Bank, its correspondent in London, to credit Baker (a company controlled by Zdiri) with the same sum. Lloyds Bank did so, being put in funds at a later stage by Agip's bank. Baker then transferred the money to Jackson. Agip's action against Jackson for money had and received failed. Since Lloyds had credited Baker before being paid by Agip's bank, the moneys received by Baker and Jackson were not genuine exchange products of Agip's funds (see (b)). And furthermore, Agip's bank could not have transferred the requisite sums to Lloyds without mixing them with other funds in the New York clearing system, thus preventing requirement (c) from being fulfilled.[37]

Common law money claims and change of position

10-12   In so far as the recipient has innocently incurred expenditure or obligations in the faith that he can keep what he has got, he may rely on the general defence of change of position. *Lipkin Gorman v Karpnale Ltd*,[38] besides establishing the general availability of this defence,[39] illustrates the process neatly. A partner in a firm of solicitors gambled the firm's money at the Playboy Club: the club, who did not count as *bona fide* purchasers, had to repay the amount staked less the partner's own winnings. Similarly, in *Agip (Africa) Ltd v Jackson*,[40] the defendants, Manx accountants, had credited to accounts controlled by them assets derived from moneys filched from Agip, but had then accounted for them to their principals, who were in fact party to the fraud. Millett J at first instance decided that even if the defendants were liable (which in the event he held they were not) their innocent change of position would have protected them in any case.[41]

(c) Tracing: the equitable jurisdiction

10-13   The common law rights mentioned above presuppose an initial proprietary right recognised at common law. The claimant who starts out with an equitable claim[42] to assets has superficially analogous, but in fact rather different, claims

---

36   [1991] Ch 547. See McKendrick [1991] LM & CLQ 378. See too *Solomons v Williams* (2001) unreported, 23 May, Ch D.

37   In the event, the plaintiffs succeeded in equity, however. On this point, see too *El Ajou v Dollar Land Holdings Ltd* [1993] 3 All ER 717, p 733 *et seq*; *Jones (FC) & Sons (Trustee) v Jones* [1997] Ch 159, p 168 *et seq*.

38   [1991] 2 AC 548.

39   On which see Chapter 13.

40   [1990] Ch 265.

41   The case was appealed to the Court of Appeal, where in the event this point did not fall for decision (see [1991] Ch 547).

42   As for what amounts to an equitable claim for these purposes, see below.

against recipients of those assets or their proceeds. These claims are of two types.[43]

First, in certain cases the recipient is liable personally to repay the value of what he has received, in rather the same way that the defendant in *Lipkin Gorman v Karpnale Ltd*[44] found itself liable in money had and received to the original owners of the moneys gambled away at their casino.

Secondly, where the property subject to the original equitable right has been exchanged or turned into something else, the owner can claim a substitutive equitable right in its product by the process known as 'tracing'.

Equitable personal claims

10-14 Suppose that, in the winding-up of an estate, assets are misdirected by the personal representatives and reach the wrong hands. The leading case is *Ministry of Health v Simpson*.[45] A philanthropist's executors distributed very substantial sums to certain charities according to a provision in his will. That provision was in fact invalid, as the House of Lords subsequently established.[46] Having recovered what they could from the executors, the real beneficiaries of the estate sued the respective charities for the balance. The House of Lords, in a judgment limited to misdistribution of estates, confirmed that the recipients were indeed liable to repay. This was, and is, a drastic liability, particularly since it is independent of fault in anyone, and (apparently) is unaffected by any change of position on the part of the recipient.[47] Its only palliation was a slightly odd one,[48] namely, that any recovery fell to be reduced by the amount that was, or could reasonably have been, recovered from the personal representatives and anyone else responsible for the payment.[49]

10-15 It is not entirely clear whether the principle in *Ministry of Health v Simpson*[50] can be extended to cover claims not involving the administration of estates. In *Re*

---

43 Leaving aside the claim against the recipient who still has the original trust property and who cannot claim the protection afforded the *bona fide* purchaser. This claim, like that of the legal owner of goods that have got into the wrong hands, is not really restitutionary at all.

44 [1991] 2 AC 548.

45 [1951] AC 251.

46 See *Chichester Diocesan Board Fund v Simpson* [1944] AC 341.

47 *Quaere*, however, how far this has survived the construction of a general change of position defence in *Lipkin Gorman v Karpnale Ltd* [1991] 2 AC 548. In New South Wales, it has been held that it has not: *Gertsch v Atsas* (1999) unreported, 1 October, SC (NSW).

48 Though established on the authorities. Smith (1991) OJLS 481 defends it on the basis that, to the extent that such recovery is available, the recipients' enrichment is not at the beneficiaries' expense, but rather at the executors'. With respect, this argument, albeit powerful, seems ultimately unconvincing. Enrichment is either at the claimant's expense or it is not: and if it is, it does not cease to be merely because there is someone else the claimant can look to. Cf *Friends Provident Life Office v Hillier Parker* [1997] QB 85.

49 Eg, a bank: cf *Re Leslie (J) Engineers Co Ltd* [1976] 2 All ER 85.

50 [1951] AC 251.

Leslie (J) Engineers Co Ltd,[51] Slade J was apparently prepared to hold it applicable in distribution on a winding-up, where a company director made certain disbursements of the company's money which were open to attack under the insolvency laws (on the facts, however, the point did not arise).[52] This is no doubt sensible, since there is a good deal in common between the processes of distributing the assets of deceased persons and defunct corporations. But the real question is whether the principle ought to be applied to misapplication of trust assets generally.[53]

The argument in favour of doing so can be simply expressed. The receiver of trust assets (assuming he cannot plead *bona fide* purchase) must, of course, disgorge them if he still has them. If he does not have them, he currently remains liable *in personam*, but only if he knew, or possibly had reason to know,[54] when he got them that they were trust assets. A number of commentators[55] have cogently argued that this liability is misconceived. They suggest that any receiver of trust property should be liable *in personam* for its value, whether or not he was at fault and whether or not he still has it; and that the defence of change of position is now adequate to protect the recipient who has innocently got rid of the assets.

10-16 Notwithstanding this, it is suggested that the case for extending *Ministry of Health v Simpson*[56] has not been adequately made out.

First, as will appear in Chapter 13, it is not certain that the defence of change of position will adequately protect the recipient who no longer has the asset concerned. It is unclear, for instance, whether a defendant is entitled to plead the defence where the change of position arises out of arrangements entered into prior to receipt.[57] Yet the innocent handler of someone else's asset ought clearly to be protected in such a case.

Secondly, where someone handles or deals with an asset which he in all innocence believes to be his own, it is submitted that this factor tells against imposing any extended liability. It is by no means clear that he should be liable even for negligence in keeping, disposing of or (for that matter) losing that asset

---

51 [1976] 2 All ER 85. See, too, *Butler v Broadhead* [1974] 2 All ER 401, where Templeman J left open the question of extending the Ministry of Health case.

52 Since the liquidator had not exhausted his remedies against the director personally.

53 Cf Denning J's *dicta* in *Nelson v Larholt* [1948] 1 KB 339, p 342, cited without disapproval by Danckwerts J in *Baker v Medway Building Supplies Ltd* [1958] 2 All ER 533.

54 The cases do not speak with one voice. *International Sales Ltd v Marcus* [1982] 3 All ER 551 holds that it is enough if the recipient ought to have known the assets were misapplied, as does *El Ajou v Dollar Land Holdings Ltd* [1993] 3 All ER 717. *Re Montagu's Settlement Trusts* [1987] Ch 264, by contrast, suggests that only actual notice will do. So does *Eagle Trust plc v SBC Securities Ltd (No 2)* [1996] 1 BCLC 121.

55 Eg, Birks, in *Commercial Aspects of Trusts* (McKendrick, ed), p 149; Birks [1989] LM and CLQ 296; Millett (1991) 107 LQR 73. See, too, Harpum, in *Frontiers of Liability* (Birks, ed), p 9 *et seq*, accepting that this ought to be the law, but cogently arguing that it is not, yet.

56 [1951] AC 251.

57 See *South Tyneside MBC v Svenska International plc* [1995] 1 All ER 545; below, § 13-16.

when, on the facts as he sees them, what he does with it is nobody's business but his own. Yet extending *Ministry of Health v Simpson*[58] would have exactly the opposite effect. Since the defence of change of position involves an absence of negligence and must be proved by the defendant,[59] the result would be a strict liability with the burden on the receiver to disprove fault. There seems no sensible justification for this at all.

Equitable claims to substitute property

10-17 We now turn to claims based on the equitable, rather than the common law rules: that is, where the claimant seeks to establish an equitable interest in some substitute property. Typically, we are dealing with a case where a trustee has misapplied trust property or a fiduciary, such as an agent, has redirected funds which ought to have gone to his principal.

To establish my right to trace assets in your hands, I have to show three things:

(a) that my claim is to a definite asset still in your hands;

(b) that I had a sufficient equitable proprietary base to start with, since otherwise my proprietary claim must fail at the outset; and

(c) that there is a sufficient connection between the asset in your hands and my original property to say that one represents the other.

(a) The nature of the claimant's interest in the substitute

10-18 The claim we are dealing with here is purely a claim to property. In particular, it applies – unlike the 'receipt-based' claim for money had and received – only to the defendant who still has property representing the claimant's. I cannot lay claim to property from you if you have not still got it:[60] all I can do is claim money in substitution, which in equity I can do only if I can show that you acted with the requisite degree of knowledge to make you guilty of knowing receipt. The facts of *Lipkin Gorman v Karpnale Ltd*,[61] where a solicitor stole partnership moneys and gambled them away, show this neatly. Although there is little doubt that Lipkin Gorman would have had the right on principle to trace their money in equity,[62] this remedy could not be used because the club clearly did not still have it. The only claim open to them was, therefore, the receipt-based

---

58 [1951] AC 251.

59 Below, § 13-6 *et seq*.

60 'The tracing claim in equity gives rise to a proprietary remedy *which depends on the continued existence of the trust property in the hands of the defendant*': *Agip (Africa) Ltd v Jackson* [1990] Ch 265, p 290 (Millett J) (italics supplied).

61 [1991] 2 AC 548.

62 Since their defaulting partner, Cass, clearly stood in a fiduciary position vis à vis them.

claim at common law which ultimately succeeded. And again, where (as we shall see) a defaulting fiduciary has placed misapplied moneys in a bank account on which he has subsequently drawn so as to reduce the balance below the amount of those moneys, any proprietary claim is limited to the lowest intermediate balance.[63] Above that amount, any remaining balance ex hypothesi cannot be the proceeds of the funds originally deposited.

As with the common law, the nature of the claimant's interest in the substitute asset is not entirely clear. Nevertheless, it seems best analysed in a similar way to the common law claim. That is, the claimant does not simply get the equitable property in the substitute,[64] but instead may elect to claim equitable rights in it. There is equally little authority on just what equitable proprietary rights he gets if he does so elect. One possibility is that, having elected to lay claim to the substitute, he counts as an equitable owner like any other. But this would raise difficulties with third parties. An innocent third party purchaser of a legal interest in the substitute would, of course, take free of any interest of the claimant: but a purchaser of an equitable interest, such as a bank with a fixed or floating charge, would not.[65] A more imaginative, and ultimately satisfactory, solution would be to regard the claimant's interest as a 'mere equity', that is, as an equitable proprietary interest which nevertheless yields to the subsequent *bona fide* purchaser of an equitable interest as much as a legal one.[66] There is indeed some, albeit weak, authority in Ireland for this approach. In *Re ffrench's Estate*,[67] a tenant for life wrongfully used capital moneys to buy land, which he later equitably mortgaged to X. It was held by the Irish Court of Appeal that X, even though his interest was merely equitable, took free of the beneficiaries under the original settlement, Sir Andrew Porter MR putting this on the basis that the interest of the latter was a mere equity. Although the majority in *Re ffrench's Estate* were prepared to decide the case on different grounds,[68] it is suggested that there is much to be said for Porter MR's view.

---

63 The rule in *Roscoe (Bolton) Ltd v Winder* [1915] 1 Ch 62: below, § 10-25.

64 Since if he did, there would arise a potential problem of exponential growth in the claimant's wealth. If T, a trustee, wrongfully takes a horse held on trust for B, a beneficiary, and exchanges it with X (who takes in bad faith) for a cow, B will retain his rights in the horse and in addition have a potential claim to the cow. But he must not be allowed to double his money by obtaining both. See above, § 10-5.

65 Since where the equities are equal, the first in time prevails. Thus, in *Re Goldcorp Exchange Ltd* [1995] 1 AC 74, the argument was between investors and a bank holding an all-moneys floating charge, which even after crystallisation could only be equitable. It never seems to have been argued that the bank could obtain priority as the *bona fide* purchaser of an equitable interest in the moneys.

66 See *Phillips v Phillips* (1862) 4 De G, F and J 208, laying down the accepted definition of a 'mere equity'.

67 (1887) 21 LR Ir 283.

68 Namely, that the other beneficiaries' claim was barred by *laches*.

(b) The equitable proprietary base

10-19   If I lay claim to substitute assets in your hands, they must clearly be substitutes for something – that is, a given asset which does, or at least did, belong to me.[69] To use Birks's terms,[70] there must obviously be a *proprietary* base of some sort.

Most significantly, this means that a mere debtor-creditor relationship will not do. Suppose I lend you money or otherwise give you credit (for instance, by paying in advance for goods or services). You are *prima facie* free to do as you like with the money you receive. From the moment of payment it is yours, not mine: all I have is a claim *in personam* against you.[71] It follows that even if you fail to repay me or satisfy my claim, I have no rights either to the money in your hands or to any proceeds of it. Take the facts of *Re Goldcorp Exchange Ltd*.[72] Hopeful, if avaricious, investors paid Goldcorp in advance for bullion to be purchased and stored on their behalf. They were allocated none, or at least a good deal less than they were entitled to. When Goldcorp collapsed, the Privy Council quite correctly denied them any claim against assets in fact purchased with the money they had paid.[73] The only way such a claimant can succeed is to show that, exceptionally, the person to whom he paid his money did not become absolute owner of it but held it on (for example) a '*Quistclose* trust',[74] so that the payer retained an equitable property in it.[75]

10-20   What kind of 'proprietary base' will suffice? An interest as *cestui que trust* is the obvious, but by no means the only, basis for a tracing claim in equity. A resulting trust will do just as well, or a constructive trust;[76] as will a '*Quistclose* trust',[77] and, indeed, any other situation where moneys are received by A to be invested on behalf of B and it is clear that A is not entitled to deal with them as

---

69   'You cannot grant a proprietary right to A who has not had it beforehand, without taking some proprietary right away from B': Mummery LJ in *Re Polly Peck Ltd (No 2)* [1998] 3 All ER 812, p 830.

70   Birks, p 378 *et seq*.

71   Compare *Box v Barclays Bank plc* (1998) *The Times*, 30 April (no proprietary claim of any kind in respect of simple loan of money to a fraudster).

72   [1995] 1 AC 74, esp pp 99–100. See, too, *Neste OY v Lloyds Bank Ltd* [1983] 2 Lloyd's Rep 658. Earlier authorities include, eg, *Moseley v Cressey's Co* (1865) LR 1 Eq 405.

73   Admittedly, the House of Lords held, in the notorious decision in *Sinclair v Brougham* [1914] AC 398, that a bank taking *ultra vires* deposits somehow counted as a fiduciary for these purposes, so as to give the would-be depositors a proprietary claim against its assets. But this decision has been heavily criticised in England (see, eg, the judgments of Lords Browne-Wilkinson, Slynn and Goff in *Westdeutsche Landesbank Girozentrale v Islington BC* [1996] AC 669) and, it is submitted, should not be followed on this point in Ireland.

74   After *Quistclose Investments Ltd v Barclays Bank Ltd* [1970] AC 567.

75   As in *Re EVTR Ltd* [1987] BCLC 646. Money was lent for a specific purpose on terms of a Quistclose trust; having been used for that purpose, thus exhausting the trust, it was recovered by the borrower's liquidator as a wrongful preference. It was held that the recovered funds were held by the liquidator on trust for the lender.

76   *AG for Hong Kong v Reid* [1994] 1 AC 324 is a straightforward case of tracing into the proceeds of moneys held on constructive trust.

77   See *Re EVTR Ltd* [1987] BCLC 646, above.

he thinks fit. For instance, in *Shanahan's Stamps Ltd v Farelly*,[78] a company solicited, and received, moneys from investors to be specifically invested in stamps on their behalf. When the company collapsed, this was held to give the investors a right against any stamps or other assets they could show had been bought with those funds. Again, it seems clear that an interest in a deceased person's estate will do. Thus, in *Re Diplock*,[79] beneficiaries were held able to trace assets transferred to those not entitled – even though technically, a person entitled to assets from an unadministered estate does not have an equitable interest in anything in particular.[80] But, something capable of being regarded as proprietary is essential: the mere fact that an asset in the defendant's hands derives from knowledge imparted in confidence, for example, will not do.[81]

Moreover – and very significantly – the claimant need not necessarily show a specifically equitable proprietary interest. At least where he can show himself to be the beneficiary of a fiduciary obligation of some sort with regard to the property, it is sufficient to show legal ownership of assets in the hands of, or under the control of, a bailee, agent, employee or similar person.[82]

10-21   It is less clear whether a claimant may lay claim in equity to the proceeds of property to which he has an unencumbered legal title in a situation where he cannot otherwise show any fiduciary relationship. The point arises in particular in the case of straightforward theft: can the owner make any claim in equity to any proceeds in the hands of the thief?[83] There are clear English *dicta* that the answer is 'No'.[84]

But, there are two powerful arguments the other way.

One is based on principles analogous to those applying to resulting trusts. Where I contribute to the purchase by you of an item of property, then unless I intend to make a gift to you I will have an interest in that property by way of resulting trust. It seems odd that my position should be any worse where I do not give you the purchase moneys, but instead you filch them from me.[85]

---

78   [1962] IR 386. See also other 'investment scheme' cases such as *Barlow Clowes International Ltd v Vaughan* [1992] 4 All ER 22.

79   [1948] Ch 465.

80   See, eg, *Comr of Stamp Duties v Livingston* [1965] AC 694, p 707.

81   *Satnam Investments Ltd v Dunlop Heywood and Co Ltd* [1999] 3 All ER 652.

82   One need only cite cases such as *Agip (Africa) Ltd v Jackson* [1991] Ch 547 or *El Ajou v Dollar Land Holdings plc* [1994] 2 All ER 688.

83   It might be thought that this did not matter, given that the owner has a perfectly good claim at common law (above, § 10-5 *et seq*). But, as we shall see, the rules in equity for identifying proceeds are a good deal more generous to the claimant than those existing at common law.

84   A proposition accepted by the CA in *Re Diplock* [1948] Ch 465, p 532, and later reiterated by Fox LJ in *Agip (Africa) Ltd v Jackson* [1991] Ch 547, p 566.

85   A point well made by Chambers: see Chambers, *Resulting Trusts*, pp 21–23 (where certain early Commonwealth authorities supporting it are usefully collected).

Secondly, it is difficult to see any sensible reason why the victim of an ordinary theft should be in any worse position than someone whose assets have been spirited away by an agent, trustee or other fiduciary: a point which has caused the traditional rule to come in for a great deal of criticism – both academic[86] and judicial.[87] In the circumstances, it is suggested that the rule must now be open to serious doubt. It should certainly be regarded as susceptible to revision in the Republic, and by the House of Lords in England.

In any case, whether or not simple theft can allow an equitable claim to proceeds is not of enormous significance in practice. Since most sizeable thefts are embezzlements committed by agents, employees, and the like, who are indubitably fiduciaries, it follows that the victim of theft or fraud will as often as not be able to use both money had and received at common law (relying on his legal ownership) and tracing in equity (relying on his fiduciary relationship with the thief), according to which is more advantageous.[88]

(c) Sufficient connection: identifying the proceeds

10-22 We now turn to the third requirement for an equitable claim to proceeds: that the asset in the defendant's hands is a genuine substitute for, or proceeds of, the claimant's original asset.

In essence, the connection required between these two assets is largely the same in equity as for common law claims. That is, the assets in the defendant's hands must represent the direct or indirect exchange product of the claimant's property. But there is one vital qualification to this. It concerns admixture of the claimant's assets with others. We have seen that this will bar identification at common law, and hence any claim for money had and received against a subsequent recipient. It will not, however, affect the process of identification in equity. Thus in *Agip (Africa) Ltd v Jackson*,[89] dealt with above, the fact that Agip's money had been mixed in the New York clearing system during its transfer into the hands of Zdiri's agents, while it barred any common law right, did not prevent equitable tracing (though in fact this was impossible for another reason,

---

86 Eg, Burrows, p 69.

87 See, particularly, the oft-cited remark in *Black v Freedman* (1910) 12 CLR 105 that even a bare thief is a trustee (and hence, inferentially, a fiduciary). This was quoted without disapproval by Lord Templeman in *Lipkin Gorman v Karpnale Ltd* [1991] 2 AC 548, pp 565–66. In *Metall und Rohstoff AG v Donaldson* [1989] 3 All ER 14, p 57, Slade LJ refused to strike out a claim based on it and in the *Westdeutsche* case Lord Browne-Wilkinson remarked laconically that he thought stolen money was traceable in equity (see [1996] AC 669, p 716). See, too, Lord Millett's comment in *Foskett v McKeown* [1999] AC 102, pp 128–29.

88 So, to take just one example, in *Banque Belge pour l'Étranger v Hambrouck* [1921] 1 KB 321, the plaintiffs relied on both money had and received and equitable tracing.

89 [1991] Ch 547.

namely that the defendants were no longer in possession of any assets representing the plaintiffs' property).

(d) Mixing assets: bank accounts and 'first in, first out'

10-23   We have seen that admixture will not prevent equitable tracing. This in turn, however, raises a further awkward question of principle, in particular where money has been laundered or transferred through one or more bank accounts. Suppose various assets, including mine, are paid by you into your bank account at various times: you then buy a picture, a car, a holiday and so on out of that account. Can I insist on claiming an interest in the picture or the car? Or has my money disappeared with the holiday? The common law ducks this issue by barring all claims at the point of mixture. Equity, by contrast, cannot do this; having decided to take mixture in its stride, it has then in the nature of things to construct some rule as to which payment in corresponds to which payment out. It must in the nature of things be a pretty arbitrary rule; given that a bank account is merely an amorphous running balance between banker and customer, swelled by credits and depleted by drawings, the question which of the former correspond to which of the latter is not susceptible of any logical or rational answer.[90] But, nevertheless, a rule there must be.

10-24   With current accounts, the principle that has been utilised is known as the rule in *Clayton's* case:[91] that is, that *prima facie* drawings on a running account are deemed to take place in the same order as credits, and that this applies to claims by the original equitable owners to the proceeds of those drawings.[92] Put more simply, 'first in, first out'. Thus, in *Re Diplock*,[93] mentioned above, where a given charity had received misapplied assets and paid them into a current account, this principle was applied to determine which of the moneys of the plaintiffs were still in the charity's hands and which had to be regarded as having disappeared. It follows that where my money is paid into your bank account and then that account is drawn on to provide an asset in your hands, I have a claim to that asset if, and only if,[94] I can show, on the 'first in, first out' basis, that my money went into that asset.[95] If on this basis an asset was bought partly with my money and partly with yours, I have a proportionate interest in it, including any rise in its value.[96]

---

90   See, generally, Smith, *The Law of Tracing*, p 183 *et seq*.
91   (1816) 1 Mer 572.
92   *Pennell v Deffell* (1853) 4 De G M & G 372.
93   *Re Diplock* [1948] Ch 465. See, too, *Hancock v Smith* (1889) 41 Ch D 456.
94   *Hancock v Smith* (1889) 41 Ch D 456; *Re Tilley's Will Trusts* [1967] Ch 1179.
95   *Re Diplock* [1948] Ch 465.
96   Cf *Scott v Scott* (1962) 109 CLR 649.

10-25   Because this whole exercise in tracing mixed funds involves the claimant identifying the proceeds of his own assets in the defendant's hands, it follows that however much of the claimant's moneys were originally incorporated in the defendant's account, once these have been drawn out the exercise stops. Moreover, this continues to be so even though there may have been subsequent credits to the account largely balancing the drawings. This is because of the rule in *Roscoe v Winder*,[97] to the effect that inpayments to an account by a defaulting trustee are *prima facie* deemed to be made for his own benefit and not that of the beneficiary whose moneys he has spent elsewhere. Thus, in *Bishopsgate Investment Trust Ltd v Homan*,[98] where the late Robert Maxwell paid stolen pension fund moneys into an account which shortly afterwards became overdrawn, it was held that the pensioners had no claim against anything subsequently bought using cheques drawn on that account. On the other hand, this is only a *prima facie* rule and there is nothing to prevent a delinquent fiduciary manifesting an intent to replace misapplied assets. Such an intent was held apparent in *Re Hughes*[99] where a solicitor, on hearing that he was under investigation by the Law Society, hurriedly took steps to make good moneys improperly removed from his client account.

10-26   On the other hand, the 'first in, first out' rule is heavily qualified. It does not apply to anything other than a running account:[100] indeed, a distinction is drawn in the banking context between current and deposit accounts, with only the former triggering the rule.[101] Nor will it obtain where the beneficial owners of money intend funds provided by them to be mixed generally with others' moneys, as where several persons give to a deserving cause,[102] or pay in to a general investment scheme hoping for substantial returns, where the whole object of the exercise is for investors' funds to be paid into a general pool, as in *Barlow Clowes International Ltd v Vaughan*.[103] Here, the moneys in the account at the time of any claim are deemed to be derived *pari passu* from the funds of those who paid in. And *Clayton's* case is also subject to the 'wrongdoers' lien' provision discussed in greater detail below.[104]

It should be noted that there are disarming *dicta* in *Barlow Clowes*[105] that even where normally *Clayton's* case would be applicable, the courts retain a general

---

97   [1915] 1 Ch 62.

98   [1995] Ch 211.

99   [1970] IR 237.

100   *The Mecca* [1897] AC 286.

101   As happened in *Re Diplock* [1948] Ch 465. This is a little curious, since in 1816, when *Clayton's* case was decided, the distinction between deposit and current accounts had hardly developed.

102   See *Re British Red Cross Balkan Fund* [1914] 2 Ch 419.

103   [1992] 4 All ER 22. See, too, *Re Money Markets International Stockbrokers Ltd* [2000] 3 IR 437, p 452, where Laffoy JJ left the point open.

104   See § 10-28 *et seq*.

105   In particular by Woolf LJ: see [1992] 4 All ER 22, p 39.

discretion to disapply it where it would not be in the interests of justice. But these are only *dicta*, and, it is submitted, they should be treated with caution. There is an inherent undesirability in treating proprietary rights as a matter in the discretion of the courts; furthermore, were such a discretion to exist, the settlement of proceedings arising from misapplied assets would be made a great deal more difficult.

(e) A conundrum: 'backwards tracing'

10-27   On the authorities, in order for me to show that my assets are represented by an exchange product in your hands, you must have received the former before you became owner of the latter. One can, in other words, only trace forwards and not back.

Thus, if you use £10,000 of trust money belonging to me to buy yourself a car, I can claim to trace into the car. But now suppose that, having previously bought the car on credit, you use the £10,000 to pay off the seller. Here, all you got in exchange for the £10,000 was discharge of your debt to the seller: and whatever remedies I might have in respect of that, there is no reason to give me any claim against the car itself. Thus, in *Bishopsgate Investment Management Ltd v Homan*,[106] where the plaintiff's moneys had been spirited away by the late Robert Maxwell and wrongfully paid into the account of a company controlled by him, the Court of Appeal was clear that no possible claim could arise in respect of assets bought out of that account before receipt of the moneys concerned.

(f) A special rule in equity: the lien against property in the wrongdoer's hands

10-28   The equitable tracing claim, as a substitutionary proprietary claim, is available against a wrongdoer mixing trust property with his own, just as it is against anyone else. You credit £1,000 of my trust money to your account which already contains £500, and then buy shares for £1,500 that double in value. I can claim two-thirds of those shares in respect of my £1,000 (and hence a windfall profit of £1,000).[107] But, as mentioned above, this only works if the necessary *nexus* can be shown to identify the trust property with what was bought. Change the facts slightly and suppose you had bought only £500 worth of shares and dissipated the other £1,000. In this situation I would, applying the rule in *Clayton's* case, be

---

106 [1995] Ch 211. But cf Smith [1995] CLJ 290 and the comments of Scott VC in *Foskett v McKeown* in the CA: [1998] Ch 265, p 283 *et seq*. Hobhouse LJ was apparently content to accept the status quo: *ibid*, p 296.
107 *Scott v Scott* (1962) 109 CLR 649.

left high and dry: what derived from my money has disappeared, and that which is left derives from your own assets.

For this reason, if you are a wrongdoer, I have a further, independent right to claim a lien against all moneys remaining in your account, and against anything bought with moneys from it. This is significant for two reasons. First, you may be insolvent and, because of the vagaries of *Clayton's* case I may not be able positively to identify my trust property with anything you still have.[108] Secondly, even if I can get over the problem of identification, the exchange product of my property may have gone down in value. You use £1,000 of my trust fund to buy shares now worth £750. I can claim the shares as the product of my £1,000, but if I do I 'use up' £1,000 of my claim: if, on the other hand, I claim a lien over them, I only exhaust £750 of my claim and can seek to recover the balance of £250 elsewhere.

10-29   At this point, however, an awkward question arises. Suppose a defaulting trustee pays £1,000 trust moneys into an account containing £1,000 of his own, buys shares for £1,000 and dissipates the rest. If the shares rise in value by 20%, can the beneficiary claim the whole £1,200 or is he limited to a charge for the original £1,000? On the basis of *Clayton's* case, the latter solution must be right: the beneficiary simply cannot show that *his* money went to buy the shares.

It is sometimes said, however, that *Clayton's* case is inapplicable to drawings by a wrongdoer,[109] and hence that the beneficiary is entitled to the full £1,200. With respect, however, it is suggested that the authorities do not bear this out. The leading case is *Re Hallett's Estate*.[110] A claim was brought against a credit in a bank account held by a defaulting trustee, in which he had previously admixed some £1,800 of trust moneys. Although the 'first in, first out' rule indicated that only a small proportion of the remaining moneys continued to represent the trust funds, the Master of the Rolls allowed the trust to claim the full £1,800. He said:[111]

> [In] the case of a trustee who has blended trust moneys with his own, it seems to me perfectly plain that he cannot be heard to say that he took away the trust money when he had a right to take away his own money.

But these words are equally consistent with a holding that the trust had a lien over the bank account, which it would have on orthodox principles anyway. Similar reasoning can be applied to *Re Oatway*,[112] where a trustee bought shares out of an improperly mixed fund: since the shares there were worth less than the trust funds originally paid in, there was no difficulty over giving the trust a lien over the entire holding. And that this is indeed the correct analysis of the

---

108 As happened in *Re Hallett's Estate* (1880) 13 Ch D 696.
109 Eg, by Budd J in *Shanahan's Stamp Auctions Ltd v Farelly* [1962] IR 386, p 428.
110 (1880) 13 Ch D 696.
111 (1880) 13 Ch D 696, p 727.
112 [1903] 2 Ch 356.

position is suggested by *Re Tilley's Will Trusts*.[113] A trustee mixed some £2,200 of trust funds in her own account: from the mixed account she then engaged in very successful property dealing over an extended period. Nevertheless, in the absence of proof that, on the basis of *Clayton's* case, her profits derived specifically from trust moneys, the beneficiaries of the trust were denied any proportionate remedy against them: they were instead limited to a charge for the original £2,200.

It is therefore respectfully suggested that, subject to the possibility of asserting a wrongdoer's lien, there is no reason not to apply *Clayton's* case to drawings by wrongdoers as to others.

(g) Equitable tracing: change of position and *bona fide* purchase

10-30 There is no doubt, since *Lipkin Gorman v Karpnale Ltd*,[114] that change of position is a defence to equitable tracing claims.

III DIVERSION CASES

(a) Generally

10-31 So far, this chapter has been concerned with diversion of *assets* – that is, gains coming to you because some third party has caused me to be deprived of property of some sort whose proceeds have ended up in your hands. But there is no necessary reason why my entitlement to restitution need be based on property: as was suggested above, § 10-1, certain other, non-proprietary, rights may equally suffice to give the claimant title to sue. It is to these other cases, where the law provides that accretions to your wealth represent diverted gains that really ought to have come to me, and hence that you must account for them to me, that we now turn.

(b) Profits of property or office

10-32 If I take something of yours and hire it out for my own profit, there is no difficulty in your suing me for that profit through the mechanism of waiver of tort, that is, restitution for wrongs.[115] But, there will not always be a wrong on which to hang a restitutionary claim. Suppose that, owing to either fraud or confusion, I receive the rent of your land without actually displacing you or

---

113 [1967] Ch 1179.
114 [1991] 2 AC 548.
115 See below, Chapter 11.

your tenant.[116] Clearly, you can sue the tenant, since he has not discharged his debt to you by paying me: equally clearly, the tenant (assuming he did not know that he was paying the wrong person) can sue me for money paid by mistake. But can you short-circuit this process and sue me direct? Here I have committed no wrongful act against you; nevertheless, the answer is yes, and I am liable to account directly to you for the rent wrongfully received.[117]

Similarly, too, it has been held, with the profits of an office. No doubt because the distinction between paid office and private investment has at times been blurred in Anglo-Irish history, it has long been held that a person who receives the perquisites of an office to which another is in fact entitled is liable in money had and received to the true holder.[118] In Ireland, where it is arguable that usurpation of office falls to be regarded as a tort,[119] it is just possible that this might be regarded as a species of restitution for wrongs: but there is no equivalent let out in England, where the action is simply for restitution independent of any tort.[120]

And, indeed, it has since been decided that the principle goes beyond office holders as such. In *Jacob v Allen*,[121] a person died apparently intestate. Letters of administration were taken out, and the would-be administrator began to collect sums due to the estate. Later, a valid will came to light. The executor successfully claimed from the administrator those sums collected by him. On a similar basis, an assignor who receives payment of a debt assigned to an assignee is bound to account to the latter. If, for example, a company, having validly assigned its book debts to A, goes into receivership and the receiver then takes payment from a customer, there is no doubt that the receiver is liable to account to A.[122] It is also probable that the liability in equity of an executor *de son tort*[123] and a trustee *de son tort*[124] to pay over assets received can be put on the same basis.[125]

---

116 If I do displace your tenant, I may be liable to you for mesne profits: cf *Official Custodian for Charities v Mackey (No 2)* [1985] 2 All ER 1016.

117 The right is well established. An early example of its successful assertion is *Tottenham v Bedingfield* (1572) Owen 35. See, too, *Arris v Stukeley* (1677) 2 Mod 260; *Asher v Wallis* (1707) 11 Mod 146.

118 Eg, *Arris v Stukeley* (1677) 2 Mod 260; *King v Alston* (1848) 12 QB 971.

119 Assuming *Lawlor v Alton* (1873) IR 8 CL 160 to be correct. It has, it seems, never been followed.

120 In the *Earl of Shrewsbury's* case (1610) 9 Rep 46b, 51a, usurpation of office was apparently regarded as a tort and an action on the case given in respect of it: but this approach was disowned in *Arris v Stukeley* (1677) 2 Mod 260.

121 (1703) Salk 27.

122 Eg, *Aluminium Industrie BV v Romalpa* [1976] 2 All ER 552; *Pfeiffer Weinkellerei GmbH v Arbuthnot Factors Ltd* [1991] BCC 484 (though in the latter case, the claim failed for other reasons).

123 See, eg, *Yardley v Arnold* (1842) C & M 434.

124 Described by AL Smith LJ in *Mara v Browne* [1896] 1 Ch 199.

125 And cf the position of the self-appointed agent, who may be held a constructive trustee of all he has received in the course his *soi-disant* office: *English v Dedham Vale Properties Ltd* [1978] 1 All ER 382.

10-33   In order to succeed in a 'diversionary' claim of this sort, the claimant must of course show he was entitled himself to sue the payer for the moneys received by the defendant.[126] Thus, a landlord cannot claim rent paid by a sub-tenant to a tenant whose lease has been forfeited,[127] nor can an improperly appointed office holder make a claim in respect of misdirected perquisites.[128] And, no doubt for the same reason, it has been held that an office holder can only claim sums he was legally entitled to, and not (for instance) gratuities.[129]

It has been suggested[130] that there is a qualification to these cases, namely that the claimant cannot succeed unless he can show that the payer by paying the defendant got a good discharge for the debt: otherwise, it is argued, the defendant's enrichment is at the payer's expense and not his (since he can still sue the payer). But this limitation is not, it is suggested, supported by any clear authority. On the contrary, what authority there is is against it.[131] Nor does there seem to be any good reason for it on principle. The claimant was clearly entitled to the money (more so, indeed, than the payer): the recipient equally clearly was not. Nor is there any reason on principle why the same enrichment should not be regarded, for the purposes of the law of restitution, as having been at the expense of two people.[132] Furthermore, it seems a waste of everyone's time and money to require two actions here, one by the person entitled against the payer and another by the payer against the actual recipient.[133]

(c) Other cases

10-34   Very commonly, the factor justifying restitution in a third party situation arises out of some existing relation between the parties. The simplest situation is where you receive £100 from X as my agent, or simply on my account. My ability to sue you in contract is decidedly doubtful;[134] nevertheless, in either case, there is

---

126 And, indeed, for precisely those sums. An unliquidated claim against the payer for a sum which may be more or less than the amount received will not do: see *Official Custodian for Charities v Mackey (No 2)* [1985] 2 All ER 1016.

127 *Ibid.*

128 *Bowell v Milbank* (1772) 1 TR 399.

129 *Boyter v Dodsworth* (1796) 6 TR 681.

130 See Smith (1991) OJLS 481.

131 See, in particular, Kelly CB's judgment in *Rusden v Pope* (1868) LR 3 Ex 269, pp 278–79, where he clearly thought that freight paid to the mortgagor of a ship when it should have been paid to the mortgagee could be recovered by the latter from the former even though the person paying for it had notice of the mortgagee's entitlement and hence (presumably) could have been sued over again.

132 See above, §1-28.

133 See also *Official Custodian for Charities v Mackey* [1985] 2 All ER 1016, p 1021, where Nourse J makes precisely this point.

134 On privity grounds, if nothing else: see *Williams v Everett* (1811) 14 East 582; *Leader v Leader* (1871) IR 6 CL 20. *Quaere* whether in England the position would be different today because of the provisions of the Contracts (Rights of Third Parties) Act 1999.

clear authority I can sue you in money had and received for the £100.[135] There is indeed room for the view that a similar rule applies where you do not actually receive £100 from X, but instead you, being debtor to X for £100, agree to pay me:[136] but this is, to say the least, doubtful in the light of certain earlier decisions.[137]

And, similar principles apply in equity. Assume a trustee, without committing a breach of fiduciary duty or using trust property, receives a sum of money deriving from, or attributable to, his trusteeship: for instance, by being appointed a director of a company in which the trust has a shareholding, and being paid as such.[138] Or assume a partner receives a sum of money that, properly construed, represents partnership profits or the price of a partnership asset. In either case, it is a necessary incident of the relationship – trusteeship, partnership, etc – that the sum concerned not be regarded as one's own, but paid over or shared, as the case may be. It is this obligation which equity duly enforces by imposing a duty on the receiver to pay over to the beneficiary.

---

135 As was early established: see, eg, *Beckingham and Lambert v Vaughan* (1616) 1 Rolle Rep 391, and subsequently *Stevens v Hill* (1805) 5 Esp 247. See, generally, Davies (1959) 75 LQR 220.
136 *Shamia v Joory* [1958] 1 QB 448.
137 Notably *Liversidge v Broadbent* (1859) 4 H and Nor 603.
138 Eg, *Re Macadam* [1946] Ch 73.

CHAPTER 11

RESTITUTION FOR WRONGS

I GENERALLY

11-1   In this chapter, there is a shift of focus. From dealing with benefits that reach the defendant through the act of the claimant himself, or by some third party, or by diversion of assets or profits, we now turn to the third logical possibility: benefits accruing to the defendant as a direct result of some wrong committed by him, where the sole ground of restitution is the defendant's own behaviour.

Three preliminary points are in order.

11-2   First, 'wrong' in this connection is used in as general a sense as possible. It covers not only torts, but also breaches of contract, trust and fiduciary duty, all of which give rise to duties of compensation (whether we call such compensation 'damages' or not).[1] It also extends to intellectual property infringements, whether extra-statutory (such as passing off and breach of confidence) or statutory (for example, patent, copyright or trademark infringement). Indeed, the meaning of 'wrong' can perhaps best be summarised as including any act amounting to a breach of duty giving consequences in civil law.[2] This is not, of course, to say that there is any all-embracing rule covering restitutionary recovery for all these varieties of wrong; only that the issues raised are similar, and they are worth dealing with together.

11-3   Secondly, this chapter deals with wrongs as a ground for, rather than merely a background to, restitution: cases, in other words, where the fact that the defendant has gained from a wrong is regarded, *without more*, as sufficient to give the claimant a right to restitution. An example can make this clearer. Suppose you induce me to give you £1,000 by a negligent misrepresentation. It is clear that I can recover the £1,000 in a restitutionary action: furthermore, if there is a suitable special relationship between us,[3] it is equally clear that you are liable to me in tort. Nevertheless, this is not a case of restitution for wrongs; my right to £1,000 from you is based on my mistake, not your tort. Now imagine, by contrast, that you are my trustee and make £1,000 from information obtained in your capacity as such. In so far as you are bound to make restitution at all,[4] this

---

1   Eg, compensation for losses caused by a breach of trust, or liability for dishonest assistance in a breach of fiduciary duty.
2   But not including, eg, confiscation by the State of the proceeds of crime, which is better regarded as a branch of criminal law.
3   Under the rule in *Hedley Byrne and Co Ltd v Heller and Partners Ltd* [1964] AC 462.
4   See below, § 11-24 *et seq*.

is genuine restitution for wrongs. Your duty to give me the £1,000 is genuinely based on the fact that you committed a wrong – in this case, a breach of trust.

11-4   Thirdly, we are dealing here with cases where remedies are *in fact* given to reverse enrichment resulting from a wrong, whatever labels the courts attach to them. As we shall see, damages can be an unjustified enrichment remedy just as much as more traditional restitutionary remedies such as waiver of tort or account of profits. The analytical point that damages are meant to reflect the claimant's loss rather than to recoup the defendant's gain is not necessarily borne out in practice; to the extent that damages exceed the loss suffered by the claimant, there is no reason not to call them restitutionary.

II THE POINT OF PRINCIPLE: WHEN SHOULD RESTITUTION FOR WRONGS BE PERMITTED?

11-5   All this, of course, leaves unanswered a more fundamental question; why do we have a category of restitution for wrongs at all? The answer is not immediately obvious. In all the other cases of restitution, there is not only a gain to the defendant, but something done, or at least lost (actually or potentially) by the claimant. The remedy is therefore aimed, at least partly, at giving effect to a form of corrective justice. No such justification exists in the case of restitution for wrongs.

One strand of thinking lying behind recovery for wrongs is the idea that the law should pursue a general policy of preventing anyone from profiting from his wrong, at least where he has acted deliberately. 'The broad proposition that a wrongdoer should not be allowed to profit from his wrong,' said Lord Nicholls, 'has an obvious attraction.'[5] Coupled with this is, of course, the idea of deterrence: deliberate infringement of others' rights ought to be discouraged, even at the cost of allowing claimants to obtain an occasional windfall. The possibility of exemplary damages for deliberate wrongs aimed at making a profit is a clear instance of such thinking. It is exemplified by Lord Devlin's *dictum* in the English case of *Rookes v Barnard*[6] that 'tort should not pay',[7] together (in England) with at least one statutory instance.[8] Largely on this basis, it has been further argued by Jones and others[9] that cynical breaches of contract and other deliberate wrongs calculated to make a profit ought to trigger a restitutionary response – a suggestion accepted, albeit *obiter*, by the High Court

---

5   *AG v Blake* [2001] 1 AC 268, p 278. The context was restitutionary damages for breach of contract: see below, § 11-8 *et seq*.

6   [1964] AC 1129.

7   *Ibid*, p 1227.

8   See Housing Act 1988, s 28 (damages for wrongful eviction to include any gain in value of house through availability of vacant possession).

9   Goff & Jones, p 521; Birks, p 326 *et seq*. Cf Edelman [2000] RLR 129.

in Ireland in *Hickey v Roches Stores Ltd*.[10] (In that case, however, the breach of contract involved was neither deliberate nor cynical, so the question did not arise.) This proposition has, however, found little favour in England. In *AG v Blake*,[11] Lord Steyn specifically rejected it as a criterion for awarding restitutionary damages for breach of contract.[12]

11-6 It is respectfully suggested that the courts have been right to be sceptical about creating a general right to restitution for deliberate wrongs. Grant that you do not deserve to keep profit made as a result of wronging me: this does not show that I – as against, say, the State in the case of a criminal act – should have any right to claim it from you, if I cannot show any other specific ground (for example, duress or mistake) to justify recovery.[13] Indeed, there is a good case for arguing precisely the contrary: that once you have paid for any losses your activities cause, *prima facie* you ought, in a free society, to be able to go about your business without further hindrance; the law ought not, without strong justification, to go further and insist that you justify your retention of the other assets you happen to have. The decision of the English Court of Appeal in *Halifax Building Society v Thomas*[14] illustrates the point nicely. T obtained a 100% mortgage on a certain property by deception, on which he later defaulted. The building society exercised its right of sale, which (unusually, because of the steeply rising housing market) left a surplus after discharging the loan. Although T had clearly profited from his wrong, the society failed in its claim against him. Instead, the court held that the profit was caught by a compensation order imposed on T in prior criminal proceedings.

11-7 If, then, it should not be enough merely for the claimant to show that the defendant has profited from what he did, some separate justification has to be found for awarding restitutionary relief for wrongs. As a matter of principle, it is suggested below that there are two particular situations which are likely to justify an exceptional award of this sort. One is where the right that has been infringed is a 'tradable' right: that is, a right which is not inalienable or essentially personal, but instead which the holder has some legitimate interest in selling or turning into money if he wishes. The other is where the duty broken includes an obligation of loyalty: more precisely, where the defendant is under some express or implied obligation not to turn his position to profit at the expense of the claimant.[15] These, it will be suggested below, inform much of the present law on the subject, though the correspondence is not exact.

---

10 (1976) (reported at [1993] RLR 196: see, esp [1993] RLR 208).
11 [2001] 1 AC 268.
12 [2001] 1 AC 268, p 291. See, too, *Surrey CC v Bredero Homes Ltd* [1993] 3 All ER 705, discussed below, § 11-21.
13 Cf *Halifax Building Society v Thomas* [1996] Ch 217, p 229.
14 [1996] Ch 217.
15 Cf the argument in Worthington (1999) 62 MLR 218.

(a) Infringement of tradable rights

11-8   The first case is where the right infringed is a property or other right which exists at least partly for the purpose of being traded or turned into money.[16] The reason for imposing restitutionary liability here is that a defendant who infringes such a right should not be able by his wrongful act to escape the bargaining process.[17]

Property rights are obviously the prime example of the kind of tradable right involved here. If I wrongfully sell your goods, I should have to account for the proceeds. The same argument must apply if I gain a benefit from dealing with them in other ways: for example, using them or hiring them out. And, of course, similar reasoning must apply to property of other sorts. If I remain on your land after my right to do so has disappeared (for example, because my licence to be there has come to an end), I should have to pay an occupation rent. Again, most intellectual property rights are freely licensable. Copyright exists to be licensed in order to provide authors with an income, and there is undoubtedly a flourishing market in know-how and other commercial information. It follows that there is a strong argument for granting restitution in cases of infringement – for example, breach of copyright or confidence.

It is not difficult to see, however, that not all rights can be looked at in this way. The right not to be assaulted or injured, for example, is not like a property or similar right, existing to be bought and sold: it is a right personal to the claimant, existing for his protection alone. It follows, it is suggested, that if someone pays you £100 to beat me up, there is no reason to allow me to recover this sum rather than the actual loss I have suffered.

11-9   Should the category of 'tradable rights' extend to contractual rights, so that the contract breaker presumptively ought to be liable to pay over any profits made as a result?

On one level, the instinctive answer appears to be 'Yes'. After all, contractual rights can be, and indeed frequently are, waived or traded for money. A person who breaks a contract without first asking his co-contractor what he would charge for release of his rights is, in a sense, bypassing the bargaining process. Moreover, if restitutionary damages are not available, certain breaches of contract will go entirely unremedied. (For example, a builder who, in breach of contract, substitutes for the materials stipulated cheaper but equally efficacious ones simply increases his profit at the expense of the client's right to get what he

---

16 This point is well made by Jackman [1989] CLJ 302. His reference to 'facilitative institutions' allowing the creation of private agreements or arrangements between people is largely equivalent to rights existing with a view to being traded.

17 Indeed, there is a great deal in common with this strand of thinking and the concept, referred to above, § 5-13, of 'advantage-taking', dealing with the situation where, without committing a wrong, the defendant takes advantage of a service which he knows is intended by the claimant providing it only to be available for payment.

contracted for.)[18] As a result, there has been considerable academic pressure for a measure of restitutionary recovery here, at least in the case of deliberate breach.[19]

Nevertheless, it is respectfully suggested that these arguments in favour of restitutionary recovery are not as strong as they seem. However unsympathetic one may be towards the builder who surreptitiously uses ersatz materials, if in fact the client gets a house as good in every respect as what he stipulated for,[20] the injustice to him is not very great if he receives no substantial recovery. There is also the well known point based on the economic doctrine of 'efficient breach' – that if a contract is broken profitably to the contract-breaker,[21] that is evidence that social goods are distributed more optimally – which, though of little practical importance, is still relevant. Two further points are also worth making. First, a contracting party, unlike the victim of other sorts of wrong, is *ex hypothesi* already in relations with his co-contractor; as a result, he can choose the terms on which he deals. Given that he is already protected against actual loss suffered as a result of breach, it does not seem unfair to say that if he wishes the extra advantage of being able to strip a contract-breaker of his profit, he should be expected to stipulate for it. Secondly, it must be remembered that a good many breaches of contract will involve breaches of a duty of loyalty, in which case there is a separate argument for restitutionary recovery anyway.

(b) Obligations of loyalty

11-10   The other category of cases where restitutionary recovery is justified concerns obligations of loyalty, or (to use the more traditional term) fiduciary duties. The reason for treating these as another special category is, it is suggested, lies in the nature of the duties themselves. Although they are extremely varied, the essence of most fiduciary duties is an obligation specifically to exercise a power in the interest of someone else, and not to turn it to one's own separate advantage.[22] Examples include the duty owed by a trustee to his beneficiary, an agent to his principal, a partner to the partnership generally, and so on. There is, as it were, built into relationships of this sort an understanding that benefits accruing as a result of the fiduciary's efforts are to accrue, in whole or in part, to the beneficiary, and are not to be diverted. If so, giving the claimant a right to profits

---

18   Cf *Samson v Proctor* [1975] NZLR 665, and the notorious Louisiana case of *City of New Orleans v Firemen's Charitable Association*, 9 So 486 (1891).

19   Jones (1983) 99 LQR 443. A more moderate line is taken by Goodhart [1995] RLR 3.

20   And, it must be remembered that this is an exacting condition. If the building is in fact below standard, there is no reason why some damages for breach of contract should not be awarded, even though the defect may be purely cosmetic. For a case of this sort, cf *Samson v Proctor* [1975] NZLR 665.

21   On which the literature is voluminous. Posner, *Economic Analysis of Law* (3rd edn), p 107, sums it up well.

22   This largely follows the instructive analysis in Shepherd (1981) 97 LQR 51.

made as a result of a breach is not so much supplementing the underlying obligation as giving full effect to it.

The contrast between relationships of this sort and ordinary contractual relations is not difficult to see. In the latter case, we simply have exchanges of goods and services for money with each side taking the risks of incidental gains and losses: there is no element of any duty to exercise powers for the other's benefit. If so, it is suggested that the idea that restitutionary recovery should be available in the former, but not the latter case immediately becomes understandable.

III CASES WHERE RESTITUTION FOR WRONGS IS AVAILABLE

(a) Restitution for torts

The availability of exemplary damages

11-11   A tort action *prima facie* lies for the claimant's loss, no more, no less. However, exemplary damages may be awarded in respect of certain deliberate torts – notably defamation, trespass, assault, false imprisonment and malicious prosecution. According to the House of Lords' judgment in *Rookes v Barnard*,[23] they are available in two cases (apart, of course, from where statute specifically allows them). One is high-handed or deliberately illegal actions by public authorities, with which we are not concerned here. The other, more significantly, is where a tort has been deliberately committed with a view to making a profit even when any possible award of damages is taken into account. To this extent (it is thought) deterrence should be applicable: tort should not pay, at least where it is committed deliberately.[24]

This latter area of recovery obviously has important restitutionary implications (although, as has been suggested above, its moral foundation may be a little shaky). Thus, in *Cassell and Co Ltd v Broome*,[25] where the plaintiff was knowingly defamed in a book with a view to the possible profits easily outstripping any likely award of damages, an award of exemplary damages in the then very substantial sum of £25,000 was upheld. Moreover, for these purposes, a saving of expense counts as a profit, as it does elsewhere in the law of restitution: thus, a decision not to withdraw an issue of a paper in order to save the costs of pulping and reprinting can give rise to exemplary recovery.[26]

---

23   [1964] AC 1129.

24   *Rookes v Barnard* [1964] AC 1129, p 1226 (Lord Devlin). See, too, *Cassell and Co Ltd v Broome* [1972] AC 1027, p 1073 (Lord Hailsham); and, more recently, *John v MGN Ltd* [1998] QB 598.

25   [1972] AC 1027. See too *Manson v Associated Newspapers* [1965] 1 WLR 1038.

26   *Maxwell v Pressdram Ltd* (1986) *The Times*, 22 November.

In Ireland, the position is probably the same. The approach in *Hickey v Roches Stores*[27] to deliberate breach of contract is presumably applicable by analogy to torts: furthermore, in *Whelan v Madigan*,[28] where a landlord deliberately interfered with his tenants' property in order to get rid of them and obtain a better rent from someone else, Kenny J apparently accepted the *Rookes v Barnard* position (though in the event, he decided in his discretion not to award punitive damages). Nevertheless, the restitutionary thinking behind exemplary damages should not be exaggerated. In particular, there is no necessary correlation between the amount of any profit and the measure of damages: indeed, it seems exemplary damages are still available even if the defendant, while he aimed to make a profit from his tort, actually made none at all.[29]

It has been held in England that punitive damages under this head are specifically limited to where the defendant knew of the wrongfulness of his act and deliberately intended his gains to exceed any compensation payable.[30] Subject to this restriction, however, they are available on principle for any tort.[31] In Ireland, the position is less clear,[32] and may well develop in a different direction.

Tort damages: gain masquerading as loss

11-12 Suppose I borrow your car and return it a week late. Suppose, further, that during that time you would not in fact have used it. Damages in conversion are at large, and there is English authority that they may in suitable cases be measured not by your loss, which is nil, but at the reasonable hire value of the car for the extra period.[33] Similar principles apply to trespass to land. If I purportedly exercise a right of way I do not have over your property,[34] or repeatedly drive my vehicles over your land in the course of my business, or use

---

27   (1976) unreported.

28   [1978] ILRM 136. Similar English cases are *Drane v Evangelou* [1978] 2 All ER 437 and *Guppys (Bridport) Ltd v Brookling* (1984) 14 HLR 1. The matter is now partly covered by statute in England: see the Housing Act 1988, s 28.

29   *John v MGN Ltd* [1998] QB 598, p 624.

30   See *Riches v News Group Newspapers Ltd* [1985] 2 All ER 845, p 861 (Parker LJ). Hence the mere fact that all newspapers are published for profit will not do: see *Broadway Approvals v Odhams Press Ltd* [1965] 1 WLR 805.

31   *Kuddus v Chief Constable of Leicestershire* [2001] 3 All ER 193.

32   In *Conway v Irish National Teachers' Organisation* [1991] 2 IR 305, exemplary damages were awarded for deprivation of the constitutional right to education, and to this extent the limitations of *Rookes v Barnard* were rejected. In *Cooper v O'Connell* (1997) unreported, 5 June, the Supreme Court left it open whether they were available in negligence, merely deciding that even if they were, this was not a suitable case to award them.

33   *Strand Electric Co v Brisford Entertainments Ltd* [1952] 2 QB 246; *Hillesden Securities Ltd v Ryjack Ltd* [1983] 2 All ER 184. But see *Saleh Farid v Theodorou* (1992) unreported, 30 January, CA. The *Strand Electric* case was accepted as rightly decided by the High Court in Ireland in *Hickey v Roches Stores Ltd* (1976) [1993] RLR 196, p 202.

34   *Jaggard v Sawyer* [1995] 2 All ER 189.

it as a dumping ground for my waste,[35] I may be liable to you not simply for any damage I do, but for a reasonable sum by way of wayleave or dumping charge. The action for *mesne* profits available against a wrongful occupier of land as part and parcel of a judgment for possession is another example.[36] Yet again, damages for infringement of patent or copyright, or for misuse of confidential commercial information, are not infrequently assessed at the sum the infringer might reasonably have expected to have to pay by way of royalty.[37]

11-13   This particular way of measuring damages is, however, in its nature limited to torts involving infringement of property rights and the like (including intellectual property); the idea of a reasonable charge for permission to commit other torts, such as libel or assault, is hardly attractive. Indeed, an extremely restrictive view was taken of it, and any substantial extension ruled out, by the English Court of Appeal in *Stoke-on-Trent CC v W and J Wass Ltd.*[38] The plaintiff was entitled to the benefit of a franchise to hold a market in Stoke-on-Trent, the effect of which was to make it an actionable nuisance for anyone to hold a rival market within some six miles. The defendants wrongfully opened their own market within that distance; nevertheless, it was held that the plaintiff's remedy against them was limited to damages for loss suffered, and that it was not open to it to rely on the 'licence fee' cases and claim a proportion of the defendants' (not inconsiderable) profits from the rival operation. This is, it must be said, a very narrow decision, and difficult to support. The plaintiff's right, being a limited monopoly, was closely analogous to an intellectual property right, such as the right to prevent passing off. Furthermore, it was the sort of right whose relaxation for a money payment would presumably have been unobjectionable. For these reasons it is to be hoped that whatever the English position, Irish courts, at least, will regard it with some scepticism.

Waiver of tort

11-14   In the previous two causes of action, restitution comes in (as it were) interstitially, on the back of some other principle. Waiver of tort,[39] by contrast, raises it directly. In certain cases, a tort victim can elect to claim not his loss, but

---

35   *Jegon v Vivian* (1871) LR 6 Ch App 742; *Whitwham v Westminster Brymbo Coal Co* [1892] 2 Ch 538; *Bracewell v Appleby* [1975] 1 All ER 993. And cf *Swordheath Properties Ltd v Tabet* [1979] 1 All ER 240, p 242.

36   On which see, eg, *Ministry of Defence v Ashman* [1993] 2 EGLR 102. Note that in that case, the restitutionary aspect of the action was emphasised: the ministry recovered the value of the wrongful occupation to the defendant, without reference to the amount they could actually have got from letting the property to someone else.

37   Eg *General Tire and Rubber Co v Firestone Tyre and Rubber Co Ltd (No 2)* [1975] 2 All ER 173 (patent); *Stovin-Bradford v Volpoint Ltd* [1971] 3 All ER 571 (copyright).

38   [1988] 3 All ER 394.

39   'Waiver' not in the sense that the claimant condones or forgives the wrong, but because he must elect between this cause of action and one for damages *tout court*. See *United Australia Ltd v Barclays Bank Ltd* [1941] AC 1.

the cash proceeds or other profits gained by the defendant. The cause of action is, technically, money had and received, and is distinct from that for the tort itself.[40] This may be significant. Thus, s 234(4) of the English Insolvency Act 1986 protects a company liquidator who innocently seizes property apparently belonging to the company from liability for 'loss or damage' suffered by the true owner (tort): but fairly clearly leaves intact the owner's ability to waive the tort and sue him for the proceeds.

The commonest use of waiver of tort is in connection with the wrongful sale or use of goods. The claimant can waive the tort of detinue[41] or conversion, and elect to claim the actual amount paid to the defendant rather than the value of what was wrongfully dealt with.[42] Liability is not dependent on knowledge by the defendant of the wrongfulness of his act.

11-15 It is nevertheless clear that waiver of tort is not limited to the property torts. It can apply equally – though perhaps with less justification – to the seduction of a menial servant,[43] and possibly to economic torts such as inducement of breach of contract.[44] What is doubtful is whether it will go further than this. The decision in *Phillips v Homfray*[45] is clear authority against extending it to trespass to land, although this is fairly unimportant in practice since, as we saw above,[46] damages themselves will often reflect the reasonable value of the defendant's use of the land in question. And despite early authority in favour of waiver of deceit,[47] *Halifax Building Society v Thomas*,[48] holding that a building society has no claim to profits accruing to a borrower guilty of mortgage fraud against it, now suggests a contrary answer. As for torts such as libel, in view of the limitations on exemplary damages there,[49] it is most unlikely that the courts will allow these controls to be sidestepped by the creation of any general right to waive that tort.

---

40 See, eg, *Chesworth v Farrer* [1967] 1 QB 107, where it was held that the action for proceeds of goods converted was not subject to limitation period applicable to actions in tort. This particular distinction is no longer relevant in either jurisdiction, but the point of principle remains. Similarly, the action was unaffected by the rule that one could not sue a dead tortfeasor: but as this rule has been abolished in all jurisdictions, this does not now matter either.

41 In the Republic only. Detinue no longer exists in England or NI: see Torts (Interference with Goods) Act 1977, s 2(1).

42 Eg, *Hambly v Trott* (1776) 1 Cowp 371.

43 Eg, *Lightly v Clouston* (1808) 1 Taunt 112. But, in Ireland, it was seemingly held not to apply to seduction of the plaintiff's wife: *Maher v Collins* [1975] IR 232.

44 See Goff & Jones, p 784.

45 (1883) 24 Ch D 439.

46 See above, § 11-12.

47 *Madden v Kempster* (1807) 1 Camp 12; *Hill v Perrott* (1810) 3 Taunt 274.

48 [1996] Ch 217.

49 See above, § 11-11.

Indeed, since the refusal by the English Court of Appeal in *AB v South West Water Services Ltd*[50] to extend exemplary damages beyond the torts for which they had traditionally been awarded (the tort in issue there being nuisance), it is likely that the courts will not allow this principle to be outflanked by similar attempts to extend the range of torts that can be waived. It is also worth remembering that in the case of intellectual property rights, the remedy of account of profits has long been available:[51] if so, it is even more likely that the courts will think there is no general need for a cause of action for actual profits made from wrongdoing.

11-16 Moreover, subject to the following paragraph, it is respectfully suggested that this reluctance is right. Exemplary damages apart (and accepted as anomalous), the torts where some remedy is available to the claimant against the profits made by the defendant are broadly those connected with the protection of property, that is, aimed at preventing the defendant from enriching himself by using that which is not his. Elsewhere, at least in the absence of knowing wrongdoing, there is less call for stripping the defendant of his gains.

Waiver of tort: non-cash gains

11-17 Most cases of waiver of tort have hitherto been for straightforward money profit. There is no reason why on principle, however, it should not extend to other sorts of gains, such as items of property,[52] or saving of inevitable expenditure. On the other hand, it is unlikely whether on present English authority it would. In the mining case of *Phillips v Homfray*,[53] the defendant and his partners unlawfully led coals over (or rather, under) the plaintiff's property. After the defendant died, and with him any cause of action for damages in tort,[54] an attempt was made to waive the tort of trespass and recover from the defendant's estate the expense thus saved. But this failed, partly on the ground that such negative savings could not form the subject of an action for money had and received. Today, the matter is of largely academic interest, since – as mentioned above – damages for trespass may include a reasonable charge for use of the land, and the action for damages will survive against the deceased's estate.[55]

---

50   [1993] QB 507.

51   See, generally, Burrows, *Remedies for Torts and Breach of Contract*, 2nd edn, p 299 *et seq*.

52   See *Hill v Perrott* (1810) 3 Taunt 274 (goods delivered as a result of fraud).

53   (1883) 24 Ch D 439.

54   As the law then stood. See, now, the Civil Liability Act 1961, s 8 (Ireland); Law Reform (Miscellaneous Provisions) Act 1934, s 1(1) (England).

55   See the statutory provisions in the previous note.

(b) Restitution for breach of contract[56]

11-18   As with tort, so, *prima facie*, with contract; if I can break my contract with you, pay you damages and still come out with a profit, there is normally[57] nothing you can do to extract that profit from me. (Indeed, I may do rather better, since at least in England, breach of contract cannot give rise to exemplary damages either.)[58]

Thus, in *Surrey CC v Bredero Homes Ltd*,[59] building land was sold subject to a stipulation limiting the number of houses to be constructed by the buyer to no more than 72. In breach of contract, the buyer built 77 houses instead. The council, having discovered this fact, but being unable to show any loss to itself, was limited to nominal damages, with no claim in respect of the extra profit made by the builder by exceeding the agreed density. Nor was the court impressed with an attempt to argue that the victim of a contractual breach should be regarded as having lost the amount a reasonable person would have charged for release of the obligation in question: as Dillon LJ remarked with some force, it was somewhat unreal to base awards of damages on a hypothetical bargain that no one ever contemplated in the first place.[60]

Again, however, as with tort, this principle is by no means absolute. Indeed, the House of Lords in *AG v Blake*[61] made it clear that, while the general rule was to limit contract damages to the claimant's loss, there was no doctrinal reason not to reckon them by the defendant's gain if justice so demanded. So, in that actual case (discussed in more detail below), an ex-member of the intelligence services was held liable to repay to the British Government the profits from a book published in breach of his employment contract.

We now turn to the various cases where, exceptionally, restitutionary damages are available.

---

56   Birks (1993) 109 LQR 518.

57   Unless, of course, you have some other independent ground of restitution, such as the existence of a fiduciary relationship. Again, a contracted vendor of land who wrongfully sells to a third party at a profit has to account for that profit to the purchaser; but this results not from his breach of contract, but from the fact that on signing the contract he held the subject matter on constructive trust for the purchaser.

58   See *Perera v Vandiyar* [1953] 1 WLR 672. In Ireland, exemplary damages have been awarded for wrongful dismissal: see *Garvey v Ireland* (1979) unreported, 19 December. But this was a case of a State employee (a Garda), where there may have been good constitutional reasons for such an award; and it is not clear whether the same result would follow against a private employer.

59   [1993] 3 All ER 705. See too *Tito v Waddell (No 2)* [1977] Ch 106, p 332 (Megarry VC).

60   See [1993] 3 All ER, pp 712–13. But cf *Jaggard v Sawyer* [1995] 2 All ER 189, and Sharpe and Waddams (1982) 2 OJLS 290.

61   [2001] 1 AC 268. Cf the similar result reached 20 years earlier in the US: *Snepp v US*, 444 US 507 (1980).

Contracts providing for payment over of profits arising from breach

11-19   It seems that there is no objection to a contract providing expressly or impliedly that certain acts are not to be done without the consent of one or other party, and that if they are, any profits must be paid over to that party. A neat example is a contract of agency: an agent who takes a bribe is guilty of a breach of contract, and has simply on this account to pay it over to his principal, quite apart from any liability for breach of fiduciary duty.[62] Express agreements to similar effect are often found in sales of potential development land: the plot concerned is sold on the basis that no development is to be carried out by the purchaser without the vendor's consent, and that if the purchaser does develop, a proportion of any planning gain goes to the vendor. Although it might seem that such a clause was open to attack as a penalty,[63] it is suggested that the better view ought to be to the contrary.[64] It would be, to say the least, surprising if such agreements turned out to be unenforceable.

Breach of contract amounting also to infringement of a property or tradable right

11-20   Suppose you agree to garage my car for a week for £10. In breach of contract, I leave it there for a fortnight. Assuming your garage would otherwise have remained empty (that is, you cannot show loss through having had to find alternative accommodation for your own car, or because of a lost opportunity to hire out the garage to somebody else), what can you recover from me? According to the decision in *Penarth Dock Engineering Co Ltd v Pounds*,[65] your measure of damages is analogous to that in tort for trespass or conversion,[66] that is, the reasonable hire value of the garage for the extra week. The fact that you might not in fact have used the garage yourself is irrelevant.

Restitution for infringement of a property right may also be the explanation for cases such as *Wrotham Park Estates Ltd v Parkside Homes Ltd*,[67] allowing an apparently restitutionary measure of damages for breach of a restrictive covenant affecting land. This point is covered in more detail below.

---

62   Eg, *Industries and General Mortgage Co Ltd v Lewis* [1949] 2 All ER 573.

63   Cf *Schiesser International Ltd v Gallagher* (1971) 106 ILTR 22 (penalty to stipulate for repayment of employee's training costs if employee resigned at any time within three years).

64   Cf *Alder v Moore* [1961] 2 QB 57 (payment to disabled footballer on terms that he was not to play professionally again: no objection to clause requiring repayment if he did).

65   [1963] 1 Lloyd's Rep 359 (defendant's property overstaying welcome at plaintiff's wharf).

66   Ie, under the principle illustrated in *Strand Electric Co Ltd v Brisford Entertainments Ltd* [1952] 2 QB 246.

67   [1974] 2 All ER 321.

Breach of contract not to do something without consent: the covenant cases

11-21   Suppose a valid restrictive covenant between two landowners, A and B, prevents A building in his garden without B's consent; suppose further that A breaks it. Assuming B's land is not depreciated as a result, can he recover anything more than nominal damages?

In *Wrotham Park Estates Ltd v Parkside Homes Ltd*,[68] a positive answer was given, on partly restitutionary reasoning. The defendant, a speculative builder, put up a number of new houses in defiance of a long standing restrictive covenant entered into by a predecessor in title in favour of the plaintiff. The plaintiff sought an injunction requiring their demolition, but failed. Instead, it was awarded damages on the basis of the savings made by the defendant through not seeking release of the covenant before beginning work, set *faute de mieux* at 5% of the defendant's profits, being the amount that might reasonably have been asked for such a release if requested.

Matters are made more awkward, however, by the later decision of the Court of Appeal in *Surrey CC v Bredero Homes Ltd*,[69] where (as we have seen) on very similar facts a remedy was denied in excess of actual loss suffered. The cases were almost identical, the only distinction between them being that: (a) whereas in *Wrotham* the covenant bound the land, and hence the defendants' acts could be referred to in a loose sense as an infringement of property rights, in *Bredero* it was only enforceable *inter partes*; and (b) damages were sought in lieu of an injunction in *Wrotham*, whereas in *Bredero* they were sought at common law.

Neither distinction, however, is very convincing. No doubt for this reason, Lord Browne Wilkinson in *AG v Blake*[70] seems to have seen the cases as contradictory.[71] His own preference was clearly for the *Wrotham Park* case, which he regarded as a 'solitary beacon' as against the 'difficult' decision in *Bredero*.[72] It is suggested, moreover, that this is in accordance with principle. Covenants with respect to land are essentially tradable rights: unlike contracts generally, they are normally entered into with one eye on their release for money. If so, there is much to be said for awarding damages based on a reasonable charge for release where the defendant has failed to bargain for the right to infringe them.

---

68   [1974] 2 All ER 321.
69   [1993] 3 All ER 705.
70   2001] 1 AC 268.
71   *Ibid*, p 283.
72   *Ibid*.

Breach of contract and breach of fiduciary duty

11-22　As mentioned above, some breaches of fiduciary duty, such as the duty of an employee or agent not to make an uncovenanted profit from his position, are also breaches of contract. Where this is so, for instance, where an ex-employee uses secret information gained from his employment in order to make a profit, there is clearly no objection to restitutionary recovery for breach of the duty concerned.[73] Nevertheless, the fact that the parties have chosen to regulate their relationship fairly closely as a matter of contract may make the courts a little reluctant to spell out a fiduciary relationship as well, as shown by the Australian decision in *US Surgical Corp v Hospital Products Corp*.[74] There, a sole distributorship agreement was flagrantly broken by the defendant distributor, causing considerable profit to itself and substantial but pretty unquantifiable losses to the plaintiff. It was held by the High Court of Australia that no fiduciary relationship arose, the plaintiffs being limited in remedy to such loss as they could prove they had suffered.

Other cases

11-23　As was briefly mentioned above, the prospect of wider recovery of restitutionary damages for breach of contract was put firmly on the agenda in 2000 by the House of Lords' decision in *AG v Blake*.[75] A notorious spy, who had been imprisoned in England for passing on secrets, but had later escaped to Russia, wrote a profitable book in which he revealed details of his work for the British security service. The publication was not a breach of confidence,[76] but it was a breach of his contract of employment. By a majority, the House of Lords decided that the defendant should be liable to pay over those profits as damages for breach of contract. Lord Nicholls, who delivered the leading judgment, said that there was no necessary bar to restitutionary damages in any kind of contract, though such damages were exceptional. Unfortunately, he gave no clear criteria for deciding when they were appropriate.[77] Nevertheless, he thought that they were justified in that case on the grounds that the disclosures, while not a breach of confidence, were closely analogous to one.

73　For a spectacular example, see *LAC Minerals v International Corona Resources* [1989] 2 SCR 574 (profitable misuse of information on mining concession: constructive trust imposed on profits).

74　(1984) 58 ALJR 587.

75　[2001] 1 AC 268.

76　Since all the information was by then in the public domain.

77　His suggestion that it was a 'useful general guide' to ask whether the claimant had a 'legitimate interest' in preventing the defendant's profitable activity ([2001] 1 AC 268, p 285), with respect, adds very little.

(c) Restitution for breach of trust or fiduciary duty

11-24 Turning from breach of contract and tort to breach of trust and other cases of infringement of fiduciary duty, the contrast is striking: the duty to account for profits wrongly made suddenly stops being an anomaly, and becomes the norm. This disparate treatment of what are, at bottom, simply different species of wrong is at first sight odd: but, as suggested above, it is explicable on the ground of the nature of the duties themselves. Trusts are about the duty to look after, and hence not profit from misusing, others' assets. The duties of agents, company directors, partners, and others normally reckoned to be in a fiduciary position are duties not only to serve those others' interests, but to provide unbiased judgment in doing so. If so, it is hardly surprising that the law should be so willing to impose on such people a *prima facie* duty not to profit from their position, and to pay over any gains when they do, and that further, it should give their beneficiaries title to sue for restitution of it.

Trustees

11-25 Two particular duties of a trustee are relevant to this chapter: his duty not to make a profit out of the trust property itself, or from his position in relation to it, and his more extensive duty not to put himself in a position where he might face a conflict of interest. If he breaks either, he will hold on constructive trust for his beneficiary any gains made as a result.[78] As regards the first of these duties, the classic example always cited is that of the renewal of a lease, where ever since *Keech v Sandford*[79] the trustee has been held to hold the renewed lease at the disposal of the beneficiary, unless he can show that his interest is in substance an entirely new lease rather than a continuation of the old, and that he did not use his position in any way to get it.[80] Other cases include a trustee being paid as a director of a company in which the trust holds shares,[81] and the notorious decision in *Boardman v Phipps*.[82] An adviser to a trust discovered in his capacity as such that a company in which the trust had a substantial holding was badly managed; there was little doubt that large profits could be made by taking it over entirely and reconstructing it. The trust being unable to provide all the necessary capital, the adviser put up part of it himself. He was held liable to repay to the beneficiaries[83] the profit he had made, even though it had been gained with his own money.

---

78 A point well made by Deane J in the Australian decision in *Chan v Zacharia* (1984) 154 CLR 178.

79 (1726) 1 Eq Cas Abr 741.

80 As happened in *Dempsey v Ward* [1899] 1 IR 463 (beneficiary's lease forfeited for breach of covenant: new lease in favour of trustee allowed to stand). And see the instructive decision in *Re Biss* [1903] 2 Ch 40.

81 *Re Macadam* [1946] Ch 73.

82 [1967] 2 AC 46.

83 Except, of course, those who had consented.

11-26 The second situation, conflict of duty, does not arise so often. It is typified by cases concerning trustees of a leasehold interest who take the opportunity to buy in the reversion, thus potentially putting themselves in the position of both lessor and lessee.[84] The rule in England has been held to apply to all such purchases whatever the merits,[85] making the trustee a constructive trustee of the reversion; but in Ireland it is arguable that it will not be invoked unless there is some real prospect of prejudice to the beneficiary's interests.[86]

In neither case does it matter whether the trustee acted honestly or otherwise;[87] nor, since we are talking here about restitution for wrongs, is it relevant that the profit could not have gone to the beneficiaries at all.[88] For obvious reasons, a similar principle attaches to an adviser to a trustee or other third party who makes use of such an opportunity, presumably on the basis that he is a joint wrongdoer and can be in no better position than the trustee himself.

At least where he acts honestly, however, the trustee will be allowed to keep a sum reflecting his own expenditure of time and skill,[89] and where appropriate, his own expenses in purchasing property which he is held to hold on trust.[90]

Other fiduciaries

11-27 The category of fiduciaries is a notoriously wide and varied one. It runs from those, like personal representatives and – to a lesser extent – company directors, who are treated very like trustees, to others, such as agents, mortgagees, joint tenants and partners, whose duties are far more limited. Fiduciaries, in other words, vary greatly in their legal treatment.[91] All on principle, however, owe a duty not to make a profit out of their position. In the case of personal representatives, directors and agents, this is presumably on the same basis as trustees, that is, their beneficiaries' need for dispassionate advice or dealing. Hence, cases such as *Regal (Hastings) Ltd v Gulliver*[92] holding company directors liable to pay over profits in a situation highly analogous to that in *Phipps v Boardman*,[93] and *Industrial Development Consultants Ltd v Cooley*,[94] deciding that a

---

84 Eg, *Gabbett v Lauder* (1883) LR 11 Ir 295; *Phillips v Phillips* (1885) 29 Ch D 673; *Thompson's Trustee v Heaton* [1974] 1 All ER 1239. Cf *Griffiths v Owen* [1907] 1 Ch 195.

85 See *Protheroe v Protheroe* [1968] 1 All ER 1111.

86 See Keane, *Equity and the law of Trusts in the Republic of Ireland*, § 13.04.

87 See *Boardman v Phipps* [1967] 2 AC 46, a classic case of an honest defendant being held liable.

88 *Keech v Sandford* (1726) 1 Eq Cas Abr 741; *Boardman v Phipps* [1967] 2 AC 46; cf *Industrial Development Consultants Ltd v Cooley* [1972] 2 All ER 162.

89 Which, for obvious reasons, he would not have been allowed to do had he been guilty of knowing wrongdoing: cf *Guinness plc v Saunders* [1990] 2 AC 663.

90 Eg, *Re Lord Ranelagh's Will* (1884) 26 Ch D 590.

91 Cf, in another context, *Re Coomber* [1911] 1 Ch 723.

92 [1942] 1 All ER 378.

93 [1967] 2 AC 46.

94 [1972] 2 All ER 162.

director could not appropriate for his own benefit a contract unsuccessfully tendered for by his employers. And, there are decisions holding joint tenants[95] and partners[96] to be under similar duties.

Again, if I employ you as my agent I have a right to expect that you will exercise judgment unclouded by possibilities of personal advantage from bribes and the like; hence my right to claim from you, without question, any bribe or other benefit you receive in the course of so acting.[97] On the other hand, the relation of principal and agent has been held to permit the retention of certain benefits by the agent that, while coming to him by virtue of his position, have nothing to do with the relations between him and his principal.[98]

It seems, moreover, that breach of fiduciary duty, like breach of a trustee's duty, is an 'anti-enrichment' wrong giving rise to restitution not only as against the fiduciary himself, but also as against anyone else knowingly participating in it. *Arab Monetary Fund v Hashim*[99] makes this reasoning clear. Builders obtained a valuable contract by bribing the building owners' agent; having performed it and been paid, they were held liable to pay over the amount of the bribe to the owners on the basis that they had participated in a breach of fiduciary duty and that the amount of the bribe must be regarded as representing extra profits made as a result of so doing. Similarly, in *Warman International Ltd v Dwyer*,[100] the High Court of Australia held that where a person incurred liability for knowing assistance[101] in a breach of fiduciary duty, this carried with it a duty to account for profits made.

(d) Infringement of intellectual property rights

11-28 By long tradition, infringements of intellectual property rights are always regarded as anti-enrichment wrongs: indeed, as pointed out above, this must be right, since their very *raison d'être* is to allow the holder to license for payment what would otherwise amount to an infringement. We have already mentioned one side of this point, namely, that damages for such infringement are often reckoned on a 'reasonable licence fee' basis, representing the sum that the defendant should be regarded as having saved vis à vis a notional reasonable claimant. But in addition to this, there is the peculiar remedy of account of profits. Originally a purely equitable creation, this is now available by statute for

---

95 See *Protheroe v Protheroe* [1968] 1 All ER 1111.

96 See, eg, *Thompson's Trustee v Heaton* [1974] 1 All ER 1239.

97 As in *Boston Deep Sea Fishing Co v Ansell* (1888) 39 Ch D 339 and *Patten v Hamilton* [1911] IR 46. See, more recently, *All wood v Clifford* (2001) unreported, 28 June, Ch D.

98 Eg, *Aas v Benham* [1891] 2 Ch 244; *NZ Netherlands Society v Kuys* [1973] 1 WLR 1126.

99 [1993] 1 Lloyd's Rep 543, esp p 565.

100 (1995) 182 CLR 544.

101 Which would now be known, at least in English law, as 'dishonest assistance': see *Royal Brunei Airlines Sdn Bhd v Tan* [1995] 2 AC 378.

breach of copyright[102] and patent;[103] in cases of breach of confidence,[104] passing off[105] and trade mark infringement,[106] the original judge-made right still has to be invoked. It is a discretionary remedy, alternative to damages,[107] and may be refused on any of the usual equitable grounds.[108] Strictly, the court must do its best to separate out that element in the defendant's profit which is attributable to the infringement rather than to the defendant's own efforts, though this can be a highly ticklish operation at times.[109]

11-29   A troublesome point here is how far a defendant should escape liability to account for profits if he did not know and had no reason to know he was infringing the claimant's rights. Logically, it is suggested that liability to account for profits should be strict, as, *prima facie*, is liability to pay damages. If a wrong is indeed categorised an 'anti-enrichment' wrong, the defendant's enrichment from committing it remains unjustified however innocent he was; indeed, it may be easier to justify making the innocent defendant account for profits than pay damages since the former remedy, at least in theory, cannot leave him out of pocket. This principle is indeed observed in copyright and design right, so much so that in at least one case, liability to account for profits is actually wider than that for damages.[110] On the other hand, in trade mark infringement, passing off and breach of confidence, the innocence of the defendant seems to be regarded as a reason for the court to exercise its discretion against granting an account.[111] And similarly with patents; by statute, a person who escapes liability to damages on account of innocence also avoids liability to an account of profits.[112] It is difficult to justify these latter provisions, and virtually impossible to support

---

102 England: Copyright, Designs and Patents Act 1988, s 96(2). Ireland: Copyright Act 1963, s 22(2).

103 England: Patents Act 1977, s 61(1)(d). Ireland: Patents Act 1992, s 47.

104 Eg *Peter Pan Mfg Co v Corsets Silhouette Ltd* [1963] 3 All ER 402; *AG v Guardian Newspapers Ltd (No 2)* [1990] 1 AC 109. Cf *AG v Blake* [2001] 1 AC 268, where restitutionary damages were awarded for a breach of contract by a member of the British security services that would have been a breach of confidence but for the fact that the information disclosed was by then in the public domain. The analogy with breach of confidence was explicitly acknowledged: see pp 287 (Lord Nicholls), 291 (Lord Steyn).

105 Eg, *Weingarten v Bayer* (1903) 22 RPC 341.

106 See Kerly's *Law of Trade Marks and Trade Names*, 13th edn, § 18-156 *et seq* and, eg, *Edelsten v Edelsten* (1863) 1 DJ and Sm 185.

107 See *Sutherland Publishing Co Ltd v Caxton Publishing Co Ltd* [1936] Ch 323, p 336 (affirmed [1939] AC 178).

108 *Van Zeller v Mason Catley* (1907) 25 RPC 37; *Young v Holt* (1947) 65 RPC 25.

109 See, eg, *My Kinda Town v Soll* [1982] FSR 147.

110 See Copyright, Designs and Patents Act 1988, ss 97(1) (copyright), 233(1) (design right). This makes it a defence to an action for damages, but not to a claim for account of profits, that the defendant had no reason to know that copyright or design right subsisted in what he copied. For Ireland, see Copyright Act 1963, s 23(3).

111 See *Seager v Copydex Ltd* [1967] 2 All ER 415, p 419 (breach of confidence); *Young v Holt* (1947) 65 RPC 25 (passing off).

112 England: Patents Act 1977, s 62(1). Ireland: Patents Act 1992, s 49(1).

the different treatment afforded to the various types of intellectual property right.

IV RESTITUTIONARY REMEDIES AVAILABLE FOR WRONGS

(a) Form

11-30   Subject to a few exceptions, there is no doubt that restitution for wrongs takes the form of a simple money liability, whether in the shape of money had and received, account of profits or an award of damages. In particular, there is no question of the claimant being able to claim equitable ownership of the unwarranted profit or priority in insolvency.

(b) The exceptions: *Taylor v Plumer*

11-31   We mentioned above that if you steal my horse and exchange it for a cow I have the right under the rule in *Taylor v Plumer*[113] to claim ownership of the cow while it is in your hands. Since this liability of yours depends on your being a wrongdoer, this provides a *de facto* exception to the above principle.

(c) The exceptions: 'property benefits'

11-32   The fact that your gain arose from the disposal, use or exploitation of something belonging to me not only provides a reason to make you accountable for that gain; it also often justifies giving me the remedies of an owner against it while it remains in your hands. If I lend you my car and you sell it, not only are you liable to me for the price you got for it: while you still have the money in your hands, you will hold it on constructive trust for me.[114] Similarly (it is submitted), where you borrow my car and without my consent hire it out to a stranger: the hire fees, while you still have them, ought to be held on trust for me.

Similarly, too, with equitable interests: there has been no doubt since *Keech v Sandford*[115] that where a trustee or other fiduciary makes a profit either from using trust property, or by virtue of his legal ownership of it, he will hold that profit on constructive trust for the beneficiary, and will not simply come under a duty to account. Although most of the cases have concerned peripheral matters such as the renewal of trust leases or the purchase of reversions thereto, there is

---

113 (1815) 3 M & S 562.

114 Cf *Clough Mill Ltd v Martin* [1984] 3 All ER 982, and the other 'retention of title' cases.

115 (1726) 1 Eq Cas Abr 741; also, *Gabbett v Lauder* (1883) LR 11 Ir 295 and *Protheroe v Protheroe* [1968] 1 All ER 1111.

no doubt that similar reasoning would apply to, for example, a trustee who hired out trust property for his own benefit.

(d) Other fiduciary profits

11-33 Suppose you, a trustee, make a profit not by using actual trust property, but merely by virtue of your position as trustee; for instance (as in *Boardman v Phipps*),[116] by using information that has come to you as such. Should the 'property benefit' reasoning nevertheless be extended to such situations, so as to make you not only accountable to me – which you clearly ought to be – but a constructive trustee of what you gained?

In *Phipps's* case itself, the original order made, declaring a trust, suggests the answer yes.[117] And, as far as English law is concerned, the point has now been put beyond doubt by the very important case of *AG for Hong Kong v Reid*.[118] A public prosecutor in Hong Kong received massive bribes in exchange for showing favour to alleged criminals; these he invested in land in New Zealand, where he had decamped, and later became insolvent. The Privy Council held that this land was held on constructive trust for the Hong Kong Government: the bribes, they said, ought to have been paid straight over to Reid's employers, and Reid could not pray in aid the fact that he had not done so.

And, indeed, at first sight this looks convincing, even if one does not take the view that information is not only a commodity, but a form of property (which is something quite different).[119] After all, why distinguish between profiteers according to whether they misused others' property or merely abused their own position in some other way? Again, the distinction between a trust and a duty to account principally matters where the profiteer is insolvent and the argument is between beneficiary and creditors: if so, why should creditors be allowed to benefit from money their debtor should never have had in the first place? And, yet again, suppose the fiduciary, having made his profit, invests cannily and increases it: should the beneficiary not have a claim against this further gain?

11-34 On the other hand, it must be said that there are strong arguments against the conclusion reached in *Reid*, and in favour of earlier cases, notably those on the liability of agents, which had reached the opposite result. The best known of these latter is *Lister v Stubbs*,[120] holding that a bribe received by an agent can be

---

116 [1967] 2 AC 46.

117 But no argument was presented on this aspect either in the Court of Appeal or the House of Lords. Nor did it matter in that case, since the defendant was perfectly solvent and the measure of recovery was the same in either case.

118 [1994] 1 AC 324.

119 [1967] 2 AC 46, p 125 (Lord Upjohn).

120 (1890) 45 Ch D 1. See, too, *AG's Reference (No 1 of 1985)* [1986] 2 All ER 219, and *Iran Shipping Co v Denby* [1987] 1 Lloyd's Rep 367.

recovered by his principal, but only by way of personal suit and not through the medium of a constructive trust.

The point is this. In order to allow a proprietary claim, whether by way of constructive trust or otherwise, one ought to have to start with some proprietary base. Put another way, to make any sense of such a claim, I must be able to say that the money in your possession derives from something I do, or did, own. It is difficult to see what such basis can be found here, without begging the question by arguing that information or opportunity coming to a fiduciary by virtue of his position must count as property for these purposes.

Nor are the policy arguments in favour of the *AG for Hong Kong v Reid*[121] solution very convincing. Distinctions between property and other claimants are as old as the law itself, and can hardly be objectionable as such; to take one obvious example from the law of restitution, if you make a profit from selling my goods, I can claim it *in specie*, whereas if you profit from libelling me I have to be satisfied with a personal claim in respect of your gain. So, too, with the argument that creditors should not gain from what their bankrupt debtor should not have had: no one has ever suggested that this reasoning should be applied, for example, to the seller who is paid for goods, but then goes bankrupt before supplying them.[122] As for the argument that the fiduciary should have to pay over not only profit, but profit on profit, this may well be true; but there are other ways of reaching that result than by inventing a bogus proprietary claim. The proper solution, it is suggested, is to say that the fiduciary is only under a personal liability, but that that liability extends not only to immediate profits, but also to all subsequent gains resulting from it, provided they are not too remote.[123] In short, it is to be hoped that Irish courts, when faced with this problem, will decline to follow *AG for Hong Kong v Reid*.[124]

(e) Profits and losses

11-35   Where benefits can be recovered on the ground that they were gained as a result of a wrongful act, a further question arises: is this right cumulative with, or alternative to, the victim's right to claim his loss? As a matter of policy, something can be said on both sides. To allow cumulation overcompensates claimants: on the other hand, it is a little odd to treat in the same way a defendant who gains while causing the claimant no loss, and one who in addition causes some loss, but still less than the amount of his gain. Nevertheless, the general rule seems to be against cumulation. This is clear in the

---

121 [1994] 1 AC 324.
122 Cf *Eldan Services Ltd v Chandag Motors Ltd* [1990] 3 All ER 459.
123 As suggested by Professor Birks: *Introduction to the Law of Restitution*, p 387 *et seq*.
124 [1994] 1 AC 324; Oakley [1994] CLJ 31; Oakley [1995] CLJ 377.

case of the equitable remedy of account of profits;[125] and elsewhere, the Privy Council has made it clear that a defaulting fiduciary can be sued for his profits or for the beneficiary's loss, but not both;[126] he must elect between the two.[127] Not surprisingly, a trustee is in the same position.[128] As for waiver of tort, it is well established that where it is available, it is an alternative to an action for damages; the claimant has to elect which he wants.[129] On the other hand, this is not an absolute rule: where exemplary damages in tort are allowed, these are traditionally awarded over and above any sum for loss suffered.[130]

---

125 *Sutherland Publishing Co Ltd v Caxton Publishing Co Ltd* [1936] Ch 323, p 336 (affirmed [1939] AC 178).

126 See *Mahesan v Malaysia Government Housing Society* [1979] AC 374.

127 Such an election, once made, is final. As to what amounts to an irrevocable election, see *Tang Man Sit v Capacious Investments Ltd* [1996] AC 514.

128 See, eg, *Tang Man Sit v Capacious Investments Ltd* [1996] AC 514.

129 *United Australia v Barclays Bank* [1941] AC 1, p 18 (the case actually turned on when such an election becomes irrevocable, which is when the plaintiff recovers judgment).

130 Thus, in *Cassell and Co Ltd v Broome* [1972] AC 1027, £15,000 was awarded for compensation and £25,000 in addition by way of exemplary damages.

CHAPTER 12

RESTITUTION AND PUBLIC AUTHORITIES

I GENERALLY

12-1   As with contract and tort, so with restitution. Public authorities, not to mention others subject to public law regulation[1] are, *prima facie*, subject to the same restitutionary rights and duties as anyone else: see, for instance, the 'swaps' cases,[2] or other instances where (for example) questions of services rendered under abortive contracts are in issue.[3] However, restitutionary claims by and against such bodies or authorities have, in practice, to be subject to qualifications and exceptions. One cannot treat the State or government in its various forms, with their unique coercive powers and correlative duty to safeguard the public interest, simply as if it were a species of private citizen or company. As La Forest J put it in the Canadian Supreme Court (in the context of recovery of overpaid tax):

> ... where one party is enriched at the expense of another it is appropriate to begin by asking if the principles of restitution would afford recovery to the losing party, whether that party is a public body or not. However ... when unconstitutional or *ultra vires* levies are in issue, special considerations do arise which may call for a different rule.[4]

It is the special rules applicable to public authorities that this chapter deals with.

However, four important preliminary points need to be made.

12-2   First, the concept of a 'public authority' in the law of restitution ought to be given a fairly wide connotation. The need for special rules arguably applies not simply to public bodies *tout court*, but to any body vested with a statutory monopoly or the right to demand compulsory payments, or saddled with specific statutory duties to supply goods or services at a given price. Thus, in *South of Scotland Electricity Board v BOC Ltd*,[5] the House of Lords, while deciding that charges levied by a public body in breach of a statutory non-discrimination principle were recoverable, applied a series of cases dealing with the similar

---

1   Eg, electricity, gas and water utilities.

2   Eg, *Westdeutsche Landesbank v Islington BC* [1996] AC 669.

3   A random example of such a case is *Sabemo v North Sydney Municipal Council* (1977) 2 NSWLR 880 (building contract case where client happened to be public authority decided on orthodox private law grounds).

4   *Air Canada v British Columbia* [1989] 1 SCR 1161, p 1201. Or, as Wilson J put it in the same case, p 1214: 'Citizens are expected to be law-abiding. They are expected to pay their taxes. Pay first and object later is the general rule.'

5   [1959] 2 All ER 225 (strictly dealing with Scots law).

situation that used to arise in connection with the carriage charges of private railway companies.[6] And again, the answer to the question of whether (for instance) overpaid water rates are recoverable should not be radically different according to whether the utility concerned has, or has not, undergone a process of privatisation (or, indeed, was ever nationalised in the first place).

12-3 The second observation is the predominance in this area of statute, not to mention in Ireland the provisions of the Constitution itself. In the nature of things a large proportion of public bodies' income takes the form of taxes and other charges raised under statutory authority, while a good deal of their expenditure consists of grants and benefits payable to private citizens or other public organisations under statutory duties or powers; as a result, restitutionary claims tend to revolve around miscalculations and overpayments by or to such authorities. And problems of this sort are very often dealt with specifically by statute, in which case common law or equitable principles of recovery are likely to be ousted. As Lord Goff put it in *Woolwich Equitable Building Society v Inland Revenue Comrs (No 2)*:[7] 'Because of the other legislative provisions dealing with repayment of various taxes it seems in any event that the number of cases where any principle of common law would need to be relied on is likely to be small.'[8] Common law recovery is only likely to be in issue where the relevant statute is silent, or payments have been made pursuant to *ultra vires* rules (as in the *Woolwich* case itself), or in Ireland where the Constitution itself is held to invalidate the statutory demand, as in *Murphy v AG*,[9] where aspects of the taxation of married couples was held to contravene Art 41, s 3 of the Constitution.[10]

12-4 The third point is related. Because public authorities (and those acting on their behalf) are at times expected to play fairer than private enterprise,[11] the grounds for restitution against them ought arguably to be wider than those elsewhere. The obvious example is the common law action dating from 1982 in Ireland,[12]

---

6 The leading case being *Great Western Rly v Sutton* (1869) LR 4 HL 226. Similar problems have arisen in Ireland; see, eg, *Great Southern and Western Rly Co v Robertson* (1878) 2 LR Ir 548.

7 [1993] AC 70, p 168.

8 But cf *Dolan v Neligan* [1967] IR 247, p 267, where in a case of overpayment of customs duty the Supreme Court managed to find that the restrictive repayment provisions of the Customs Consolidation Act 1876 did not apply there, and allowed common law recovery. And see, too, *R v Secretary of State for the Environment ex p London Borough of Camden* (1995) unreported, 17 February, QBD (statute not exhaustive source of right to recoup grants mistakenly paid by central government to local authority).

9 [1982] IR 241. (See too *Muckley v Ireland* [1985] IR 472, where a statutory attempt to reverse the effect of *Murphy* was itself struck down.)

10 Indeed, it is noteworthy that in cases following *Murphy*, the issue of recovery has normally turned on statutory provisions: Eg, *Mooney v Ó Coindealbhóin* [1992] 2 IR 23; *Texaco (Ireland) Ltd v Murphy (No 2)* [1992] 1 IR 399; *Texaco (Ireland) Ltd v Murphy (No 3)* [1992] 2 IR 300.

11 Witness, in another context, the 'officers of the court' exception to the old rule disallowing recovery of money paid under a mistake of law: *Ex p James* (1874) LR 9 Ch App 609.

12 *Murphy v AG* [1982] IR 241.

and now established in England by the massively important case of *Woolwich Building Society v IRC (No 2)*,[13] for recovery of tax overpaid (in the rare cases where it lies). But there are others as well, for instance, the principle known as extortion *colore officii*, whereby an unwarranted demand by someone clothed with public authority to collect payments may give rise *ipso facto* to restitution even in the absence of any of the other traditional unjust factors.

12-5   The fourth point is a converse one: public authorities may need to be given certain advantages not shared by other litigants, in terms either of specific defences available specifically to them, or of defences denied to those in conflict with them. Possible limitations on the right to recover overpaid taxes, such as a defence of excessive financial disruption, or limits on the extent to which a public authority can be estopped from asserting a claim, are good examples.

II PARTICULAR PUBLIC LAW RIGHTS TO RESTITUTION

(a) Payments *colore officii*

12-6   In many cases, public authorities and numerous other bodies and office holders are bound to do things, such as providing services, issuing licences, and so on, either for no charge or for a limited fee. There is no doubt that a decision by an authority to demand a fee for what it is bound to provide for nothing, or ask for a larger fee than that allowed, is susceptible to judicial review;[14] but what if the fee is paid and then demanded back? The answer is that *prima facie* recovery is allowed; see, for instance, *Morgan v Palmer*,[15] where a publican successfully sued to recover a sum demanded as a condition of renewal of his licence which the defendant had no authority to charge, and the Supreme Court's decision in *Dolan v Neligan*[16] that import duties paid by the Irish distributors of Babycham were recoverable on proof that they were not in fact due. A similar principle applies to non-public bodies, such as utilities, which are charged with specific statutory duties to provide services at particular prices.[17]

It might be argued that these are really cases of duress, and in a sense they are. The defendant will nearly always have declined (expressly or impliedly) to carry out his duty if not paid as demanded. (It is notable that in at least one

---

13   [1993] AC 70.

14   Eg, *R v Richmond-on-Thames BC ex p McCarthy & Stone Ltd* [1991] 4 All ER 897 (practice of levying charges for preliminary consultations on planning applications successfully challenged by judicial review).

15   (1824) 2 B & C 729. See, too, *Steele v Williams* (1853) 8 Ex 625, and the discussion of the whole matter in *Woolwich Building Society v Inland Revenue Comrs (No 2)* [1993] AC 70.

16   [1967] IR 247, p 267. See, too, *Rogers v Louth CC* [1981] IR 265, and the important case of *Hooper v Exeter Corp* (1887) 56 LJQB 457.

17   Eg, *Great Western Rly Co v Sutton* (1869) LR 4 HL 226 (railway); *South of Scotland Electricity Board v BOC Ltd* [1959] 2 All ER 225 (electricity supplier).

established authority going the other way, *Twyford v Manchester Corp*,[18] recovery seems to have been denied at least partly on the basis of the absence of any such threat). But this analysis is not entirely satisfactory. Duress normally depends on a wrongful threat. Refusal to perform a public duty is, however, wrongful only in a wide sense: it may well not give rise to any liability in damages, and indeed, in England, may be challengeable only by an application for judicial review.[19] Yet, on principle, it is difficult to see why this should make any difference. Furthermore, in at least some cases where recovery was allowed, there seems to have been no evidence of any threat at all.[20] For these reasons, it is suggested that it is better to cut the link between duress and payments made *colore officii*,[21] and to say that the latter is an independent, though related, head of recovery, based simply on the fact that the demand was unjustified and that 'the parties were not on an equal footing'.[22]

(b) Overpaid taxes

12-7 In the rare case where statute does not regulate recovery, overpaid taxes create problems for traditional restitution law. The difficulty is twofold. First, while some overpayments are covered by traditional restitution concepts (for example, where a taxpayer miscomputes his income, and thus pays under a mistake of fact, or where he pays under a mistake of law), many are not. For example, there may well have been a genuine dispute with the taxing authorities as to what is exigible, in which case there will not have been any relevant mistake or other ground for restitution. In such a case, given Anglo-Irish law's adherence to the view that to found restitution, there must be an 'unjust factor', there will be no traditional peg on which to hang a claim for recompense.

Secondly, many tax payments – at least those which are clearly disputed – are made against the background of an overt or implicit threat of legal proceedings; and, in general, a claimant who chooses to pay in response to a legal demand rather than take the risk of disputing it in court will lose any right to impugn it later.[23] But that is arguably not satisfactory in the context of public imposts: as Wilson J has pointed out in the Supreme Court of Canada, the

---

18 [1946] Ch 236.

19 Because of the principle in *O'Reilly v Mackman* [1983] 2 AC 237, requiring essentially public law issues to be litigated under RSC Ord 53 or not at all. In Ireland, the position under the equivalent provision, namely, the Rules of the Superior Courts Ord 84, is less restrictive: cf *O'Donnell v Dún Laoghaire Corp* [1991] ILRM 301.

20 Eg, *Hooper v Exeter Corp* (1887) 56 LJQB 457, or *Rogers v Louth CC* [1981] IR 265.

21 Cf La Forest J's deprecation, in the context of overpaid tax, of attempts to shoehorn the case into the duress category by using the concept of 'practical compulsion' – *Air Canada v British Columbia* [1989] 1 SCR 1161, p 1209.

22 See Windeyer J in *Mason v New South Wales* (1959) 102 CLR 108, p 140.

23 See above, § 4-18 (in the context of duress claims).

expectation that taxpayers will be law-abiding and pay on the nail ought perhaps to carry with it a correlative duty to return revenues not in fact due.[24]

12-8 Nevertheless, in *Woolwich Equitable Building Society v Inland Revenue Comrs (No 2)*,[25] a case where the plaintiff society had overpaid some £50 m in tax but relevant statutory provisions did not apply,[26] the House of Lords by a bare majority overcame both these problems. The lack of any traditional head of restitution was countered by reference to English constitutional principle in the shape of the prohibition in the Bill of Rights 1688[27] against the levying of taxes not authorised by Parliament. This, coupled with a judgment that public authorities were in a peculiarly powerful position vis à vis the taxpayer, and ought for that reason to be under particular duties of probity, was held sufficient to create a specific head of recovery. As for the point of payment against a threat of litigation, this again fell victim to the principle that the State should be distinguished from other claimants. While any other citizen who threatened litigation in good faith could reasonably expect to keep the fruits of his endeavour, however unwilling the payer, the overwhelming power of the State dictated that it should not share this privilege. Only in the event of a truly voluntary intent on the part of the taxpayer to pay to close the transaction would recovery be barred.

12-9 Lord Goff, delivering the leading judgment, left it open whether taxes demanded as a result of misapplication of valid taxing provisions, rather than in reliance on invalid ones, ought to be treated similarly: but he inclined to the view that they should.[27a] In practice, however, this is an issue most unlikely to arise since, in nearly every such case, the statutory provisions for repayment will apply in any case. Such specific statutory schemes cover (for example) overpaid income tax,[28] residential property taxes[29] and VAT.[30] Although they vary, a common feature of these provisions is that there is no specific requirement of duress or some other 'unjust factor' that would be necessary in an action between private persons. Subject to a number of specific defences, all that has to be shown is that tax has been paid that was not properly exigible, thus getting close to a general *conditio indebiti*, or legal principle that payments of money not

---

24 In *Air Canada v British Columbia* [1989] 1 SCR 1161, p 1214.

25 [1993] AC 70. Although the Revenue later returned the sum involved, the case was litigated over the claimants' desire for interest on the sums concerned while in the Revenue's hands (totalling nearly £8 m). If the claimants had no right to recovery, interest was not payable; if they had such a right, it was. See generally Beatson (1993) 109 LQR 401.

26 Because the tax concerned had been demanded under the provisions of a statutory instrument that was simply void as being *ultra vires*, the relevant provisions did not cover it.

27 Article 4.

27a As did Elias J in *BSkyB plc v Comrs of Customs & Excise* [2001] STC 437.

28 (England) Taxes Management Act 1970, s 33; (Ireland) Taxes Consolidation Act 1997, s 930.

29 See (England) SI 1992/613, s 24 (council tax); (Ireland) Finance Act 1986, s 114 (residential property tax).

30 Value Added Tax Act 1994, s 80 (England); Value Added Tax Act 1972, s 20 (Ireland).

owed are *prima facie* recoverable.[31] In both jurisdictions, however, the legislator has in certain cases taken steps to safeguard the public coffers by precluding recovery where tax has been paid in accordance with a prevailing, albeit wrong, understanding of the relevant taxing statute.[32]

12-10 A further important feature of the statutory schemes is that sometimes, the right of the taxpayer to reimbursement is not absolute, but qualified by a reference to reasonableness[33] or conditional on some overriding discretion given by statute to the public authority concerned. To some extent this negatives the idea of any 'right' to repayment existing at all. On the other hand, this difference is not as important as it might seem. Such statutory discretions, whether to seek or to withhold repayment, are on principle subject to judicial review: and in *Tower Hamlets BC v Chetnik Developments Ltd*,[34] where a local authority's discretion to refund overpaid rates was in issue, the House of Lords explicitly relied on analogies from the private law of restitution in striking down the authority's decision to refuse a refund.[35]

12-11 There seems little doubt that the principles adumbrated in the Woolwich case are applicable in Ireland. In addition, however, and quite independently of them, there is a constitutional dimension. In *Murphy v AG*,[36] the statutory scheme of taxation of married persons in the Republic was held to contravene the provisions of Art 40, s 3 of the Constitution. It was also held that, as a necessary inference from the Constitution, payments made pursuant to the unconstitutional demand ought to be recoverable – though, as appears below, the Supreme Court managed to keep this recovery within manageable proportions by limiting both the taxpayers by whom, and the tax years in respect of which, recoupment was to be allowed.

(c) Recovery by the State or Crown of unauthorised payments

12-12 On the basis of the constitutional maxim that any expenditure by the Crown must be sanctioned by Parliament, it has long been held in England that any payment by the Crown specifically found to be unauthorised is *ipso facto* recoverable from the recipient as money had and received (and probably by way of equitable proprietary claim in so far as the recipient, or any subsequent person other than a *bona fide* purchaser, still has it): see the decision in *Auckland*

---

31 Which does not, of course, exist as a general rule: see *Woolwich Building Society v IRC (No 2)* [1992] 3 All ER 737, p 759 (Lord Goff).

32 Eg (England), Taxes Management Act 1970, s 33(2A)(a); (Ireland) Taxes Consolidation Act 1997, s 930(2).

33 As in the (English) Taxes Management Act 1970, s 33, and the (Irish) Taxes Consolidation Act , s 930.

34 [1988] 1 AC 858.

35 In any case, the *Chetnik* decision is now academic, since in the case of rates, the discretion to repay has now been replaced by a right to reimbursement – see SI 1989/1058, s 22.

36 [1982] IR 241.

Harbour Board v R.[37] Although there seems no Irish case directly in point, the *Auckland* case has since been cited without disapproval in the Republic,[38] and presumably applies there as well.

This principle clearly has affinities with that covering reimbursement of *ultra vires* payments generally;[39] but it is not entirely clear whether it is in fact the same. In particular, while actions to recoup *ultra vires* payments are clearly subject to general restitutionary defences such as change of position,[40] there is also authority that actions by the Crown in this connection are not.[41] It remains to be seen whether they will in due course be assimilated to the general rule. On principle, they clearly ought to be.[42]

(d) Restrictions on recovery against public authorities

Procedural

12-13   Restitutionary claims against public authorities based on overpaid tax or on the invalidity of a demand may face one of two extra procedural hurdles.

The first concerns the place of judicial review. Under the rule in *O'Reilly v Mackman*,[43] a person wishing to challenge the exercise of a public law power must in general do so by way of judicial review rather than by a private law action. It is therefore arguable that an action seeking to recover an overpayment without first seeking judicial review will be struck out as an abuse of process.[44] If so, this may be highly important. Not only is judicial review, unlike restitutionary recovery, a discretionary remedy; it is also subject to a very short time limit. However, the point is by no means clear. There is authority that the rule in *O'Reilly v Mackman*[45] does not apply to a case where private law rights are in issue, at least where these 'dominate' the proceedings;[46] and it may well

---

37   [1924] AC 318. The possibility of a proprietary remedy is mentioned in the same case, p 327. See too *Eastbourne BC v Foster* [2001] EWCA 1091.

38   See *Kenny v Cosgrave* [1926] IR 515, p 528.

39   See above, Chapter 7.

40   *Westdeutsche Landesbank Girozentrale v Islington BC* [1994] 4 All ER 890 (affirmed on another point [1996] AC 669).

41   So held in Australia: *Commonwealth v Burns* [1971] VR 825. Despite *Lipkin Gorman*, the point of whether change of position applies in such cases was left open by Schiemann J in *R v Secretary of State for the Environment ex p London Borough of Camden* (1995) unreported, 17 February.

42   See below, § 13-18.

43   [1983] 2 AC 237.

44   In the *Woolwich Building Society* case itself the taxpayers, before suing to recover the excess, first brought judicial review proceedings (see [1991] 4 All ER 92) to establish that the demand was unlawful. It followed that no *O'Reilly v Mackman* point could conceivably be taken.

45   [1983] 2 AC 237

46   See, in particular, *Roy v Kensington FPC* [1992] 1 All ER 705, p 729.

be that this exception would apply so as to allow actions to be brought directly for the repayment of tax or for restitution of payments made *colore officii* without the necessity of a prior challenge by way of application for judicial review.[47]

12-14   The second problem concerns rights of appeal. In most cases of tax,[48] and in many concerning other charges by public authorities, a statutory right of appeal against a charge is given. Does the existence of such a right preclude restitutionary proceedings in the ordinary courts? Glidewell LJ in the *Woolwich* case in the Court of Appeal[49] left the point open; but, on principle, it is submitted that it must, at least where it provides machinery for repayment. It is a general rule that statutory rights of challenge preclude private law actions;[50] and there is no reason to treat actions based on unjustified enrichment any differently. Furthermore, even if the right of appeal does not oust restitution proceedings entirely, it is suggested that failure to exercise it before bringing those proceedings may give cause for striking out as an abuse of process, or at least for penalisation in costs.[51]

Substantive – change of position and analogous arguments

12-15   Since *Westdeutsche Landesbank Girozentrale v Islington BC*,[52] it is clear that the defence of change of position is available to public authorities as it is to anyone else. On the other hand, in the nature of things, its ambit of the defence in the hands of public authorities is likely to be rather different. The idea of central government being able to show a change of position resulting from a belief in the security of a given tax receipt from a particular person is, to say the least, far-fetched – though not impossible.[53] On the other hand, it is a good deal more plausible that local government may well be able to show that, by budgeting for a given receipt from a large class of taxpayers, it has changed its position:[54] indeed, it may be able to raise the defence in a number of situations where it

---

47   See, eg, *British Steel plc v Customs and Excise Comrs* [1997] 2 All ER 366. If so, did the Woolwich Building Society waste its money (and the taxpayer's) in bringing its original proceedings for judicial review?

48   Though not on the special facts of the *Woolwich* case, where no such right existed.

49   See [1991] 4 All ER 577, p 602.

50   See, eg, *Calveley v Merseyside Chief Constable* [1989] 1 All ER 1025 (statutory right of appeal precludes negligence proceedings).

51   Cf *Roy v Kensington FPC* [1992] 1 All ER 705, p 715 (Lord Lowry).

52   [1994] 4 All ER 890 (affirmed on another point [1996] AC 669). In fact, the defendants failed to show any relevant change of position; the evidence was that it had – on the contrary – from an early stage budgeted against a possible repayment liability. See, too, *South Tyneside MBC v Svenska International plc* [1995] 1 All ER 545.

53   In *Air Canada v British Columbia* [1989] 1 SCR 1161, p 1204, La Forest J observed that the 1936 decision of the US Supreme Court in *US v Butler* 297 US 1 (1935) could potentially have required the return of the then unimaginable sum of $1 bn in wrongly paid taxes.

54   Or, where a local authority has paid over rating receipts to another authority under 'precepting' provisions: *Spiers and Pond v Finsbury BC* (1956) 1 Ryde's Rating Cas 219 (semble).

would not be available to a private litigant – for example, if it could show that it has lost the right to raise taxation in a subsequent year, or has lost the opportunity to claim some grant or rebate from another source.[55]

12-16   A variety of the 'change of position' point is the 'fiscal chaos' argument sometimes raised against claims for repayment of tax. But this has been treated with some scepticism, and probably rightly so. In *Air Canada v British Columbia*,[56] La Forest J in the Supreme Court of Canada castigated the principle as unworkably uncertain, and it has not impressed the High Court of Australia either.[57] In England, Lord Goff in the *Woolwich* case[58] pointed out that limitations on the statutory schemes for recovery would, in the vast majority of cases, provide adequate protection in any case. And even in the case of unconstitutional taxes, where statute cannot apply and the argument for recovery is especially strong, the Supreme Court in *Murphy v AG*[59] was able to deal with the problem in another way, by limiting recovery: (a) to the taxpayers involved in that case and others who had brought proceedings prior to the decision of the High Court; and (b) to those tax years in which the taxpayers had protested their non-liability. Up to that time, said Henchy J:

> ... the State was entitled, in the absence of any claim of unconstitutionality, to act on the assumption that the taxes in question were validly imposed, that they were properly transmissible to the central fund, and that from there they were liable to be expended, according to the will of Parliament, for the multiplicity of purposes for which drawings are made on the central fund.[60]

12-17   There is, however, another problem. Suppose a local authority charges large numbers of ratepayers with an *ultra vires* business rate or other tax, in reliance on which it incurs additional irrecoverable expenditure; later, one taxpayer sues to recover what he has paid. Can the authority show change of position? Taken in aggregate, it clearly can; as against the individual claimant, it will probably be unable to. Presumably the change of position defence will be flexible enough to take account of this problem and, where necessary, allow reduction *pro rata* of claims.[61]

---

55   Argued, unsuccessfully on the facts, by Islington Council in *Westdeutsche Landesbank Girozentrale v Islington BC* [1994] 4 All ER 890.

56   See [1989] 1 SCR 1161, p 1204.

57   See Mason CJ in *Comr of Revenue v Royal Insurance (Australia) Ltd* (1994) 69 ALJR 51, p 57.

58   *Woolwich Equitable Building Society v Inland Revenue Comrs (No 2)* [1993] AC 70, p 177.

59   [1982] IR 241.

60   *Ibid*, p 318.

61   Cf the expansive approach to change of position adopted by the House of Lords in *Lipkin Gorman v Karpnale Ltd* [1991] 2 AC 548: the gambling there took place over a long period, but no exact exercise in tying individual payments of winnings to particular receipts was attempted. A similarly generous view was taken in *Scottish Equitable plc v Derby* (2001) unreported, 16 March, where the English Court of Appeal emphasised that the court should not require detailed correlation between the receipt and every individual payment by the taxpayer: the matter was to be looked at in the round.

Substantive – unjust enrichment of the claimant if recovery permitted

12-18   On occasion, taxes or other charges payable to public authorities are recoverable by the taxpayer from third parties, whether in the form of increased charges or otherwise. The working of VAT is a classic example: the taxpayer's liability to the central authorities is simply added to the price of its goods and services. It follows that if recovery is allowed against the authority, the claimant may effectively get a windfall. Should this affect the question of recovery?

In the case of VAT, statute provides an affirmative answer in both jurisdictions: recovery of overpaid VAT is not to be granted where the effect would be to enrich the claimant unjustly.[62] But what should happen elsewhere in cases where statute provides no answer? Canadian and Australian authority differ here;[63] and in *Woolwich Equitable Building Society v Inland Revenue Comrs (No 2)*,[64] Lord Goff left the point open.

12-19   Although the provision of a 'passing on' defence along these lines is superficially attractive, it is tentatively suggested that recovery should be allowed even here. First, it is quite possible that the third party from whom the tax was recouped would himself have a right to restitution[65] against the taxpayer, at least where the latter got his payment back from the authority.[66] If so, justice would be done all round; and even if not, arrangements between the taxpayer and third parties ought, it is suggested, to be *res inter alios acta* as regards the taxing authority. Secondly, it is not immediately apparent why the taxing authority should itself be entitled to a windfall arising from arrangements between the taxpayer and third parties.[67] And thirdly, it is worth noting that a defence similar to 'passing on' has been rejected by the English Court of Appeal in the analogous case of *ultra vires* payments: hence, in litigation over unlawful interest rate swaps entered into by a local authority, it was held to be irrelevant that the claimant had in fact recouped its losses elsewhere.[68]

---

62   England: Value Added Tax Act 1994, ss 80(3), 80(3A–3C). Ireland: Value Added Tax Act 1972, s 20(5)(b) (inserted in 1992). The fact that a company is in insolvent liquidation and therefore cannot lawfully return the tax in full to its customers has been held in England not to oust this defence (Manchester VAT Tribunal MAN/92/1157, MAN/92/1158). But a specific undertaking so to return it may do so (see *Lamdec Ltd v Customs and Excise Comrs* MAN/90/1018 No 6078).

63   Canada apparently allows the defence (*Air Canada v British Columbia* [1989] 1 SCR 1161, but cf *Air Canada v Ontario (Liquor Control Board)* (1995) 126 DLR (4th) 301). Australia does not (*Comr of Revenue v Royal Insurance (Australia) Ltd* (1994) 69 ALJR 51, p 57).

64   See [1993] AC 70, pp 177–78.

65   Eg, for money paid by mistake. The Federal Court of Australia has seemingly accepted that this might be the case (see *Roxborough v Rothmans of Pall Mall (Australia) Ltd* (1999) 167 ALR 326, where, however, the claim failed on the facts).

66   If he did not, presumably he would have a defence of change of position.

67   Cf the position on damages. A claimant has a right to recover his loss from a wrongdoer, and it is nil ad rem that because of arrangements between himself and a third party, he did not in fact pay out of his own pocket. See, eg, *Jones v Stroud DC* [1988] 1 All ER 5, and *Linden Gardens Developments Ltd v Lenesta Sludge Disposals Ltd* [1994] 1 AC 85.

68   See *Kleinwort Benson Ltd v Birmingham CC* [1997] QB 380.

CHAPTER 13

DEFENCES

I GENERALLY

13-1   This book draws a rough and ready distinction between two kinds of factor which will negative restitutionary recovery. The first category, which has been dealt with in Chapter 1,[1] covers matters such as *bona fide* purchase, receipt under contract or the presumption against forced exchange. While these may indeed bar a restitutionary claim that would otherwise arise, they are better regarded not so much as autonomous defences, but as matters that prevent the defendant's enrichment being unjust. In other words, they prevent the issue of restitution arising at all.

13-2   The second category, by contrast, deals with cases where there is a *prima facie* case of unjust enrichment, but the defendant has the right to plead some extraneous matter which has the effect of barring the claim. That is the subject of this chapter, which will deal in particular with five such defences: exclusion by agreement and intent to close the transaction; change of position; estoppel; illegality; and statute.

II EXCLUSION OF RESTITUTION BY AGREEMENT AND SIMILAR CASES

(a) Exclusion by contract or compromise

13-3   Restitutionary rights, like any others, may be excluded by contract inter partes. Assume I order goods from you, sending a deposit which is agreed to be non-refundable in any event, even if you are in breach of contract. Or again, assume I have a running account with you subject to an agreement that no claim will lie for inadvertent overpayment unless made within one month. Such exclusions of restitutionary rights are perfectly valid at common law.[2] Similarly, with *bona fide* compromises – which are, after all, merely a species of contract, but which frequently in practice affect restitutionary claims. If you demand £1,000 from me

---

1   See above, § 1-29 *et seq*.

2   Indeed, they are probably not covered either by the Unfair Contract Terms Act 1977 in England, or in Ireland by the amended Sale of Goods Act 1893, s 55(4). These provisions only cover exclusion of one's duty to perform one's contract; whereas restitutionary liability arises extra-contractually. But they may well be covered by Council Directive (93/13/EEC) on unfair contract terms: see Annex, §§ 1(b) and 1(f).

by threatening to commit what is in fact a breach of contract (though you, in good faith, think it is not), whereupon I pay you £500 to end the dispute, I recover nothing. I cannot go back on our agreement to compromise the matter.[3]

(b) Finality: intent to close a transaction

13-4 As observed in connection with mistake and duress (see above, Chapters 3 and 4), there are many cases of payments or other benefits held to give rise to no right of recovery on the basis that they are 'once-and-for-all', but which nevertheless cannot be explained as compromises. An agreement to compromise is only effective as such if there is indeed a genuine dispute to compose,[4] and if the person seeking to rely on it was acting in good faith in giving up his supposed rights:[5] if either of these factors is lacking, the agreement will be ineffective for lack of consideration.

Nevertheless, even here there is no reason in principle why a person should not waive his restitutionary rights extra-contractually, however unlikely in practice this may be. Suppose I give you £1,000 as a reward for passing the Bar exams, but say it will not worry me if there has been a mistake in the assessment and in fact you failed them.[6] Again, imagine you contract to do work on my house, but later, in full knowledge that you have no right to do so, refuse to perform unless I pay you a further £250 to cover increased costs. Feeling sympathetic, and in order to cement our business relationship, I do so; I cannot recover my payment.[7]

(c) Donative intent

13-5 For obvious reasons, benefits rendered with the intent of making a gift of them cannot form the subject of restitutionary recovery; Anglo-Irish law does not generally allow people, however deserving, to repent of largesse.

In many cases, indeed, absence of donative intent does not need to be specifically mentioned since it is implicit in the requirements for restitution to be granted in the first place. Free acceptance, for instance, means free acceptance on the basis that what was accepted was to be paid for. If you freely accept goods or

---

3 Eg, *Cooke v Wright* (1861) 1 B & S 559; *Callisher v Bischoffsheim* (1870) LR 5 QB 449.

4 Eg *Sneath v Valley Gold* [1893] 1 QB 477; Foskett, D, *The Law and Practice of Compromise*, 3rd edn, § 2-01.

5 See *Callisher v Bischoffsheim* (1870) LR 5 QB 449, p 451.

6 'If, indeed, the money is intentionally paid, without reference to the truth or falsehood of the fact, the plaintiff meaning to waive all enquiry into it, and that the person receiving shall have the money at all events, whether the fact be true or false, the latter is certainly entitled to retain it': Parke B in *Kelly v Solari* (1841) 9 M & W 54, p 59. See, too, *Scottish Equitable plc v Derby* [2001] 3 All ER 818, p 824 (Robert Walker LJ).

7 Cf *Williams v Roffey Bros Ltd* [1991] 1 QB 1. It is inconceivable that the court in that case would have allowed restitution of the extra payment if it had been made.

services which I offer to you *gratis*, my claim to be paid for them simply cannot get off the ground. Again, the right of a would-be contractor to recover for services rendered in the expectation that a contract would later materialise is well established; but it only applies where there is no understanding that the services are to be rendered without payment (for example, as a 'loss leader', in order to encourage the recipient to do business in future).

Nevertheless, it is suggested that in other cases, donative intent does provide an independent defence to a restitutionary claim that would otherwise exist. Take a typical duress case, as where a robber threatens to stab me unless I give him my purse. It is possible, if unlikely, that I will genuinely decide that I wish to give it to him out of sympathy for his plight. If I do, I cannot later get it back.[8] Or imagine necessity; if I am your agent of necessity or someone else who would otherwise have a claim against you for necessitous intervention, but act purely out of motives of friendship, or otherwise make it clear that I will not charge for my services, it is submitted that that is an end of the matter: I cannot later change my mind.[9]

Presumably, in all these cases, what matters is not so much the claimant's actual state of mind, but the outward manifestation of it: if a reasonable person would have thought he was acting *gratis*, then that should have been sufficient.[10]

III   CHANGE OF POSITION

(a) Generally

13-6   Even before the significant decision of the House of Lords in *Lipkin Gorman v Karpnale Ltd*,[11] there is no doubt that a change of position by the defendant in reliance on being allowed to keep the benefit would sometimes amount to a defence to a restitutionary claim. An agent, for instance, who received moneys for his principal was immune to an action for money paid by mistake once he had in good faith accounted over.[12] Again, in *Re Diplock*,[13] it had been held that

---

8   Cf *The Siboen and The Sibotre* [1976] 1 Lloyd's Rep 293.

9   Cf the rendering of emergency medical attention in England: arguably the most convincing reason for denying a claim against the victim is the universal acceptance that such services are rendered gratis.

10   This is another reason for doubting the decision in *Upton RDC v Powell* [1942] 1 All ER 220. Would not a reasonable householder, seeing a fire engine draw up outside his house and begin to put out a fire, assume the fire brigade was acting gratuitously?

11   [1991] 2 AC 548.

12   A long established principle: *Buller v Harrison* (1777) 2 Cowp 565. See, too, eg, *Kleinwort, Sons and Co v Dunlop Rubber Co* (1907) 97 LT 263; *Gowers v Lloyds and National Provincial Foreign Bank Ltd* [1938] 1 All ER 766; *Bank Tejarat v Hong Kong and Shanghai Bank* [1995] 1 Lloyd's Rep 239.

13   [1948] Ch 465.

a claim against a wrongful recipient of assets comprised in an estate could be resisted on the grounds that the latter had sunk the funds in improvements to property or discharge of a mortgage.[14] In England, the provisions of s 1(3) of the Law Reform (Frustrated Contracts) Act 1943 were interpreted by Goff J in *BP (Exploration) Ltd v Hunt*[15] as giving rise to a *de facto* change of position defence. And the Supreme Court in *Murphy v AG*[16] gave relief on a related basis against the possibility of a potentially ruinous demand for repayment of tax following a declaration that a substantial pillar of the Irish income tax system was unconstitutional. But further than this, the concept did not go: the general rule was that unless the defendant to a restitutionary action could show some kind of estoppel binding the claimant, such as a relied-on assurance that a payment to him was in order,[17] the mere fact of change of position would not avail him.[18]

13-7   However, following Commonwealth developments[19] and a few suggestions in the lower courts,[20] the House of Lords in *Lipkin Gorman v Karpnale*[21] has now decided that *prima facie* it is a defence to any action based on unjust enrichment[22] that the defendant has changed his position in good faith on the faith of his receipt such that it would be inequitable to demand repayment. It would seem that no distinction is drawn in this context between personal and proprietary claims: provided they are restitutionary in nature, the defence will be available in respect of them.

The facts of *Lipkin Gorman* illustrate the point nicely. A partner in the plaintiff firm helped himself to funds belonging to it and gambled them at the Playboy Club. His losses, predictably, much exceeded his winnings. When he had been caught, imprisoned and bankrupted, the firm sued the club for the return of its money. The House of Lords, having held that the club could not raise the defence of *bona fide* purchase, held that they were nevertheless protected, to the extent that they had paid out winnings to the errant partner, by a defence of

---

14   Another arguable example was the rule in *Price v Neal* (1762) 3 Burr 1364 and *Cocks v Masterman* (1829) 9 B & C 902, precluding recovery of money paid on a forged bill of exchange in the absence of timely protest by the payee.

15   [1982] 1 All ER 925, affirmed [1983] 2 AC 352.

16   [1982] IR 241.

17   Which might, admittedly, be inferred on pretty slender evidence, as in *Holt v Markham* [1923] 1 KB 504.

18   Eg, *Durrant v Ecclesiastical Comrs* (1880) 6 QBD 234; *Baylis v Bishop of London* [1913] 1 Ch 127.

19   Eg, the Canadian decision in *Storthoaks Rural Municipality v Mobil Oil Canada* (1975) 55 DLR (3d) 1.

20   Notably by Goff J in *Barclays Bank Ltd v WJ Simms Ltd* [1980] QB 677; see, too, *Midland Bank plc v Brown Shipley Ltd* [1991] 2 All ER 690, pp 701–02 (Waller J).

21   [1991] 2 AC 548.

22   Except, perhaps, in the case of *ultra vires* payments by the State or Crown covered by the rule in *Auckland Harbour Board v R* [1924] AC 318. The point was left open by Schiemann J in *R v Secretary of State for the Environment ex p London Borough of Camden* (1995) unreported, 17 February, QBD. The English Law Commission believes the defence is, and should be, available here: Law Com No 227, 17.20.

change of position. Although *Lipkin Gorman* has not yet come up for discussion in the Irish courts, it is thought that it is likely to be followed there too.

13-8   Why should change of position be a defence in restitution, given that no such defence exists to an action in contract or tort?[23] Birks argues at one point[24] that it is allied to the principle against forced exchange. If you pay me £1,000 by mistake and I spend it on fripperies I would not otherwise have bought, making me repay you is tantamount to making me pay out of my own pocket for something I reasonably thought I was getting for free. But this is a little difficult to apply to cases of, say, charitable donation: if I have given the £1,000 to charity, I cannot say any benefit is being forced on me against my will, and yet I ought to remain able to invoke the defence.

A better ground for distinguishing in this connection between restitution and other cases is that a defendant who has committed some wrong, or owes a sum of money, can normally[25] be expected to have notice of this fact and to take steps to meet that liability: it should not be open to him to say he has changed his position in the mistaken belief that he will not have to pay. Restitution, by contrast, does not depend on any debt incurred, or – restitution for wrongs aside – wrong committed. The equities are therefore stronger in the defendant's favour. This argument also has the advantage that to some extent it explains the hesitancy of Lord Goff in *Lipkin Gorman*[26] over the application of change of position to the wrongdoing defendant.[27]

(b) Change of position: extent and scope of the defence

13-9   The first point to note is that, for obvious reasons, change of position is only a *pro tanto* defence (a point of importance when comparing it with estoppel, which is dealt with below). If you pay me £1,000 by mistake, whereupon I give £300 to charity and keep the rest, your claim remains good to the extent of £700.

On principle, the defendant, to make good the defence, must show three things:

---

23 But note that even here, change of position may be relevant on occasion. It is, for instance, far easier to resist an application to extend a limitation period if the defendant has changed his position in the meantime – as indeed it is to raise the defence of laches in equity.

24 Birks, p 410 *et seq*.

25 Except in the case of genuine strict liability torts, such as detinue or conversion. But then, the liability in damages of an entirely innocent handler of another's goods who no longer has them is itself open to considerable criticism.

26 See [1991] 2 AC 548, p 580.

27 And cf *Saronic v Liberia Huron* [1979] 1 Lloyd's Rep 341, p 365, where it was said that change of position could not be available to a defendant whose own misrepresentation had caused him to be paid in the first place. A similar suggestion was made by Schiemann J in *R v Secretary of State for the Environment ex p London Borough of Camden* (1995) unreported, 17 February (where a council unsuccessfully pleaded change of position to resist a clawback of block grant which had been paid to it because of its own misrepresentation).

(1) that he assumed that, having got the benefit in question, he would be allowed to retain it;

(2) that he had no reason to know of the possibility of his being liable to restitutionary action;

and

(3) that he has as a result disposed of the benefit received, or been deprived of it, such that it would be unjust to make him refund.

13-10 Points (1) and (2) are straightforward, and indeed are often two sides of the same coin. They are neatly illustrated by the facts of *United Overseas Bank v Jiwani*[28] (which was, in fact, an estoppel case, but raised the same issues). Instructed to credit its customer's account by $11,000, a bank mistakenly did so twice. The customer immediately used the excess in part payment for a hotel. His claim that this amounted to a change of position so as to estop the bank from reclaiming its $11,000 failed; he must, said McKenna J, have had at least a suspicion that something was wrong (and in any case, his Lordship added, it was clear that he would have made the part payment from other funds in any event). Similarly, a solicitor who acted professionally as executor of a will that was in fact invalid was held disentitled to retain payment for doing so, despite his plea of change of position: he was regarded as being on notice of possible testamentary invalidity and hence as taking the risk of a liability to repay what he received.[29] But the requirements are nevertheless separate: a person who receives a benefit in all innocence, but discovers the possibility of a claim against him before acting to his detriment, clearly ought not to be allowed the defence.[30]

13-11 Point (3) is slightly more problematical.

To begin with, it is obviously not enough merely to show that the defendant has spent the money he got. The expenditure, however extraordinary, may be one the defendant would have made anyway[31] (though it seems the courts will not be over-demanding in demanding detailed accounts).[32] Again, if the defendant spent it on ordinary living expenses, this must be irrelevant: such expenditure cannot be argued to have been incurred in reliance on the receipt, and in any case it can hardly be regarded as unfair to make him refund.[33] Yet again, expenditure does not imply total loss. If funds have gone on something

---

28 [1977] 1 All ER 733. Cf *National Westminster Bank v Barclays Bank International* [1974] 3 All ER 834.

29 See *Gray v Richards Butler* (1996) *The Times*, 23 July. With respect, this seems an unduly harsh decision on the facts.

30 For what counts as knowledge in this context, see *Bank Tejarat v Hong Kong and Shanghai Bank* [1995] 1 Lloyd's Rep 239.

31 As in *Jiwani's* case, above: see, too, *Lipkin Gorman* [1991] 2 AC 548, p 580 (Lord Goff); *Scottish Equitable plc v Derby* [2000] 3 All ER 793, p 801 (Harrison J); *Philip Collins Ltd v Davis* [2000] 3 All ER 808, p 827 (Jonathan Parker J).

32 Cf *Philip Collins Ltd v Davis* [2000] 3 All ER 808.

33 See the authorities above, fn 31.

clearly appraisable and simply realisable, such as gilt-edged stock, it is hardly inequitable for the claimant to continue to insist on repayment up to the present value of what was bought (less, presumably, any direct expenses of realisation).[34] Similarly, with payment of existing debts that would have had to be paid anyway: thus in *Scottish Equitable plc v Derby*,[35] an overpaid life policyholder was held to have no defence to an action for reimbursement merely because he had used £40,000 odd to pay off part of his mortgage. He only had a defence as to £9,000 or thereabouts of extraordinary expenditure. Presumably, in such cases, the criterion is whether the money has gone beyond the possibility of reasonable recall by the defendant; if, and only if, it has, there will be a defence of change of position. A gift to charity[36] is perhaps the best example.[37]

13-12   In some cases, the defence of change of position may be unavailable on the basis that the defendant willingly took a particular risk. Thus in *Goss v Chilcott*,[38] a defendant sought to resist a claim for restitution of funds lent under a void mortgage on the basis that the moneys had been lent on to an uncreditworthy and judgment-proof borrower. He failed: in the circumstances, he had taken the risk of losing the money in these circumstances.[39]

A further point concerns timing. What if the defendant has made a payment to X which would normally be irrecoverable, but X has subsequently agreed *ex gratia* to refund it? Despite a possible argument that this is *res inter alios acta* as regards the claimant, it seems that repayment will be ordered. Thus, in the *Scottish Equitable* case, above, the defendant had spent some of his payout on a life policy with another company, but in the light of the fact that the latter was prepared to unwind the transaction, no deduction was made on this account from the amount the defendant had to refund.

(c) Does change of position require an act by the defendant?

13-13   A much more tricky point is whether change of position requires an act by the defendant himself, or whether any worsening in his position that can be shown

---

34   An example given by McKenna J in *United Overseas Bank v Jiwani* [1977] 1 All ER 733, p 737. See, too, *Scottish Equitable plc v Derby* [2001] 3 All ER 818 (purchase of life policy).

35   [2001] 3 All ER 818.

36   This also emphasises the necessity for a 'reasonableness' criterion. At least in some cases of gifts to charity, the gifts themselves might be recoverable on the ground of mistake if made on the basis of funds received by the donor; but a court would, it is suggested, be loath to require the donor in such circumstances to engage in litigation against the charity in order to repay his own transferor.

37   But would the money be directly recoverable by the payer from the charity? I argue in Chapter 1 that it should not, on the basis that receipt from a third party ought to be a factor justifying retention; but this view is subjected to searching criticism by Burrows (see Burrows, p 46).

38   [1997] AC 788.

39   See *ibid*, p 799.

to result from his enrichment ought to be in account. Take the case of the recipient of £100 paid by mistake. Grant that he should not have to refund if he has given away £100 in reliance; should it make any difference if the £100 has been not spent, but lost or stolen? It is submitted that it should not. The injustice to the defendant that would arise from making him repay in full is the same in both cases. Furthermore, to limit change of position to the defendant's own acts would lead to some very nice distinctions. It would be odd, to say the least, if my liability to repay you money I did not have depended on whether I had handed it over to a confidence trickster (which presumably would count as spending it), or alternatively had my pocket picked in the street (which would count as losing it). Despite one clear contrary decision at first instance in England,[40] it now seems that this view is accepted.[41]

In any event, it is worth pointing out that cases where a defendant could rely on theft or loss as a defence are likely in the nature of things to be very rare: he will still have to show that the theft or loss would not have happened but for the enrichment, and this will probably be impossible except in the fairly unlikely event that, having received (say) £100 by mistake, the defendant was robbed of it before he had a chance to bank it.

(d) Change of position and double recovery

13-14 One advantage of allowing an 'extended' defence covering extraneous factors depriving the defendant of the benefit of his receipt is that it provides a neat solution to the problem of double liability. This concerns the fact, already mentioned in Chapter 1,[42] that there is no reason on principle why the same gain in the hands of the defendant should not give rise to liability to two different claimants. The sergeant in *Reading v AG*,[43] for example, could potentially have faced claims both from the Crown as his employers and from the Egyptian Government as taxing authority. The trustee-director who profits from his position is in the same unenviable position vis à vis both the company and the beneficiary. It is suggested, however, that in such a situation, there is no reason why the handing over of the gain to one claimant, whether as a result of threatened legal action or otherwise, should not have the same effect as any other change of position. Once the defendant has been stripped of his illegitimate gain by one claimant, it should be regarded as unjust for him to be stripped of it again by the other so as to end up out of pocket. It could then be

---

40 *Streiner v Bank Leumi* (1985) unreported, 31 October, QBD.
41 See *Scottish Equitable plc v Derby* [2001] 3 All ER 818, p 827 (Robert Walker LJ). In *Euroactividade AG v Moeller* (1995) unreported, 1 February, CA, Simon Brown LJ was similarly prepared to accept that third party actions could amount to a relevant change of position (though the defence failed on the facts).
42 See above, § 1-28.
43 [1951] AC 507.

left to the ordinary law of restitution whether the second claimant who thus lost out could then claim over against the first, or whether the loss would lie where it fell.[44]

(e) Change of position: acts other than paying money

13-15   A point not touched on in *Lipkin Gorman* is how far change of position goes beyond payment of money. Transfer of property doubtless suffices: but what about more abstract reliance, such as the rendering of services? Presumably, the answer must be yes;[45] it certainly suffices for estoppel (see below), and if it did not equally work in change of position cases, the anomalies would be glaring indeed. A fraudster who has stolen £100,000 from X gives £10,000 to his son, who trustingly squanders it, and pays £10,000 to his counsel,[46] who unsuccessfully defends him. It would be, to say the least, peculiar if nothing were recoverable from the son whereas counsel had to refund in full.

(f) Prior and subsequent change of position[47]

13-16   Most cases of change of position involve events subsequent to receipt of the benefit concerned – for instance, where, having been paid £100 by mistake, I give that sum to charity. But is the defence equally available to me if I made the donation in anticipation of the payment? The point is a nice one. On the one hand, it seems over-technical to worry too much about the precise time of payment, since it does not seem to affect the equities at all: the unfairness, if any, is precisely the same whether my expenditure occurred one hour before or one hour after the time when the payment was credited to my defendant's account.[48] But, conversely, if my act in reliance would not have allowed me to sue for the £100 if I did not get it,[49] why should it give me a subsequent title to keep it if I did? Justice, it is suggested, on balance favours the former argument,

---

44   Eg, would the British Government in *Reading v AG* [1951] AC 507, by claiming Sgt Reading's ill-gotten gains, be regarded as having adopted the sergeant's actions so as themselves to face an action by the Egyptian Government? There seems no reason why not.

45   As was assumed by Carnwath J in *Gray v Richards Butler* (1996) *The Times*, 23 July (services rendered by executor pursuant to invalid will), though the defence failed for other reasons. See, too, *Scottish Equitable plc v Derby* [2000] 3 All ER 793, p 801, where Harrison J seemingly accepted that a generous view of change of position ought to be taken.

46   Who does not, of course, act under a contract, and therefore by parity of reasoning with *Lipkin Gorman* cannot plead *bona fide* purchase.

47   See (2000) 117 LQR 14.

48   As now suggested by Burrows: see [1995] RLR 15, p 20. See, too, *Lipkin Gorman v Karpnale Ltd* [1991] 2 AC 548, where all winnings and losses by the Playboy Club were lumped together without minute inquiry as to the order in which they took place.

49   Because of the rule in *Combe v Combe* [1951] 2 KB 215.

as do Goff & Jones.[50] But, in *South Tyneside MBC v Svenska International plc*,[51] Clarke J plumped for the latter. He therefore held that a defendant in a 'swaps' action[52] which had entered into a back-to-back hedging transaction before signing the main contract could not plead change of position on that basis.

(g) Who can invoke change of position? – the problem of 'wrongdoers'

13-17 Lord Goff in *Lipkin Gorman* suggested that change of position was a general defence, applicable to all restitutionary claims, subject to one caveat: 'It is commonly accepted that the defence should not be open to a wrongdoer.'[53] With respect, this is a little difficult to understand; and indeed, whether such a blanket exception is either necessary or desirable is rather doubtful. It is no doubt aimed at such unsympathetic characters as the thief, or the agent who takes a bribe, who later tries to avoid disgorging his ill-gotten gains by saying he has spent them. But such people are unlikely to be able to invoke the principle anyway, since however much they may have changed their position, they can hardly claim to have done so in good faith. And what about the innocent wrongdoer, such as the unwitting converter? It is hard to see why he should not have the benefit of the defence if the claimant chooses to waive the tort and sue for money had and received.[54] If the recipient of the claimant's money can claim change of position, why not the recipient of the claimant's goods who is sued for the amount he got for them when he resold them?

It may be possible, however, to justify a slightly different exception in this context. There are dicta in two cases[55] that a defendant who has received money as a result of a misrepresentation by him cannot plead change of position to an action for money paid by mistake.[56] This is presumably on the basis that the

---

50 Goff & Jones, pp 822–23. In *Philip Collins Ltd v Davis* [2000] 3 All ER 808, p 827, Jonathan Parker J was not unreceptive to it, though the point did not fall for decision.

51 [1995] 1 All ER 545. See, too, *Hinckley and Bosworth BC v Shaw* [2000] LGR 9, reaching much the same result on the basis that the anticipatory spender relies not on the receipt, but on the validity of the contract under which it is paid; but on this, cf *Eastbourne BC v Foster* [2001] EWCA 1091.

52 Ie, an action for repayment of sums paid by a local authority under an *ultra vires* interest rate swap.

53 [1991] 2 AC 548, p 580.

54 True, it could be argued that he would be liable in conversion for the full value of the goods, and so to give him a defence of change of position to a restitutionary claim would be quixotic. But he may have sold the goods for more than their value; and in any case the arbitrary measure of damages in conversion is itself difficult to defend.

55 *Saronic v Liberia Huron* [1979] 1 Lloyd's Rep 341, p 365, and *R v Secretary of State for the Environment ex p London Borough of Camden* (1995) unreported, 17 February.

56 Presumably, the same will apply to the person who takes prepayment for goods and services which he then does not supply.

equities are very weak in favour of a person who has himself caused the events leading to the restitution claim against him.

(h) Possible other exceptions to change of position

13-18 One further problem needs to be mentioned. In two situations there are clear decisions, one by the House of Lords and one by the Privy Council, that change of position is inapplicable: and neither was overruled in *Lipkin Gorman v Karpnale*.[57]

First, in *Ministry of Health v Simpson*[58] it was said that the defence did not apply to a personal claim by an executor or administrator to recover estate moneys wrongly disbursed. That specific holding was referred to, but not specifically discountenanced, in *Lipkin Gorman*;[59] it remains to be seen whether it remains good law.[60] And secondly, there is the decision in *Auckland Harbour Board v R*[61] that the same is true of unauthorised payments by the State or Crown. Once again, it remains uncertain how far this is still good law.[62]

IV ESTOPPEL

13-19 Unlike change of position, which is not a defence to causes of action other than those based on unjustified enrichment, there is nothing peculiarly restitutionary about estoppel. Any private right, whatever its origin, may be barred by an express or implied statement that it will not be exercised, coupled with change of position on the faith of it, in circumstances such that it would be inequitable to assert it. Nevertheless, estoppel is commonly relevant in practice to restitutionary claims, in particular where payment by mistake is concerned.

In contrast to change of position, the defendant seeking to invoke estoppel needs to show not only a change of position, but change of position resulting from a positive representation, express or implied, that restitutionary rights will not be relied on. This latter requirement is strictly applied: in particular, the mere fact that I pay you money does not, without more, carry with it a

---

57 [1991] 2 AC 548.

58 [1951] AC 251.

59 [1991] 2 AC 548 (Lord Goff).

60 In *Gertsch v Atsas* (1999) unreported, 1 October, the Supreme Court of New South Wales held the defence applicable.

61 [1924] AC 318: see, too, *Commonwealth v Burns* [1971] VR 825.

62 The point was pointedly left open by Schiemann J in *R v Secretary of State for the Environment ex p London Borough of Camden* (1995) unreported, 17 February. Goff & Jones, p 231, seem to suggest that the defence remains inapplicable.

representation that you will not have to pay it back.[63] On the other hand, if I query the payment and you assure me that there is no mistake, then the matter is different: witness *Avon CC v Howlett*,[64] where such an assurance was given to a teacher who had been overpaid and relied on by him, and as a result was held to bar the employer's action for recovery of the excess. Similarly, in *Holt v Markham*,[65] a demand for money paid by mistake was refused by the payee on apparently plausible grounds, whereupon the payer said nothing for two months and the payee spent the money. The payer was held barred by estoppel.

As for the change of position, this must obviously be on the faith of the representation; it must be *bona fide* and reasonable (that is, without notice of the existence of a potential claim). The facts of *United Overseas Bank v Jiwani*,[66] already given, amply illustrate this. Although there is no case directly concerning restitutionary recovery, there is plenty of authority that in other kinds of estoppel, such as proprietary estoppel, reliance by act is just as efficacious as reliance by paying hard cash or transferring property.

13-20 Given the availability of change of position as a defence, why plead estoppel at all, since it is in general harder to make out? There are two obvious reasons.

The first is relatively straightforward. There are cases where change of position will not avail the defendant: for example, where he is a wrongdoer,[67] and (arguably) where the change of position occurs before receipt of the benefit.[68] There seems no reason, however, why, in a suitable case, estoppel should not be available to the defendant who can prove a suitable representation, together with some act in reliance on it such that it would be inequitable for the claimant to seek restitution.

13-21 The second is more problematical. Traditionally, estoppel, unlike change of position, has been regarded as a matter of evidence rather than the substantive law: once a representation has been relied on, the representor is not allowed to lead evidence contradicting it. Logically, therefore, estoppel (unlike change of position) should operate on an 'all-or-nothing' basis, rather than merely *pro tanto*. Suppose you pay me £1,000 by mistake; you then assure me all is in order, whereupon I squander £600. If I plead change of position, you recover £400. If I establish estoppel, on the traditional reasoning, you recover nothing (since you are precluded from denying that the payment was entirely in order) and I get a welcome, if dubiously just, windfall of £400. And indeed, in the restitution case

---

63 See *Lipkin Gorman v Karpnale Ltd* [1991] 2 AC 548, p 579 (Lord Goff); *Philip Collins Ltd v Davis* [2000] 3 All ER 808 (Jonathan Parker J).

64 [1983] 1 All ER 1073.

65 [1923] 1 KB 504.

66 [1977] 1 All ER 733, above, § 13-10. Cf *National Westminster Bank v Barclays Bank International* [1974] 3 All ER 834.

67 Above, § 13-17.

68 Above, § 13-16.

of *Avon CC v Howlett*,[69] precisely this happened. A teacher was overpaid by about £1,000, assured that all was correct, and spent some £550. Recovery was denied *in toto*.

However, all three members of the Court of Appeal in *Howlett* expressed disquiet at the result,[70] stated that estoppel would not necessarily be available where it led to serious injustice, and left it open whether, if the matter were more fully argued, the defence available to an overpaid defendant might not be more closely tailored to the justice of the case. A later Court of Appeal took up these suggestions in *Scottish Equitable plc v Derby*,[71] where, it will be remembered, an overpaid life policyholder's plea of change of position to a demand for £170,000 failed except as to £9,000 odd. The court declined to accede to the defendant's alternative plea that he had a complete defence based on estoppel, on the basis that estoppel could not be used where (as here) the result would be wholly inequitable. The defendant was therefore limited to his *pro tanto* defence based on change of position. The practical result of this case appears to be that, at least where there is a substantial difference between the benefit to the defendant and any expenditure in reliance on it, the defence of estoppel is a dead letter.

13-22 Having said this, however, a further point arises: why retain estoppel at all as a defence in restitution cases, rather than force all defendants to rely on the more subtle protection of change of position (as has been done in Canada)?[72] Although this is on principle an attractive solution,[73] the Court of Appeal declined to take this radical route in *Scottish Equitable*. It was probably right to do so, for three reasons. First, there are the cases referred to above where the application of change of position is, to say the least, problematical. Secondly, abolishing estoppel in restitution cases would create an odd imbalance between different kinds of claim. There is no doubt that the defence of estoppel applies, for instance, to statements that contractual claims will not be exercised: it would be peculiar if the legal consequence of such statements varied according to how the claimant's case happened to be classified. If there is to be reform, a promising line of development would seem to be to hone the defence of estoppel so as to limit it to the actual reliance interest, rather than to abolish it entirely. And thirdly, getting rid of estoppel would give rise to an awkward mismatch between restitution and the law of agency. Suppose A, acting with the ostensible (but not actual) authority of B, transfers a sum of money to C. Can B recover the payment from C? As the law currently stands, the answer is no: he is deemed,

69 See *Avon CC v Howlett* [1983] 1 All ER 1073, leaving the point open to future argument; but the point was apparently accepted by Lord Goff in *Lipkin Gorman v Karpnale* [1992] 4 All ER 512, p 533.

70 See [1983] 1 All ER 1073, pp 1076, 1078, 1089.

71 [2001] 3 All ER 818. See too *Philip Collins Ltd v Davies* [2000] 3 All ER 808 and *National Westminster Bank plc v Somer* [2001] EWCA 970.

72 See *Royal Bank of Canada v Dawson* (1994) 111 DLR (4th) 230 and, generally, Key [1995] CLJ 525.

73 And indeed attracted Jonathan Parker J in *Philip Collins Ltd v Davies* [2000] 3 All ER 808, p 826.

and rightly so, to have been paid with B's authority. But ostensible authority is itself a species of estoppel:[74] and it would be unfortunate if cases such as this were to be overturned, as it were, by a sidewind.

V ILLEGALITY AND STATUTORY INVALIDITY

(a) Generally

13-23 There is no doubt that, just as a knowing participant in illegality or immorality may be barred from suing in contract or tort, so he may be barred in restitution as well. There is no reason, in a suitable case, not to apply the maxim *ex turpi causa non oritur actio* to any cause of action, whatever its classification.

Most of the cases concern failure of consideration. Thus, since *Parkinson v College of Ambulance*[75] it has been established that where money is paid for an illegal performance that the payee then declines to provide, there can be no claim for failure of consideration. No doubt this is on the same basis as in the rest of the law of contract: those who knowingly engage in illegality should do so at their own risk, and the courts should not lend their aid to them when things go wrong. The leading authority is *Bigos v Bousted*,[76] dismissing an action to recover securities deposited as security for the price of foreign currency which was not forthcoming (such conduct then being an illegal contravention of exchange controls). Pritchard J specifically distinguished between 'repentance cases' where the claimant withdrew and 'frustration cases' where the defendant did so, confirming the rule of non-recoverability in the latter class.[77]

13-24 Nevertheless, it would seem that similar principles apply to other sorts of restitutionary claim. An action to recover a payment demanded to stifle a prosecution, brought on the ground of duress, may thus be defeated by *ex turpi causa* (cf the Irish decision in *Brady v Flood*).[78] And it seems pretty clear that a similar result will follow in other areas of restitution. Suppose a builder agrees to carry out improvements to premises he knows are to be used as a brothel, but is dismissed by the client before he has finished: it is highly unlikely that he

---

74 See, eg, *Freeman & Lockyer v Buckhurst Park Properties Ltd* [1964] 2 QB 480, p 502 (Diplock LJ).

75 [1925] 2 KB 1 (payment for inclusion in honours list: no recovery when payer duly disappointed). In the earlier case of *Kearley v Thomson* (1890) 24 QBD 742, recovery was also denied: but there, there was no failure of consideration in any case, and hence no independent ground for restitution.

76 [1951] 1 All ER 92. See too *Berg v Sadler and Moore* [1937] 2 KB 158 (no recovery of money paid for cigarettes not delivered, when purchaser had fraudulently stated that he was not on a 'stop list').

77 [1951] 1 All ER 92, p 100.

78 (1841) 6 Circuit Cases 309.

would be allowed to claim a *quantum meruit* for the work done.[79] Again, take mistake. If I agree to pay you £100 to beat up X, but then inadvertently pay you £200, it would (it is suggested) be very odd if I could recover the overpayment.

The illegality defence in restitution is, however, not an absolute one, and there are a number of exceptions to it, to which we now turn.

(b) Exception: unknowing participation

13-25 Just as in contract a party can normally sue on an agreement if he does not know the facts making it illegal,[80] so in restitution. Thus in *Oom v Bruce*,[81] premiums paid under an insurance policy to carry goods from Russia to England in ignorance of facts that made it an illegal contract (because war had broken out shortly before) were held recoverable by the assured.[82] A similar decision is *Tappenden v Randall*[83] in 1801.

(c) Exception: 'repentance cases'

13-26 Although, as a general rule, a knowing participant in illegality cannot rely on failure of consideration to ground recovery, it seems an exception is made where the person seeking recovery withdrew from the transaction before any of the consideration was received. An early example is *Aubert v Walsh*,[84] holding that an assured can recover premiums paid on an illegal contract of insurance before the risk has started to run,[85] but the leading case is *Taylor v Bowers*.[86] An insolvent industrialist turned over certain machinery to his nephew in order to appear even more bereft of assets than he really was, and hence deceive his creditors into agreeing to accept less than their entitlement. He later gave up this dishonest enterprise, but the nephew refused to return the machinery. The

---

79 *Jackson Stansfield v Butterworth* [1948] 2 All ER 558 arguably was a case of this sort. An action for the value of unlicensed building work (which then required a licence) failed; and it appears the action was on a *quantum meruit*. The awkward decision in *Cotronic v Dezonie* [1991] BCLC 721, allowing a *quantum meruit* to a plaintiff illegally performing work in the name of a struck-off company, can only be justified (if at all) as turning on the interpretation of the purpose of the legislation concerned.

80 Eg, *Fielding & Platt Ltd v Najjar* [1969] 2 All ER 150.

81 (1810) 12 East 225.

82 The unjust factor being mistake, or (arguably) failure of consideration.

83 (1801) 2 B & P 467. For other examples, see Goff & Jones, 5th edn, p 616.

84 (1810) 3 Taunt 277. The same rule applies if the contract is lawful: *Stevenson v Snow* (1761) 3 Burr 1237.

85 *Sed quaere*, whether in the specialised case of marine insurance the doctrine can now stand with the Marine Insurance Act 1906, s 84. This section, having provided for recovery of the premium in the case of a void policy, specifically excepts cases of 'illegality on the part of the assured'.

86 (1876) 1 QBD 291.

industrialist was held entitled to get it back. But the right is limited to where the claimant withdrew: as was made clear in the recent Court of Appeal decision in *Tribe v Tribe*,[87] if the failure of consideration arose from the refusal of the other party to provide the contemplated exchange, the action will fail.[88]

13-27 Although these cases are said to turn on the 'repentance' of the claimant,[89] it is not easy to see how repentance as such can give anyone title to sue. It is suggested that they are really examples of recovery on a total failure of consideration, exceptionally not subject to the illegality bar.[90] Admittedly Burrows[91] denies that this can be so, contending that there can be no claim for failure of consideration where the claimant withdraws and the defendant remains ready and willing to perform (for which he cites *Thomas v Brown*.[92] But, for the reasons given in Chapter 6, it is submitted that this argument is unsound.

The view that failure of consideration is the proper ground is supported by the fact that, however repentant the claimant, he recovers nothing once he has received any benefit under the contract. So in *Kearley v Thomson*[93] the plaintiff, the friend of a bankrupt, paid £40 to one of his creditors not to appear at the public examination, with a view to the bankrupt obtaining an easier discharge. The creditor stayed away, but the bankrupt did not proceed with his application to be discharged. The plaintiff's action for return of the £40 failed, Fry LJ deciding the case squarely on the basis that 'where there has been a partial carrying into effect of an illegal purpose in a substantial manner, it is impossible, though there remains something not performed, that the money paid under that illegal contract can be recovered back'.[94] Nor does this seem unreasonable: if a party to a lawful contract cannot recover except by showing total failure, it is not easy to see why the illegality of the agreement should make any difference.

---

87 [1996] Ch 107.

88 As in *Bigos v Bousted* [1951] 1 All ER 92, above. See, too, *Berg v Sadler and Moore* [1937] 2 KB 158. The contrary suggestion by Lord Denning MR in *Shaw v Shaw* [1967] 1 All ER 638, p 639, cannot (with respect) be supported.

89 A point clearly adumbrated in *Parkinson v College of Ambulance* [1925] 2 KB 1 and *Alexander v Rayson* [1936] 1 KB 169. Similar *dicta* appear in *Harry Parker v Mason* [1940] 4 All ER 199, pp 202, 203.

90 See *Aubert v Walsh* (1810) 3 Taunt 277, p 283 (Lord Mansfield); and cf *Re Cavalier Insurance Ltd* [1989] 2 Lloyd's Rep 430, p 449. Thus, the right of an assured to recover premiums by cancelling the contract before the risk has started to run applies equally to lawful insurance contracts: *Stevenson v Snow* (1761) 3 Burr 1237. And note the deprecation of the diffuse concept of 'repentance' by Millett LJ in *Tribe v Tribe* [1996] Ch 107, p 135.

91 Burrows, p 335, following Birks, p 301.

92 (1876) 1 QBD 714.

93 (1890) 24 QBD 742.

94 *Ibid*, p 747.

(d) Exception: claimant not *in pari delicto*

13-28   A further exception arises where the claimant was not *in pari delicto* – meaning either that he was substantially less morally to blame than the defendant, or that the sole purpose of making the transaction illegal was to protect him from the other party. The first point can be illustrated by *Shelley v Paddock*,[95] where the plaintiff paid £9,500 to a fraudster for a house in Spain, contrary to the then exchange control legislation. When the house was not forthcoming, an action in deceit for the price succeeded. The fact that the plaintiff had not known of the exchange control legislation, coupled with the defendant's fraud, was sufficient to outweigh the illegality of the whole transaction. Although strictly, the action was in tort, there is no reason to think that an action for money paid on a total failure of consideration would have fared any worse.[96] In a similar vein, other cases have held that premiums paid under illegal insurance contracts can be recovered when made as a result of fraudulent statements by the insurer or his agents that the policy was valid.[97]

The 'protective' exception to the illegality bar appears in a number of guises. Statutory rent control provides a straightforward instance. Where housing legislation imposes limits on rents or forbids practices such as acceptance of premiums or 'key money', it was held in *Gray v Southouse*[98] that the lessee can recover moneys so paid, even in the absence of the statutory provision to that effect which is now near-universal.[99] Similarly with legislation making it illegal for an insurance company to carry on business without authorisation: this exists to protect policyholders from the effects of the underwriter's insolvency, and should not prevent recovery of premiums by the assured.[100]

13-29   Occasionally, extra-statutory illegality is treated in the same way. Equity, for example, has long held marriage brokerage contracts illegal: but it has gone further, and held in a series of cases culminating in *Hermann v Charlesworth*[101] that moneys paid by the hopeful would-be bride can be recovered back from the

---

95   [1980] 1 All ER 1009.

96   Another possible case is recovery of illegal premiums from a lessor, discussed below. In *Kiriri Cotton v Dewani* [1960] AC 192, p 205, Lord Denning emphasised that the tenant was not 'so much to blame' as the landlord.

97   Eg, *Hughes v Liverpool Victoria Friendly Society* [1916] 2 QB 482 (life policy illegal under Life Assurance Act 1774 as made without interest).

98   [1949] 2 All ER 1019. The principle was upheld by the Privy Council in *Kiriri Cotton Ltd v Dewani* [1960] AC 192. The basis of recovery is either duress (presumed from the provisions of the statute) or failure of consideration (the claimant has paid a capital sum for something – a lease – which the lessor was bound to provide, if at all, without such payment).

99   There is now such provision in the equivalent English legislation: see, eg, Rent Act 1977, s 57.

100   See *Re Cavalier Insurance Co* [1989] 2 Lloyd's Rep 430, p 450. The position in England has now been regularised by statute: Financial Services Act 1986, s 132.

101   [1905] 2 KB 123.

marriage broker. Another instance is cases of 'oppression', coming close to duress. For instance, in *Atkinson v Denby*[102] a preferential payment made by an insolvent debtor in fraud of his other creditors was held recoverable from the payee, who had illegitimately demanded it as the price of agreeing to an otherwise *pro rata* distribution.

(e) A particular case: restitution and the impact of existing property rights

13-30   We have seen above that certain types of restitutionary rights are enforced through manipulation of the law of property, whether legal or equitable. Examples include transfers of money or chattels under a mistake, and improvements to property acquiesced in by the owner. Presumably, these are equally affected by the illegality defence: to take an example already used, if I agree to pay you £100 to beat X up and then inadvertently pay you twice, it is highly unlikely that I would be able to assert a constructive trust over the extra £100.[103]

Nevertheless, this must be read subject to the rule that in so far as proprietary rights (legal or equitable) can be established without relying explicitly on the underlying illegality, they can be enforced. Apart from contract cases such as *Bowmaker Ltd v Barnet Instruments Ltd*,[104] the principle is neatly illustrated by *Tinsley v Milligan*[105] and *Tribe v Tribe*.[106] In the former case, M contributed to the price of a house shared by her and T in circumstances that gave rise to an inference of a resulting trust. The house, however, was put in T's name in order to allow M to plead destitution and defraud the social security system. The House of Lords, by a majority, held M entitled to a proportionate share in the house: the illegality of the scheme was irrelevant, since M could establish the resulting trust without invoking it. It is only if a claimant needs to plead his own illegal conduct in order to rebut the presumed ordering of property that he will fail. This nearly happened in *Tribe v Tribe*,[107] where a father transferred shares to his son to defraud his creditors. The son refused to give them back, and would have prevailed (on the basis that the father had to pray in aid his own turpitude to rebut the presumption of advancement that would otherwise arise) had not the father been able to use the 'repentance cases' to recover notwithstanding his own conduct.

---

102 (1862) 7 H & N 934.

103 Under the principle in *Chase Manhattan NV v Israel-British Bank Ltd* [1981] Ch 105 or *Re Irish Shipping Ltd* [1986] ILRM 518.

104 [1945] KB 65.

105 [1994] 1 AC 340.

106 [1996] Ch 107.

107 [1996] Ch 107. See, too, eg, *Tinker v Tinker* [1970] P 136 (fraud on creditors); *Chettiar v Chettiar* [1962] AC 294 (evasion of land-holding restrictions).

13-31 Neither of these cases is strictly restitutionary, since both involved claims to enforce arrangements according to the parties' intentions, rather than to reverse uncontemplated enrichments. But they may be relevant to restitutionary situations. Suppose a son transfers shares *gratis* to his father with a view to their fraudulent sale by the latter to the public at an inflated price: suppose, further, that the father then abandons the scheme. While ordinarily, a claim by the son based on failure of consideration would have to fail, on the reasoning in *Tinsley v Milligan*[108] he would be able to recover the shares by relying on the presumption of a resulting trust;[109] or, again, if you were to acquiesce in my making improvements to your property[110] which, to the knowledge of both of us, you intended to use as a brothel, I could validly assert a claim to an interest in the property.

On the other hand, this principle will not apply where the sole ground of the claimant's claim to the proprietary interest concerned is the illegal agreement itself and not the presumption of a resulting trust. Suppose an uncle transfers shares to his nephew (in favour of whom there is no presumption of advancement) for an illegal purpose, it being agreed between them that the nephew is to own them absolutely. Evidence of this latter agreement will not be admissible and the shares will remain vested in equity in the uncle.[111]

It must be admitted that this is hardly an intellectually satisfying position for the law to take. Nevertheless, short of a general discretion in the courts to adjust property rights arising out of illegal transaction,[112] any reconciliation of the principle *ex turpi causa non oritur actio* with the principle of security of property rights is bound to yield arbitrary answers in particular cases.

(f) Statutory bars to recovery

13-32 It goes without saying that the question whether a restitutionary claim exists must be looked at in the light of relevant statutory provisions: whatever the position under the general law, it must be a defence that allowing a claim would contravene the letter or intention of a relevant statute. The difficulty, of course, is

---

108 [1994] 1 AC 340.

109 Lord Goff, who dissented in *Tinsley v Milligan*, clearly thought this followed from the decision of the majority: see [1994] 1 AC 340, p 362.

110 Thus potentially allowing me to invoke the rule in *Unity Joint Stock Bank v King* (1858) 25 Beav 72.

111 See, eg, *Tinker v Tinker* [1970] P 136 (fraud on creditors); *Chettiar v Chettiar* [1962] AC 294 (evasion of land-holding restrictions). Ironically, however, it has also been held that if evidence is led in order to negative the presumption of a resulting trust, that evidence may in turn be rebutted by evidence of the parties' intentions despite the illegality involved: *Silverwood v Silverwood* (1997) 74 P & CR 453. Evidence of illegality, in other words, may not be led in order to rebut a presumption of a resulting trust, but may be used to rebut the rebuttal! On this bizarre state of affairs, the reader will no doubt form his own opinion.

112 Cf the suggestions of the English Law Commission on the matter: Consultation Paper No 154 (1999), § 8.72 *et seq*.

the practical one of construing the statute concerned. The point arises particularly in relation to statutes that make particular contracts unenforceable: requirements of form (such as writing), provisions restricting the enforcement of contracts by those not licensed to conduct a given business, gaming contracts and the like. We know these prevent an action being brought on the contract – for example, for sums owing, or for damages for breach. But how far do they also preclude restitutionary actions?

13-33 Although the cases do not all speak with one voice, the *prima facie* rule is that actions in restitution, being not actions on the contract, but proceedings against the background of it, are *prima facie* unaffected by any statutory unenforceability. Provisions requiring writing for certain kinds of contract are a straightforward example – notably, contracts for the disposition of an interest in land,[113] and (in Ireland) agreements in consideration of marriage, contracts not to be performed within one year,[114] and contracts for the sale of goods over £10.[115]

13-34 Thus, actions based on failure of consideration, where the claimant paid for land he never got, have succeeded despite the provisions of the Statute of Frauds[116] and its quondam English successor, s 40 of the Law of Property Act 1925,[117] and (it is submitted) would equally succeed under the present English legislation.[118] Similarly, deposits paid under gaming contracts, which are declared void by statute,[119] can be recovered[120] until appropriated to losses by the payee[121] (that is, so long as the consideration continues to fail).[122] So, too, with premiums paid under insurance policies that, owing to lack of insurable interest, are treated as gambling transactions.[123] Similarly, too, it is suggested, with mistake. Suppose you sell me Blackacre for £100,000 pursuant to an oral agreement; by mistake I pay you £120,000. Presumably, I can recover the odd £20,000.[124]

13-35 Again, where goods are transferred, or services rendered, under a contract which is unenforceable (for instance, because of the Statute of Frauds), the fact

---

113 (Ireland) Statute of Frauds (Ireland) 1695, s 2; (England) Law of Property (Miscellaneous Provisions) Act 1989, s 2.

114 Both covered by the Statute of Frauds (Ireland) 1695, s 2.

115 Sale of Goods Act 1893, s 4.

116 (England) Statute of Frauds 1677, s 4; (Ireland) Statute of Frauds (Ireland) 1695, s 2.

117 Eg, *Gosbell v Archer* (1835) 2 A & E 500.

118 See, now, Law of Property (Miscellaneous Provisions) Act 1989, s 2.

119 (England) Gaming Act 1845, s 18; (Ireland) Gaming and Lotteries Act 1956, s 36. Both statutory provisions are effectively the same.

120 *Graham v Thompson* (1867) IR 2 CL 64; *Universal Stock Exchange v Strachan* [1896] AC 166; *Re Cronmire* [1898] 2 QB 383.

121 *Strachan v Universal Stock Exchange (No 2)* [1895] 2 QB 697.

122 Once losses have been paid, they are of course irrecoverable: there is simply no ground for restitution that the claimant can rely on. Cf *Phelan v Stewards of Kilmacthomas Races* (1896) ICT 36; *Toner v Livingston* (1896) 30 ILTR 80.

123 *Re London Commercial County Reinsurance* [1922] 2 Ch 67.

124 But cf *Morgan v Ashcroft*, below.

that no action will lie for any agreed price will not necessarily prevent an action in *quantum meruit* or *quantum valebat* for a reasonable sum. In practice, today, such cases are likely to turn on promises to convey real property in exchange for services and similar arrangements. Thus, in the leading Canadian decision of *Deglman v Guaranty Trust*,[125] the Supreme Court held that where X agreed to provide housekeeping services to Y in exchange for Y's oral promise to leave her house to him on her death, but Y failed to do so, X could recover the reasonable value of his services. But, a similar principle applies in other cases of unenforceable contracts. Thus, in *Savage v Canning*,[126] recovery in *quantum meruit* was allowed in respect of work performed under a contract otherwise unenforceable as not falling to be performed within one year. Even where a contract is ineffective as a matter of public policy, it may be held that the public policy does not prevent a limited degree of restitutionary recovery. Hence, in *Mohamed v Alaga and Co*,[127] a solicitor's tout was held able to sue on a *quantum meruit* for services rendered by bringing business to the solicitor, despite the fact that his agreement with the solicitor had involved taking a percentage of the latter's fees and was, for that reason, illegal.

13-36 Nevertheless, the fundamental issue remains whether the statute concerned ought to be interpreted so as to allow its effect to be watered down by restitutionary recovery, and statutes other than the Statute of Frauds may well be applied more strictly. For instance, under the English Consumer Credit Act 1974, it is specifically provided that an agreement caught by the Act is entirely unenforceable against the debtor unless signed by the latter.[128] It has been understandably held that this provision cannot be circumvented by suing on a *quantum valebat* or *quantum meruit*.[129] Again, if statute provides that loans to minors are irrecoverable, even where they have lied about their age, then this equally precludes the lender suing for money had and received arising out of that deceit: one cannot very well allow a remedy in by the back door which has been specifically excluded at the front.[130] Perhaps less defensibly, the fact that a minor cannot be held liable in breach of contract for failure to deliver goods has equally been held to preclude an action for return of a prepayment on the ground of failure of consideration.[131] Again, in *Orakpo v Manson Investments*

---

125 [1954] 3 DLR 785.

126 (1867) IR 1 CL 432. See, too, *Scott v Pattison* [1923] 2 KB 723 (though this bit of the Statute of Frauds no longer applies in England).

127 [1999] 3 All ER 699; Enonchong [2000] RLR 241.

128 Another doubtless similar example in Ireland is the Hire Purchase Act 1946, s 3(2).

129 *Dimond v Lovell* [2000] 2 All ER 897.

130 *Leslie (R) Ltd v Shiell* [1914] 3 KB 607 (the relevant statute being the Infants' Relief Act 1874). But although this remains the position in Ireland, in England statute now seems to allow recovery, at least where the minor still has the money – see the Minors' Contracts Act 1987, s 3.

131 *Cowern v Nield* [1912] 2 KB 419.

Ltd,[132] a property developer bought a house with money borrowed from a moneylender, to whom he mortgaged it, in circumstances where statute[133] provided that the loan and any security thereunder were not enforceable. It was held that the statute equally prohibited the moneylender from being subrogated to the previous mortgages paid off with his money.[134]

13-37 The need for a close reading of the statute concerned was well underlined by the important Australian decision in *Pavey and Matthews Pty Ltd v Paul*.[135] A builder carried out work on the defendant's premises under a contract which was stated to be unenforceable for lack of statutory formalities. A great deal of the reasoning of the High Court of Australia was taken up with detailed discussion of the wording and purposes of the statute concerned, and whether it would amount to an unacceptable evasion to allow the builder to succeed on a *quantum meruit* for the value of the work he had done. It was only after deciding this question in the negative that the High Court was prepared to allow the restitutionary claim to succeed. In other cases, it may well be that the statute is intended to preclude restitutionary, as well as contractual, recovery.[136]

---

132 [1978] AC 95.

133 The then Moneylenders Act 1927, s 6(1) (since replaced by less draconian provisions in the Consumer Credit Act 1974).

134 See, too, the decision in *Morgan v Ashcroft* [1938] 1 KB 49, holding that s 18 of the Gaming Act 1845 (Irish equivalent: Gaming and Lotteries Act 1956, s 36) precluded recovery of moneys paid by mistake under a gambling contract. With respect, this is a little hard to justify.

135 (1986) 162 CLR 221.

136 As in *Dimond v Lovell* [2000] 3 All ER 897.

SELECTED BIBLIOGRAPHY

Arrowsmith, S, 'Ineffective transactions, unjust enrichment and questions of policy' (1989) 9 LS 307

Barker, C, '*Bona fide* purchase as a defence to unjust enrichment' [1999] RLR 75

Beatson, J, 'Restitution of taxes' (1993) 109 LQR 401

Beatson, J, *The Use and Abuse of Unjust Enrichment*, 1991, Oxford: OUP

Birks, P and Beatson, J, 'Unrequested payment of another's debt' (1976) 92 LQR 188

Birks, P (ed), *Frontiers of Liability*, 1994, Oxford: OUP

Birks, P, *An Introduction to the Law of Restitution*, rev edn, 1988, Oxford: OUP

Birks, P, 'The English recognition of unjust enrichment' [1991] LM & CLQ 473

Burrows, A, *Essays on the Law of Restitution*, 1991, Oxford: OUP

Burrows, A, 'Free acceptance and the law of restitution' (1988) 104 LQR 576

Burrows, A, 'Quadrating restitution and unjust enrichment' [2000] RLR 257

Burrows, A, 'Swaps and the friction between law and equity' [1995] RLR 15

Burrows, A, *The Law of Restitution*, 1993, London: Butterworths

Chambers, R, *Resulting Trusts*, 1997, Oxford: OUP

Cornish, W *et al* (eds), *Restitution: Past, Present and Future*, 1998, Oxford: Hart

Crilley, D, 'A case of proprietary overkill' [1994] RLR 57

Dawson, J, *Unjust Enrichment: A Comparative Survey*, 1999, New York: William S Hein, Buffalo

Edelman, J, 'Restitutionary and disengorgement damages' [2000] RLR 129

Enonchong, N, 'Illegal transactions: the future' [2001] RLR 241

Evans, D, 'Rethinking tracing and the law of restitution' (1999) 115 LQR 469

Fox, D, 'Common law claims to substituted assets' [1999] RLR 55

Fox, D, 'Legal title as a ground of restitutionary liability' [2000] RLR 465

Friedmann, D, 'Payment of another's debt' (1983) 99 LQR 534

Garner, M, 'The role of subjective benefit' (1990) 10 OJLS 42

Goff, R and Jones, G, *The Law of Restitution*, 5th edn, 1998, London: Sweet & Maxwell

Goode, R, 'The right to trace and its impact on commercial transactions' (1976) 92 LQR 360, p 528

Goodhart, W, 'Restitutionary damages and breach of contract' [1995] RLR 3

Grantham, R and Rickett, C, 'Trust money as an enrichment' [1998] LM & CLQ 514

Hedley, S, 'Unjust enrichment' [1995] CLJ 578

Jackman, I, 'Restitution for wrongs' [1989] CLJ 302

Jackson, R, History of Quasi-Contract, 1936, Cambridge: CUP

Jones, G, 'Recovery of benefits gained from breach of contract' (1983) 99 LQR 443

Khurshid, S and Mathews, P, 'Tracing confusion' (1975) 95 LQR 78

McInnes, M, 'Restitution, unjust enrichment and the perfect quadration thesis' [1999] RLR 118

McKendrick, E, 'Tracing misdirected funds' [1991] LM & CLQ 378

Mead, G, 'Free acceptance: some further considerations' (1989) 105 LQR 460

Millett, P, 'Restitution and constructive trusts' (1998) 114 LQR 399

Mitchell, R, The Law of Subrogation, 1994, Oxford: OUP

Oakley, A, 'Proprietary claims and priority in insolvency' [1995] CLJ 377

Palmer, G, Law of Restitution, 1978, Boston: Little, Brown

Rose, F (ed), Failure of Contracts, 1997, Oxford: Hart

Rose, F (ed), Restitution and Insolvency, 2000, Mansfield

Smith, L, 'Equity in the Court of King's Bench' [1995] LM & CLQ 240

Smith, L, The Law of Tracing, 1997, Oxford: OUP

Smith, L, 'Three-party restitution' (1991) OJLS 481

Stewart, A and Carter, J, 'Frustrated contracts and statutory adjustment' [1992] CLJ 66

Stoljar, S, Law of Quasi-Contract, 2nd edn, 1989, Sydney: Law Book Co

Swadling, W, 'A new role for resulting trusts' (1996) 16 LS 110

Swadling, W, 'Restitution for no consideration' [1994] RLR 73

Tettenborn, A, 'Lawful receipt - a justifying factor?' [1997] RLR 1

Tettenborn, A, 'Third party cheques, security or snare?' [1998] RLR 63

Virgo, G, *Principles of the Law of Restitution*, 1999, Oxford: OUP

Worthington, S, 'Reconsidering disengorgement for wrongs' (1999) 62 MLR 218

Zimmerman, R, 'Unjust enrichment: the modern civilian approach' (1995) 15 OJLS 403

INDEX

Acceptance
and necessitous intervention....... 207–08
non-contractual 145–46
See also Free acceptance

Account.............................. 3
and intellectual
property rights................. 253–54
See also Bank accounts

Acquiescence
and free acceptance........... 115, 117–19
and services 86–87

Animals, and
necessitous intervention.............. 205

Assets
swollen assets theory 49
See also Tracing, mixed assets;
Tracing, substituted assets

Assumptions
See Failure of assumptions

Bailment, and
necessitous intervention.............. 202

Bank accounts
'first in, first out' 228–30
unauthorised debits 60–61

Bargains
See Losing bargain effect

Benefits
and change of position........... 277–78
and contractual
restitution.............. 136–37, 141–42
and duress 100–101
and failure of assumptions 127–28
and frustration of contracts 150–51
and frustration of
contracts in Ireland 147–48
incidental benefits
and retention 30–31
incontrovertible benefits 88–89
and remedies for
property wrongs 255–56
third parties and tracing.............. 213
and void contracts................ 161–62
and voidable contracts 163

Bills of exchange,
and recoupment..................... 192

Bona fide purchase
and proprietary claims 47
and retention 25–27

Breach of contract 43, 247–50
amounting to
infringement of property
or tradable right.................... 248
and breach of fiduciary duty.......... 250
and contribution 195
as covenant........................ 249
not to act without consent 249
payment over of profits
arising from breach................. 248

Breach of fiduciary duty................ 250
See also Breach of trust

Breach of trust 251–53
categories of fiduciaries 252–53
trustees 251–52
See also Constructive trust;
Trust property; Wrongs

Bribes........................ 45, 46–47, 253

Building works......................... 9

Change of position 271–73, 279
as act by defendant................ 275–76
and double recovery.............. 276–77
and estoppel...................... 280–81
extent of defence 273–75
invocation by wrongdoers.......... 278–79
prior to receipt of benefits 277–78
and public authorities.............. 266–67
and rendering of services............. 277
scope of defence.................. 273–75
subsequent to
receipt of benefits 277–78
and tracing 220, 232
and transfer of property.............. 277
See also Defences

Chattels............................. 45
and property mistake.............. 82–83

Children
See Minors

Claimants
and contractual restitution......... 143–46
and enrichment at
claimant's expense 17–20
and illegality...................... 285–86

and proprietary claims 51
and tracing 219–20, 223–24
Clayton's case rule 228–30, 231
Co-owners and recoupment 190–92
Coercion and duress 96–99
Colore officii payments 261–62
Compromise
   as defence 269–70
   and mistake 90
Consideration
   defined 132
   and total failure 13, 135
   See also Failure of
     consideration
Constructive trust 43
Contracts
   anticipated 175–79
   and duress 91, 163–64
   and exclusion defence 269–70
   and failure of assumptions 126–27
   and illegality
     See Illegality, and contracts
   and lack of formality 174–75
   and minors
     See Minors, and contract
   and mistake 77–78, 82,
                             160–61
     See also Void contracts,
       for mistake
   and non-contractual cases 175–79
   and *ultra vires*
     See Ultra vires, and contracts
   and undue influence 163–64
   void
     See Void contracts
   voidable
     See Voidable contracts
Contractual restitution 131, 137–39,
                              143–45
   benefits defined 141–42
   with benefits freely accepted 142
   with claimant in breach 143–46
   consideration defined 132
   with defendant in breach 140–43
   frustration cases 147–48
   goods and services 139–40
   in Ireland 141

and losing bargain effect 137
losing bargain effect 142–43
money paid 133–39
with neither party in breach 146–52
no recovery rule 143–45
non-contractual acceptance 145–46
non-frustration cases 146–47
total failure
   and collateral benefits 136–37
   and consideration 13, 135
   need for 133–35, 140
   See also Breach of contract
Contribution 3, 193–97
   and co-sureties 193–94
   and contract-breakers 195
   and debtors 193
   extension of principle 197–98
   general average doctrine 197–98
   and insurers 194–95
   tortfeasors 195
   and trustees 195
   and wrongdoers 195–96
   See also Recoupment
Counter-restitution
   and failure of assumptions 128
   and voidable contracts 153–54

Damages 43
   exemplary 242–43
   and intellectual
     property rights 253
   and profits 3
   and torts 242–44
Defective loan cases,
   and subrogation 57–60
Defences
   donative intent 270–71
   exclusion by compromise 269–70
   exclusion by contract 269–70
   finality 270
   intent to close a transaction 270
   See also Change of position;
     Estoppel; Illegality
Devaluation
   and mistake 83–84
   and retention 23–25
   subjective 83–84

Diversion 232–35
  and profits of
    property or office............... 232–34
  See also Tracing

Donative intent
  as defence 270–71
  and duress 99–100
  and retention 31

Duress 91
  benefits rendered under
    threat of litigation 100–101
  causation and reasonableness 96–99
  coercion and reasonableness 96–99
  and contracts 91, 163–64
  and donative intention............ 99–100
  economic pressure.................. 92–95
  need for unlawfulness 95–96
  ratification of transaction............. 100
  remedies 101
    for money paid..................... 109
    position of third parties 111–12
    for property transferred 109–10
    for services 110
  statutory 108
  unlawful pressure 92–95
  violence............................. 92
  waiver of right to recovery 99–100
  See also Undue influence

Emergencies
  See Necessitous intervention

Enrichment........................... 6–13
  at claimant's expense 17–20
  and expense saved 7–8
  measuring the gain 12–13
  and property receipt 7
  and receipt of services.............. 9–11
  See also Unjust enrichment

Equitable lien 43

Equity 45
  equitable lien 43
  and estoppel.......................... 87

Estoppel 279–82
  and change of position............. 280–81
  equitable 87
  See also Defences

Ex turpi causa non oritur actio 287

Expense
  and enrichment at
    claimant's expense 17–20
  and set-off expenses 152

Expense saved, as enrichment 7–8

Failure of assumptions 15–16, 76–77,
                        125–26
  contractual and
    non-contractual
    expectations 126–27
  counter-restitution problem........... 128
  and free acceptance................... 126
  kinds of benefits covered 127–28
  and mistake 125–26

Failure of consideration
  contract cases 131
    See also Contractual
    restitution, total failure
  and mistake 130
  and proprietary claims............ 129–30
  and *quantum meruit* 131
  and void contracts......... 153–54, 157–58
  and voidable contracts 153–54
  See also Consideration

Fiduciary duty
  and breach of contract 250
  and gains in breach of................. 52
  and remedies for
    fiduciary profits................. 256–57

Forced exchange
  and mistake 83–84
  and retention 21–23

Fraud, and tracing.................. 213–14

Free acceptance 16–17, 113–16
  acquiescence................. 115, 117–19
  advantage-taking.......... 115–16, 119–20
  exclusions 114
  and failure
    of assumptions.................... 126
  as genuine choice.................. 120–22
  and gratuitous intent 113, 119, 122–23
  and presumption..................... 116
  request.................... 114–15, 116–17
  and silence.......................... 118
  and wrongs.......................... 119

Frustration of contracts 147–52
  benefits in kind, in Ireland......... 147–48
  'just sum' computation............ 151–52
  money paid....................... 149–50
  in Ireland........................ 148–49
  and set-off expenses 152
  and valuable benefits 150–51
  valued after event 151
  See also Contractual restitution,
    with neither party in breach

Gain............................... 38–40
  in breach of fiduciary duty 52
  unjustified, factors................. 13–20
  See also Enrichment

General average doctrine............ 197–98

Goods and contractual
  restitution 139–40

Gratuitous intent 113, 119, 122–23

Illegality 282–83
  claimant not *in pari delicto* 285–86
  and contracts 168–71
  and *ex turpi causa*
    non oritur actio..................... 287
  and existing property rights 286–87
  protective illegality 169–71
  and repentance.................... 283–84
  as unjust factor................... 169–71
  and unknowing participation......... 283
  See also Defences; Statutory
    bars to recovery

Incidental benefits, and retention...... 30–31

Incontrovertible benefits 88–89
  and retention 21–23

Insurance and subrogation 65–66

Intellectual property rights 253–55
  and account of profits............. 253–54
  and damages 253
  as tort............................ 244

Ireland
  contractual restitution,
    with defendant in breach.......... 141
  frustration of contracts............ 147–49

necessitous intervention.............. 204
and salvage..................... 191, 207
ultra vires and contracts 171, 173
void contracts...................... 160

Laches 106

Lack of formality, and contracts 174–75

Land improvement
  cases and proprietary claims........... 52

Leases, and recoupment............. 189–90

Liability 4–5
  and recoupment..................... 192
  and unjust enrichment 32–36
  and wrongs......................... 4–5

Lien
  against property in
    wrongdoer's hands.............. 230–32
  equitable lien 43
  and tracing 230–32

Litigation
  as duress 100–101
  and mistake 90

Lloyd's Open Form............... 210, 211

Loans, defective loan cases,
  and subrogation................... 57–60

Losing bargain effect
  and contractual restitution............ 137
  with defendant in breach.......... 142–43
  and void contracts................ 159–60

Loss
  and damages 243–44
  and wrongs...................... 257–58

Maritime law, and
  general average doctrine 197–98

Maritime salvage
  and necessitous intervention....... 209–12
    extra-contractual rules 210–11
    Lloyd's Open Form............ 210, 211
    'no cure, no pay' principle 211
    voluntariness requirement.......... 210
  and proprietary claims 54
  and restitution law 212

Minors
    and contracts 164–68
        claims against minors 167–68
        for money paid 163–64
        for property and services 166
    and necessitous intervention 205

Mistake
    and compromise 90
    and contract 77–78
    and contracts 77–78,
                                                82, 160–61
    exceptions to recovery 89–90
    of fact, and mistake of law 70–72
    and failure of assumptions 125–26
    and incontrovertible benefits 88–89
    kinds of 74–77
    and payment in the
        face of litigation 90
    present and future 69–70
    and property 80–84
        forced exchange 83–84
        pecuniary remedies 81
        proprietary remedies 81–83
        subjective devaluation 83–84
    and recovery of money 78–80
    and risk 89–90
    and services
        See Services, and mistake
    and subjective devaluation 83–84
    and void contracts 161–62
    and voidable contracts 163

Mistake of law
    changes in the law 73–74
    definition 72–73
    limitations on recovery 74
    and mistake of fact 70–72

Money
    and contractual restitution 133–39
    and duress 109
    and frustration of contracts 149–50
    in Ireland 148–49
    receipt 6–7
    recovery of 78–80
    and undue influence 109
    and void contracts 161
    and voidable contracts 162–63
    and wrongs 255

Necessitous intervention 14, 32
    and acceptance for
        honour of a bill
        of exchange 207–08
    agency of 200–201
    and bailment 202
    and caring for animals 205
    general principle 208–09
    for incompetents 204–05
    in Ireland 191, 204, 207
    and liquidators 203
    and maritime salvage 209–12
    for medical attention 204
    for minors 205
    and non-recovery 199–200
    and officiousness 209
    for performance of
        public duties 206–07
    and receivers 203
    and salvage, in Ireland 191, 207
    and trustees' rights 202–03
    and voluntariness 14

Non contractual cases 175–79

Non-pecuniary remedies,
    for services and mistake 88

Non-recovery
    See Recovery

Obligation and recoupment 182–84, 187,
                                                241–42

Officiousness, and retention 32

Payment
    and breach of contract 248
    colore officii 261–62
    and mistake 90
    and proprietary claims 53
    and public authorities 261–62, 264–65
    and recoupment 183–84
    and taxes repayment 262–65, 267, 268
    ultra vires 53
    unauthorised 264–65

Pecuniary restitution 44–45
    and mistake 81, 88
    and proprietary claims 48–50
    and quantum meruit 44

and *quantum valebat* 44
See also Non-pecuniary
remedies, for services
and mistake

Performance of public duties 206–07

Personal restitution
See pecuniary restitution

Plaintiffs
See Claimants

Profits, and damages. 3

Property
and change of position 277
as chattels 82–83
and diversion 232–34
and duress 109–10
and enrichment 7
and illegality. 286–87
and lien against 230–32
and minors 166
and mistake 80–84
and proprietary claims 51
and *quantum valebat*. 81, 110
receipt, as enrichment. 7
and restitution 34–36
and subrogation. 57
and torts 244
and tracing 223–32
trust 45
and undue influence. 109–10
and unjustified gains 14–15
and wrongs. 255–56
See also Intellectual
property rights

Property claims,
and subrogation. 57

Property rights, and
unjustified gains 14–15

Proprietary claims. 45–54
and claimant's property 51
and failure of consideration. 129–30
from mistakes. 51–52, 79–80
and gains in breach of duty 52
and land improvement cases. 52
and maritime salvors 54
and pecuniary restitution. 48–50
and recovery of money. 79–80
and rescission. 50–51
and *ultra vires* payments. 53

Protective illegality 169–71

Public authorities 259–61
and change of position 266–67
and judicial review 265–66
and overpaid taxes. 262–65,
267, 268
and payments *colore officii* 261–62
recovery of
unauthorised payments 264–65
and rights of appeal 266
and unjust enrichment
if recovery permitted 268

Public duties. 206–07

Quantum meruit 3, 43
and contracts void for mistake 162
and duress remedies 101
and failure of consideration,
contract cases 131
and pecuniary restitution. 44
and services rendered
under duress. 110
and statutory bars to recovery 289

Quantum valebat 3
and pecuniary restitution. 44
and property mistake 81
and property transferred
under duress. 110
and statutory bars to recovery 289

Quasi-contract 3–4

Ratification 100

Receipt
and change of position 277–78
from third parties 27–30
of property as enrichment 7
and retention 27–31
of services as enrichment 9–11
under contract 31

Recoupment. 181–87
and bills of exchange. 192
and co-owners 190–92
compellability 184–87
and defendant's obligation 187
discharge of obligation. 182–84
and unrequested payment
of another's debt 183–84

extension of principle 197–98
general average doctrine 197–98
and leases 189–90
rights of recourse 192
and shares 192
and statutory liability 192
and sureties 188
See also Contribution

Recovery 3
and change of position 276–77
and contractual restitution 143–45
and duress 99–100
and mistake 74, 78–80, 89–90
and necessitous
  intervention 199–200
and public authorities 264–65, 268
and quantum meruit 289
and quantum valebat 289
Statutory bars to 287–90
See also Money, recovery of

Remedies 43–44
and duress 101, 109–10,
                                                          111–12
for fiduciary profits 256–57
and mistake 81–83, 88
for property wrongs 255–56
and quantum meruit 101
and rights 43–44
and undue influence 109–10, 111–12
and wrongs 255–56, 256–57
See also Pecuniary restitution;
  Proprietary claims;
  Subrogation

Repayment of taxes 262–65, 267, 268

Rescission 47–48
and proprietary claims 50–51

Restitution
as coherent legal category 36–42
definition 1–2

Retention
bona fide purchase 25–27
and donative intent 31
factors justifying 23–25
and forced exchange 21–23
and incidental benefits 30–31
and incontrovertible benefits 21–23
justification 20–32

and officiousness 32
and receipt from third parties 27–30
and receipt under contract 31
and subjective devaluation 23–25
Rights, and remedies 43–44
Risk, and mistake 89–90

Salvage
and Ireland 191, 207
See also Maritime salvage
Services
and acquiescence 86–87
and change of position 277
and contractual restitution 139–40
and duress 110
and enrichment 9–11
and mistake 84–88, 86–87
non-pecuniary remedies 88
and quantum meruit 110
receipt as enrichment 9–11
and undue influence 110
Statutory bars to recovery 287–90
Statutory duress,
and undue influence 108
Statutory liability, and recoupment 192
Subjective devaluation
and devaluation 23–25
and mistake 83–84
Subrogation 54–67
contractual 56
and defective loan cases 57–60
definition 54–56
and insolvent trustees 66–67
and insurance 65–66
and property claims 57
as restitution 63–64
and sureties 61–62
and trustees 66–67
and unauthorised debits 60–61
and underwriter's remedy 65–66
and unjust enrichment 62–63
Sureties
and contribution 193–94
and recoupment 188
and subrogation 61–62
Swollen assets theory 49

Taxes, repayment 262–65, 267, 268
Taylor v Plumer rule 255
Third parties
  and duress remedies 111–12
  receipt from 27–30
  and subrogation.................... 66–67
  and tracing 213
  and undue influence 111–12
  and undue influence remedies 111–12
Third parties, benefits
  conferred through and tracing 213
Threats, as undue influence.......... 102–03
Torts 43
  damages, gain
    masquerading as loss 243–44
  and exemplary damages 242–43
  and infringement of
    property rights.................... 244
  and intellectual
    property rights.................... 244
  waiver of tort 3, 244–46
  waiver of tort,
    non-cash gains 246
Total failure........................... 129
  and contractual
    restitution................. 13, 133–35,
                   135, 136–37, 140
Tracing........................ 213–15, 230
  bank accounts and
    'first in, first out' 228–30
  and benefits conferred
    through third parties............... 213
  and change of position 220
  claims to substitute
    property 223–32
  Clayton's case rule 228–30, 231
  'first in, first out' 228–30
  and fraud 213–14
  identifying the proceeds........... 227–28
  lien against property in
    wrongdoer's hands.............. 230–32
  mixed assets 228–31
  nature of claimant's interest 223–24
  personal claims 221–23
  of position....................... 232
  proceeds identified to
    the use of claimant 219–20

proprietary base................... 225–27
substituted assets................. 214–19
sufficient connection.............. 227–28
and theft 226–27
  See also Diversion
Trust property 45
Trustees
  breach of trust 251–52
  and contribution 195
  and necessitous
    intervention 202–03
  and subrogation................... 66–67

Ultra vires
  and contracts 171–74
    claims against corporation....... 172–74
    claims by corporation........... 171–72
    in Ireland..................... 171, 173
Ultra vires payments,
  and proprietary claims 53
Underwriter's remedy,
  and subrogation................... 65–66
Undue influence 102–08
  and contracts 163–64
  contrary to legislative
    provisions 108
  defences........................... 106
  and moral authority 103–06
  'poor and ignorant' cases.......... 106–08
  reliant relationships 103–06
  remedies
    for money paid..................... 109
    position of third parties 111–12
    for property transferred 109–10
    for services 110
  statutory duress................... 108
  threats 102–03
  See also Duress
Unjust enrichment 4–5, 37–38,
                    40–42, 43
  and illegality...................... 169–71
  and liability....................... 32–36
  and public authorities................. 268
  requirements for claim 5–13
  and subrogation.................... 62–63
  See also Enrichment

Valuable benefits, and
   frustration of contracts 150–51
Violence 92
Vitiated contracts
   See Void contracts;
Void contracts
   and failure of
      consideration 153–54, 157–58
   and Ireland 160
   losing bargain effect 159–60
   for mistake
      and benefits in kind 161–62
      and money paid 161
Voidable contracts
   and counter-restitution 153–54
   and failure of consideration 153–54
   for mistake
      and benefits in kind 163
      and money paid 162–63
Voluntariness
   factors qualifying 14
   and maritime salvage 210
   necessitous intervention 14

Waiver of tort 3, 244–46
Wrongs 237–38
   obligations of loyalty 241–42
   remedies
      for fiduciary profits 256–57
      as money liability 255
      for profits or losses 257–58
      for property benefits 255–56
      Taylor v Plumer rule 255
   and restitution 238–41
   tradable rights infringement 240–41
   as unjust factors 17
   See also Breach of contract;
      Breach of trust;
      Intellectual property rights,
      infringement; Torts